JUDY HOPKINS
501
ROTARY-CUT
QUILT BLOCKS

501 Rotary-Cut Quilt Blocks
© 2008 by Judy Hopkins

That Patchwork Place® is an imprint of
Martingale & Company®.

Martingale & Company
20205 144th Ave. NE
Woodinville, WA 98072-8478 USA
www.martingale-pub.com

Credits

President & CEO ~ Tom Wierzbicki
Publisher ~ Jane Hamada
Editorial Director ~ Mary V. Green
Managing Editor ~ Tina Cook
Technical Editors ~ Laurie Baker, Ursula Reikes,
                and Laura M. Reinstatler
Copy Editor ~ Durby Peterson
Design Director ~ Stan Green
Production Manager ~ Regina Girard
Illustrator ~ Laurel Strand
Cover & Text Designer ~ Stan Green
Photographer ~ Brent Kane

Printed in China
13 12 11 10 09 08   8 7 6 5 4 3 2 1

Library of Congress Cataloging-in-Publication Data
Library of Congress Control Number: 2008022882

ISBN: 978-1-56477-893-2

MISSION STATEMENT

Dedicated to providing quality products and service to inspire creativity.

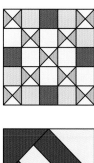 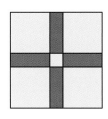 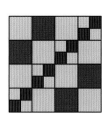

 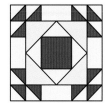 

 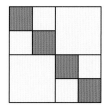 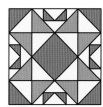

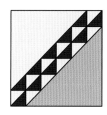 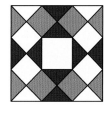 

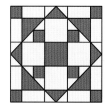 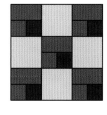 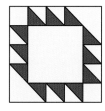

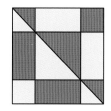 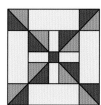 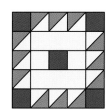

CONTENTS

INTRODUCTION

Some of my earliest quilting books were block-reference books, and they're still among my favorites. I've spent many hours contentedly studying pieced blocks, learning their names, and figuring out how to cut and stitch them.

My introduction to the wealth of traditional blocks was Mary Ellen Hopkins' *The It's Okay If You Sit On My Quilt Book.* Its delicious array of designs was printed on graph paper, so one could see the underlying structure of the blocks. Later, I expanded my block-pattern horizons with Jinny Beyer's *The Quilter's Album of Blocks and Borders,* which came with a transparent overlay on which grids were printed "to aid in understanding how to draft even the most complicated designs." When I found Judy Rehmel's *The Quilt I.D. Book* and Barbara Brackman's *Encyclopedia of Pieced Quilt Patterns*—first issued as a compilation of loose-leaf pages—I was in block heaven! But in all of these wonderful resource books, something was missing: instructions for cutting and sewing the blocks.

Many of the landmark block books were compiled and published before the rotary-cutting revolution. Most of them are reference books geared toward pattern identification—tantalizing collections of possibilities that are out of reach of the quilter who is unwilling, or unable, to do the calculations necessary to translate line drawings into usable quick-cut blocks. Books that give rotary-cutting instructions for traditional blocks are more readily available now, but in many of these the pattern for each block is given in just one size. The same is true of most block patterns published in quilting magazines.

This block book—a compilation of the 501 best blocks from my original three-volume *Around the Block* series—is different. Designed for the quilter who loves both old patterns and modern rotary-cutting techniques, it provides clear, complete instructions *in six different sizes* for each block. I hope you'll use and enjoy the patterns in this book—from Acrobats to Zigzag—for years to come!

USING THE BLOCK PATTERNS

The block patterns appear in alphabetical order. Many blocks have more than one familiar name; a block you refer to as Snail's Trail may be known by other quilters as Monkey Wrench or Indiana Puzzle. If you don't readily find the block you are looking for, it may appear under a different name.

Block designs typically are drafted on regular, underlying grids. For example, a six-unit block is based on a grid that is six squares across and six down. In this book, a grid notation is included as part of each pattern.

Each block pattern includes a shaded drawing and a lettered drawing, both keyed to the cutting instructions, and a piecing diagram.

Most of the patterns produce a single block. For a few of the blocks, it is a more efficient use of fabric to cut the pieces for two or even four blocks at a time. *Check each pattern to see how many blocks the instructions will yield.*

You can choose from one of six different finished sizes for each block. The finished sizes range from 4" to 15⅛", depending on the particular block and the number of units it contains. You will find cutting instructions for the "standard" 12" block in many, but not all, of the patterns. Blocks based on 5-, 7-, 9-, 10-, and 11-unit grids simply do not translate well to a 12" format, as 12 is not divisible into quarters or eighths by either 5, 7, 9, 10, or 11. It would be difficult to accurately measure and cut the 3.1666" and 3.9166" pieces that might be needed to make a 12" block from a design based on a 9-unit grid!

We run into the same kind of measuring and cutting problems with the on-point squares and rectangles that are a feature of many blocks in this book. Templates are given for those shapes, so you can be sure your blocks will be accurately cut.

MAKING AND USING TEMPLATES

Templates appear on pages 280–288. Trace any needed templates on paper or clear template plastic. Transfer all the information that is printed on the templates in the book to your paper or plastic templates, including the template numbers and the arrows that show grain lines. Carefully cut out the templates.

Accurate paper templates can be taped to the bottom of your cutting ruler with removable tape, giving you a guide for rotary cutting your shape. Or, place stiffened paper or plastic templates on your fabric, trace around them with a sharp pencil, and use scissors or your rotary cutter to cut on the traced lines.

Paper template taped
to bottom of ruler

BOY'S NONSENSE

3-Unit Grid

Color Illustration: page 12

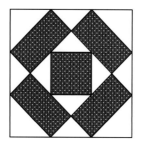 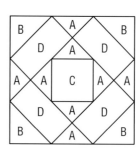 

FOR 1 BLOCK:			FINISHED BLOCK SIZE *Single dimensions in the cutting chart indicate the size of the cut square (3" = 3" x 3").*					
			4½"	6"	7½"	9"	10½"	12"
Light	A: 2 ⊠ → ⊠		2¾"	3¼"	3¾"	4¼"	4¾"	5¼"
	B: 2 ◺ → ◺		2⅜"	2⅞"	3⅜"	3⅞"	4⅜"	4⅞"
Dark	C: 1 □		2"	2½"	3"	3½"	4"	4½"
	D: 4 ◇		T41	T51	T59	T67	T70	T72
Try this:	Reverse the lights and darks in every other block.							

CUTTING THE BLOCKS

The block cutting directions are displayed in charts. These instructions are easy to follow once you are familiar with the terms and notations used throughout the book. Let's use the Boy's Nonsense pattern as an example. Note that the block is based on a three-unit grid, and that the cutting instructions produce one block.

The general instructions for this block call for a light fabric and a dark fabric. Refer to the shaded drawing to see where these values appear in the block. Some of the block patterns call for three values: light, medium, and dark. Others may require two different light fabrics (Light and Light 2) and/or two different medium fabrics (Medium and Medium 2) to define the pattern. When a pattern calls for two lights or two mediums, you could use two different prints of the same color, or two different colors of the same value.

Letters identify the various pattern pieces to cut. Check the lettered drawing to see where each of these pieces appears in the block.

In the cutting chart, a number and an icon follow each piece's letter designation. The number tells you *how many pieces* to cut, and the icon tells you *what to cut*. Six simple icons are used throughout the book:

□	=	Square(s)
◺ → ◺	=	Square(s) cut once diagonally to make half-square triangles
⊠ → ⊠	=	Square(s) cut twice diagonally to make quarter-square triangles
▭	=	Rectangle(s)
◇	=	On-point square(s); use template
◇	=	On-point rectangle(s); use template

If the general cutting instruction says "A: 2 □," cut two squares. If the cutting instruction says "B: 4 ◺ → ◹," cut four squares, then cut the squares once diagonally to make the eight "Piece B" half-square triangles needed for the block. If the cutting instruction says "C: 1 ⊠ → ⧖," cut one square, then cut the square twice diagonally to make the four "Piece C" quarter-square triangles required. If the cutting instruction says "D: 2 ▭," cut two rectangles. If it says "E: 1 ◇," or "E: 1 ◇," you will need to make a template.

The cutting dimensions or template number for these pieces appear in the columns to the right of the general cutting instructions. For example, if you want to make a Boy's Nonsense block that finishes to 9", follow the general cutting instructions using the dimensions given in the 9" Finished Block Size column:

- The first cutting instruction (A: 2 ⊠ → ⧖) tells you to cut two squares from the light fabric and to cut each square twice diagonally to make a total of eight quarter-square triangles. For a 9" block, cut 4¼" x 4¼" squares.
- The second cutting instruction (B: 2 ◺ → ◹) tells you to cut two squares from the light fabric and to cut each square once diagonally to make a total of four half-square triangles. For a 9" block, cut 3⅞" x 3⅞" squares.
- The third cutting instruction (C: 1 □) tells you to cut one square from the dark fabric. For a 9" block, cut a 3½" x 3½" square.
- The final cutting instruction (D: 4 ◇) tells you to cut four on-point rectangles from the dark fabric. For a 9" block, use Template 67.

Both the templates and the rotary-cutting dimensions given include ¼"-wide seam allowances; *do not add seam allowances!*

VARIATIONS

Each block pattern includes a "Try this" notation that suggests a variation on the block. For the Boy's Nonsense block, I suggest reversing the lights and darks in every other block. This means that for your second block, you would cut A and B from the dark fabric and C and D from the light.

Sometimes a "Try this" note will say something like "Use several different mediums for E." Increasing the number of fabrics used in the block while retaining the suggested value arrangement is a strategy worth considering for any of the block patterns. For the Boy's Nonsense block, for example, you could cut A from one light fabric and B from a different light. These could be two prints of the same color (or similar in color) but different in design scale or visual texture. Or, you could use two different colors, both light.

The "Try this" note for one block might well apply to several others. Read through the "Try this" notations throughout the book to get more ideas.

Many other variations are possible. Vary the contrast by combining lights and mediums or mediums and darks instead of lights and darks. Play with the value placement to create blocks with an entirely different look.

ROTARY CUTTING INDIVIDUAL PIECES

When cutting just a few pieces from a single fabric, use a small cutting ruler like the Bias Square®. If you want to cut several pieces at one time, fold or stack the fabric into as many as four layers. Place the Bias Square on one corner of the fabric, aligning the edges with the fabric grain (sometimes it is easier to see the grain from the wrong side of the fabric). If the fabric edges are uneven, make sure that the ruler markings for the dimensions you wish to cut do not extend beyond the fabric or overlap the selvage. For example, if you need a

3" square, make sure the 3" markings on the Bias Square are well within the fabric edges. Cut the first two sides. Rotate your cutting mat or turn the cut piece of fabric. Align the proper measurement on the Bias Square along the edges you just cut, and cut the opposite two sides.

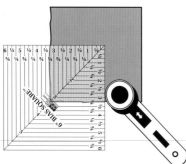

Cut the first two sides.

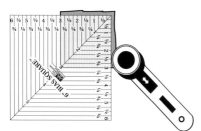

Cut the opposite two sides.

STITCHING TIPS FOR SQUARE-IN-A-SQUARE UNITS

1. Join the opposing triangles first, centering the triangles on the square. The triangle points will be sticking out about ⅜" beyond the edges of the square. Press the seam allowances toward the triangles.

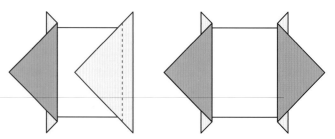

2. Join the remaining triangles. Your ¼"-wide seam should exactly intersect the 90° angle where the two triangles meet at both the top and bottom ends of the seam, as in the magnified areas of the drawing. Adjust the position of the loose triangle until the seam lines up correctly at A. Take a few stitches. Then adjust the points at B and finish stitching the seam. Press the seam allowances toward the triangles.

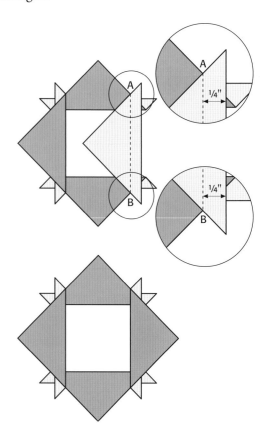

STITCHING TIPS FOR FLYING-GEESE UNITS

1. Join the left-hand triangle: Match points (A) and bottom edges; sew in the direction of the arrow. Press the seam allowances toward the smaller triangle.

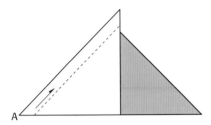

2. Join the right-hand triangle. Start at the arrow. Your ¼"-wide seam should exactly intersect the 90° angle where the two smaller triangles meet, as in the magnified portion of the drawing. Adjust the position of the loose triangle until the seam lines up correctly. Take a few stitches, then match points (B) and finish stitching the seam. Press the seam allowances toward the smaller triangle.

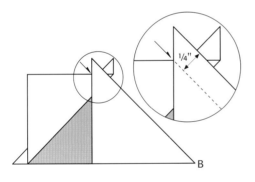

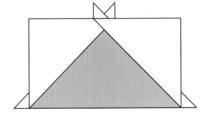

MAKING MULTIPLE BLOCKS

When you use these block patterns to make a repeat-block quilt, you will not want to cut out the blocks one a time. Instead, multiply the numbers in the cutting-instruction column by the number of blocks you wish to make, and cut all the identical pieces at the same time. Before you do these calculations, check to see if the block pattern yields more than one block. The Boy's Nonsense pattern on page 6 produces one block. To make 20 Boy's Nonsense blocks, multiply the numbers in the cutting-instruction column by 20, and cut 40 A, 40 B, 20 C, and 80 D. To make 20 blocks from a pattern that yields 2 blocks, multiply the numbers in the cutting-instruction column by 10, not 20.

When cutting many identical pieces from a single fabric, common practice is to cut selvage-to-selvage strips to the proper width, and then subcut the strips into squares or rectangles. To make half- or quarter-square triangles, these squares would be subcut once or twice diagonally. For a refresher on basic rotary-cutting techniques, refer to *101 Fabulous Rotary-Cut Quilts*, which I wrote with Nancy J. Martin (Martingale & Company).

Remember, it is always wise to make a sample block to test the pattern and confirm your fabric choices before cutting up yards of fabric!

When you make several blocks from a single pattern, watch for opportunities to use quick triangle-piecing techniques, strip-piecing methods, or other shortcuts from your own arsenal of tricks. A number of the blocks in this book contain four-patch units, for instance. Construct them with your favorite strip-piecing method instead of cutting and joining the individual squares.

CALCULATING YARDAGE REQUIREMENTS

The first step in calculating yardage requirements for multiple blocks is to figure out how many of each shape you can get from a selvage-to-selvage strip cut to one of the shape's dimensions. Pattern writers commonly count on 42" of usable width from commercial fabrics. So if you need a total of forty 2" x 2" squares, first determine how many squares you can get from one 2" x 42" strip. Divide 42" by 2 to get 21.

Next, determine how many strips you will need. Divide the total number of squares needed (40) by the number of squares per strip (21) and round up to the next whole number to get 2.

Finally, multiply the cut width of the strips (2") by the number of strips needed (2) to get 4".

Do these calculations for each of the shapes, and then add the results to find the total number of inches needed from each fabric. I usually add 10% to the total to allow for fabric shrinkage and distortion, and then divide the final figure by 36 to determine the total yardage required.

Let's calculate the total amount of light fabric needed for twenty 9" Boy's Nonsense blocks as an example (refer to the cutting instructions on page 6).

PIECE A:

For 20 blocks you need 40 squares, each 4¼" x 4¼".

1. One strip, 4¼" x 42", yields 9 squares (42 divided by 4.25 = 9.88).
2. You need 5 strips to get 40 squares (40 divided by 9 = 4.44; round up to 5).
3. So you need 21¼" of fabric for A (4.25" x 5).

PIECE B:

For 20 blocks you need 40 squares, each 3⅞" x 3⅞".

1. One strip, 3⅞" x 42", yields 10 squares (42 divided by 3.875 = 10.84).
2. You need 4 strips to get 40 squares (40 divided by 10 = 4).
3. So you need 15½" of fabric for B (3.875" x 4).

The total yardage needed for pieces A and B is 36¾". Adding 10% to allow for distortion and shrinkage brings the final figure to about 40½", or 1⅛ yards of a light fabric.

DECIMAL-TO-INCH CONVERSIONS

.0625 = ¹⁄₁₆"	.5625 = ⁹⁄₁₆"
.125 = ⅛"	.625 = ⅝"
.1875 = ³⁄₁₆"	.6875 = ¹¹⁄₁₆"
.25 = ¼"	.75 = ¾"
.3125 = ⁵⁄₁₆"	.8125 = ¹³⁄₁₆"
.375 = ⅜"	.875 = ⅞"
.4375 = ⁷⁄₁₆"	.9375 = ¹⁵⁄₁₆"
.5 = ½"	

GALLERY OF BLOCKS

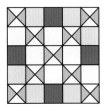
ACROBATS
(page 28)

AIR CASTLE
(page 28)

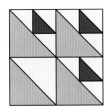
AIRCRAFT
(page 29)

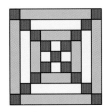
ALABAMA
(page 29)

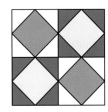
ALAMANIZER
(page 30)

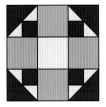
ALBUM
(page 30)

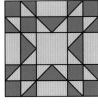
AMISH STAR
(page 31)

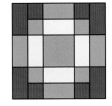
ANTIQUE TILE BLOCK
(page 31)

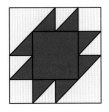
ANVIL
(page 32)

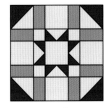
ARMY STAR
(page 32)

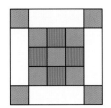
AROUND THE BLOCK
(page 33)

AROUND THE CORNER
(page 33)

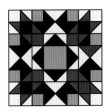
ARROW CROWN
(page 34)

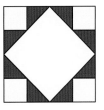
ART SQUARE
(page 34)

AT THE DEPOT
(page 35)

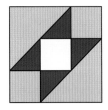
ATTIC WINDOWS
(page 35)

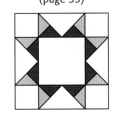
AUNT ADDIE'S ALBUM
(page 36)

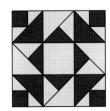
AUNT DINAH
(page 36)

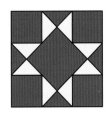
AUNT ELIZA'S STAR
(page 37)

AUNT MARY'S DOUBLE IRISH CHAIN
(page 37)

AUNT NANCY'S FAVORITE
(page 38)

AUNT RACHEL'S STAR
(page 38)

AUNT RUTH'S FANCY
(page 39)

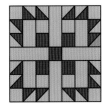
AUTUMN TINTS
(page 39)

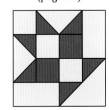
BABY BUNTING
(page 40)

BALTIMORE BELLE
(page 40)

BASKET
(page 41)

BASKET II
(page 41)

BASKET OF CHIPS
(page 42)

BASKET OF TRIANGLES
(page 42)

BASKET OF TULIPS
(page 43)

BEACON LIGHTS
(page 44)

BEAR'S PAW
(page 44)

BEGINNER'S DELIGHT
(page 45)

BERRY PATCH
(page 45)

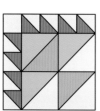

BEST FRIEND
(page 46)

BIG T
(page 46)

BIRDS IN AIR
(page 47)

BIRDS IN THE AIR
(page 47)

BIRD'S NEST
(page 48)

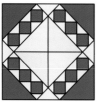

BIRTHDAY CAKE
(page 48)

BLACK SPRUCE
(page 49)

BLACKS AND WHITES
(page 49)

BLAZED TRAIL
(page 50)

BLOCKS IN A BOX
(page 50)

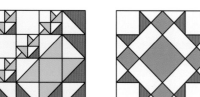

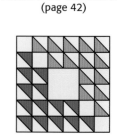
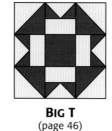

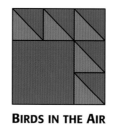

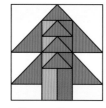
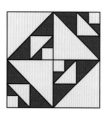
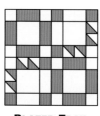
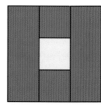

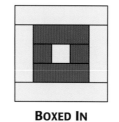
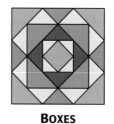

BLUE FIELDS
(page 51)

BLYTHE'S BEST
(page 51)

BOXED IN
(page 52)

BOXES
(page 52)

BOY'S NONSENSE
(page 53)

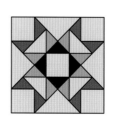
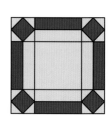

BRACED STAR
(page 53)

BROKEN DISHES
(page 54)

BROKEN SASH
(page 54)

BROKEN STAR
(page 55)

THE BROKEN WHEEL
(page 55)

BROKEN WINDOWS
(page 56)

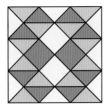

BUCKWHEAT
(page 56)

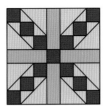

BUFFALO RIDGE
(page 57)

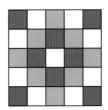

BUILDING BLOCKS
(page 57)

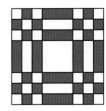

BUILDING BLOCKS II
(page 58)

CAKE STAND
(page 58)

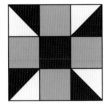

CALICO PUZZLE
(page 59)

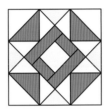

CARD BASKET
(page 59)

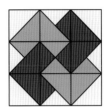

CARD TRICK
(page 60)

**CAROL'S SCRAP
TIME QUILT**
(page 60)

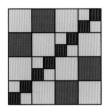

CARRIE NATION
(page 61)

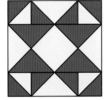

CASTLES IN SPAIN
(page 61)

CATS AND MICE
(page 62)

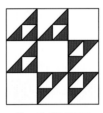

CAT'S CRADLE
(page 62)

CENTENNIAL
(page 63)

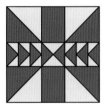

CHAIN AND BAR
(page 63)

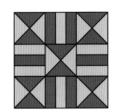

CHAIN AND HOURGLASS
(page 64)

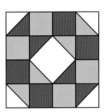

CHEYENNE
(page 64)

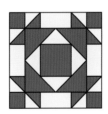

**THE CHINESE
BLOCK QUILT**
(page 65)

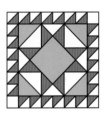

CHINOOK
(page 65)

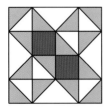

CHISHOLM TRAIL
(page 66)

CHRISTMAS STAR
(page 66)

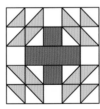

CHRISTMAS STAR II
(page 67)

CHUCK A LUCK
(page 67)

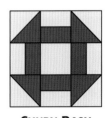

CHURN DASH
(page 68)

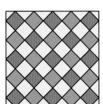

COBBLESTONES
(page 68)

COCK'S COMB
(page 69)

COFFIN STAR
(page 69)

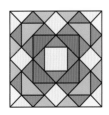

COLONIAL GARDEN
(page 70)

COMBINATION STAR
(page 70)

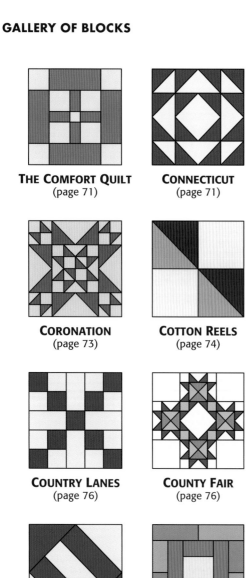

THE COMFORT QUILT
(page 71)

CONNECTICUT
(page 71)

CONTRARY WIFE
(page 72)

CORN AND BEANS
(page 72)

CORNER STAR
(page 73)

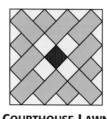

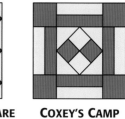

CORONATION
(page 73)

COTTON REELS
(page 74)

COUNTERCHANGE CROSS
(page 74)

COUNTERPANE
(page 75)

COUNTRY CHECKERS
(page 75)

COUNTRY LANES
(page 76)

COUNTY FAIR
(page 76)

COURTHOUSE LAWN
(page 77)

COURTHOUSE SQUARE
(page 77)

COXEY'S CAMP
(page 78)

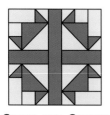

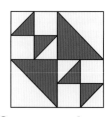

CRACKER
(page 78)

THE CRAYON BOX
(page 79)

CRAZY ANN
(page 79)

CROCKETT CABIN
(page 80)

CROSS AND CHAINS
(page 80)

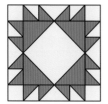

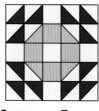
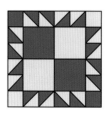
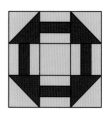

CROSS AND CROWN
(page 81)

CROSS ROADS
(page 81)

**CROSS ROADS
TO JERICHO**
(page 82)

CROSSED SQUARES
(page 82)

CROSSES AND LOSSES
(page 83)

CROWN
(page 83)

CROWN AND STAR
(page 84)

CROWN OF THORNS
(page 84)

CROW'S FOOT
(page 85)

CROW'S NEST
(page 85)

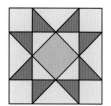

CRYSTAL STAR
(page 86)

CUPS AND SAUCERS
(page 86)

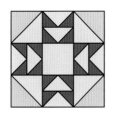

CUT THE CORNERS
(page 87)

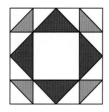

CYPRESS
(page 87)

DARIEN'S DILEMMA
(page 88)

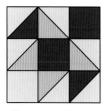

DARTING BIRDS
(page 88)

DENALI
(page 89)

DEVIL'S CLAWS
(page 89)

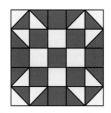

DEWEY DREAM QUILT
(page 90)

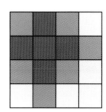

DIAGONAL SQUARE
(page 90)

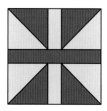

DIAMOND PANES
(page 91)

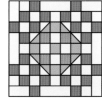

DIAMOND PLAID BLOCK
(page 91)

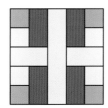

DOES DOUBLE DUTY
(page 92)

DOMINO AND SQUARE
(page 92)

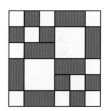

DOMINO NET
(page 93)

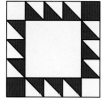

DOUBLE SAWTOOTH
(page 93)

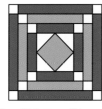

THE DOUBLE SQUARE
(page 94)

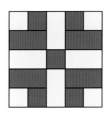

THE DOUBLE V
(page 94)

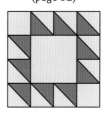

DOUBLE X
(page 95)

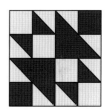

DOUBLE X #3
(page 95)

DOUBLE X #4
(page 96)

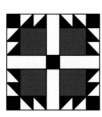

DOVES IN THE WINDOW
(page 96)

DUCK AND DUCKLINGS
(page 97)

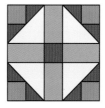

DUCK'S FOOT
(page 97)

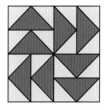

DUTCHMAN'S PUZZLE
(page 98)

EAGLE'S NEST
(page 98)

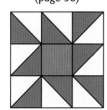

ECCENTRIC STAR
(page 99)

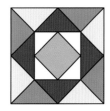

ECONOMY
(page 99)

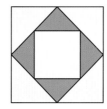

ECONOMY PATCH
(page 100)

EDDYSTONE LIGHT
(page 100)

EIGHT HANDS AROUND
(page 101)

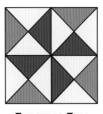

ELECTRIC FAN
(page 101)

ENVELOPE
(page 102)

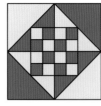

EQUINOX
(page 102)

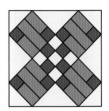

EVA'S DELIGHT
(page 103)

FAIR AND SQUARE
(page 103)

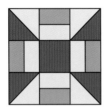

FARM FRIENDLINESS
(page 104)

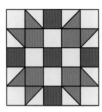

FATHER'S CHOICE
(page 104)

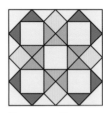

FEDERAL SQUARE
(page 105)

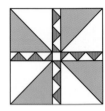

FIELDS AND FENCES
(page 105)

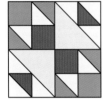

FIREFLIES
(page 106)

FIVE CROSSES
(page 106)

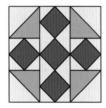

FIVE DIAMONDS
(page 107)

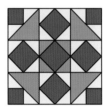

FIVE SPOT
(page 107)

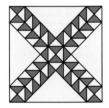

FLOCK OF BIRDS
(page 108)

FLOCK OF GEESE
(page 108)

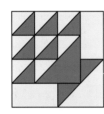

FLOWER BASKET
(page 109)

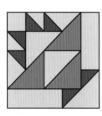

FLOWER POT
(page 109)

FLOWER POT II
(page 110)

FLYING BIRDS
(page 110)

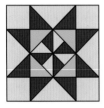

FLYING CLOUD
(page 111)

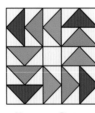

FLYING GEESE
(page 111)

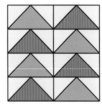

FLYING GEESE II
(page 112)

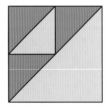

FLYING GOOSE
(page 112)

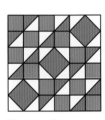

FLYING SHUTTLES
(page 113)

FOGGY MOUNTAIN BREAKDOWN
(page 113)

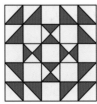

FOOT STOOL
(page 114)

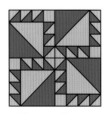

FOREST PATH
(page 114)

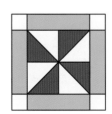

FOREST PATHS
(page 115)

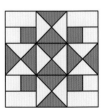

FOUR CORNERS
(page 115)

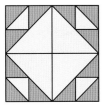

FOUR KNAVES
(page 116)

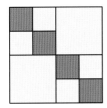

FOUR PATCH
(page 116)

FOUR SQUARES
(page 117)

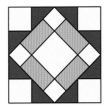

FOUR-FOUR TIME
(page 117)

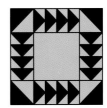

FOX AND GEESE
(page 118)

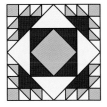

FOX PAWS
(page 118)

FOXY GRANDPA
(page 119)

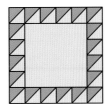

FRAMED SQUARES
(page 119)

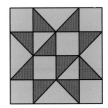

FREE TRADE
(page 120)

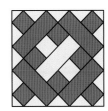

FRIENDSHIP CHAIN
(page 120)

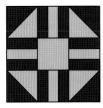

FRIENDSHIP QUILT
(page 121)

FRIENDSHIP QUILT II
(page 121)

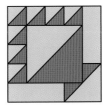

FRUIT BASKET
(page 122)

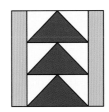

GAGGLE OF GEESE
(page 122)

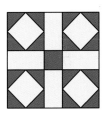

GARDEN OF EDEN
(page 123)

GEM BLOCK
(page 123)

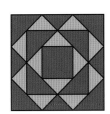

GENTLEMAN'S FANCY
(page 124)

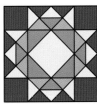

**GEORGETOWN
CIRCLE**
(page 124)

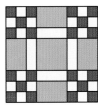

**GLORIFIED
NINE PATCH**
(page 125)

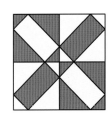

GOOD FORTUNE
(page 125)

GOOSE IN THE POND
(page 126)

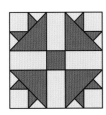

GOOSE TRACKS
(page 126)

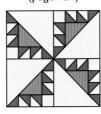

**GRAND RIGHT
AND LEFT**
(page 127)

GRANDMA'S FAVORITE
(page 127)

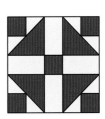

**GRANDMOTHER'S
CHOICE**
(page 128)

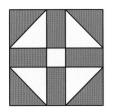

**GRANDMOTHER'S
CHOICE II**
(page 128)

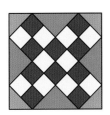

**GRANDMOTHER'S
CROSS**
(page 129)

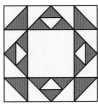

**GRANDMOTHER'S
FAVORITE**
(page 129)

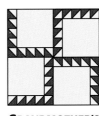

**GRANDMOTHER'S
PINWHEEL**
(page 130)

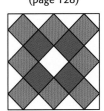

**GRANDMOTHER'S
PRIDE**
(page 130)

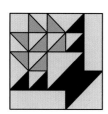

GRAPE BASKET
(page 131)

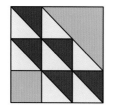

GREAT BLUE HERON
(page 131)

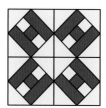

**THE H SQUARE
QUILT**
(page 132)

HANDY ANDY
(page 132)

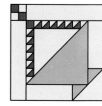

HANGING BASKET
(page 133)

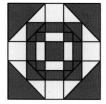

HARMONY SQUARE
(page 134)

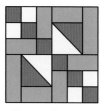

HAYES CORNER
(page 134)

HAZY DAISY
(page 135)

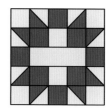

HEARTH AND HOME
(page 135)

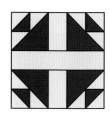

HEN AND CHICKENS
(page 136)

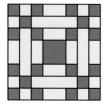

**THE HEN AND
HER CHICKS**
(page 136)

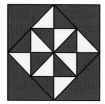

HERM'S SHIRT
(page 137)

HILL AND CRAG
(page 137)

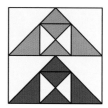

HILL AND VALLEY
(page 138)

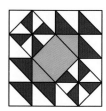

HITHER AND YON
(page 138)

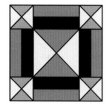

HOBSON'S KISS
(page 139)

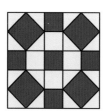

HOME CIRCLE
(page 139)

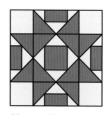

HOME TREASURE
(page 140)

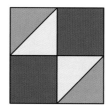

HOMEWARD BOUND
(page 140)

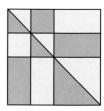

HOPKINS SQUARE
(page 141)

HOPSCOTCH
(page 141)

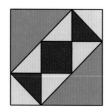

HOUR GLASS
(page 142)

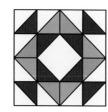

HOUR GLASS II
(page 142)

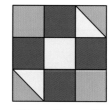

HOUR GLASS III
(page 143)

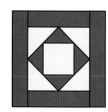

HOUR GLASS IV
(page 143)

**THE HOUSE
JACK BUILT**
(page 144)

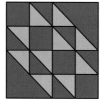

HOVERING HAWKS
(page 144)

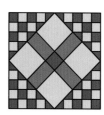

IDITAROD TRAIL
(page 145)

IMPERIAL T
(page 145)

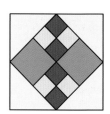

**IMPROVED
FOUR PATCH**
(page 146)

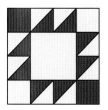

INDIAN
(page 146)

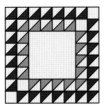

INDIAN PLUMES
(page 147)

INDIAN STAR
(page 147)

INDIANA PUZZLE
(page 148)

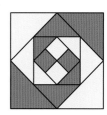

INDIANA PUZZLE II
(page 148)

IRISH CHAIN
(page 149)

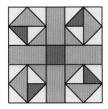

JACK IN THE BOX
(page 149)

JACK IN THE PULPIT
(page 150)

JACK'S DELIGHT
(page 150)

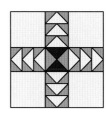

JACOB'S LADDER
(page 151)

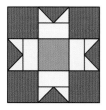

JANET'S STAR
(page 151)

JEFFERSON CITY
(page 152)

JOSEPH'S COAT
(page 152)

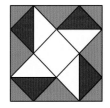

JULY FOURTH
(page 153)

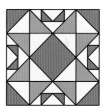

JUNEAU
(page 153)

KALEIDOSCOPE
(page 154)

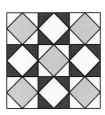

KANSAS STAR
(page 154)

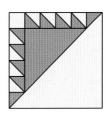

KANSAS TROUBLES
(page 155)

**KENTUCKY
CROSSROADS**
(page 155)

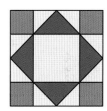

KING'S CROWN
(page 156)

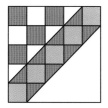

KING'S CROWN II
(page 156)

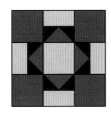

LADIES' AID ALBUM
(page 157)

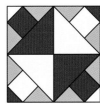

LADIES' AID BLOCK
(page 157)

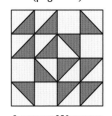

LADIES' WREATH
(page 158)

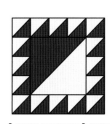

LADY OF THE LAKE
(page 158)

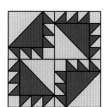

LAWYER'S PUZZLE
(page 159)

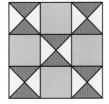

THE LETTER X
(page 159)

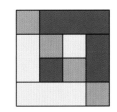

LIGHT AND SHADOWS
(page 160)

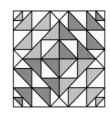

LIGHTHOUSE
(page 160)

LINCOLN
(page 161)

LINCOLN'S PLATFORM
(page 161)

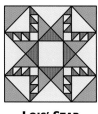

LOIS' STAR
(page 162)

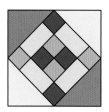

LOLA
(page 162)

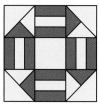

LONDON ROADS
(page 163)

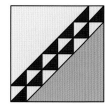

LONDON SQUARE
(page 163)

LOST SHIP
(page 164)

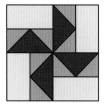

LOUISIANA
(page 164)

LOVER'S LANE
(page 165)

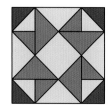

MAGIC CROSS
(page 165)

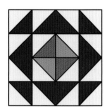

MAGIC TRIANGLES
(page 166)

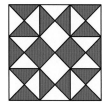

MALVINA'S CHAIN
(page 166)

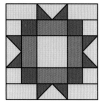

MAPLE STAR
(page 167)

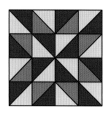

MARGARET'S CHOICE
(page 167)

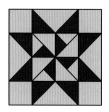

**MARTHA
WASHINGTON STAR**
(page 168)

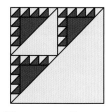

MARYLAND BEAUTY
(page 168)

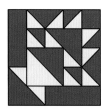

MAY BASKET
(page 169)

MEMORY
(page 169)

MEMORY BLOCKS
(page 170)

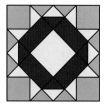

MEMORY BLOCKS II
(page 170)

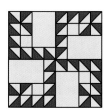

MERRY GO ROUND
(page 171)

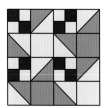

MILKY WAY
(page 171)

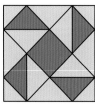

MILL WHEEL
(page 172)

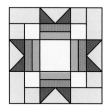

MILLENNIUM
(page 172)

MINERAL WELLS
(page 173)

MINNESOTA
(page 173)

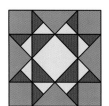

MISSOURI STAR
(page 174)

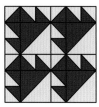

MIXED T
(page 174)

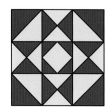

MOSAIC
(page 175)

MOSAIC #3
(page 175)

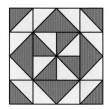

MOSAIC #8
(page 176)

MOSAIC #10
(page 176)

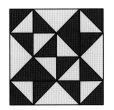
MOSAIC #11
(page 177)

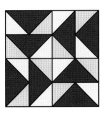
MOSAIC #12
(page 177)

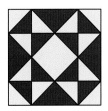
MOSAIC #19
(page 178)

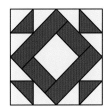
MOSAIC #21
(page 178)

MOSAIC ROSE
(page 179)

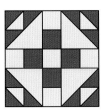
**MRS. KELLER'S
NINE PATCH**
(page 179)

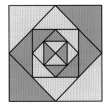
NAUTILUS
(page 180)

NEW ALBUM
(page 180)

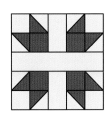
NEW ENGLAND BLOCK
(page 181)

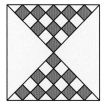
NEW HOUR GLASS
(page 181)

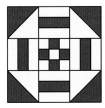
NEW WATERWHEEL
(page 182)

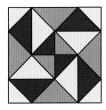
**NEXT DOOR
NEIGHBOR**
(page 182)

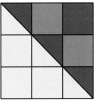
**NINE PATCH
STRAIGHT FURROW**
(page 183)

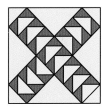
**THE NORTH
CAROLINA BEAUTY**
(page 183)

**NORTHUMBERLAND
STAR**
(page 184)

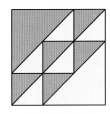
NORTHWIND
(page 184)

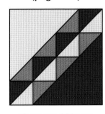
OCEAN WAVE
(page 185)

ODD FELLOWS
(page 185)

ODD FELLOWS CHAIN
(page 186)

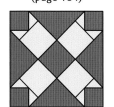
ODD FELLOW'S CROSS
(page 186)

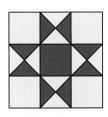
OHIO STAR
(page 187)

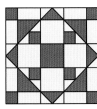
OLD FAVORITE
(page 187)

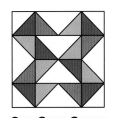
OLD GREY GOOSE
(page 188)

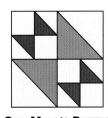
OLD MAID'S PUZZLE
(page 188)

OLD MAID'S PUZZLE II
(page 189)

**OLD MAID'S
RAMBLE**
(page 189)

**THE OLD RUGGED
CROSS**
(page 190)

OLD TIME BLOCK
(page 190)

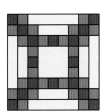
ON THE SQUARE
(page 191)

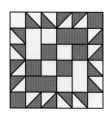

ONE MORE BLOCK
(page 191)

AN ORIGINAL DESIGN
(page 192)

OUR EDITOR
(page 192)

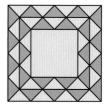

OUR VILLAGE GREEN
(page 193)

THE OZARK TRAIL
(page 193)

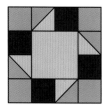

PAPER PINWHEELS
(page 194)

PATH THRU THE WOODS
(page 194)

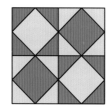

PAVEMENT PATTERN
(page 195)

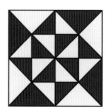

PEACE AND PLENTY
(page 195)

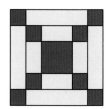

PENNSYLVANIA
(page 196)

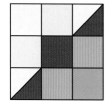

PERKIOMEN VALLEY
(page 196)

PHILADELPHIA PAVEMENT
(page 197)

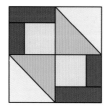

PICKET FENCE
(page 197)

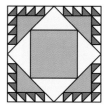

PINE BURR
(page 198)

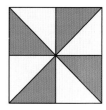

PINWHEEL
(page 198)

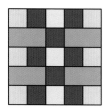

PLAID
(page 199)

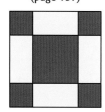

A PLAIN BLOCK
(page 199)

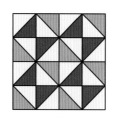

PORT AND STARBOARD
(page 200)

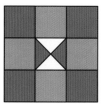

PRACTICAL ORCHARD
(page 200)

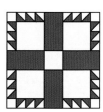

PREMIUM STAR
(page 201)

THE PRESIDENTIAL ARMCHAIR
(page 201)

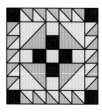

PRICKLY PEAR
(page 202)

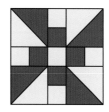

PROPELLER
(page 202)

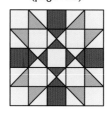

PROVIDENCE
(page 203)

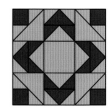

PUSS IN THE CORNER
(page 203)

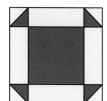

PUSS IN THE CORNER II
(page 204)

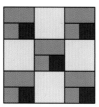

PUSSY IN THE CORNER
(page 204)

PYRAMIDS
(page 205)

QUILT IN LIGHT AND DARK
(page 205)

RAILROAD CROSSING
(page 206)

RAMBLER
(page 206)

RED CROSS
(page 207)

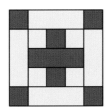

RED CROSS II
(page 207)

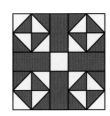

RED CROSS III
(page 208)

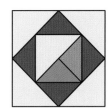

REMEMBER ME
(page 208)

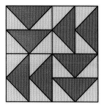

**RETURN OF
THE SWALLOWS**
(page 209)

REVERSE X
(page 209)

RHODE ISLAND
(page 210)

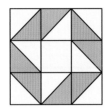

RIBBON QUILT
(page 210)

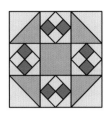

RICHMOND
(page 211)

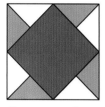

RIGHT AND LEFT
(page 211)

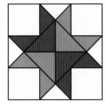

**RIGHT HAND
OF FRIENDSHIP**
(page 212)

RISING STAR
(page 212)

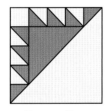

RISING SUN
(page 213)

**ROAD TO THE
WHITE HOUSE**
(page 213)

**ROBBING PETER
TO PAY PAUL**
(page 214)

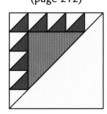

ROCKY GLEN
(page 214)

ROCKY GLEN II
(page 215)

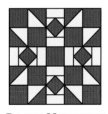

**ROCKY MOUNTAIN
CHAIN**
(page 215)

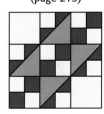

ROCKY ROAD
(page 216)

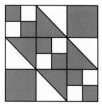

**ROCKY ROAD
TO CALIFORNIA**
(page 216)

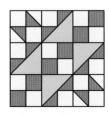

**ROCKY ROAD
TO DUBLIN**
(page 217)

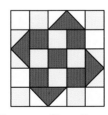

ROLLING NINE PATCH
(page 217)

ROLLING PINWHEEL
(page 218)

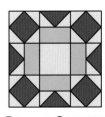

ROLLING SQUARES
(page 218)

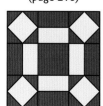

ROLLING STONE
(page 219)

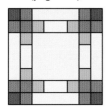

THE ROSEBUD
(page 219)

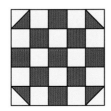

ROUND THE CORNER
(page 220)

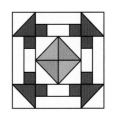

RUINS OF JERICHO
(page 220)

SAIL BOATS
(page 221)

SALLY'S FAVORITE
(page 221)

SALT LAKE CITY
(page 222)

A SALUTE TO THE COLORS
(page 222)

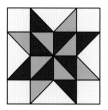

SARAH'S CHOICE
(page 223)

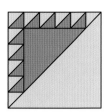

SAWTOOTH
(page 223)

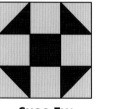

SAWTOOTH II
(page 224)

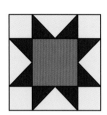

SAWTOOTH STAR
(page 224)

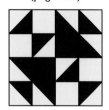

SCHOOL GIRL'S PUZZLE
(page 225)

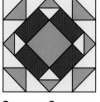

SCOTCH SQUARES
(page 225)

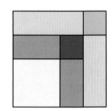

SCOT'S PLAID
(page 226)

SHOO FLY
(page 226)

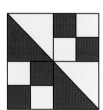

THE SICKLE
(page 227)

THE SILENT STAR
(page 227)

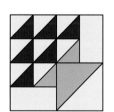

SIMPLE FLOWER BASKET
(page 228)

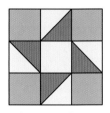

SIMPLEX STAR
(page 228)

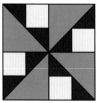

SINGLE CHAIN AND KNOT
(page 229)

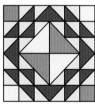

SMOKEHOUSE
(page 229)

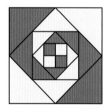

SNAIL'S TRAIL
(page 230)

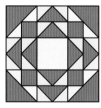

SNOWY OWL
(page 231)

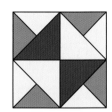

SOUTHERN BELLE
(page 231)

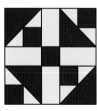

SPINNER
(page 232)

SPINNING TOPS
(page 232)

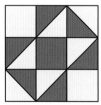

SPLIT NINE PATCH
(page 233)

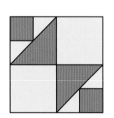

SPOOL AND BOBBIN
(page 233)

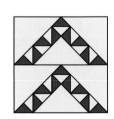

SPRING AND FALL
(page 234)

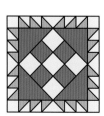

SPRING HAS COME
(page 234)

SQUARE AND STAR
(page 235)

THE SQUARE DEAL
(page 235)

SQUARE ON SQUARE
(page 236)

SQUARE SURROUNDED
(page 236)

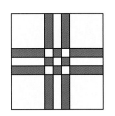

SQUARES AND STRIPS
(page 237)

ST. JOHN PAVEMENT
(page 237)

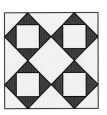

**THE STAR
AND BLOCK**
(page 238)

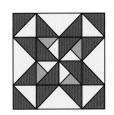

STAR AND PINWHEELS
(page 238)

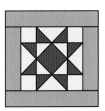

STAR OF VIRGINIA
(page 239)

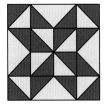

STAR PUZZLE
(page 239)

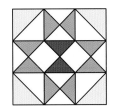

STAR X
(page 240)

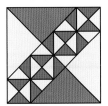

STARRY PATH
(page 240)

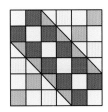

STEPPING STONES
(page 241)

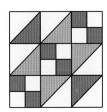

STEPS TO THE ALTAR
(page 241)

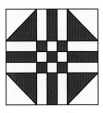

STILES AND PATHS
(page 242)

STORM SIGNAL
(page 242)

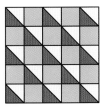

STRENGTH IN UNION
(page 243)

STRIP HEART
(page 243)

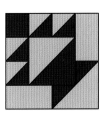

SUGAR BOWL
(page 244)

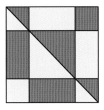

SUMMER SOLSTICE
(page 244)

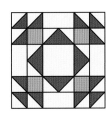

SUMMER WINDS
(page 245)

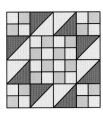

SUNNY LANES
(page 245)

SUNSHINE
(page 246)

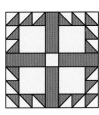

SURPRISE PACKAGE
(page 246)

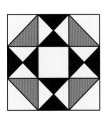

SWAMP ANGEL
(page 247)

T SQUARE
(page 247)

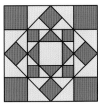

TEMPLE COURT
(page 248)

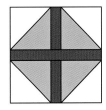

TEXAS PUZZLE
(page 248)

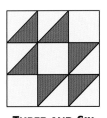

THREE AND SIX
(page 249)

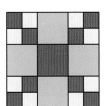

THRIFTY
(page 249)

**THUNDER AND
LIGHTNING**
(page 250)

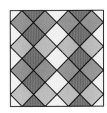

TINTED CHAINS
(page 250)

TOAD IN A PUDDLE
(page 251)

TOMBSTONE QUILT
(page 251)

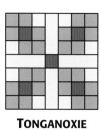

**TONGANOXIE
NINE PATCH**
(page 252)

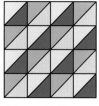

TRAIL OF TEARS
(page 252)

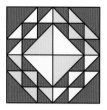

TRIANGLE
(page 253)

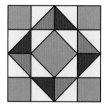

TRIANGLE SQUARES
(page 253)

TRIANGLES
(page 254)

TRIPLET
(page 254)

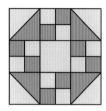

TRUE BLUE
(page 255)

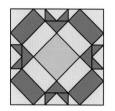

TURKEY IN THE STRAW
(page 255)

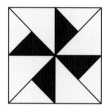

TURNSTILE
(page 256)

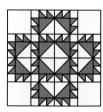

TWELVE CROWNS
(page 256)

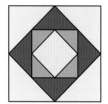

TWELVE TRIANGLES
(page 257)

TWINKLING STAR
(page 257)

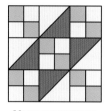

**UNDERGROUND
RAILROAD**
(page 258)

UNION
(page 258)

UNION SQUARE
(page 259)

UNNAMED STAR
(page 259)

VERMONT
(page 260)

VINES AT THE WINDOW
(page 260)

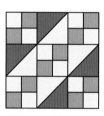

WAGON TRACKS
(page 261)

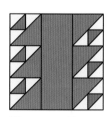

WAMPUM BLOCK
(page 261)

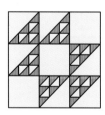

WANDERING LOVER
(page 262)

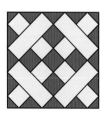

**WASHINGTON
PAVEMENT**
(page 262)

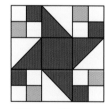

WATER WHEEL
(page 263)

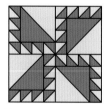

WAVES OF THE SEA
(page 263)

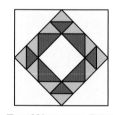

THE WEDDING RING
(page 264)

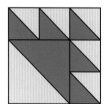

WEST WIND
(page 264)

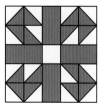

WHEEL OF CHANCE
(page 265)

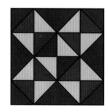

WHEEL OF TIME
(page 265)

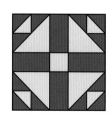

WHIRLING FIVE PATCH
(page 266)

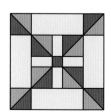

WHIRLING SQUARE
(page 266)

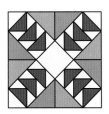

WHIRLWIND
(page 267)

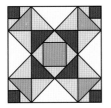

WHITE HEMSTITCH
(page 267)

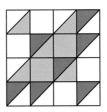

WILD DUCK
(page 268)

WILD GOOSE
(page 268)

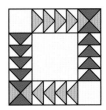

WILD GOOSE CHASE
(page 269)

**WILD GOOSE
CHASE II**
(page 269)

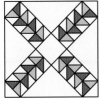

**WILD GOOSE
CHASE III**
(page 270)

WILLOW HAVEN
(page 270)

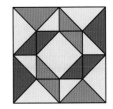

WINDBLOWN SQUARE
(page 271)

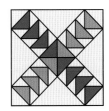

WINDMILL
(page 271)

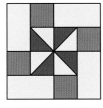

WINDMILL II
(page 272)

WINDMILL III
(page 272)

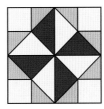

WINDMILL SQUARE
(page 273)

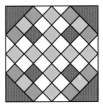

**WINDOWS
AND DOORS**
(page 273)

THE WINGED 9 PATCH
(page 274)

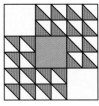

WINGED SQUARE
(page 274)

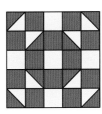

WISHING RING
(page 275)

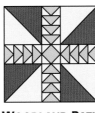

WOODLAND PATH
(page 275)

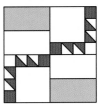

**WORLD'S FAIR
PUZZLE**
(page 276)

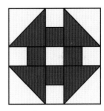

WRENCH
(page 276)

THE X
(page 277)

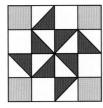

X QUARTET
(page 277)

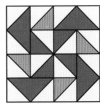

YANKEE PUZZLE
(page 278)

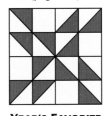

YEAR'S FAVORITE
(page 278)

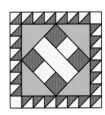

ZENOBIA'S PUZZLE
(page 279)

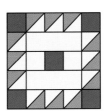

ZIGZAG
(page 279)

BLOCK PATTERNS

ACROBATS

5-Unit Grid
Color Illustration: page 11

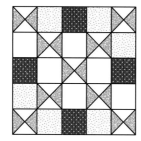 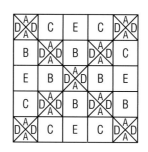 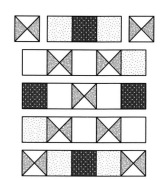

		FINISHED BLOCK SIZE					
		Single dimensions in the cutting chart indicate the size of the cut square (3" = 3" x 3").					
FOR 2 BLOCKS:		**5"**	**6¼"**	**7½"**	**8¾"**	**10"**	**12½"**
Light	A: 9 ⊠ → ⊠	2¼"	2½"	2¾"	3"	3¼"	3¾"
	B: 12 □	1½"	1¾"	2"	2¼"	2½"	3"
Light 2	C: 12 □	1½"	1¾"	2"	2¼"	2¾"	3"
Medium	D: 9 ⊠ → ⊠	2¼"	2½"	2¾"	3"	3¼"	3¾"
Dark	E: 8 □	1½"	1¾"	2"	2¼"	2¾"	3"
Try this:	Use many different mediums for D.						

AIR CASTLE

6-Unit Grid
Color Illustration: page 11

 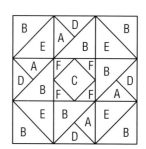 

		FINISHED BLOCK SIZE					
		Single dimensions in the cutting chart indicate the size of the cut square (3" = 3" x 3").					
FOR 1 BLOCK:		**4½"**	**6"**	**7½"**	**9"**	**10½"**	**12"**
Light	A: 1 ⊠ → ⊠	2¾"	3¼"	3¾"	4¼"	4¾"	5¼"
	B: 4 ◻ → ◺	2⅜"	2⅞"	3⅜"	3⅞"	4⅜"	4⅞"
	C: 1 ◇	T5	T7	T9	T11	T12	T14
Dark	D: 1 ⊠ → ⊠	2¾"	3¼"	3¾"	4¼"	4¾"	5¼"
	E: 2 ◻ → ◺	2⅜"	2⅞"	3⅜"	3⅞"	4⅜"	4⅞"
	F: 2 ◻ → ◺	1⅝"	1⅞"	2⅛"	2⅜"	2⅝"	2⅞"
Try this:	Use one light for A and C and a different light for B.						

AIRCRAFT

4-Unit Grid
Color Illustration: page 11

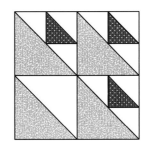
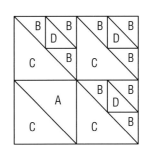
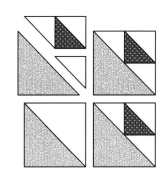

		FINISHED BLOCK SIZE *Single dimensions in the cutting chart indicate the size of the cut square (3" = 3" x 3").*					
FOR 2 BLOCKS:		**4"**	**6"**	**8"**	**9"**	**10"**	**12"**
Light	A: 1 ☐→◤	2⅞"	3⅞"	4⅞"	5⅜"	5⅞"	6⅞"
	B: 9 ☐→◤	1⅞"	2⅜"	2⅞"	3⅛"	3⅜"	3⅞"
Medium	C: 4 ☐→◤	2⅞"	3⅞"	4⅞"	5⅜"	5⅞"	6⅞"
Dark	D: 3 ☐→◤	1⅞"	2⅜"	2⅞"	3⅛"	3⅜"	3⅞"

Try this: Use several different mediums for C.

ALABAMA

9-Unit Grid
Color Illustration: page 11

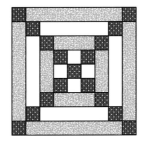
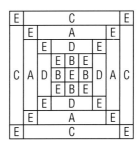
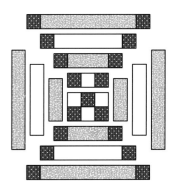

		FINISHED BLOCK SIZE *Single dimensions in the cutting chart indicate the size of the cut square (3" = 3" x 3").*					
FOR 1 BLOCK:		**6¾"**	**9"**	**10⅛"**	**11¼"**	**12⅜"**	**13½"**
Light	A: 4 ▭	1¼" x 4¼"	1½" x 5½"	1⅝" x 6⅛"	1¾" x 6¾"	1⅞" x 7⅜"	2" x 8"
	B: 4 ☐	1¼"	1½"	1⅝"	1¾"	1⅞"	2"
Medium	C: 4 ▭	1¼" x 5¾"	1½" x 7½"	1⅝" x 8⅜"	1¾" x 9¼"	1⅞"x 10⅛"	2" x 11"
	D: 4 ▭	1¼" x 2¾"	1½" x 3½"	1⅝" x 3⅞"	1¾" x 4¼"	1⅞" x 4⅝"	2" x 5"
Dark	E: 17 ☐	1¼"	1½"	1⅝"	1¾"	1⅞"	2"

Try this: Use one medium for C and a different medium for D.

ALAMANIZER

4-Unit Grid
Color Illustration: page 11

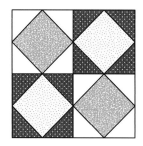 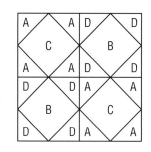 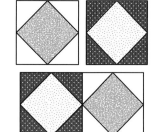

FOR 1 BLOCK:		FINISHED BLOCK SIZE *Single dimensions in the cutting chart indicate the size of the cut square (3" = 3" x 3").*					
		4"	**6"**	**8"**	**9"**	**10"**	**12"**
Light	A: 4 ◻→◻	1⅞"	2⅜"	2⅞"	3⅛"	3⅜"	3⅞"
Light 2	B: 2 ◇	T7	T11	T14	T15	T16	T19
Medium	C: 2 ◇	T7	T11	T14	T15	T16	T19
Dark	D: 4 ◻→◻	1⅞"	2⅜"	2⅞"	3⅛"	3⅜"	3⅞"

Try this: Use several different fabrics for B and C.

ALBUM

6-Unit Grid
Color Illustration: page 11

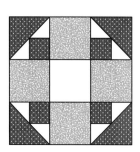 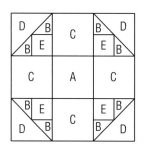 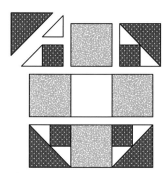

FOR 1 BLOCK:		FINISHED BLOCK SIZE *Single dimensions in the cutting chart indicate the size of the cut square (3" = 3" x 3").*					
		4½"	**6"**	**7½"**	**9"**	**10½"**	**12"**
Light	A: 1 ◻	2"	2½"	3"	3½"	4"	4½"
	B: 4 ◻→◻	1⅝"	1⅞"	2⅛"	2⅜"	2⅝"	2⅞"
Medium	C: 4 ◻	2"	2½"	3"	3½"	4"	4½"
Dark	D: 2 ◻→◻	2⅜"	2⅞"	3⅜"	3⅞"	4⅜"	4⅞"
	E: 4 ◻	1¼"	1½"	1¾"	2"	2¼"	2½"

Try this: Reverse the mediums and darks in every other block.

◻ Light ◻ Light 2 ◻ Medium ◻ Medium 2 ◼ Dark

AMISH STAR

6-Unit Grid
Color Illustration: page 11

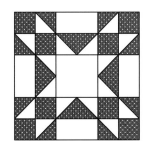
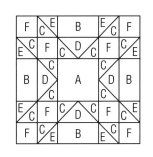
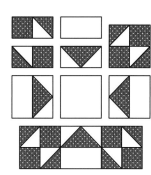

		FINISHED BLOCK SIZE *Single dimensions in the cutting chart indicate the size of the cut square (3" = 3" x 3").*					
FOR 1 BLOCK:			**4½"**	**6"**	**7½"**	**9"**	**10½"**	**12"**
Light	A: 1 ☐		2"	2½"	3"	3½"	4"	4½"
	B: 4 ▭		1¼" x 2"	1½" x 2½"	1¾" x 3"	2" x 3½"	2¼" x 4"	2½" x 4½"
	C: 8 ◻→◺		1⅝"	1⅞"	2⅛"	2⅜"	2⅝"	2⅞"
Dark	D: 1 ⊠→◹		2¾"	3¼"	3¾"	4¼"	4¾"	5¼"
	E: 4 ◻→◺		1⅝"	1⅞"	2⅛"	2⅜"	2⅝"	2⅞"
	F: 8 ☐		1¼"	1½"	1¾"	2"	2¼"	2½"

Try this: Reverse the lights and darks in every other block.

ANTIQUE TILE BLOCK

6-Unit Grid
Color Illustration: page 11

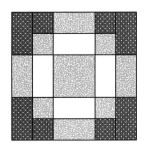
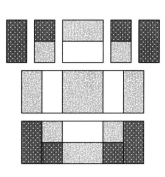

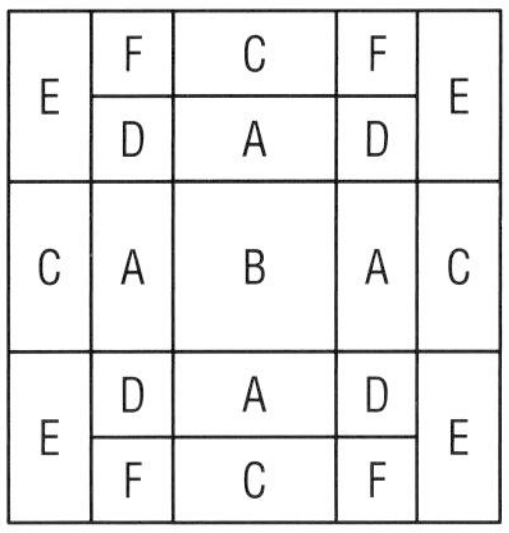

		FINISHED BLOCK SIZE *Single dimensions in the cutting chart indicate the size of the cut square (3" = 3" x 3").*					
FOR 1 BLOCK:			**4½"**	**6"**	**7½"**	**9"**	**10½"**	**12"**
Light	A: 4 ▭		1¼" x 2"	1½" x 2½"	1¾" x 3"	2" x 3½"	2¼" x 4"	2½" x 4½"
Medium	B: 1 ☐		2"	2½"	3"	3½"	4"	4½"
	C: 4 ▭		1¼" x 2"	1½" x 2½"	1¾" x 3"	2" x 3½"	2¼" x 4"	2½" x 4½"
	D: 4 ☐		1¼"	1½"	1¾"	2"	2¼"	2½"
Dark	E: 4 ▭		1¼" x 2"	1½" x 2½"	1¾" x 3"	2" x 3½"	2¼" x 4"	2½" x 4½"
	F: 4 ☐		1¼"	1½"	1¾"	2"	2¼"	2½"

Try this: Use one medium for B and C and a different medium for D.

ANVIL

4-Unit Grid

Color Illustration: page 11

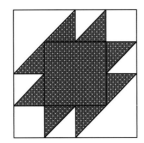
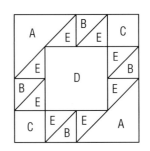
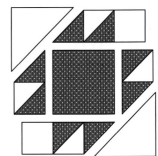

FOR 1 BLOCK:		FINISHED BLOCK SIZE *Single dimensions in the cutting chart indicate the size of the cut square (3" = 3" x 3").*					
		4"	**6"**	**8"**	**9"**	**10"**	**12"**
Light	A: 1 ◻ → ◹	2⅞"	3⅞"	4⅞"	5⅜"	5⅞"	6⅞"
	B: 2 ◻ → ◹	1⅞"	2⅜"	2⅞"	3⅛"	3⅜"	3⅞"
	C: 2 ◻	1½"	2"	2½"	2¾"	3"	3½"
Dark	D: 1 ◻	2½"	3½"	4½"	5"	5½"	6½"
	E: 4 ◻ → ◹	1⅞"	2⅜"	2⅞"	3⅛"	3⅜"	3⅞"

Try this: Use a large-scale print for D.

ARMY STAR

8-Unit Grid

Color Illustration: page 11

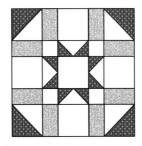
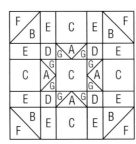
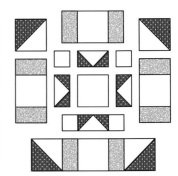

FOR 1 BLOCK:		FINISHED BLOCK SIZE *Single dimensions in the cutting chart indicate the size of the cut square (3" = 3" x 3").*					
		6"	**8"**	**9"**	**10"**	**12"**	**14"**
Light	A: 1 ⊠ → ⊠	2¾"	3¼"	3½"	3¾"	4¼"	4¾"
	B: 2 ◻ → ◹	2⅜"	2⅞"	3⅛"	3⅜"	3⅞"	4⅜"
	C: 5 ◻	2"	2½"	2¾"	3"	3½"	4"
	D: 4 ◻	1¼"	1½"	1⅝"	1¾"	2"	2¼"
Medium	E: 8 ▭	1¼" x 2"	1½" x 2½"	1⅝" x 2¾"	1¾" x 3"	2" x 3½"	2¼" x 4"
Dark	F: 2 ◻ → ◹	2⅜"	2⅞"	3⅛"	3⅜"	3⅞"	4⅜"
	G: 4 ◻ → ◹	1⅝"	1⅞"	2"	2⅛"	2⅜"	2⅝"

Try this: Reverse the lights and darks.

AROUND THE BLOCK

5-Unit Grid

Color Illustration: page 11

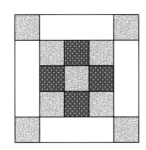

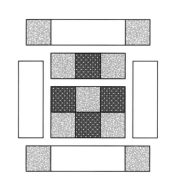

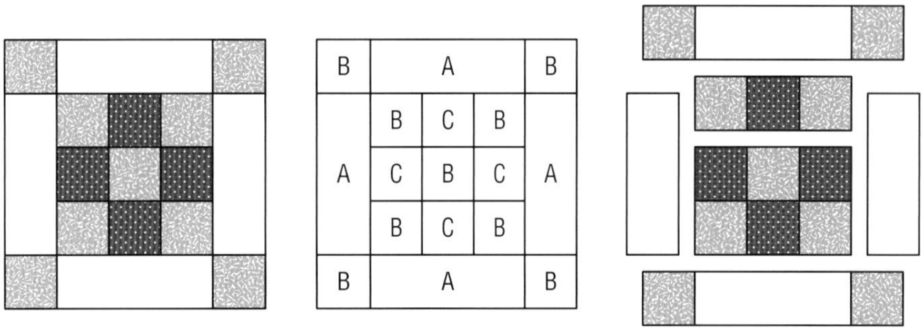

		FINISHED BLOCK SIZE					
		Single dimensions in the cutting chart indicate the size of the cut square (3" = 3" x 3").					
FOR 1 BLOCK:		**5"**	**6¼"**	**7½"**	**8¾"**	**10"**	**12½"**
Light	A: 4 ▭	1½" x 3½"	1¾" x 4¼"	2" x 5"	2¼" x 5¾"	2½" x 6½"	3" x 8"
Medium	B: 9 ☐	1½"	1¾"	2"	2¼"	2½"	3"
Dark	C: 4 ☐	1½"	1¾"	2"	2¼"	2½"	3"

Try this: Use a different dark in every block.

AROUND THE CORNER

4-Unit Grid

Color Illustration: page 11

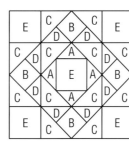

		FINISHED BLOCK SIZE					
		Single dimensions in the cutting chart indicate the size of the cut square (3" = 3" x 3").					
FOR 1 BLOCK:		**4"**	**6"**	**8"**	**9"**	**10"**	**12"**
Light	A: 1 ⊠→⊠	2¼"	2¾"	3¼"	3½"	3¾"	4¼"
	B: 4 ◇	T2	T5	T7	T8	T9	T11
Medium	C: 6 ◺→◹	1⅞"	2⅜"	2⅞"	3⅛"	3⅜"	3⅞"
Dark	D: 2 ⊠→⊠	2¼"	2¾"	3¼"	3½"	3¾"	4¼"
	E: 5 ☐	1½"	2"	2½"	2¾"	3"	3½"

Try this: Reverse the mediums and darks in every other block.

☐ *Light*   ▦ *Light 2*   ▨ *Medium*   ▤ *Medium 2*   ■ *Dark*

ARROW CROWN

8-Unit Grid

Color Illustration: page 11

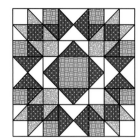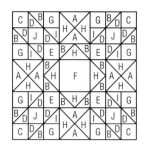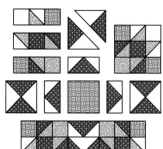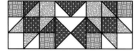

		FINISHED BLOCK SIZE *Single dimensions in the cutting chart indicate the size of the cut square (3" = 3" x 3").*					
FOR 1 BLOCK:		**6"**	**8"**	**9"**	**10"**	**12"**	**14"**
Light	A: 2 ⊠ → ⊠	2¾"	3¼"	3½"	3¾"	4¼"	4¾"
	B: 8 ◺ → ◺	1⅝"	1⅞"	2"	2⅛"	2⅜"	2⅝"
	C: 4 □	1¼"	1½"	1⅝"	1¾"	2"	2¼"
Medium	D: 8 ◺ → ◺	1⅝"	1⅞"	2"	2⅛"	2⅜"	2⅝"
	E: 4 □	1¼"	1½"	1⅝"	1¾"	2"	2¼"
Medium 2	F: 1 □	2"	2½"	2¾"	3"	3½"	4"
	G: 8 □	1¼"	1½"	1⅝"	1¾"	2"	2¼"
Dark	H: 3 ⊠ → ⊠	2¾"	3¼"	3½"	3¾"	4¼"	4¾"
	I: 4 ◺ → ◺	1⅝"	1⅞"	2"	2⅛"	2⅜"	2⅝"
	J: 4 □	1¼"	1½"	1⅝"	1¾"	2"	2¼"

Try this: Use several different mediums for D.

ART SQUARE

4-Unit Grid

Color Illustration: page 11

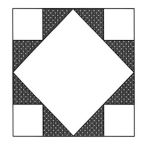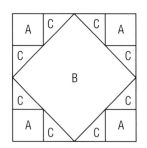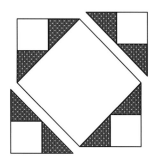

		FINISHED BLOCK SIZE *Single dimensions in the cutting chart indicate the size of the cut square (3" = 3" x 3").*					
FOR 1 BLOCK:		**4"**	**6"**	**8"**	**9"**	**10"**	**12"**
Light	A: 4 □	1½"	2"	2½"	2¾"	3"	3½"
	B: 1 ◇	T14	T19	T23	T24	T25	T27
Dark	C: 4 ◺ → ◺	1⅞"	2⅜"	2⅞"	3⅛"	3⅜"	3⅞"

Try this: Use a large-scale print for B.

AT THE DEPOT

6-Unit Grid
Color Illustration: page 11

 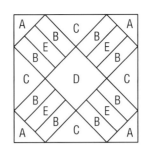 

	FINISHED BLOCK SIZE					
	Single dimensions in the cutting chart indicate the size of the cut square (3" = 3" x 3").					
FOR 1 BLOCK:	**4½"**	**6"**	**7½"**	**9"**	**10½"**	**12"**
Light A: 2 ▢ ▸ ◱	2"	2⅜"	2¾"	3⅛"	3½"	3⅞"
B: 8 ◇	T29	T33	T37	T42	T47	T52
Medium C: 1 ⊠ ▸ ⊠	3½"	4¼"	5"	5¾"	6½"	7¼"
Dark D: 1 ◇	T8	T11	T13	T15	T17	T19
E: 4 ◇	T29	T33	T37	T42	T47	T52
Try this: Use a medium instead of a light for A.						

ATTIC WINDOWS

3-Unit Grid
Color Illustration: page 11

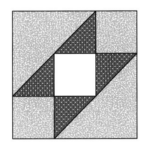 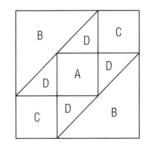 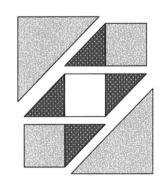

	FINISHED BLOCK SIZE					
	Single dimensions in the cutting chart indicate the size of the cut square (3" = 3" x 3").					
FOR 1 BLOCK:	**4½"**	**6"**	**7½"**	**9"**	**10½"**	**12"**
Light A: 1 ▢	2"	2½"	3"	3½"	4"	4½"
Medium B: 1 ▢ ▸ ◲	3⅞"	4⅞"	5⅞"	6⅞"	7⅞"	8⅞"
C: 2 ▢	2"	2½"	3"	3½"	4"	4½"
Dark D: 2 ▢ ▸ ◲	2⅜"	2⅞"	3⅜"	3⅞"	4⅜"	4⅞"
Try this: Reverse the mediums and darks in every other block.						

AUNT ADDIE'S ALBUM

4-Unit Grid

Color Illustration: page 11

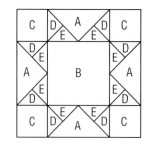
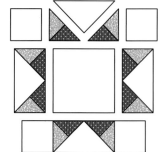

FOR 1 BLOCK:		FINISHED BLOCK SIZE *Single dimensions in the cutting chart indicate the size of the cut square (3" = 3" x 3").*					
		4"	**6"**	**8"**	**9"**	**10"**	**12"**
Light	A: 1 ⊠→⊠	3¼"	4¼"	5¼"	5¾"	6¼"	7¼"
	B: 1 ☐	2½"	3½"	4½"	5"	5½"	6½"
	C: 4 ☐	1½"	2"	2½"	2¾"	3"	3½"
Medium	D: 2 ⊠→⊠	2¼"	2¾"	3¼"	3½"	3¾"	4¼"
Dark	E: 2 ⊠→⊠	2¼"	2¾"	3¼"	3½"	3¾"	4¼"

Try this: Use a large-scale print or an autographed square for B.

AUNT DINAH

6-Unit Grid

Color Illustration: page 11

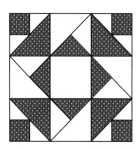
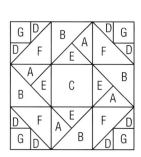

FOR 1 BLOCK:		FINISHED BLOCK SIZE *Single dimensions in the cutting chart indicate the size of the cut square (3" = 3" x 3").*					
		4½"	**6"**	**7½"**	**9"**	**10½"**	**12"**
Light	A: 1 ⊠→⊠	2¾"	3¼"	3¾"	4¼"	4¾"	5¼"
	B: 2 ◻→◻	2⅜"	2⅞"	3⅜"	3⅞"	4⅜"	4⅞"
	C: 1 ☐	2"	2½"	3"	3½"	4"	4½"
	D: 4 ◻→◻	1⅝"	1⅞"	2⅛"	2⅜"	2⅝"	2⅞"
Dark	E: 1 ⊠→⊠	2¾"	3¼"	3¾"	4¼"	4¾"	5¼"
	F: 2 ◻→◻	2⅜"	2⅞"	3⅜"	3⅞"	4⅜"	4⅞"
	G: 4 ☐	1¼"	1½"	1¾"	2"	2¼"	2½"

Try this: Use a medium instead of a dark for F.

AUNT ELIZA'S STAR

3-Unit Grid
Color Illustration: page 11

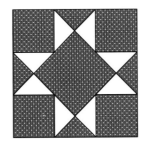 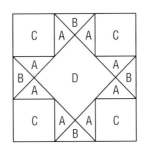 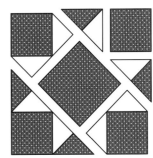

FOR 1 BLOCK:	FINISHED BLOCK SIZE *Single dimensions in the cutting chart indicate the size of the cut square (3" = 3" x 3").*					
	4½"	**6"**	**7½"**	**9"**	**10½"**	**12"**
Light A: 2 ⊠ → ⊠	2¾"	3¼"	3¾"	4¼"	4¾"	5¼"
Dark B: 1 ⊠ → ⊠	2¾"	3¼"	3¾"	4¼"	4¾"	5¼
C: 4 ☐	2"	2½"	3"	3½"	4"	4½"
D: 1 ◇	T11	T14	T16	T19	T21	T23

Try this: Reverse the lights and darks in every other block.

AUNT MARY'S DOUBLE IRISH CHAIN

8-Unit Grid
Color Illustration: page 11

 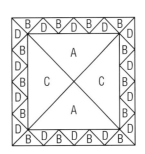 

FOR 2 BLOCKS:	FINISHED BLOCK SIZE *Single dimensions in the cutting chart indicate the size of the cut square (3" = 3" x 3").*					
	4"	**6"**	**8"**	**9"**	**10"**	**12"**
Light A: 1 ⊠ → ⊠	4¼"	5¾"	7¼"	8"	8¾"	10¼"
B: 7 ⊠ → ⊠	2¼"	2¾"	3¼"	3½"	3¾"	4¼"
Dark C: 1 ⊠ → ⊠	4¼"	5¾"	7¼"	8"	8¾"	10¼"
D: 7 ⊠ → ⊠	2¼"	2¾"	3¼"	3½"	3¾"	4¼"

Try this: Use several different lights and darks for B and D.

Aunt Nancy's Favorite

4-Unit Grid

Color Illustration: page 11

 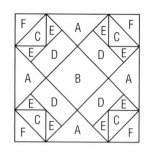 

		FINISHED BLOCK SIZE					
		Single dimensions in the cutting chart indicate the size of the cut square (3" = 3" x 3").					
FOR 1 BLOCK:		**4"**	**6"**	**8"**	**9"**	**10"**	**12"**
Light	A: 1 ⊠→⊠	3¼"	4¼"	5¼"	5¾"	6¼"	7¼"
	B: 1 ◇	T7	T11	T14	T15	T16	T19
Medium	C: 2 ◻→◺	1⅞"	2⅜"	2⅞"	3⅛"	3⅜"	3⅞"
	D: 4 ◇	T32	T41	T51	T56	T59	T67
Dark	E: 2 ⊠→⊠	2¼"	2¾"	3¼"	3½"	3¾"	4¼"
	F: 2 ◻→◺	1⅞"	2⅜"	2⅞"	3⅛"	3⅜"	3⅞"

Try this: Use one medium for C and a different medium for D.

Aunt Rachel's Star

12-Unit Grid

Color Illustration: page 11

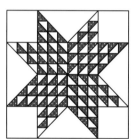 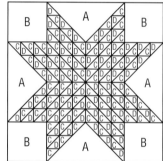 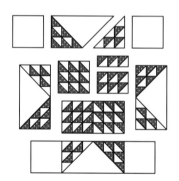

		FINISHED BLOCK SIZE					
		Single dimensions in the cutting chart indicate the size of the cut square (3" = 3" x 3").					
FOR 1 BLOCK:		**6"**	**7½"**	**9"**	**12"**	**13½"**	**15"**
Light	A: 1 ⊠→⊠	4¼"	5"	5¾"	7¼"	8"	8¾"
	B: 4 ◻	2"	2⅜"	2¾"	3½"	3⅞"	4¼"
	C: 36 ◻→◺	1⅜"	1½"	1⅝"	1⅞"	2"	2⅛"
Dark	D: 36 ◻→◺	1⅜"	1½"	1⅝"	1⅞"	2"	2⅛"

Try this: Use many different darks for D.

Aunt Ruth's Fancy

7-Unit Grid
Color Illustration: page 11

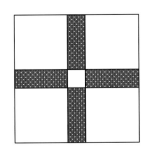
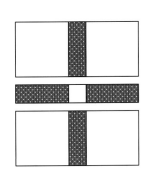

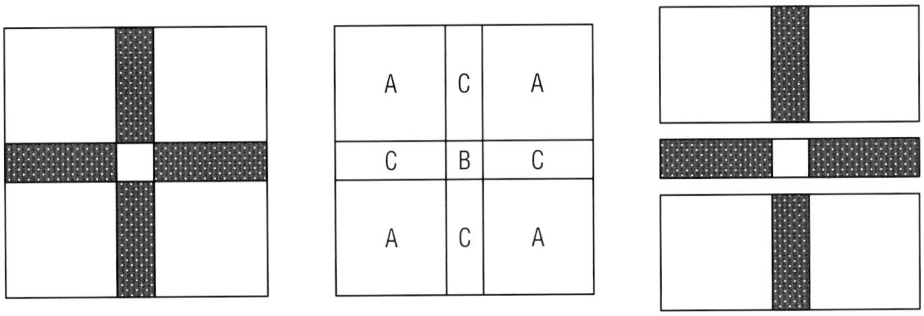

FOR 1 BLOCK:		FINISHED BLOCK SIZE *Single dimensions in the cutting chart indicate the size of the cut square (3" = 3" x 3").*					
		5¼"	**7"**	**8¾"**	**10½"**	**12¼"**	**14"**
Light	A: 4 ☐	2¾"	3½"	4¼"	5"	5¾"	6½"
	B: 1 ☐	1¼"	1½"	1¾"	2"	2¼"	2½"
Dark	C: 4 ▭	1¼" x 2¾"	1½" x 3½"	1¾" x 4¼"	2" x 5"	2¼" x 5¾"	2½" x 6½"

Try this: Reverse the lights and darks.

Autumn Tints

7-Unit Grid
Color Illustration: page 11

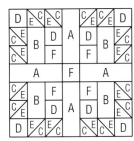

FOR 1 BLOCK:		FINISHED BLOCK SIZE *Single dimensions in the cutting chart indicate the size of the cut square (3" = 3" x 3").*					
		5¼"	**7"**	**8¾"**	**10½"**	**12¼"**	**14"**
Light	A: 4 ▭	1¼" x 2¾"	1½" x 3½"	1¾" x 4¼"	2" x 5"	2¼" x 5¾"	2½" x 6½"
	B: 4 ▭	1¼" x 2"	1½" x 2½"	1¾" x 3"	2" x 3½"	2¼" x 4"	2½" x 4½"
	C: 8 ◲→◹	1⅝"	1⅞"	2⅛"	2⅜"	2⅝"	2⅞"
	D: 8 ☐	1¼"	1½"	1¾"	2"	2¼"	2½"
Dark	E: 8 ◲→◹	1⅝"	1⅞"	2⅛"	2⅜"	2⅝"	2⅞"
	F: 5 ☐	1¼"	1½"	1¾"	2"	2¼"	2½"

Try this: Use a different light or a medium for A.

BABY BUNTING

4-Unit Grid
Color Illustration: page 11

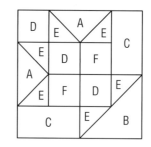

FOR 2 BLOCKS:	FINISHED BLOCK SIZE Single dimensions in the cutting chart indicate the size of the cut square (3" = 3" x 3").					
	4"	**6"**	**8"**	**9"**	**10"**	**12"**
Light A: 1 ⊠ → ⊠	3¼"	4¼"	5¼"	5¾"	6¼"	7¼"
B: 1 ◱ → ◲	2⅞"	3⅞"	4⅞"	5⅜"	5⅞"	6⅞"
C: 4 ▭	1½" x 2½"	2" x 3½"	2½" x 4½"	2¾" x 5"	3" x 5½"	3½" x 6½"
D: 6 ☐	1½"	2"	2½"	2¾"	3"	3½"
Dark E: 6 ◱ → ◲	1⅞"	2⅜"	2⅞"	3⅛"	3⅜"	3⅞"
F: 4 ☐	1½"	2"	2½"	2¾"	3"	3½"

Try this: Reverse the lights and darks in every other block.

BALTIMORE BELLE

6-Unit Grid
Color Illustration: page 12

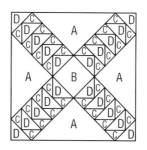

FOR 1 BLOCK:	FINISHED BLOCK SIZE Single dimensions in the cutting chart indicate the size of the cut square (3" = 3" x 3").					
	4½"	**6"**	**7½"**	**9"**	**10½"**	**12"**
Light A: 1 ⊠ → ⊠	4¼"	5¼"	6¼"	7¼"	8¼"	9¼"
B: 1 ◇	T5	T7	T9	T11	T12	T14
Medium C: 8 ⊠ → ⊠	2"	2¼"	2½"	2¾"	3"	3¼"
Dark D: 10 ◱ → ◲	1⅝"	1⅞"	2⅛"	2⅜"	2⅝"	2⅞"

Try this: Use many different mediums for C.

BASKET

5-Unit Grid
Color Illustration: page 12

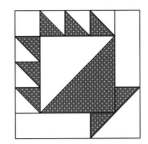
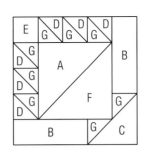
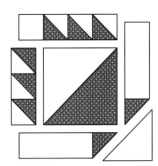

		FINISHED BLOCK SIZE Single dimensions in the cutting chart indicate the size of the cut square (3" = 3" x 3").					
FOR 2 BLOCKS:		**5"**	**6¼"**	**7½"**	**8¾"**	**10"**	**12½"**
Light	A: 1 ◻→◻	3⅞"	4⅝"	5⅜"	6⅛"	6⅞"	8⅜"
	B: 4 ▭	1½" x 3½"	1¾" x 4¼"	2" x 5"	2¼" x 5¾"	2½" x 6½"	3" x 8"
	C: 1 ◻→◻	2⅞"	3⅜"	3⅞"	4⅜"	4⅞"	5⅞"
	D: 6 ◻→◻	1⅞"	2⅛"	2⅜"	2⅝"	2⅞"	3⅜"
	E: 2 ◻	1½"	1¾"	2"	2¼"	2½"	3"
Dark	F: 1 ◻→◻	3⅞"	4⅝"	5⅜"	6⅛"	6⅞"	8⅜"
	G: 8 ◻→◻	1⅞"	2⅛"	2⅜"	2⅝"	2⅞"	3⅜"

Try this: Use several different darks for G.

BASKET II

4-Unit Grid
Color Illustration: page 12

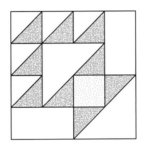
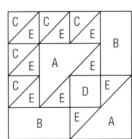
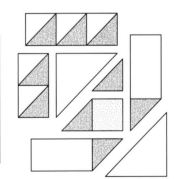

		FINISHED BLOCK SIZE Single dimensions in the cutting chart indicate the size of the cut square (3" = 3" x 3").					
FOR 2 BLOCKS:		**4"**	**6"**	**8"**	**9"**	**10"**	**12"**
Light	A: 2 ◻→◻	2⅞"	3⅞"	4⅞"	5⅜"	5⅞"	6⅞"
	B: 4 ▭	1½" x 2½"	2" x 3½"	2½" x 4½"	2¾" x 5"	3" x 5½"	3½" x 6½"
	C: 5 ◻→◻	1⅞"	2⅜"	2⅞"	3⅛"	3⅜"	3⅞"
Light 2	D: 2 ◻	1½"	2"	2½"	2¾"	3"	3½"
Medium	E: 9 ◻→◻	1⅞"	2⅜"	2⅞"	3⅛"	3⅜"	3⅞"

Try this: Use a dark instead of light 2 for D.

BASKET OF CHIPS

5-Unit Grid
Color Illustration: page 12

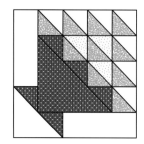 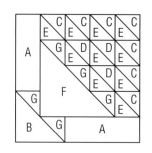 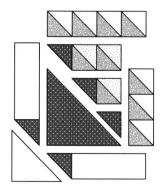

FOR 2 BLOCKS:		FINISHED BLOCK SIZE *Single dimensions in the cutting chart indicate the size of the cut square (3" = 3" x 3").*					
		5"	**6¼"**	**7½"**	**8¾"**	**10"**	**12½"**
Light	A: 4	1½" x 3½"	1¾" x 4¼"	2" x 5"	2¼" x 5¾"	2½" x 6½"	3" x 8"
	B: 1 →	2⅞"	3⅜"	3⅞"	4⅜"	4⅞"	5⅞"
	C: 7 →	1⅞"	2⅛"	2⅜"	2⅝"	2⅞"	3⅜"
Light 2	D: 3 →	1⅞"	2⅛"	2⅜"	2⅝"	2⅞"	3⅜"
Medium	E: 10 →	1⅞"	2⅛"	2⅜"	2⅝"	2⅞"	3⅜"
Dark	F: 1 →	3⅞"	4⅝"	5⅜"	6⅛"	6⅞"	8⅜"
	G: 5 →	1⅞"	2⅛"	2⅜"	2⅝"	2⅞"	3⅜"

Try this: Use several different mediums for D.

BASKET OF TRIANGLES

6-Unit Grid
Color Illustration: page 12

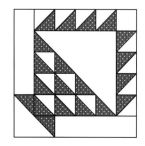 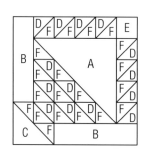 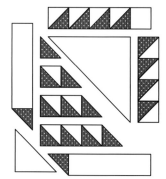

FOR 2 BLOCKS:		FINISHED BLOCK SIZE *Single dimensions in the cutting chart indicate the size of the cut square (3" = 3" x 3").*					
		4½"	**6"**	**7½"**	**9"**	**10½"**	**12"**
Light	A: 1 →	3⅞"	4⅞"	5⅞"	6⅞"	7⅞"	8⅞"
	B: 4	1¼" x 3½"	1½" x 4½"	1¾" x 5½"	2" x 6½"	2¼" x 7½"	2½" x 8½"
	C: 1 →	2⅜"	2⅞"	3⅜"	3⅞"	4⅜"	4⅞"
	D: 14 →	1⅝"	1⅞"	2⅛"	2⅜"	2⅝"	2⅞"
	E: 2	1¼"	1½"	1¾"	2"	2¼"	2½"
Dark	F: 20 →	1⅝"	1⅞"	2⅛"	2⅜"	2⅝"	2⅞"

Try this: Use several different darks for F.

BASKET OF TULIPS

8-Unit Grid

Color Illustration: page 12

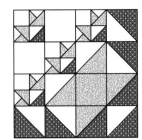
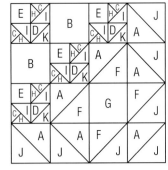
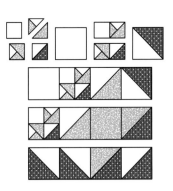

		FINISHED BLOCK SIZE *Single dimensions in the cutting chart indicate the size of the cut square (3" = 3" x 3").*					
FOR 2 BLOCKS:		**6"**	**8"**	**9"**	**10"**	**12"**	**14"**
Light	A: 7 ☐→◩	2⅜"	2⅞"	3⅛"	3⅜"	3⅞"	4⅜"
	B: 4 ☐	2"	2½"	2¾"	3"	3½"	4"
	C: 4 ☒→⊠	2"	2¼"	2⅜"	2½"	2¾"	3"
	D: 4 ☐→◩	1⅝"	1⅞"	2"	2⅛"	2⅜"	2⅝"
	E: 8 ☐	1¼"	1½"	1⅝"	1¾"	2"	2¼"
Medium	F: 4 ☐→◩	2⅜"	2⅞"	3⅛"	3⅜"	3⅞"	4⅜"
	G: 2 ☐	2"	2½"	2¾"	3"	3½"	4"
	H: 4 ☒→⊠	2"	2¼"	2⅜"	2½"	2¾"	3"
	I: 8 ☐→◩	1⅝"	1⅞"	2"	2⅛"	2⅜"	2⅝"
Dark	J: 7 ☐→◩	2⅜"	2⅞"	3⅛"	3⅜"	3⅞"	4⅜"
	K: 4 ☐→◩	1⅝"	1⅞"	2"	2⅛"	2⅜"	2⅝"

Try this: Reverse the mediums and darks.

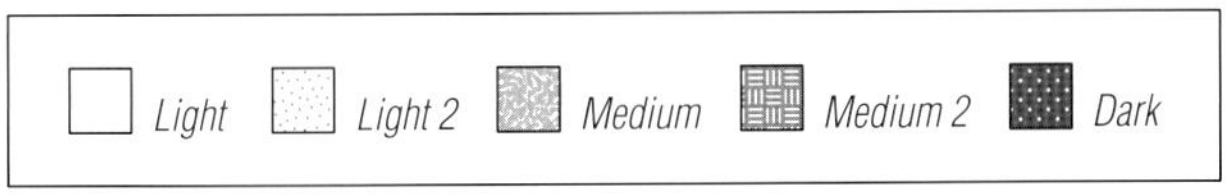

☐ Light ☐ Light 2 ☐ Medium ☐ Medium 2 ■ Dark

BEACON LIGHTS

4-Unit Grid

Color Illustration: page 12

		FINISHED BLOCK SIZE					
		Single dimensions in the cutting chart indicate the size of the cut square (3" = 3" x 3").					
FOR 1 BLOCK:		**4"**	**6"**	**8"**	**9"**	**10"**	**12"**
Light	A: 2 ⊠ → ⊠	2¼"	2¾"	3¼"	3½"	3¾"	4¼"
	B: 4 ▢	1½"	2"	2½"	2¾"	3"	3½"
	C: 4 ◇	T32	T41	T51	T56	T59	T67
Medium	D: 1 ◇	T7	T11	T14	T15	T16	T19
	E: 4 ◇	T2	T5	T7	T8	T9	T11
Dark	F: 2 ⊠ → ⊠	2¼"	2¾"	3¼"	3½"	3¾"	4¼"

Try this: Use one light for A and B and a different light for C.

BEAR'S PAW

7-Unit Grid

Color Illustration: page 12

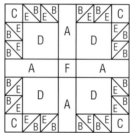
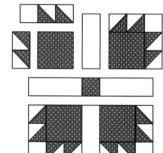

		FINISHED BLOCK SIZE					
		Single dimensions in the cutting chart indicate the size of the cut square (3" = 3" x 3").					
FOR 1 BLOCK:		**5¼"**	**7"**	**8¾"**	**10½"**	**12¼"**	**14"**
Light	A: 4 ▭	1¼" x 2¾"	1½" x 3½"	1¾" x 4¼"	2" x 5"	2¼" x 5¾"	2½" x 6½"
	B: 8 ◺ → ◹	1⅝"	1⅞"	2⅛"	2⅜"	2⅝"	2⅞"
	C: 4 ▢	1¼"	1½"	1¾"	2"	2¼"	2½"
Dark	D: 4 ▢	2"	2½"	3"	3½"	4"	4½"
	E: 8 ◺ → ◹	1⅝"	1⅞"	2⅛"	2⅜"	2⅝"	2⅞"
	F: 1 ▢	1¼"	1½"	1¾"	2"	2¼"	2½"

Try this: Use a large-scale print for D.

BEGINNER'S DELIGHT

10-Unit Grid

Color Illustration: page 12

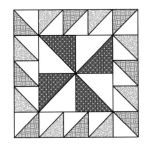
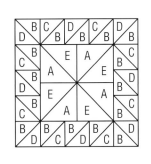
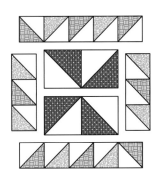

		FINISHED BLOCK SIZE Single dimensions in the cutting chart indicate the size of the cut square (3" = 3" x 3").					
FOR 1 BLOCK:		**5"**	**6¼"**	**7½"**	**8¾"**	**10"**	**12½"**
Light	A: 2 ▢ → ◩	2⅜"	2¾"	3⅛"	3½"	3⅞"	4⅝"
	B: 8 ▢ → ◩	1⅞"	2⅛"	2⅜"	2⅝"	2⅞"	3⅜"
Medium	C: 4 ▢ → ◩	1⅞"	2⅛"	2⅜"	2⅝"	2⅞"	3⅜"
Medium 2	D: 4 ▢ → ◩	1⅞"	2⅛"	2⅜"	2⅝"	2⅞"	3⅜"
Dark	E: 2 ▢ → ◩	2⅜"	2¾"	3⅛"	3½"	3⅞"	4⅝"

Try this: Reverse the lights and mediums around the outside edges of the block.

BERRY PATCH

6-Unit Grid

Color Illustration: page 12

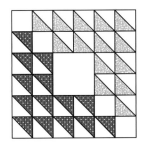
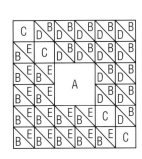
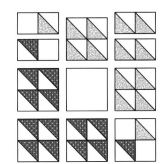

		FINISHED BLOCK SIZE Single dimensions in the cutting chart indicate the size of the cut square (3" = 3" x 3").					
FOR 1 BLOCK:		**4½"**	**6"**	**7½"**	**9"**	**10½"**	**12"**
Light	A: 1 ▢	2"	2½"	3"	3½"	4"	4½"
	B: 14 ▢ → ◩	1⅝"	1⅞"	2⅛"	2⅜"	2⅝"	2⅞"
	C: 4 ▢	1¼"	1½"	1¾"	2"	2¼"	2½"
Medium	D: 7 ▢ → ◩	1⅝"	1⅞"	2⅛"	2⅜"	2⅝"	2⅞"
Dark	E: 7 ▢ → ◩	1⅝"	1⅞"	2⅛"	2⅜"	2⅝"	2⅞"

Try this: Use many different mediums and darks.

BEST FRIEND

7-Unit Grid

Color Illustration: page 12

 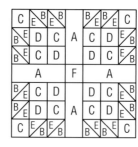 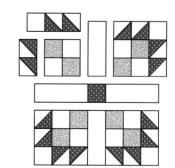

		FINISHED BLOCK SIZE					
		Single dimensions in the cutting chart indicate the size of the cut square (3" = 3" x 3").					
FOR 1 BLOCK:		**5¼"**	**7"**	**8¾"**	**10½"**	**12¼"**	**14"**
Light	A: 4 ▭	1¼" x 2¾"	1½" x 3½"	1¾" x 4¼"	2" x 5"	2¼" x 5¾"	2½" x 6½"
	B: 8 ◻→◨	1⅝"	1⅞"	2⅛"	2⅜"	2⅝"	2⅞"
	C: 12 ☐	1¼"	1½"	1¾"	2"	2¼"	2½"
Medium	D: 8 ☐	1¼"	1½"	1¾"	2"	2¼"	2½"
Dark	E: 8 ◻→◨	1⅝"	1⅞"	2⅛"	2⅜"	2⅝"	2⅞"
	F: 1 ☐	1¼"	1½"	1¾"	2"	2¼"	2½"

Try this: Use one light for A and a different light for B and C.

BIG T

6-Unit Grid

Color Illustration: page 12

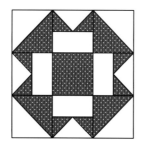 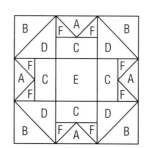 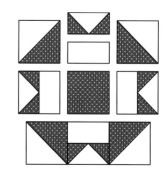

		FINISHED BLOCK SIZE					
		Single dimensions in the cutting chart indicate the size of the cut square (3" = 3" x 3").					
FOR 1 BLOCK:		**4½"**	**6"**	**7½"**	**9"**	**10½"**	**12"**
Light	A: 1 ⊠→⊠	2¾"	3¼"	3¾"	4¼"	4¾"	5¼"
	B: 2 ◻→◨	2⅜"	2⅞"	3⅜"	3⅞"	4⅜"	4⅞"
	C: 4 ▭	1¼" x 2"	1½" x 2½"	1¾" x 3"	2" x 3½"	2¼" x 4"	2½" x 4½"
Dark	D: 2 ◻→◨	2⅜"	2⅞"	3⅜"	3⅞"	4⅜"	4⅞"
	E: 1 ☐	2"	2½"	3"	3½"	4"	4½"
	F: 4 ◻→◨	1⅝"	1⅞"	2⅛"	2⅜"	2⅝"	2⅞"

Try this: Reverse the lights and darks in every other block.

BIRDS IN AIR

7-Unit Grid

Color Illustration: page 12

 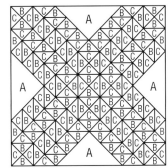 

	FINISHED BLOCK SIZE Single dimensions in the cutting chart indicate the size of the cut square (3" = 3" x 3").					
FOR 1 BLOCK:	**5¼"**	**7"**	**8¾"**	**10½"**	**12¼"**	**14"**
Light A: 1 ⊠ → ⊠	3½"	4¼"	5"	5¾"	6½"	7¼"
B: 20 ⊠ → ⊠	2"	2¼"	2½"	2¾"	3"	3¼"
Dark C: 20 ⊠ → ⊠	2"	2¼"	2½"	2¾"	3"	3¼"

Try this: Reverse the darks and lights in every other block.

BIRDS IN THE AIR

3-Unit Grid

Color Illustration: page 12

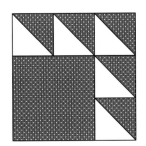 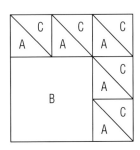 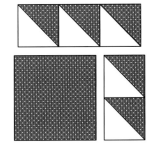

	FINISHED BLOCK SIZE Single dimensions in the cutting chart indicate the size of the cut square (3" = 3" x 3").					
FOR 2 BLOCKS:	**4½"**	**6"**	**7½"**	**9"**	**10½"**	**12"**
Light A: 5 ◻ → ◻	2⅜"	2⅞"	3⅜"	3⅞"	4⅜"	4⅞"
Dark B: 2 ◻	3½"	4½"	5½"	6½"	7½"	8½"
C: 5 ◻ → ◻	2⅜"	2⅞"	3⅜"	3⅞"	4⅜"	4⅞"

Try this: Reverse the lights and darks.

◻ Light   ▦ Light 2   ▦ Medium   ▦ Medium 2   ■ Dark

BIRD'S NEST

10-Unit Grid

Color Illustration: page 12

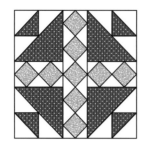 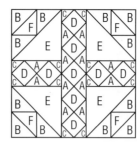  

		FINISHED BLOCK SIZE *Single dimensions in the cutting chart indicate the size of the cut square (3" = 3" x 3").*					
FOR 1 BLOCK:		**6¼"**	**7½"**	**8¾"**	**10"**	**12½"**	**13¾"**
Light	A: 3 ⊠ → ⊠	2½"	2¾"	3"	3¼"	3¾"	4"
	B: 6 ◰ → ◲	2⅛"	2⅜"	2⅝"	2⅞"	3⅜"	3⅝"
	C: 6 ◰ → ◲	1½"	1⅝"	1¾"	1⅞"	2⅛"	2¼"
Medium	D: 9 ◇	T4	T5	T6	T7	T9	T10
Dark	E: 2 ◰ → ◲	3⅜"	3⅞"	4⅜"	4⅞"	5⅞"	6⅜"
	F: 2 ◰ → ◲	2⅛"	2⅜"	2⅝"	2⅞"	3⅜"	3⅝"

Try this: Use several different mediums for D.

BIRTHDAY CAKE

5-Unit Grid

Color Illustration: page 12

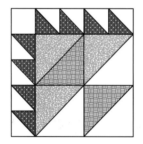 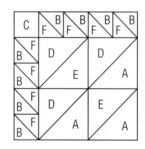 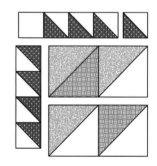

		FINISHED BLOCK SIZE *Single dimensions in the cutting chart indicate the size of the cut square (3" = 3" x 3").*					
FOR 2 BLOCKS:		**5"**	**6¼"**	**7½"**	**8¾"**	**10"**	**12½"**
Light	A: 3 ◰ → ◲	2⅞"	3⅜"	3⅞"	4⅜"	4⅞"	5⅞"
	B: 8 ◰ → ◲	1⅞"	2⅛"	2⅜"	2⅝"	2⅞"	3⅜"
	C: 2 □	1½"	1¾"	2"	2¼"	2½"	3"
Medium	D: 3 ◰ → ◲	2⅞"	3⅜"	3⅞"	4⅜"	4⅞"	5⅞"
Medium 2	E: 2 ◰ → ⊠	2⅞"	3⅜"	3⅞"	4⅜"	4⅞"	5⅞"
Dark	F: 8 ◰ → ◲	1⅞"	2⅛"	2⅜"	2⅝"	2⅞"	3⅜"

Try this: Use a different medium in every block.

□ Light　▨ Light 2　▨ Medium　▨ Medium 2　■ Dark

BLACK SPRUCE

6-Unit Grid

Color Illustration: page 12

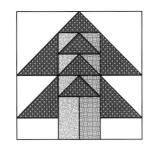
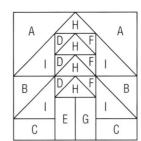
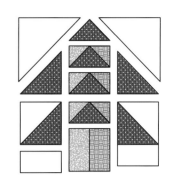

		FINISHED BLOCK SIZE					
		Single dimensions in the cutting chart indicate the size of the cut square (3" = 3" x 3").					
FOR 2 BLOCKS:		**4½"**	**6"**	**7½"**	**9"**	**10½"**	**12"**
Light	A: 2 ◻→◹	3⅛"	3⅞"	4⅝"	5⅜"	6⅛"	6⅞"
	B: 2 ◻→◹	2⅜"	2⅞"	3⅜"	3⅞"	4⅜"	4⅞"
	C: 4 ▭	1¼" x 2"	1½" x 2½"	1¾" x 3"	2" x 3½"	2¼" x 4"	2½" x 4½"
Medium	D: 3 ◻→◹	1⅝"	1⅞"	2⅛"	2⅜"	2⅝"	2⅞"
	E: 2 ▭	1¼" x 2"	1½" x 2½"	1¾" x 3"	2" x 3½"	2¼" x 4"	2½" x 4½"
Medium 2	F: 3 ◻→◹	1⅝"	1⅞"	2⅛"	2⅜"	2⅝"	2⅞"
	G: 2 ▭	1¼" x 2"	1½" x 2½"	1¾" x 3"	2" x 3½"	2¼" x 4"	2½" x 4½"
Dark	H: 2 ⊠→⊠	2¾"	3¼"	3¾"	4¼"	4¾"	5¼"
	I: 4 ◻→◹	2⅜"	2⅞"	3⅜"	3⅞"	4⅜"	4⅞"

Try this: Use one dark for H and a different dark for I.

BLACKS AND WHITES

8-Unit Grid

Color Illustration: page 12

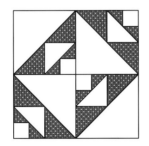
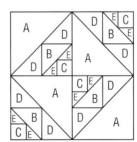

		FINISHED BLOCK SIZE					
		Single dimensions in the cutting chart indicate the size of the cut square (3" = 3" x 3").					
FOR 1 BLOCK:		**6"**	**8"**	**9"**	**10"**	**12"**	**14"**
Light	A: 2 ◻→◹	3⅞"	4⅞"	5⅜"	5⅞"	6⅞"	7⅞"
	B: 2 ◻→◹	2⅜"	2⅞"	3⅛"	3⅜"	3⅞"	4⅜"
	C: 4 ◻	1¼"	1½"	1⅝"	1¾"	2"	2¼"
Dark	D: 4 ◻→◹	2⅜"	2⅞"	3⅛"	3⅜"	3⅞"	4⅜"
	E: 4 ◻→◹	1⅝"	1⅞"	2"	2⅛"	2⅜"	2⅝"

Try this: Use a medium instead of a light for A.

BLAZED TRAIL

8-Unit Grid

Color Illustration: page 12

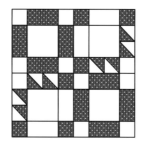

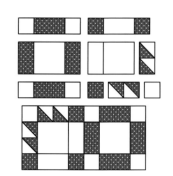

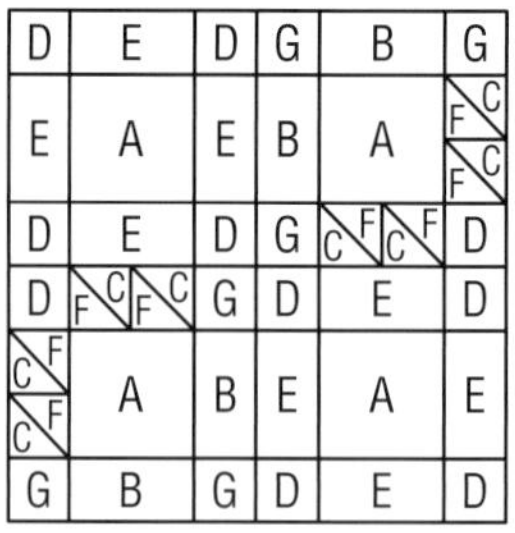

		FINISHED BLOCK SIZE					
		Single dimensions in the cutting chart indicate the size of the cut square (3" = 3" x 3").					
FOR 1 BLOCK:		**6"**	**8"**	**9"**	**10"**	**12"**	**14"**
Light	A: 4 ☐	2"	2½"	2¾"	3"	3½"	4"
	B: 4 ▭	1¼" x 2"	1½" x 2½"	1⅝" x 2¾"	1¾" x 3"	2" x 3½"	2¼" x 4"
	C: 4 ◻ → ◩	1⅝"	1⅞"	2"	2⅛"	2⅜"	2⅝"
	D: 10 ☐	1¼"	1½"	1⅝"	1¾"	2"	2¼"
Dark	E: 8 ▭	1¼" x 2"	1½" x 2½"	1⅝" x 2¾"	1¾" x 3"	2" x 3½"	2¼" x 4"
	F: 4 ◻ → ◩	1⅝"	1⅞"	2"	2⅛"	2⅜"	2⅝"
	G: 6 ☐	1¼"	1½"	1⅝"	1¾"	2"	2¼"

Try this: Use a medium instead of a light for A.

BLOCKS IN A BOX

3-Unit Grid

Color Illustration: page 12

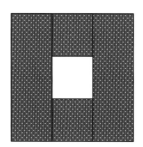

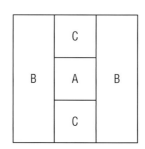

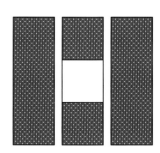

		FINISHED BLOCK SIZE					
		Single dimensions in the cutting chart indicate the size of the cut square (3" = 3" x 3").					
FOR 1 BLOCK:		**4½"**	**6"**	**7½"**	**9"**	**10½"**	**12"**
Light	A: 1 ☐	2"	2½"	3"	3½"	4"	4½"
Dark	B: 2 ▭	2" x 5"	2½" x 6½"	3" x 8"	3½" x 9½"	4" x 11"	4½" x 12½"
	C: 2 ☐	2"	2½"	3"	3½"	4"	4½"

Try this: Use a medium instead of a dark in every other block.

☐ Light   ▨ Light 2   ▨ Medium   ▨ Medium 2   ▨ Dark

BLUE FIELDS

8-Unit Grid

Color Illustration: page 12

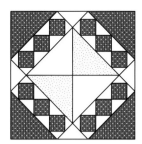
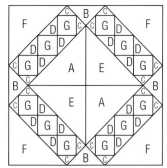
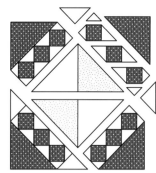

FOR 1 BLOCK:		FINISHED BLOCK SIZE *Single dimensions in the cutting chart indicate the size of the cut square (3" = 3" x 3").*					
		6"	**8"**	**9"**	**10"**	**12"**	**14"**
Light	A: 1 ◻→◺	3⅛"	3⅞"	4¼"	4⅝"	5⅜"	6⅛"
	B: 1 ⊠→⊠	2¾"	3¼"	3½"	3¾"	4¼"	4¾"
	C: 4 ⊠→⊠	2"	2¼"	2⅜"	2½"	2¾"	3"
	D: 8 ◻→◺	1⅝"	1⅞"	2"	2⅛"	2⅜"	2⅝"
Light 2	E: 1 ◻→◺	3⅛"	3⅞"	4¼"	4⅝"	5⅜"	6⅛"
Dark	F: 2 ◻→◺	3⅛"	3⅞"	4¼"	4⅝"	5⅜"	6⅛"
	G: 12 ◻	1¼"	1½"	1⅝"	1¾"	2"	2¼"

Try this: Use several different darks for G.

BLYTHE'S BEST

8-Unit Grid

Color Illustration: page 12

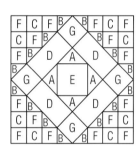

FOR 1 BLOCK:		FINISHED BLOCK SIZE *Single dimensions in the cutting chart indicate the size of the cut square (3" = 3" x 3").*					
		6"	**8"**	**9"**	**10"**	**12"**	**14"**
Light	A: 1 ⊠→⊠	2¾"	3¼"	3½"	3¾"	4¼"	4¾"
	B: 8 ◻→◺	1⅝"	1⅞"	2"	2⅛"	2⅜"	2⅝"
	C: 8 ◻	1¼"	1½"	1⅝"	1¾"	2"	2¼"
Medium	D: 4 ◇	T41	T51	T56	T59	T67	T70
Dark	E: 1 ◻	2"	2½"	2¾"	3"	3½"	4"
	F: 16 ◻	1¼"	1½"	1⅝"	1¾"	2"	2¼"
	G: 4 ◇	T5	T7	T8	T9	T11	T12

Try this: Use one light for A and a different light for B and C.

BOXED IN

5-Unit Grid
Color Illustration: page 12

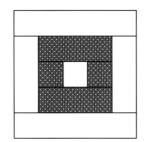 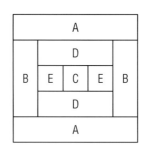 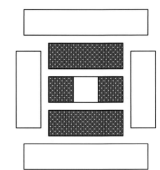

FOR 1 BLOCK:		**FINISHED BLOCK SIZE** Single dimensions in the cutting chart indicate the size of the cut square (3" = 3" x 3").					
		5"	**6¼"**	**7½"**	**8¾"**	**10"**	**12½"**
Light	A: 2 ▭	1½" x 5½"	1¾" x 6¾"	2" x 8"	2¼" x 9¼"	2½" x 10½"	3" x 13"
	B: 2 ▭	1½" x 3½"	1¾" x 4¼"	2" x 5"	2¼" x 5¾"	2½" x 6½"	3" x 8"
	C: 1 □	1½"	1¾"	2"	2¼"	2½"	3"
Dark	D: 2 ▭	1½" x 3½"	1¾" x 4¼"	2" x 5"	2¼" x 5¾"	2½" x 6½"	3" x 8"
	E: 2 □	1½"	1¾"	2"	2¼"	2½"	3"

Try this: Reverse the lights and darks in every other block.

BOXES

6-Unit Grid
Color Illustration: page 12

 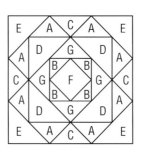 

FOR 1 BLOCK:		**FINISHED BLOCK SIZE** Single dimensions in the cutting chart indicate the size of the cut square (3" = 3" x 3").					
		4½"	**6"**	**7½"**	**9"**	**10½"**	**12"**
Light	A: 2 ⊠ → ⊠	2¾"	3¼"	3¾"	4¼"	4¾"	5¼"
	B: 2 ◺ → ◿	1⅝"	1⅞"	2⅛"	2⅜"	2⅝"	2⅞"
Medium	C: 1 ⊠ → ⊠	2¾"	3¼"	3¾"	4¼"	4¾"	5¼"
	D: 2 ◺ → ◺	2⅜"	2⅞"	3⅜"	3⅞"	4⅜"	4⅞"
Medium 2	E: 2 ◺ → ◺	2⅜"	2⅞"	3⅜"	3⅞"	4⅜"	4⅞"
	F: 1 ◇	T5	T7	T9	T11	T12	T14
Dark	G: 1 ⊠ → ⊠	2¾"	3¼"	3¾"	4¼"	4¾"	5¼"

Try this: Use a dark instead of a medium for E.

BOY'S NONSENSE

3-Unit Grid

Color Illustration: page 12

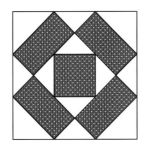
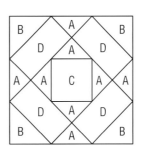

FOR 1 BLOCK:	FINISHED BLOCK SIZE Single dimensions in the cutting chart indicate the size of the cut square (3" = 3" x 3").					
	4½"	**6"**	**7½"**	**9"**	**10½"**	**12"**
Light A: 2 ⊠ → ⊠	2¾"	3¼"	3¾"	4¼"	4¾"	5¼"
B: 2 ◨ → ◨	2⅜"	2⅞"	3⅜"	3⅞"	4⅜"	4⅞"
Dark C: 1 ☐	2"	2½"	3"	3½"	4"	4½"
D: 4 ◇	T41	T51	T59	T67	T70	T72

Try this: Reverse the lights and darks in every other block.

BRACED STAR

6-Unit Grid

Color Illustration: page 12

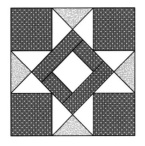
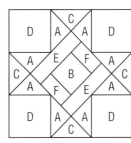

FOR 1 BLOCK:	FINISHED BLOCK SIZE Single dimensions in the cutting chart indicate the size of the cut square (3" = 3" x 3").					
	4½"	**6"**	**7½"**	**9"**	**10½"**	**12"**
Light A: 2 ⊠ → ⊠	2¾"	3¼"	3¾"	4¼"	4¾"	5¼"
B: 1 ◇	T5	T7	T9	T11	T12	T14
Medium C: 1 ⊠ → ⊠	2¾"	3¼"	3¾"	4¼"	4¾"	5¼"
Dark D: 4 ☐	2"	2½"	3"	3½"	4"	4½"
E: 2 ◇	T30	T34	T38	T43	T48	T53
F: 2 ◇	T28	T32	T36	T41	T46	T51

Try this: Use a medium instead of a light for B.

Light | Light 2 | Medium | Medium 2 | Dark

BROKEN DISHES

10-Unit Grid
Color Illustration: page 12

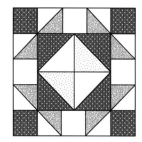
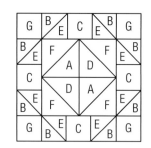
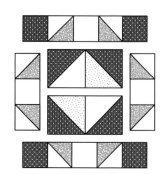

FOR 1 BLOCK:	FINISHED BLOCK SIZE *Single dimensions in the cutting chart indicate the size of the cut square (3" = 3" x 3").*					
	5"	6¼"	7½"	8¾"	10"	12½"
Light A: 1 ◻→◪	2⅜"	2¾"	3⅛"	3½"	⅞"	4⅝"
B: 4 ◻→◪	1⅞"	2⅛"	2⅜"	2⅝"	2⅞"	3⅜"
C: 4 ◻	1½"	1¾"	2"	2¼"	2½"	3"
Light 2 D: 1 ◻→◪	2⅜"	2¾"	3⅛"	3½"	3⅞"	4⅝"
Medium E: 4 ◻→◪	1⅞"	2⅛"	2⅜"	2⅝"	2⅞"	3⅜"
Dark F: 2 ◻→◪	2⅜"	2¾"	3⅛"	3½"	3⅞"	4⅝"
G: 4 ◻	1½"	1¾"	2"	2¼"	2½"	3"

Try this: Reverse the mediums and darks in every other block.

BROKEN SASH

2-Unit Grid
Color Illustration: page 12

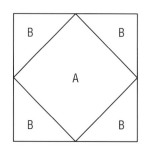
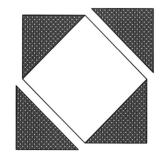

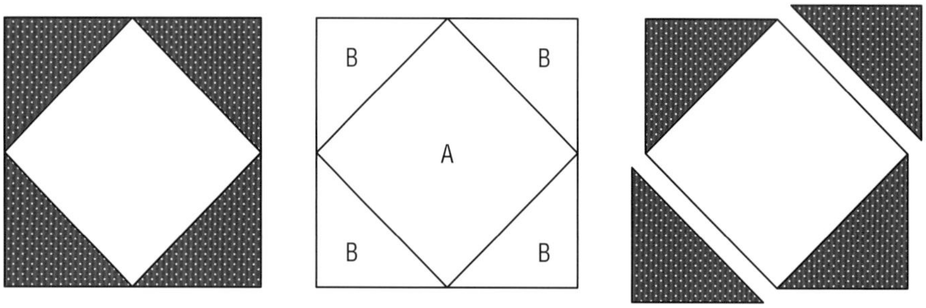

FOR 1 BLOCK:	FINISHED BLOCK SIZE *Single dimensions in the cutting chart indicate the size of the cut square (3" = 3" x 3").*					
	4"	6"	8"	9"	10"	12"
Light A: 1 ◇	T14	T19	T23	T24	T25	T27
Dark B: 2 ◻→◪	2⅞"	3⅞"	4⅞"	5⅜"	5⅞"	6⅞"

Try this: Use a large-scale print for A.

BROKEN STAR

8-Unit Grid

Color Illustration: page 12

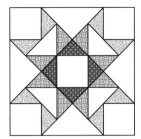 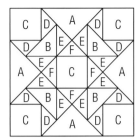 

			FINISHED BLOCK SIZE					
			Single dimensions in the cutting chart indicate the size of the cut square (3" = 3" x 3").					
FOR 1 BLOCK:			**4"**	**6"**	**8"**	**9"**	**10"**	**12"**
Light	A: 1 ⊠ → ⊠		3¼"	4¼"	5¼"	5¾"	6¼"	7¼"
	B: 2 ◻ → ◻		1⅞"	2⅜"	2⅞"	3⅛"	3⅜"	3⅞"
	C: 5 ☐		1½"	2"	2½"	2¾"	3"	3½"
Medium	D: 2 ⊠ → ⊠		2¼"	2¾"	3¼"	3½"	3¾"	4¼"
Medium 2	E: 2 ⊠ → ⊠		2¼"	2¾"	3¼"	3½"	3¾"	4¼"
Dark	F: 1 ⊠ → ⊠		2¼"	2¾"	3¼"	3½"	3¾"	4¼"

Try this: Use several different mediums for D and E.

THE BROKEN WHEEL

8-Unit Grid

Color Illustration: page 12

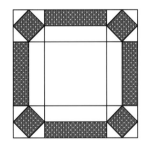 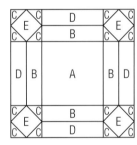 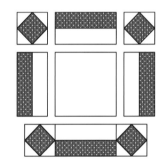

			FINISHED BLOCK SIZE					
			Single dimensions in the cutting chart indicate the size of the cut square (3" = 3" x 3").					
FOR 1 BLOCK:			**6"**	**8"**	**9"**	**10"**	**12"**	**14"**
Light	A: 1 ☐		3½"	4½"	5"	5½"	6½"	7½"
	B: 4 ▭		1¼" x 3½"	1½" x 4½"	1⅝" x 5"	1¾" x 5½"	2" x 6½"	2¼" x 7½"
	C: 8 ◻ → ◻		1⅝"	1⅞"	2"	2⅛"	2⅜"	2⅝"
Dark	D: 4 ▭		1¼" x 3½"	1½" x 4½"	1⅝" x 5"	1¾" x 5½"	2" x 6½"	2¼" x 7½"
	E: 4 ◇		T5	T7	T8	T9	T11	T12

Try this: Use a medium instead of a light for B.

☐ Light ▨ Light 2 ▨ Medium ▨ Medium 2 ▨ Dark

56

BROKEN WINDOWS

6-Unit Grid
Color Illustration: page 13

 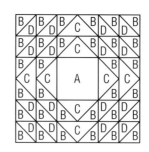 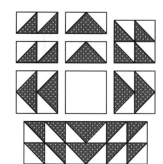

	FINISHED BLOCK SIZE					
	Single dimensions in the cutting chart indicate the size of the cut square (3" = 3" x 3").					
FOR 1 BLOCK:	**4½"**	**6"**	**7½"**	**9"**	**10½"**	**12"**
Light A: 1 ☐	2"	2½"	3"	3½"	4"	4½"
B: 16 ◻→◻	1⅝"	1⅞"	2⅛"	2⅜"	2⅝"	2⅞"
Dark C: 2 ⊠→⊠	2¾"	3¼"	3¾"	4¼"	4¾"	5¼"
D: 8 ◻→◻	1⅝"	1⅞"	2⅛"	2⅜"	2⅝"	2⅞"

Try this: Use several different lights and darks.

BUCKWHEAT

3-Unit Grid
Color Illustration: page 13

 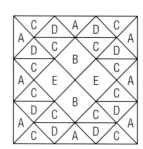 

	FINISHED BLOCK SIZE					
	Single dimensions in the cutting chart indicate the size of the cut square (3" = 3" x 3").					
FOR 1 BLOCK:	**4½"**	**6"**	**7½"**	**9"**	**10½"**	**12"**
Light A: 2 ⊠→⊠	2¾"	3¼"	3¾"	4¼"	4¾"	5¼"
B: 2 ◇	T5	T7	T9	T11	T12	T14
Medium C: 3 ⊠→⊠	2¾"	3¼"	3¾"	4¼"	4¾"	5¼"
Dark D: 2 ⊠→⊠	2¾"	3¼"	3¾"	4¼"	4¾"	5¼"
E: 2 ◇	T5	T7	T9	T11	T12	T14

Try this: Use several different mediums for C.

BUFFALO RIDGE

7-Unit Grid

Color Illustration: page 13

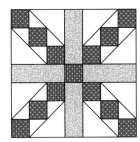 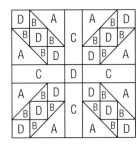 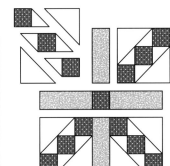

		FINISHED BLOCK SIZE Single dimensions in the cutting chart indicate the size of the cut square (3" = 3" x 3").					
FOR 1 BLOCK:		**5¼"**	**7"**	**8¾"**	**10½"**	**12¼"**	**14"**
Light	A: 4 ◻ → ◿	2⅜"	2⅞"	3⅜"	3⅞"	4⅜"	4⅞"
	B: 8 ◻ → ◿	1⅝"	1⅞"	2⅛"	2⅜"	2⅝"	2⅞"
Medium	C: 4 ▭	1¼" x 2¾"	1½" x 3½"	1¾" x 4¼"	2" x 5"	2¼" x 5¾"	2½" x 6½"
Dark	D: 13 ◻	1¼"	1½"	1¾"	2"	2¼"	2½"

Try this: Use one light for A and several different lights for B.

BUILDING BLOCKS

5-Unit Grid

Color Illustration: page 13

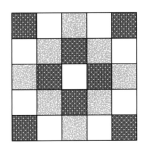 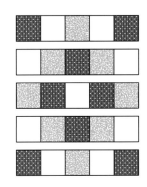

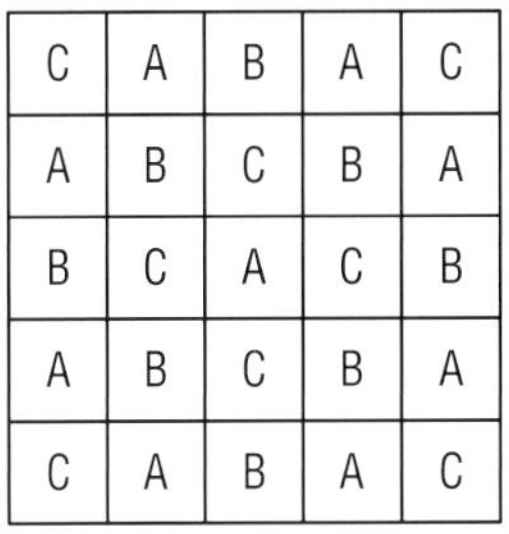

		FINISHED BLOCK SIZE Single dimensions in the cutting chart indicate the size of the cut square (3" = 3" x 3").					
FOR 1 BLOCK:		**5"**	**6¼"**	**7½"**	**8¾"**	**10"**	**12½"**
Light	A: 9 ◻	1½"	1¾"	2"	2¼"	2½"	3"
Medium	B: 8 ◻	1½"	1¾"	2"	2¼"	2½"	3"
Dark	C: 8 ◻	1½"	1¾"	2"	2¼"	2½"	3"

Try this: Use several different lights for A.

BUILDING BLOCKS II

9-Unit Grid
Color Illustration: page 13

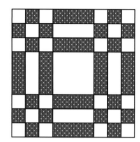
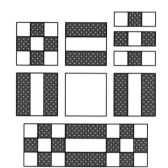

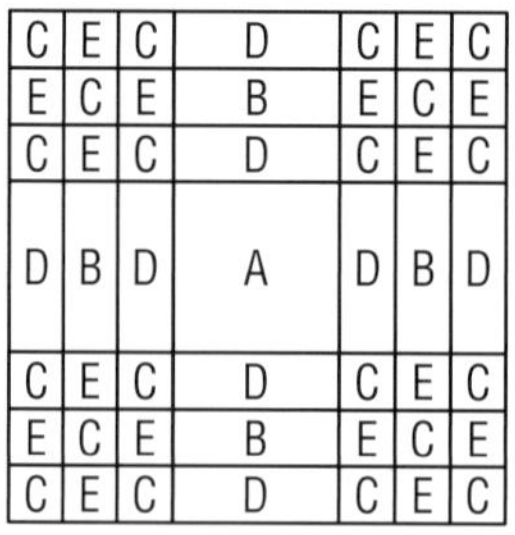

	FINISHED BLOCK SIZE *Single dimensions in the cutting chart indicate the size of the cut square (3" = 3" x 3").*					
FOR 1 BLOCK:	**6¾"**	**9"**	**10⅛"**	**11¼"**	**12⅜"**	**13½"**
Light A: 1 ▫	2¾"	3½"	3⅞"	4¼"	4⅝"	5"
B: 4 ▭	1¼" x 2¾"	1½" x 3½"	1⅝" x 3⅞"	1¾" x 4¼"	1⅞" x 4⅝"	2" x 5"
C: 20 ▫	1¼"	1½"	1⅝"	1¾"	1⅞"	2"
Dark D: 8 ▭	1¼" x 2¾"	1½" x 3½"	1⅝" x 3⅞"	1¾" x 4¼"	1⅞" x 4⅝"	2" x 5"
E: 16 ▫	1¼"	1½"	1⅝"	1¾"	1⅞"	2"

Try this: Use a medium instead of a light for A and B.

CAKE STAND

4-Unit Grid
Color Illustration: page 13

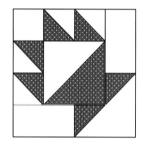
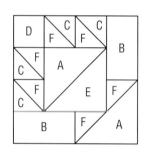
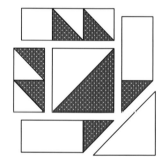

	FINISHED BLOCK SIZE *Single dimensions in the cutting chart indicate the size of the cut square (3" = 3" x 3").*					
FOR 2 BLOCKS:	**4"**	**6"**	**8"**	**9"**	**10"**	**12"**
Light A: 2 ◻→◪	2⅞"	3⅞"	4⅞"	5⅜"	5⅞"	6⅞"
B: 4 ▭	1½" x 2½"	2" x 3½"	2½" x 4½"	2¾" x 5"	3" x 5½"	3½" x 6½"
C: 4 ◻→◪	1⅞"	2⅜"	2⅞"	3⅛"	3⅜"	3⅞"
D: 2 ▫	1½"	2"	2½"	2¾"	3"	3½"
Dark E: 1 ◻→◪	2⅞"	3⅞"	4⅞"	5⅜"	5⅞"	6⅞"
F: 6 ◻→◪	1⅞"	2⅜"	2⅞"	3⅛"	3⅜"	3⅞"

Try this: Reverse the lights and darks in every other block.

CALICO PUZZLE

3-Unit Grid
Color Illustration: page 13

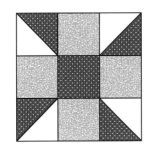
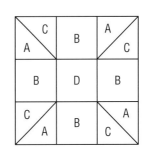
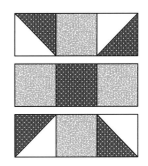

FOR 1 BLOCK:		FINISHED BLOCK SIZE *Single dimensions in the cutting chart indicate the size of the cut square (3" = 3" x 3").*					
		4½"	**6"**	**7½"**	**9"**	**10½"**	**12"**
Light	A: 2 ◻→◹	2⅜"	2⅞"	3⅜"	3⅞"	4⅜"	4⅞"
Medium	B: 4 ◻	2"	2½"	3"	3½"	4"	4½"
Dark	C: 2 ◻→◹	2⅜"	2⅞"	3⅜"	3⅞"	4⅜"	4⅞"
	D: 1 ◻	2"	2½"	3"	3½"	4"	4½"

Try this: Use one dark for C and a different dark for D.

CARD BASKET

6-Unit Grid
Color Illustration: page 13

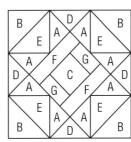

FOR 1 BLOCK:		FINISHED BLOCK SIZE *Single dimensions in the cutting chart indicate the size of the cut square (3" = 3" x 3").*					
		4½"	**6"**	**7½"**	**9"**	**10½"**	**12"**
Light	A: 2 ⊠→⧖	2¾"	3¼"	3¾"	4¼"	4¾"	5¼"
	B: 2 ◻→◹	2⅜"	2⅞"	3⅜"	3⅞"	4⅜"	4⅞"
	C: 1 ◇	T5	T7	T9	T11	T12	T14
Light 2	D: 1 ⊠→⧖	2¾"	3¼"	3¾"	4¼"	4¾"	5¼"
Dark	E: 2 ◻→◹	2⅜"	2⅞"	3⅜"	3⅞"	4⅜"	4⅞"
	F: 2 ◇	T30	T34	T38	T43	T48	T53
	G: 2 ◇	T28	T32	T36	T41	T46	T51

Try this: Use a medium instead of a light for B and C.

CARD TRICK

3-Unit Grid
Color Illustration: page 13

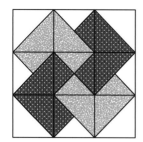
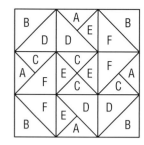
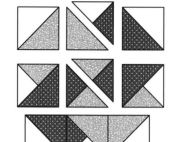

| | | | **FINISHED BLOCK SIZE** | | | | |
| | | | Single dimensions in the cutting chart indicate the size of the cut square (3" = 3" x 3"). | | | | |
FOR 1 BLOCK:			**4½"**	**6"**	**7½"**	**9"**	**10½"**	**12"**
Light	A: 1 ⊠ → ⊠		2¾"	3¼"	3¾"	4¼"	4¾"	5¼"
	B: 2 ◻ → ◹		2⅜"	2⅞"	3⅜"	3⅞"	4⅜"	4⅞"
Medium	C: 1 ⊠ → ⊠		2¾"	3¼"	3¾"	4¼"	4¾"	5¼"
	D: 2 ◻ → ◹		2⅜"	2⅞"	3⅜"	3⅞"	4⅜"	4⅞"
Dark	E: 1 ⊠ → ⊠		2¾"	3¼"	3¾"	4¼"	4¾"	5¼"
	F: 2 ◻ → ◹		2⅜"	2⅞"	3⅜"	3⅞"	4⅜"	4⅞"

Try this: Make each "card" from a different fabric.

CAROL'S SCRAP TIME QUILT

6-Unit Grid
Color Illustration: page 13

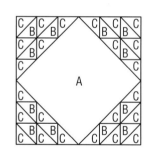

| | | | **FINISHED BLOCK SIZE** | | | | |
| | | | Single dimensions in the cutting chart indicate the size of the cut square (3" = 3" x 3"). | | | | |
FOR 1 BLOCK:			**4½"**	**6"**	**7½"**	**9"**	**10½"**	**12"**
Light	A: 1 ◇		T15	T19	T22	T24	T26	T27
Medium	B: 6 ◻ → ◹		1⅝"	1⅞"	2⅛"	2⅜"	2⅝"	2⅞"
Dark	C: 12 ◻ → ◹		1⅝"	1⅞"	2⅛"	2⅜"	2⅝"	2⅞"

Try this: Use a medium- or large-scale print for A.

CARRIE NATION

8-Unit Grid
Color Illustration: page 13

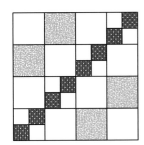

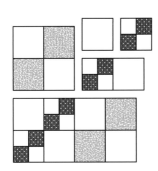

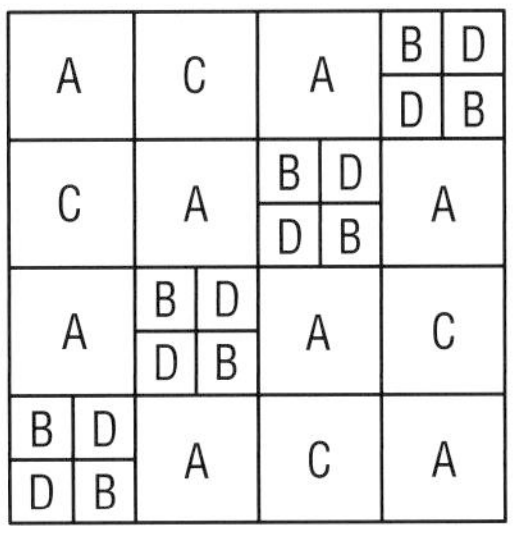

FOR 1 BLOCK:	FINISHED BLOCK SIZE Single dimensions in the cutting chart indicate the size of the cut square (3" = 3" x 3").					
	6"	**8"**	**9"**	**10"**	**12"**	**14"**
Light A: 8 □	2"	2½"	2¾"	3"	3½"	4"
B: 8 □	1¼"	1½"	1⅝"	1¾"	2"	2¼"
Medium C: 4 □	2"	2½"	2¾"	3"	3½"	4"
Dark D: 8 □	1¼"	1½"	1⅝"	1¾"	2"	2¼"

Try this: Use several different mediums for C and several different darks for D.

CASTLES IN SPAIN

4-Unit Grid
Color Illustration: page 13

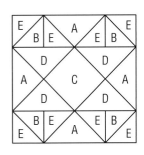

FOR 1 BLOCK:	FINISHED BLOCK SIZE Single dimensions in the cutting chart indicate the size of the cut square (3" = 3" x 3").					
	4"	**6"**	**8"**	**9"**	**10"**	**12"**
Light A: 1 ⊠ → ⊠	3¼"	4¼"	5¼"	5¾"	6¼"	7¼"
B: 2 ◿ → ◺	1⅞"	2⅜"	2⅞"	3⅛"	3⅜"	3⅞"
C: 1 ◇	T7	T11	T14	T15	T16	T19
Dark D: 1 ⊠ → ⊠	3¼"	4¼"	5¼"	5¾"	6¼"	7¼"
E: 4 ◿ → ◺	1⅞"	2⅜"	2⅞"	3⅛"	3⅜"	3⅞"

Try this: Use a medium instead of a dark for E.

☐ Light   ☐ Light 2   ☐ Medium   ☐ Medium 2   ☐ Dark

CATS AND MICE

6-Unit Grid
Color Illustration: page 13

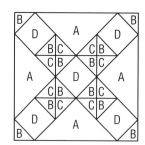

FOR 1 BLOCK:		FINISHED BLOCK SIZE Single dimensions in the cutting chart indicate the size of the cut square (3" = 3" x 3").					
		4½"	**6"**	**7½"**	**9"**	**10½"**	**12"**
Light	A: 1 ⊠ → ⊠	4¼"	5¼"	6¼"	7¼"	8¼"	9¼"
	B: 6 ◻ → ◸	1⅝"	1⅞"	2⅛"	2⅜"	2⅝"	2⅞"
Dark	C: 4 ◻ → ◸	1⅝"	1⅞"	2⅛"	2⅜"	2⅝"	2⅞"
	D: 5 ◇	T5	T7	T9	T11	T12	T14

Try this: Reverse the lights and darks.

CAT'S CRADLE

6-Unit Grid
Color Illustration: page 13

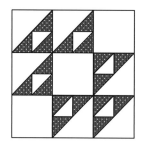
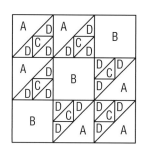
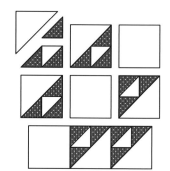

FOR 1 BLOCK:		FINISHED BLOCK SIZE Single dimensions in the cutting chart indicate the size of the cut square (3" = 3" x 3").					
		4½"	**6"**	**7½"**	**9"**	**10½"**	**12"**
Light	A: 3 ◻ → ◸	2⅜"	2⅞"	3⅜"	3⅞"	4⅜"	4⅞"
	B: 3 ◻	2"	2½"	3"	3½"	4"	4½"
	C: 3 ◻ → ◸	1⅝"	1⅞"	2⅛"	2⅜"	2⅝"	2⅞"
Dark	D: 9 ◻ → ◸	1⅝"	1⅞"	2⅛"	2⅜"	2⅝"	2⅞"

Try this: Reverse the lights and darks in every other block.

CENTENNIAL

4-Unit Grid
Color Illustration: page 13

 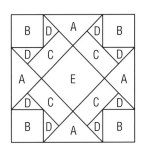 

		FINISHED BLOCK SIZE					
		Single dimensions in the cutting chart indicate the size of the cut square (3" = 3" x 3").					
FOR 1 BLOCK:		**4"**	**6"**	**8"**	**9"**	**10"**	**12"**
Light	A: 1 ⊠→⊠	3¼"	4¼"	5¼"	5¾"	6¼"	7¼"
	B: 4 ☐	1½"	2"	2½"	2¾"	3"	3½"
	C: 4 ◇	T32	T41	T51	T56	T59	T67
Dark	D: 2 ⊠→⊠	2¼"	2¾"	3¼"	3½"	3¾"	4¼"
	E: 1 ◇	T7	T11	T14	T15	T16	T19

Try this: Use a medium instead of a light for C.

CHAIN AND BAR

8-Unit Grid
Color Illustration: page 13

 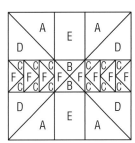 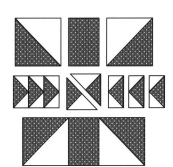

		FINISHED BLOCK SIZE					
		Single dimensions in the cutting chart indicate the size of the cut square (3" = 3" x 3").					
FOR 2 BLOCKS:		**6"**	**8"**	**9"**	**10"**	**12"**	**14"**
Light	A: 4 ☐→◩	3⅛"	3⅞"	4¼"	4⅝"	5⅜"	6⅛"
	B: 1 ⊠→⊠	2¾"	3¼"	3½"	3¾"	4¼"	4¾"
	C: 12 ☐→◩	1⅝"	1⅞"	2"	2⅛"	2⅜"	2⅝"
Dark	D: 4 ☐→◩	3⅛"	3⅞"	4¼"	4⅝"	5⅜"	6⅛"
	E: 4 ▭	2" x 2¾"	2½" x 3½"	2¾" x 3⅞"	3" x 4¼"	3½" x 5"	4" x 5¾"
	F: 4 ⊠→⊠	2¾"	3¼"	3½"	3¾"	4¼"	4¾"

Try this: Use several different darks for F.

CHAIN AND HOURGLASS

9-Unit Grid
Color Illustration: page 13

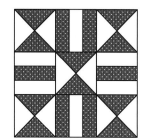 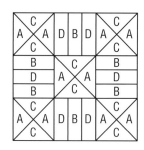 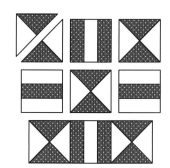

		FINISHED BLOCK SIZE					
		Single dimensions in the cutting chart indicate the size of the cut square (3" = 3" x 3").					
FOR 2 BLOCKS:		6¾"	9"	10⅛"	11¼"	12⅜"	13½"
Light	A: 5 ⊠ → ⊠	3½"	4¼"	4⅝"	5"	5⅜"	5¾"
	B: 12 ▭	1¼" x 2¾"	1½" x 3½"	1⅝" x 3⅞"	1¾" x 4¼"	1⅞" x 4⅝"	2" x 5"
Dark	C: 5 ⊠ → ⊠	3½"	4¼"	4⅝"	5"	5⅜"	5¾"
	D: 12 ▭	1¼" x 2¾"	1½" x 3½"	1⅝" x 3⅞"	1¾" x 4¼"	1⅞" x 4⅝"	2" x 5"

Try this: Reverse the lights and darks in every other block.

CHEYENNE

4-Unit Grid
Color Illustration: page 13

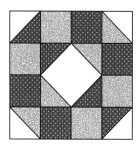 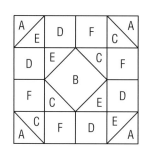 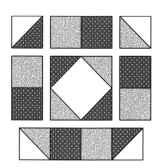

		FINISHED BLOCK SIZE					
		Single dimensions in the cutting chart indicate the size of the cut square (3" = 3" x 3").					
FOR 1 BLOCK:		4"	6"	8"	9"	10"	12"
Light	A: 2 ◻ → ◻	1⅞"	2⅜"	2⅞"	3⅛"	3⅜"	3⅞"
	B: 1 ◇	T7	T11	T14	T15	T16	T19
Medium	C: 2 ◻ → ◻	1⅞"	2⅜"	2⅞"	3⅛"	3⅜"	3⅞"
	D: 4 ◻	1½"	2"	2½"	2¾"	3"	3½"
Dark	E: 2 ◻ → ◻	1⅞"	2⅜"	2⅞"	3⅛"	3⅜"	3⅞"
	F: 4 ◻	1½"	2"	2½"	2¾"	3"	3½"

Try this: Use several different mediums and darks.

THE CHINESE BLOCK QUILT

6-Unit Grid

Color Illustration: page 13

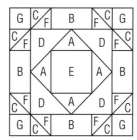

FOR 1 BLOCK:		**FINISHED BLOCK SIZE** Single dimensions in the cutting chart indicate the size of the cut square (3" = 3" x 3").					
		4½"	**6"**	**7½"**	**9"**	**10½"**	**12"**
Light	A: 1 ⊠ → ⊠	2¾"	3¼"	3¾"	4¼"	4¾"	5¼"
	B: 4 ▭	1¼" x 2"	1½" x 2½"	1¾" x 3"	2" x 3½"	2¼" x 4"	2½" x 4½"
	C: 4 ◻ → ◻	1⅝"	1⅞"	2⅛"	2⅜"	2⅝"	2⅞"
Dark	D: 2 ◻ → ◻	2⅜"	2⅞"	3⅜"	3⅞"	4⅜"	4⅞"
	E: 1 ☐	2"	2½"	3"	3½"	4"	4½"
	F: 4 ◻ → ◻	1⅝"	1⅞"	2⅛"	2⅜"	2⅝"	2⅞"
	G: 4 ☐	1¼"	1½"	1¾"	2"	2¼"	2½"

Try this: Use a medium instead of a dark for F.

CHINOOK

8-Unit Grid

Color Illustration: page 13

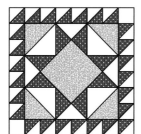
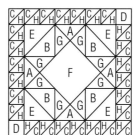

FOR 1 BLOCK:		**FINISHED BLOCK SIZE** Single dimensions in the cutting chart indicate the size of the cut square (3" = 3" x 3").					
		6"	**8"**	**9"**	**10"**	**12"**	**14"**
Light	A: 1 ⊠ → ⊠	2¾"	3¼"	3½"	3¾"	4¼"	4¾"
	B: 2 ◻ → ◻	2⅜"	2⅞"	3⅛"	3⅜"	3⅞"	4⅜"
	C: 13 ◻ → ◻	1⅝"	1⅞"	2"	2⅛"	2⅜"	2⅝"
	D: 2 ☐	1¼"	1½"	1⅝"	1¾"	2"	2¼"
Medium	E: 2 ◻ → ◻	2⅜"	2⅞"	3⅛"	3⅜"	3⅞"	4⅜"
	F: 1 ◇	T11	T14	T15	T16	T19	T21
Dark	G: 2 ⊠ → ⊠	2¾"	3¼"	3½"	3¾"	4¼"	4¾"
	H: 13 ◻ → ◻	1⅝"	1⅞"	2"	2⅛"	2⅜"	2⅝"

Try this: Use many different darks for H.

CHISHOLM TRAIL

4-Unit Grid
Color Illustration: page 13

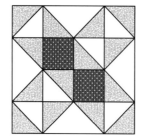 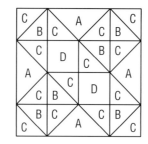 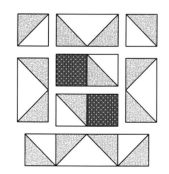

FOR 1 BLOCK:	FINISHED BLOCK SIZE Single dimensions in the cutting chart indicate the size of the cut square (3" = 3" x 3").					
	4"	**6"**	**8"**	**9"**	**10"**	**12"**
Light A: 1 ⊠ → ⊠	3¼"	4¼"	5¼"	5¾"	6¼"	7¼"
B: 3 ◲ → ◲	1⅞"	2⅜"	2⅞"	3⅛"	3⅜"	3⅞"
Medium C: 7 ◲ → ◲	1⅞"	2⅜"	2⅞"	3⅛"	3⅜"	3⅞"
Dark D: 2 □	1½"	2"	2½"	2¾"	3"	3½"

Try this: Use several different mediums for C.

CHRISTMAS STAR

6-Unit Grid
Color Illustration: page 13

 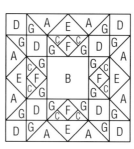 

FOR 1 BLOCK:	FINISHED BLOCK SIZE Single dimensions in the cutting chart indicate the size of the cut square (3" = 3" x 3").					
	4½"	**6"**	**7½"**	**9"**	**10½"**	**12"**
Light A: 2 ⊠ → ⊠	2¾"	3¼"	3¾"	4¼"	4¾"	5¼"
B: 1 □	2"	2½"	3"	3½"	4"	4½"
C: 2 ⊠ → ⊠	2"	2¼"	2½"	2¾"	3"	3¼"
D: 8 □	1¼"	1½"	1¾"	2"	2¼"	2½"
Medium E: 1 ⊠ → ⊠	2¾"	3¼"	3¾"	4¼"	4¾"	5¼"
F: 4 ◇	T1	T2	T4	T5	T6	T7
Dark G: 8 ◲ → ◲	1⅝"	1⅞"	2⅛"	2⅜"	2⅝"	2⅞"

Try this: Use a pictorial holiday print for B.

CHRISTMAS STAR II

5-Unit Grid
Color Illustration: page 13

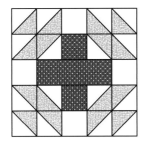 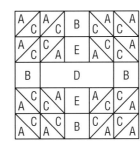 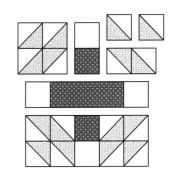

		FINISHED BLOCK SIZE					
		Single dimensions in the cutting chart indicate the size of the cut square (3" = 3" x 3").					
FOR 1 BLOCK:			**5"**	**6¼"**	**7½"**	**8¾"**	**10"**	**12½"**
Light	A: 8 ◻→◹		1⅞"	2⅛"	2⅜"	2⅝"	2⅞"	3⅜"
	B: 4 ◻		1½"	1¾"	2"	2¼"	2½"	3"
Medium	C: 8 ◻→◹		1⅞"	2⅛"	2⅜"	2⅝"	2⅞"	3⅜"
Dark	D: 1 ▭		1½" x 3½"	1¾" x 4¼"	2" x 5"	2¼" x 5¾"	2½" x 6½"	3" x 8"
	E: 2 ◻		1½"	1¾"	2"	2¼"	2½"	3"

Try this: Reverse the darks and mediums in every other block.

CHUCK A LUCK

6-Unit Grid
Color Illustration: page 13

 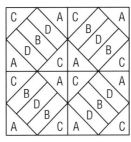 

		FINISHED BLOCK SIZE					
		Single dimensions in the cutting chart indicate the size of the cut square (3" = 3" x 3").					
FOR 1 BLOCK:			**4½"**	**6"**	**7½"**	**9"**	**10½"**	**12"**
Light	A: 4 ◻→◹		2"	2⅜"	2¾"	3⅛"	3½"	3⅞"
	B: 6 ◇		T29	T33	T37	T42	T47	T52
Dark	C: 4 ◻→◹		2"	2⅜"	2¾"	3⅛"	3½"	3⅞"
	D: 6 ◇		T29	T33	T37	T42	T47	T52

Try this: Use a different combination of lights and darks in each quadrant of the block.

◻ *Light*   ▨ *Light 2*   ▨ *Medium*   ▨ *Medium 2*   ■ *Dark*

CHURN DASH

6-Unit Grid

Color Illustration: page 13

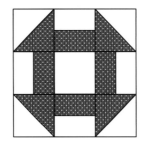
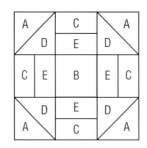
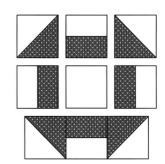

FOR 1 BLOCK:		FINISHED BLOCK SIZE *Single dimensions in the cutting chart indicate the size of the cut square (3" = 3" x 3").*					
		4½"	**6"**	**7½"**	**9"**	**10½"**	**12"**
Light	A: 2 ◻→◩	2⅜"	2⅞"	3⅜"	3⅞"	4⅜"	4⅞"
	B: 1 ◻	2"	2½"	3"	3½"	4"	4½"
	C: 4 ▭	1¼" x 2"	1½" x 2½"	1¾" x 3"	2" x 3½"	2¼" x 4"	2½" x 4½"
Dark	D: 2 ◻→◩	2⅜"	2⅞"	3⅜"	3⅞"	4⅜"	4⅞"
	E: 4 ▭	1¼" x 2"	1½" x 2½"	1¾" x 3"	2" x 3½"	2¼" x 4"	2½" x 4½"

Try this: Reverse the lights and darks.

COBBLESTONES

10-Unit Grid

Color Illustration: page 13

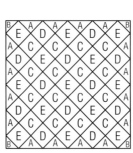
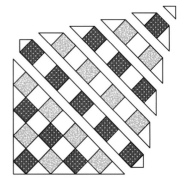

FOR 1 BLOCK:		FINISHED BLOCK SIZE *Single dimensions in the cutting chart indicate the size of the cut square (3" = 3" x 3").*					
		6¼"	**7½"**	**8¾"**	**10"**	**12½"**	**13¾"**
Light	A: 4 ⊠→⧖	2½"	2¾"	3"	3¼"	3¾"	4"
	B: 2 ◻→◩	1½"	1⅝"	1¾"	1⅞"	2⅛"	2¼"
	C: 16 ◇	T4	T5	T6	T7	T9	T10
Medium	D: 12 ◇	T4	T5	T6	T7	T9	T10
Dark	E: 13 ◇	T4	T5	T6	T7	T9	T10

Try this: Use many different fabrics for D and E.

COCK'S COMB

4-Unit Grid

Color Illustration: page 13

 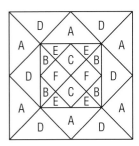 

		FINISHED BLOCK SIZE					
		Single dimensions in the cutting chart indicate the size of the cut square (3" = 3" x 3").					
FOR 2 BLOCKS:		**4"**	**6"**	**8"**	**9"**	**10"**	**12"**
Light	A: 3 ⊠ → ⊠	3¼"	4¼"	5¼"	5¾"	6¼"	7¼"
	B: 2 ⊠ → ⊠	2¼"	2¾"	3¼"	3½"	3¾"	4¼"
	C: 4 ◇	T2	T5	T7	T8	T9	T11
Dark	D: 3 ⊠ → ⊠	3¼"	4¼"	5¼"	5¾"	6¼"	7¼"
	E: 2 ⊠ → ⊠	2¼"	2¾"	3¼"	3½"	3¾"	4¼"
	F: 4 ◇	T2	T5	T7	T8	T9	T11

Try this: Use a light and a medium instead of a light and a dark in every other block.

COFFIN STAR

4-Unit Grid

Color Illustration: page 13

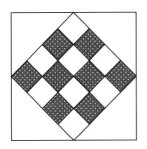 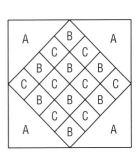 

		FINISHED BLOCK SIZE					
		Single dimensions in the cutting chart indicate the size of the cut square (3" = 3" x 3").					
FOR 1 BLOCK:		**4"**	**6"**	**8"**	**9"**	**10"**	**12"**
Light	A: 2 ◻ → ◺	2⅞"	3⅞"	4⅞"	5⅜"	5⅞"	6⅞"
	B: 8 ◇	T2	T5	T7	T8	T9	T11
Dark	C: 8 ◇	T2	T5	T7	T8	T9	T11

Try this: Use a different light or a medium for A.

COLONIAL GARDEN

4-Unit Grid

Color Illustration: page 13

 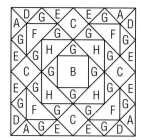 

FOR 1 BLOCK:		FINISHED BLOCK SIZE *Single dimensions in the cutting chart indicate the size of the cut square (3" = 3" x 3").*					
		4"	**6"**	**8"**	**9"**	**10"**	**12"**
Light	A: 1 ⊠ → ⊠	2¼"	2¾"	3¼"	3½"	3¾"	4¼"
	B: 1 □	1½"	2"	2½"	2¾"	3"	3½"
	C: 4 ◇	T2	T5	T7	T8	T9	T11
Light 2	D: 1 ⊠ → ⊠	2¼"	2¾"	3¼"	3½"	3¾"	4¼"
Medium	E: 2 ⊠ → ⊠	2¼"	2¾"	3¼"	3½"	3¾"	4¼"
	F: 2 ◺ → ◺	1⅞"	2⅜"	2⅞"	3⅛"	3⅜"	3⅞"
Medium 2	G: 5 ⊠ → ⊠	2¼"	2¾"	3¼"	3½"	3¾"	4¼"
Dark	H: 2 ◺ → ◺	1⅞"	2⅜"	2⅞"	3⅛"	3⅜"	3⅞"

Try this: Reverse the mediums and darks in every other block.

COMBINATION STAR

6-Unit Grid

Color Illustration: page 13

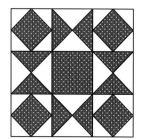 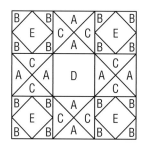 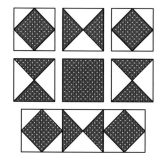

FOR 1 BLOCK:		FINISHED BLOCK SIZE *Single dimensions in the cutting chart indicate the size of the cut square (3" = 3" x 3").*					
		4½"	**6"**	**7½"**	**9"**	**10½"**	**12"**
Light	A: 2 ⊠ → ⊠	2¾"	3¼"	3¾"	4¼"	4¾"	5¼"
	B: 8 ◺ → ◺	1⅝"	1⅞"	2⅛"	2⅜"	2⅝"	2⅞"
Dark	C: 2 ⊠ → ⊠	2¾"	3¼"	3¾"	4¼"	4¾"	5¼"
	D: 1 □	2"	2½"	3"	3½"	4"	4½"
	E: 4 ◇	T5	T7	T9	T11	T12	T14

Try this: Use a medium instead of a dark for D and E.

THE COMFORT QUILT

9-Unit Grid
Color Illustration: page 14

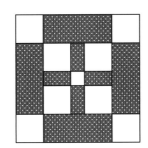

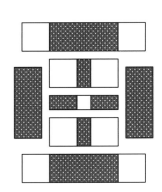

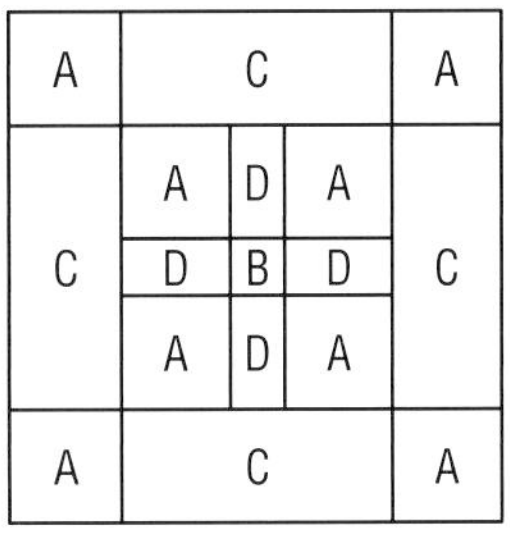

FOR 1 BLOCK:			**FINISHED BLOCK SIZE** Single dimensions in the cutting chart indicate the size of the cut square (3" = 3" x 3").					
			6¾"	**9"**	**10⅛"**	**11¼"**	**12⅜"**	**13½"**
Light	A: 8 ☐		2"	2½"	2¾"	3"	3¼"	3½"
	B: 1 ☐		1¼"	1½"	1⅝"	1¾"	1⅞"	2"
Dark	C: 4 ▭		2" x 4¼"	2½" x 5½"	2¾" x 6⅛"	3" x 6¾"	3¼" x 7⅜"	3½" x 8"
	D: 4 ▭		1¼" x 2"	1½" x 2½"	1⅝" x 2¾"	1¾" x 3"	1⅞" x 3¼"	2" x 3½"
Try this:	Use one dark for C and a different dark for D.							

CONNECTICUT

4-Unit Grid
Color Illustration: page 14

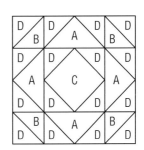

FOR 1 BLOCK:			**FINISHED BLOCK SIZE** Single dimensions in the cutting chart indicate the size of the cut square (3" = 3" x 3").					
			4"	**6"**	**8"**	**9"**	**10"**	**12"**
Light	A: 1 ⊠ → ⊠		3¼"	4¼"	5¼"	5¾"	6¼"	7¼"
	B: 2 ◩ → ◪		1⅞"	2⅜"	2⅞"	3⅛"	3⅜"	3⅞"
	C: 1 ◇		T7	T11	T14	T15	T16	T19
Dark	D: 8 ◩ → ◪		1⅞"	2⅜"	2⅞"	3⅛"	3⅜"	3⅞"
Try this:	Reverse the lights and darks.							

☐ Light   ☐ Light 2   ▦ Medium   ▤ Medium 2   ▨ Dark

Contrary Wife

3-Unit Grid
Color Illustration: page 14

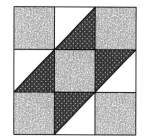
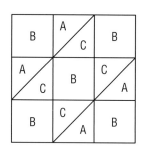
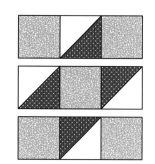

FOR 1 BLOCK:		FINISHED BLOCK SIZE *Single dimensions in the cutting chart indicate the size of the cut square (3" = 3" x 3").*					
		4½"	6"	7½"	9"	10½"	12"
Light	A: 2 ◻→◹	2⅜"	2⅞"	3⅜"	3⅞"	4⅜"	4⅞"
Medium	B: 5 ◻	2"	2½"	3"	3½"	4"	4½"
Dark	C: 2 ◻→◹	2⅜"	2⅞"	3⅜"	3⅞"	4⅜"	4⅞"

Try this: Use several different mediums for B.

Corn and Beans

6-Unit Grid
Color Illustration: page 14

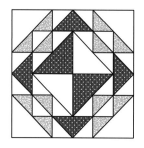
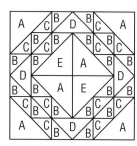

FOR 1 BLOCK:		FINISHED BLOCK SIZE *Single dimensions in the cutting chart indicate the size of the cut square (3" = 3" x 3").*					
		4½"	6"	7½"	9"	10½"	12"
Light	A: 3 ◻→◹	2⅜"	2⅞"	3⅜"	3⅞"	4⅜"	4⅞"
	B: 10 ◻→◹	1⅝"	1⅞"	2⅛"	2⅜"	2⅝"	2⅞"
Medium	C: 6 ◻→◹	1⅝"	1⅞"	2⅛"	2⅜"	2⅝"	2⅞"
Dark	D: 1 ⊠→⊠	2¾"	3¼"	3¾"	4¼"	4¾"	5¼"
	E: 1 ◻→◹	2⅜"	2⅞"	3⅜"	3⅞"	4⅜"	4⅞"

Try this: Use one light for A and a different light for B.

◻ Light   ▨ Light 2   ▨ Medium   ▦ Medium 2   ■ Dark

CORNER STAR

8-Unit Grid

Color Illustration: page 14

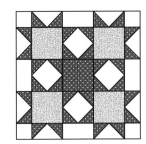
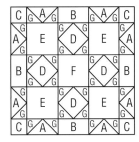
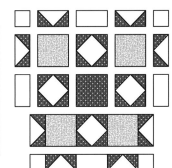

		FINISHED BLOCK SIZE					
		Single dimensions in the cutting chart indicate the size of the cut square (3" = 3" x 3").					
FOR 1 BLOCK:		**6"**	**8"**	**9"**	**10"**	**12"**	**14"**
Light	A: 2 ⊠ → ⊠	2¾"	3¼"	3½"	3¾"	4¼"	4¾"
	B: 4 ▭	1¼" x 2"	1½" x 2½"	1⅝" x 2¾"	1¾" x 3"	2" x 3½"	2¼" x 4"
	C: 4 □	1¼"	1½"	1⅝"	1¾"	2"	2¼"
	D: 4 ◇	T5	T7	T8	T9	T11	T12
Medium	E: 4 □	2"	2½"	2¾"	3"	3½"	4"
Dark	F: 1 □	2"	2½"	2¾"	3"	3½"	4"
	G: 16 ◻ → ◻	1⅝"	1⅞"	2"	2⅛"	2⅜"	2⅝"

Try this: Use several different mediums for E.

CORONATION

8-Unit Grid

Color Illustration: page 14

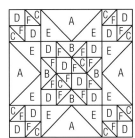

		FINISHED BLOCK SIZE					
		Single dimensions in the cutting chart indicate the size of the cut square (3" = 3" x 3").					
FOR 1 BLOCK:		**6"**	**8"**	**9"**	**10"**	**12"**	**14"**
Light	A: 1 ⊠ → ⊠	4¼"	5¼"	5¾"	6¼"	7¼"	8¼"
	B: 1 ⊠ → ⊠	2¾"	3¼"	3½"	3¾"	4¼"	4¾"
	C: 5 ◻ → ◻	1⅝"	1⅞"	2"	2⅛"	2⅜"	2⅝"
	D: 14 □	1¼"	1½"	1⅝"	1¾"	2"	2¼"
Dark	E: 4 ◻ → ◻	2⅜"	2⅞"	3⅛"	3⅜"	3⅞"	4⅜"
	F: 9 ◻ → ◻	1⅝"	1⅞"	2"	2⅛"	2⅜"	2⅝"

Try this: Use one dark for E and a medium or a different dark for F.

Cotton Reels

2-Unit Grid

Color Illustration: page 14

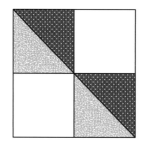
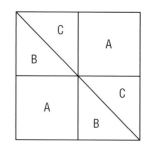
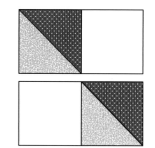

FOR 1 BLOCK:	FINISHED BLOCK SIZE Single dimensions in the cutting chart indicate the size of the cut square (3" = 3" x 3").					
	4"	**6"**	**8"**	**9"**	**10"**	**12"**
Light A: 2 ☐	2½"	3½"	4½"	5"	5½"	6½"
Medium B: 1 ◺ → ◹	2⅞"	3⅞"	4⅞"	5⅜"	5⅞"	6⅞"
Dark C: 1 ◺ → ◹	2⅞"	3⅞"	4⅞"	5⅜"	5⅞"	6⅞"

Try this: Use two different lights for A.

Counterchange Cross

6-Unit Grid

Color Illustration: page 14

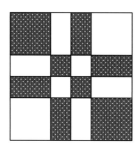
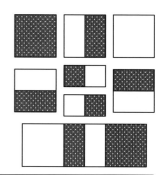

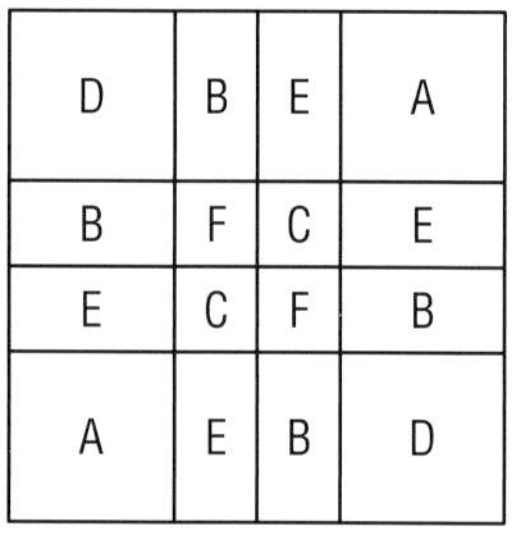

FOR 1 BLOCK:	FINISHED BLOCK SIZE Single dimensions in the cutting chart indicate the size of the cut square (3" = 3" x 3").					
	4½"	**6"**	**7½"**	**9"**	**10½"**	**12"**
Light A: 2 ☐	2"	2½"	3"	3½"	4"	4½"
B: 4 ▭	1¼" x 2"	1½" x 2½"	1¾" x 3"	2" x 3½"	2¼" x 4"	2½" x 4½"
C: 2 ☐	1¼"	1½"	1¾"	2"	2¼"	2½"
Dark D: 2 ☐	2"	2½"	3"	3½"	4"	4½"
E: 4 ▭	1¼" x 2"	1½" x 2½"	1¾" x 3"	2" x 3½"	2¼" x 4"	2½" x 4½"
F: 2 ☐	1¼"	1½"	1¾"	2"	2¼"	2½"

Try this: Use a different combination of lights and darks in each quadrant of the block.

COUNTERPANE

6-Unit Grid

Color Illustration: page 14

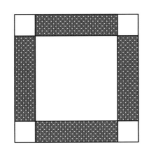
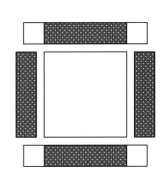

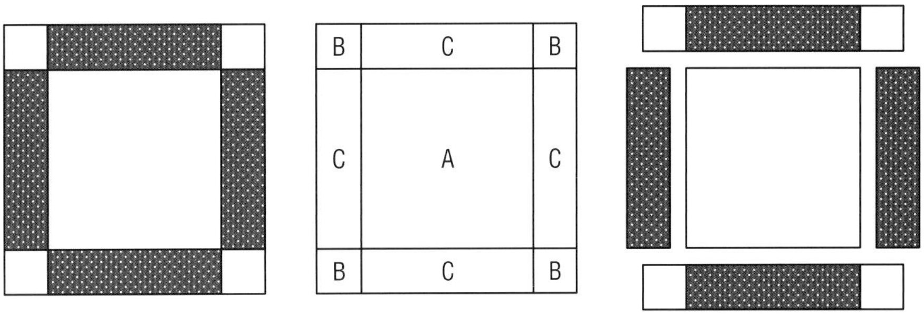

	FINISHED BLOCK SIZE *Single dimensions in the cutting chart indicate the size of the cut square (3" = 3" x 3").*					
FOR 1 BLOCK:	**4½"**	**6"**	**7½"**	**9"**	**10½"**	**12"**
Light A: 1 ▢	3½"	4½"	5½"	6½"	7½"	8½"
B: 4 ▢	1¼"	1½"	1¾"	2"	2¼"	2½"
Dark C: 4 ▭	1¼" x 3½"	1½" x 4½"	1¾" x 5½"	2" x 6½"	2¼" x 7½"	2½" x 8½"

Try this: Use a large-scale print for A.

COUNTRY CHECKERS

5-Unit Grid

Color Illustration: page 14

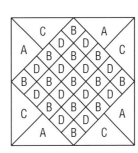

	FINISHED BLOCK SIZE *Single dimensions in the cutting chart indicate the size of the cut square (3" = 3" x 3").*					
FOR 1 BLOCK:	**5"**	**6¼"**	**7½"**	**8¾"**	**10"**	**12½"**
Light A: 1 ⊠ → ⧅	3¾"	4⅜"	5"	5⅝"	6¼"	7½"
B: 13 ◇	T2	T4	T5	T6	T7	T9
Light 2 C: 1 ⊠ → ⧅	3¾"	4⅜"	5"	5⅝"	6¼"	7½"
Dark D: 12 ◇	T2	T4	T5	T6	T7	T9

Try this: Use many different darks for D.

COUNTRY LANES

5-Unit Grid
Color Illustration: page 14

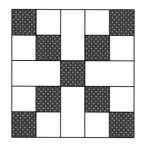

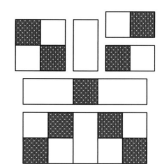

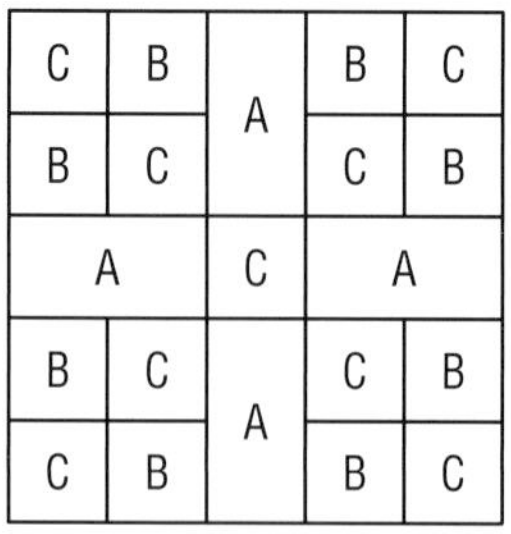

FOR 1 BLOCK:		FINISHED BLOCK SIZE *Single dimensions in the cutting chart indicate the size of the cut square (3" = 3" x 3").*					
		5"	**6¼"**	**7½"**	**8¾"**	**10"**	**12½"**
Light	A: 4	1½" x 2½"	1¾" x 3"	2" x 3½"	2¼" x 4"	2½" x 4½"	3" x 5½"
	B: 8	1½"	1¾"	2"	2¼"	2½"	3"
Dark	C: 9	1½"	1¾"	2"	2¼"	2½"	3"

Try this: Use a medium instead of a light for A.

COUNTY FAIR

10-Unit Grid
Color Illustration: page 14

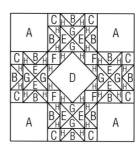

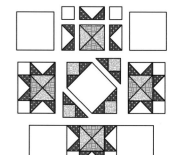

FOR 1 BLOCK:		FINISHED BLOCK SIZE *Single dimensions in the cutting chart indicate the size of the cut square (3" = 3" x 3").*					
		6¼"	**7½"**	**8¾"**	**10"**	**12½"**	**13¾"**
Light	A: 4	2⅜"	2¾"	3⅛"	3½"	4¼"	4⅝"
	B: 3 →	2½"	2¾"	3"	3¼"	3¾"	4"
	C: 8	1⅛"	1¼"	1⅜"	1½"	1¾"	1⅞"
	D: 1	T9	T11	T12	T14	T16	T18
Medium	E: 2 →	2½"	2¾"	3"	3¼"	3¾"	4"
	F: 4	1⅛"	1¼"	1⅜"	1½"	1¾"	1⅞"
Medium 2	G: 2 →	2½"	2¾"	3"	3¼"	3¾"	4"
Dark	H: 16 →	1½"	1⅝"	1¾"	1⅞"	2⅛"	2¼"

Try this: Use many different mediums for E and G.

COURTHOUSE LAWN

8-Unit Grid
Color Illustration: page 14

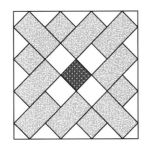
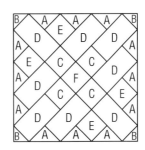
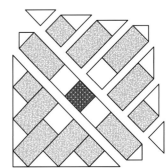

FOR 1 BLOCK:		FINISHED BLOCK SIZE *Single dimensions in the cutting chart indicate the size of the cut square (3" = 3" x 3").*					
		6"	8"	9"	10"	12"	14"
Light	A: 3 ⊠ → ⊠	2¾"	3¼"	3½"	3¾"	4¼"	4¾"
	B: 2 ◺ → ◺	1⅝"	1⅞"	2"	2⅛"	2⅜"	2⅝"
	C: 4 ◇	T5	T7	T8	T9	T11	T12
Medium	D: 8 ◇	T41	T51	T56	T59	T67	T70
	E: 4 ◇	T5	T7	T8	T9	T11	T12
Dark	F: 1 ◇	T5	T7	T8	T9	T11	T12

Try this: Use one light for A and B and a different light for C.

COURTHOUSE SQUARE

6-Unit Grid
Color Illustration: page 14

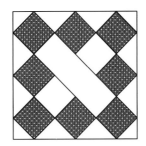
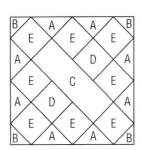
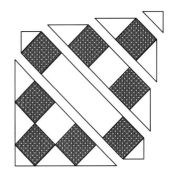

FOR 1 BLOCK:		FINISHED BLOCK SIZE *Single dimensions in the cutting chart indicate the size of the cut square (3" = 3" x 3").*					
		4½"	6"	7½"	9"	10½"	12"
Light	A: 2 ⊠ → ⊠	2¾"	3¼"	3¾"	4¼"	4¾"	5¼"
	B: 2 ◺ → ◺	1⅝"	1⅞"	2⅛"	2⅜"	2⅝"	2⅞"
	C: 1 ◇	T42	T52	T60	T68	T71	T73
	D: 2 ◇	T5	T7	T9	T11	T12	T14
Dark	E: 8 ◇	T5	T7	T9	T11	T12	T14

Try this: Use a medium instead of a dark for E.

☐ Light ▦ Light 2 ▦ Medium ▦ Medium 2 ■ Dark

78

COXEY'S CAMP

8-Unit Grid
Color Illustration: page 14

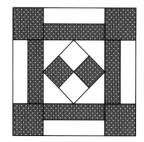

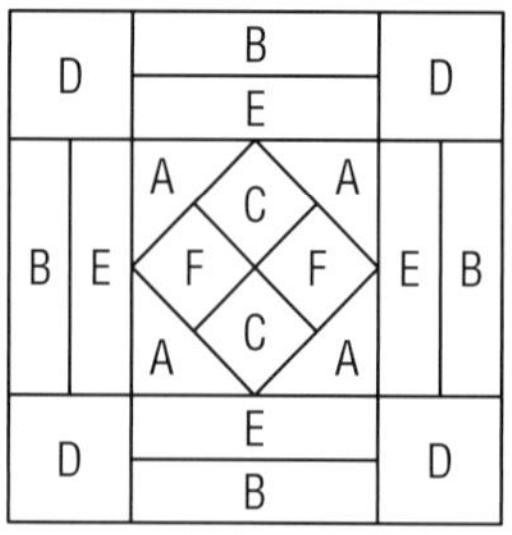

		FINISHED BLOCK SIZE *Single dimensions in the cutting chart indicate the size of the cut square (3" = 3" x 3").*					
FOR 1 BLOCK:		**6"**	**8"**	**9"**	**10"**	**12"**	**14"**
Light	A: 2 ◻→◪	2⅜"	2⅞"	3⅛"	3⅜"	3⅞"	4⅜"
	B: 4 ▭	1¼" x 3½"	1½" x 4½"	1⅝" x 5"	1¾" x 5½"	2" x 6½"	2¼" x 7½"
	C: 2 ◇	T5	T7	T8	T9	T11	T12
Dark	D: 4 ◻	2"	2½"	2¾"	3"	3½"	4"
	E: 4 ▭	1¼" x 3½"	1½" x 4½"	1⅝" x 5"	1¾" x 5½"	2" x 6½"	2¼" x 7½"
	F: 2 ◇	T5	T7	T8	T9	T11	T12

Try this: Use a medium instead of a light for A.

CRACKER

3-Unit Grid
Color Illustration: page 14

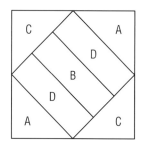
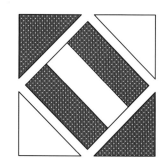

		FINISHED BLOCK SIZE *Single dimensions in the cutting chart indicate the size of the cut square (3" = 3" x 3").*					
FOR 1 BLOCK:		**4½"**	**6"**	**7½"**	**9"**	**10½"**	**12"**
Light	A: 1 ◻→◪	3⅛"	3⅞"	4⅝"	5⅜"	6⅛"	6⅞"
	B: 1 ◇	T42	T52	T60	T68	T71	T73
Dark	C: 1 ◻→◪	3⅛"	3⅞"	4⅝"	5⅜"	6⅛"	6⅞"
	D: 2 ◇	T42	T52	T60	T68	T71	T73

Try this: Use a medium instead of a light for A and B.

THE CRAYON BOX

6-Unit Grid
Color Illustration: page 14

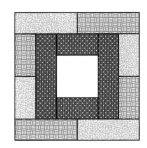
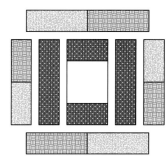

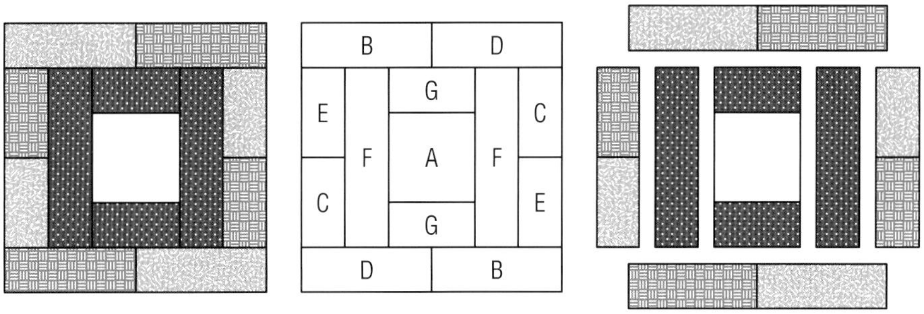

FOR 1 BLOCK:			**FINISHED BLOCK SIZE**					
			Single dimensions in the cutting chart indicate the size of the cut square (3" = 3" x 3").					
			4½"	**6"**	**7½"**	**9"**	**10½"**	**12"**
Light	A: 1		2"	2½"	3"	3½"	4"	4½"
Medium	B: 2		1¼" x 2¾"	1½" x 3½"	1¾" x 4¼"	2" x 5"	2¼" x 5¾"	2½" x 6½"
	C: 2		1¼" x 2"	1½" x 2½"	1¾" x 3"	2" x 3½"	2¼" x 4"	2½" x 4½"
Medium 2	D: 2		1¼" x 2¾"	1½" x 3½"	1¾" x 4¼"	2" x 5"	2¼" x 5¾"	2½" x 6½"
	E: 2		1¼" x 2"	1½" x 2½"	1¾" x 3"	2" x 3½"	2¼" x 4"	2½" x 4½"
Dark	F: 2		1¼" x 3½"	1½" x 4½"	1¾" x 5½"	2" x 6½"	2¼" x 7½"	2½" x 8½"
	G: 2		1¼" x 2"	1½" x 2½"	1¾" x 3"	2" x 3½"	2¼" x 4"	2½" x 4½"

Try this: Use a scrappy assortment of mediums for B, C, D and E.

CRAZY ANN

8-Unit Grid
Color Illustration: page 14

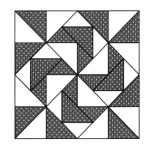
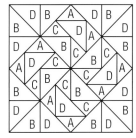

FOR 1 BLOCK:			**FINISHED BLOCK SIZE**					
			Single dimensions in the cutting chart indicate the size of the cut square (3" = 3" x 3").					
			6"	**8"**	**9"**	**10"**	**12"**	**14"**
Light	A: 2		2¾"	3¼"	3½"	3¾"	4¼"	4¾"
	B: 6		2⅜"	2⅞"	3⅛"	3⅜"	3⅞"	4⅜"
Dark	C: 2		2¾"	3¼"	3½"	3¾"	4¼"	4¾"
	D: 6		2⅜"	2⅞"	3⅛"	3⅜"	3⅞"	4⅜"

Try this: Reverse the lights and darks in every other block.

CROCKETT CABIN

4-Unit Grid
Color Illustration: page 14

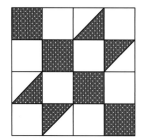
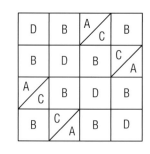
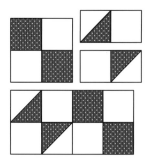

		FINISHED BLOCK SIZE					
		Single dimensions in the cutting chart indicate the size of the cut square (3" = 3" x 3").					
FOR 1 BLOCK:		**4"**	**6"**	**8"**	**9"**	**10"**	**12"**
Light	A: 2 ◻→◩	1⅞"	2⅜"	2⅞"	3⅛"	3⅜"	3⅞"
	B: 8 ◻	1½"	2"	2½"	2¾"	3"	3½"
Dark	C: 2 ◻→◩	1⅞"	2⅜"	2⅞"	3⅛"	3⅜"	3⅞"
	D: 4 ◻	1½"	2"	2½"	2¾"	3"	3½"

Try this: Use one dark for C and a different dark for D.

CROSS AND CHAINS

6-Unit Grid
Color Illustration: page 14

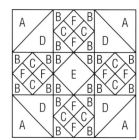

		FINISHED BLOCK SIZE					
		Single dimensions in the cutting chart indicate the size of the cut square (3" = 3" x 3").					
FOR 1 BLOCK:		**4½"**	**6"**	**7½"**	**9"**	**10½"**	**12"**
Light	A: 2 ◻→◩	2⅜"	2⅞"	3⅜"	3⅞"	4⅜"	4⅞"
	B: 10 ◻→◩	1⅝"	1⅞"	2⅛"	2⅜"	2⅝"	2⅞"
	C: 8 ◇	T1	T2	T4	T5	T6	T7
Dark	D: 2 ◻→◩	2⅜"	2⅞"	3⅜"	3⅞"	4⅜"	4⅞"
	E: 1 ◇	T5	T7	T9	T11	T12	T14
	F: 8 ◇	T1	T2	T4	T5	T6	T7

Try this: Use a medium instead of a light for B.

CROSS AND CROWN

7-Unit Grid

Color Illustration: page 14

 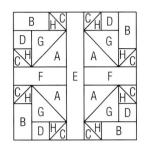 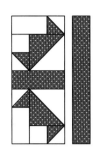 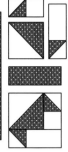

		FINISHED BLOCK SIZE *Single dimensions in the cutting chart indicate the size of the cut square (3" = 3" x 3").*					
FOR 1 BLOCK:		**5¼"**	**7"**	**8¾"**	**10½"**	**12¼"**	**14"**
Light	A: 2 ☐→◺	2⅜"	2⅞"	3⅜"	3⅞"	4⅜"	4⅞"
	B: 4 ▭	1¼" x 2"	1½" x 2½"	1¾" x 3"	2" x 3½"	2¼" x 4"	2½" x 4½"
	C: 4 ☐→◺	1⅝"	1⅞"	2⅛"	2⅜"	2⅝"	2⅞"
	D: 4 ☐	1¼"	1½"	1¾"	2"	2¼"	2½"
Dark	E: 1 ▭	1¼" x 5¾"	1½" x 7½"	1¾" x 9¼"	2" x 11"	2¼" x 12¾"	2½" x 14½"
	F: 2 ▭	1¼" x 2¾"	1½" x 3½"	1¾" x 4¼"	2" x 5"	2¼" x 5¾"	2½" x 6½"
	G: 2 ☐→◺	2⅜"	2⅞"	3⅜"	3⅞"	4⅜"	4⅞"
	H: 4 ☐→◺	1⅝"	1⅞"	2⅛"	2⅜"	2⅝"	2⅞"

Try this: Use a medium instead of a dark for E and F.

CROSS ROADS

6-Unit Grid

Color Illustration: page 14

 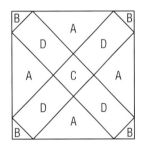 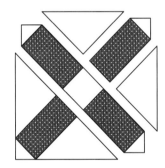

		FINISHED BLOCK SIZE *Single dimensions in the cutting chart indicate the size of the cut square (3" = 3" x 3").*					
FOR 1 BLOCK:		**4½"**	**6"**	**7½"**	**9"**	**10½"**	**12"**
Light	A: 1 ⊠→⧄	4¼"	5¼"	6¼"	7¼"	8¼"	9¼"
	B: 2 ☐→◺	1⅝"	1⅞"	2⅛"	2⅜"	2⅝"	2⅞"
	C: 1 ◇	T5	T7	T9	T11	T12	T14
Dark	D: 4 ▱	T41	T51	T59	T67	T70	T72

Try this: Reverse the lights and darks in every other block.

CROSS ROADS TO JERICHO

3-Unit Grid
Color Illustration: page 14

 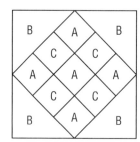 

FOR 1 BLOCK:	**FINISHED BLOCK SIZE** *Single dimensions in the cutting chart indicate the size of the cut square (3" = 3" x 3").*					
	4½"	**6"**	**7½"**	**9"**	**10½"**	**12"**
Light A: 5 ◇	T5	T7	T9	T11	T12	T14
Medium B: 2 ◺ → ◳	3⅛"	3⅞"	4⅝"	5⅜"	6⅛"	6⅞"
Dark C: 4 ◇	T5	T7	T9	T11	T12	T14

Try this: Reverse the mediums and darks in every other block.

CROSSED SQUARES

5-Unit Grid
Color Illustration: page 14

 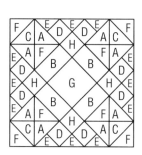 

FOR 1 BLOCK:	**FINISHED BLOCK SIZE** *Single dimensions in the cutting chart indicate the size of the cut square (3" = 3" x 3").*					
	5"	**6¼"**	**7½"**	**8¾"**	**10"**	**12½"**
Light A: 4 ◺ → ◳	1⅞"	2⅛"	2⅜"	2⅝"	2⅞"	3⅜"
B: 4 ◇	T32	T36	T41	T46	T51	T59
Light 2 C: 2 ◺ → ◳	1⅞"	2⅛"	2⅜"	2⅝"	2⅞"	3⅜"
D: 8 ◇	T2	T4	T5	T6	T7	T9
Dark E: 3 ⊠ → ⊠	2¼"	2½"	2¾"	3"	3¼"	3¾"
F: 4 ◺ → ◳	1⅞"	2⅛"	2⅜"	2⅝"	2⅞"	3⅜"
G: 1 ◇	T7	T9	T11	T12	T14	T16
H: 4 ◇	T2	T4	T5	T6	T7	T9

Try this: Use a medium instead of a light for A.

CROSSES AND LOSSES

4-Unit Grid
Color Illustration: page 14

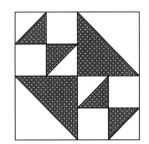
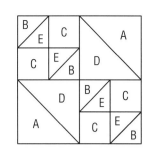
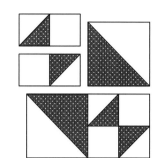

	FINISHED BLOCK SIZE Single dimensions in the cutting chart indicate the size of the cut square (3" = 3" x 3").					
FOR 1 BLOCK:	**4"**	**6"**	**8"**	**9"**	**10"**	**12"**
Light A: 1 ▱ → ◨	2⅞"	3⅞"	4⅞"	5⅜"	5⅞"	6⅞"
B: 2 ▱ → ◨	1⅞"	2⅜"	2⅞"	3⅛"	3⅜"	3⅞"
C: 4 ☐	1½"	2"	2½"	2¾"	3"	3½"
Dark D: 1 ▱ → ◨	2⅞"	3⅞"	4⅞"	5⅜"	5⅞"	6⅞"
E: 2 ▱ → ◨	1⅞"	2⅜"	2⅞"	3⅛"	3⅜"	3⅞"

Try this: Use a medium instead of a dark for E.

CROWN

6-Unit Grid
Color Illustration: page 14

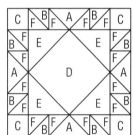

	FINISHED BLOCK SIZE Single dimensions in the cutting chart indicate the size of the cut square (3" = 3" x 3").					
FOR 1 BLOCK:	**4½"**	**6"**	**7½"**	**9"**	**10½"**	**12"**
Light A: 1 ⊠ → ⊠	2¾"	3¼"	3¾"	4¼"	4¾"	5¼"
B: 4 ▱ → ◨	1⅝"	1⅞"	2⅛"	2⅜"	2⅝"	2⅞"
C: 4 ☐	1¼"	1½"	1¾"	2"	2¼"	2½"
D: 1 ◇	T11	T14	T16	T19	T21	T23
Dark E: 2 ▱ → ◨	2⅜"	2⅞"	3⅜"	3⅞"	4⅜"	4⅞"
F: 8 ▱ → ◨	1⅝"	1⅞"	2⅛"	2⅜"	2⅝"	2⅞"

Try this: Use a different fabric for each "crown."

CROWN AND STAR

8-Unit Grid
Color Illustration: page 14

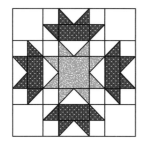
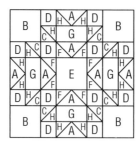
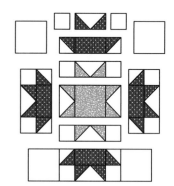

		FINISHED BLOCK SIZE Single dimensions in the cutting chart indicate the size of the cut square (3" = 3" x 3").					
FOR 1 BLOCK:		**6"**	**8"**	**9"**	**10"**	**12"**	**14"**
Light	A: 2 ⊠ → ⊠	2¾"	3¼"	3½"	3¾"	4¼"	4¾"
	B: 4 □	2"	2½"	2¾"	3"	3½"	4"
	C: 4 ◻ → ◺	1⅝"	1⅞"	2"	2⅛"	2⅜"	2⅝"
	D: 12 □	1¼"	1½"	1⅝"	1¾"	2"	2¼"
Medium	E: 1 □	2"	2½"	2¾"	3"	3½"	4"
	F: 4 ◻ → ◺	1⅝"	1⅞"	2"	2⅛"	2⅜"	2⅝"
Dark	G: 4 ▭	1¼" x 2"	1½" x 2½"	1⅝" x 2¾"	1¾" x 3"	2" x 3½"	2¼" x 4"
	H: 8 ◻ → ◺	1⅝"	1⅞"	2"	2⅛"	2⅜"	2⅝"
Try this:	Reverse the mediums and darks.						

CROWN OF THORNS

5-Unit Grid
Color Illustration: page 14

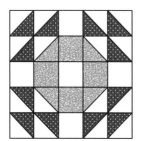
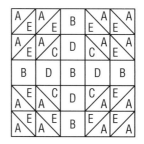
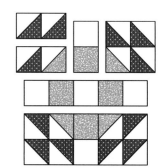

		FINISHED BLOCK SIZE Single dimensions in the cutting chart indicate the size of the cut square (3" = 3" x 3").					
FOR 1 BLOCK:		**5"**	**6¼"**	**7½"**	**8¾"**	**10"**	**12½"**
Light	A: 8 ◻ → ◺	1⅞"	2⅛"	2⅜"	2⅝"	2⅞"	3⅜"
	B: 5 □	1½"	1¾"	2"	2¼"	2½"	3"
Medium	C: 2 ◻ → ◺	1⅞"	2⅛"	2⅜"	2⅝"	2⅞"	3⅜"
	D: 4 □	1½"	1¾"	2"	2¼"	2½"	3"
Dark	E: 6 ◻ → ◺	1⅞"	2⅛"	2⅜"	2⅝"	2⅞"	3⅜"
Try this:	Use several different darks for E.						

CROW'S FOOT

6-Unit Grid
Color Illustration: page 14

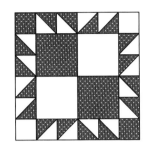 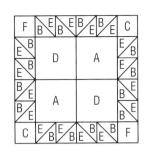 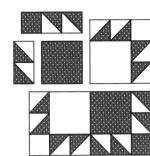

		FINISHED BLOCK SIZE					
		Single dimensions in the cutting chart indicate the size of the cut square (3" = 3" x 3").					
FOR 1 BLOCK:		4½"	6"	7½"	9"	10½"	12"
Light	A: 2 ☐	2"	2½"	3"	3½"	4"	4½"
	B: 8 ◺→◹	1⅝"	1⅞"	2⅛"	2⅜"	2⅝"	2⅞"
	C: 2 ☐	1¼"	1½"	1¾"	2"	2¼"	2½"
Dark	D: 2 ☐	2"	2½"	3"	3½"	4"	4½"
	E: 8 ◺→◹	1⅝"	1⅞"	2⅛"	2⅜"	2⅝"	2⅞"
	F: 2 ☐	1¼"	1½"	1¾"	2"	2¼"	2½"

Try this: Use a medium instead of a light for A.

CROW'S NEST

9-Unit Grid
Color Illustration: page 14

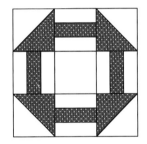 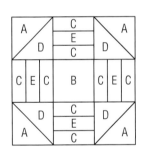 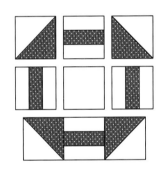

		FINISHED BLOCK SIZE					
		Single dimensions in the cutting chart indicate the size of the cut square (3" = 3" x 3").					
FOR 1 BLOCK:		6¾"	9"	10⅛"	11¼"	12⅜"	13½"
Light	A: 2 ◺→◹	3⅛"	3⅞"	4¼"	4⅝"	5"	5⅜"
	B: 1 ☐	2¾"	3½"	3⅞"	4¼"	4⅝"	5"
	C: 8 ▭	1¼" x 2¾"	1½" x 3½"	1⅝" x 3⅞"	1¾" x 4¼"	1⅞" x 4⅝"	2" x 5"
Dark	D: 2 ◺→◹	3⅛"	3⅞"	4¼"	4⅝"	5"	5⅜"
	E: 4 ▭	1¼" x 2¾"	1½" x 3½"	1⅝" x 3⅞"	1¾" x 4¼"	1⅞" x 4⅝"	2" x 5"

Try this: Use a medium instead of a light for B.

CRYSTAL STAR

4-Unit Grid

Color Illustration: page 15

 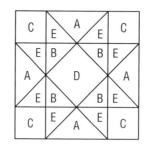 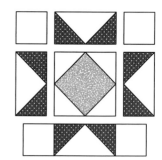

		FINISHED BLOCK SIZE					
		Single dimensions in the cutting chart indicate the size of the cut square (3" = 3" x 3").					
FOR 1 BLOCK:		**4"**	**6"**	**8"**	**9"**	**10"**	**12"**
Light	A: 1 ⊠ → ⊠	3¼"	4¼"	5¼"	5¾"	6¼"	7¼"
	B: 2 ◺ → ◹	1⅞"	2⅜"	2⅞"	3⅛"	3⅜"	3⅞"
	C: 4 ☐	1½"	2"	2½"	2¾"	3"	3½"
Medium	D: 1 ◇	T7	T11	T14	T15	T16	T19
Dark	E: 4 ◺ → ◹	1⅞"	2⅜"	2⅞"	3⅛"	3⅜"	3⅞"

Try this: Use one light for A and C and a different light for B.

CUPS AND SAUCERS

6-Unit Grid

Color Illustration: page 15

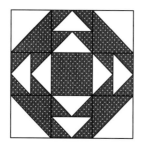 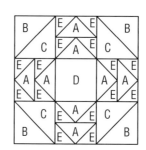 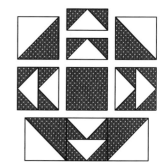

		FINISHED BLOCK SIZE					
		Single dimensions in the cutting chart indicate the size of the cut square (3" = 3" x 3").					
FOR 1 BLOCK:		**4½"**	**6"**	**7½"**	**9"**	**10½"**	**12"**
Light	A: 2 ⊠ → ⊠	2¾"	3¼"	3¾"	4¼"	4¾"	5¼"
	B: 2 ◺ → ◹	2⅜"	2⅞"	3⅜"	3⅞"	4⅜"	4⅞"
Dark	C: 2 ◺ → ◹	2⅜"	2⅞"	3⅜"	3⅞"	4⅜"	4⅞"
	D: 1 ☐	2"	2½"	3"	3½"	4"	4½"
	E: 8 ◺ → ◹	1⅝"	1⅞"	2⅛"	2⅜"	2⅝"	2⅞"

Try this: Reverse the lights and darks in every other block.

CUT THE CORNERS

6-Unit Grid
Color Illustration: page 15

 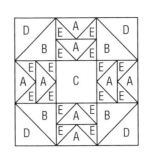 

FOR 1 BLOCK:		FINISHED BLOCK SIZE					
		Single dimensions in the cutting chart indicate the size of the cut square (3" = 3" x 3").					
		4½"	6"	7½"	9"	10½"	12"
Light	A: 2 ⊠ → ⊠	2¾"	3¼"	3¾"	4¼"	4¾"	5¼"
	B: 2 ◺ → ◺	2⅜"	2⅞"	3⅜"	3⅞"	4⅜"	4⅞"
	C: 1 ☐	2"	2½"	3"	3½"	4"	4½"
Light 2	D: 2 ◺ → ◺	2⅜"	2⅞"	3⅜"	3⅞"	4⅜"	4⅞"
Dark	E: 8 ◺ → ◺	1⅝"	1⅞"	2⅛"	2⅜"	2⅝"	2⅞"

Try this: Use a medium instead of lights for C and D.

CYPRESS

4-Unit Grid
Color Illustration: page 15

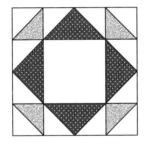 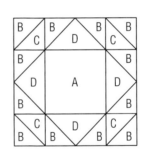 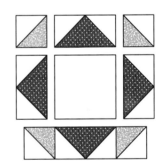

FOR 1 BLOCK:		FINISHED BLOCK SIZE					
		Single dimensions in the cutting chart indicate the size of the cut square (3" = 3" x 3").					
		4"	6"	8"	9"	10"	12"
Light	A: 1 ☐	2½"	3½"	4½"	5"	5½"	6½"
	B: 6 ◺ → ◺	1⅞"	2⅜"	2⅞"	3⅛"	3⅜"	3⅞"
Medium	C: 2 ◺ → ◺	1⅞"	2⅜"	2⅞"	3⅛"	3⅜"	3⅞"
Dark	D: 1 ⊠ → ⊠	3¼"	4¼"	5¼"	5¾"	6¼"	7¼"

Try this: Use one light for A and a different light for B.

☐ Light	Light 2	Medium	Medium 2	Dark

DARIEN'S DILEMMA

5-Unit Grid

Color Illustration: page 15

 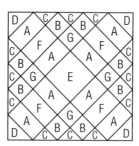 

		FINISHED BLOCK SIZE *Single dimensions in the cutting chart indicate the size of the cut square (3" = 3" x 3").*					
FOR 1 BLOCK:		**5"**	**6¼"**	**7½"**	**8¾"**	**10"**	**12½"**
Light	A: 8 ◇	T32	T36	T41	T46	T51	T59
	B: 8 ◇	T2	T4	T5	T6	T7	T9
Dark	C: 3 ⊠→⊠	2¼"	2½"	2¾"	3"	3¼"	3¾"
	D: 2 ◻→◻	1⅞"	2⅛"	2⅜"	2⅝"	2⅞"	3⅜"
	E: 1 ◇	T7	T9	T11	T12	T14	T16
	F: 4 ◇	T32	T36	T41	T46	T51	T59
	G: 4 ◇	T2	T4	T5	T6	T7	T9

Try this: Use a light and a medium instead of a light and a dark for every other block.

DARTING BIRDS

3-Unit Grid

Color Illustration: page 15

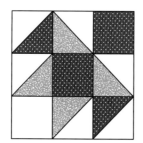 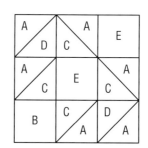 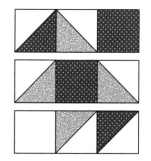

		FINISHED BLOCK SIZE *Single dimensions in the cutting chart indicate the size of the cut square (3" = 3" x 3").*					
FOR 1 BLOCK:		**4½"**	**6"**	**7½"**	**9"**	**10½"**	**12"**
Light	A: 3 ◻→◻	2⅜"	2⅞"	3⅜"	3⅞"	4⅜"	4⅞"
	B: 1 ◻	2"	2½"	3"	3½"	4"	4½"
Medium	C: 2 ◻→◻	2⅜"	2⅞"	3⅜"	3⅞"	4⅜"	4⅞"
Dark	D: 1 ◻→◻	2⅜"	2⅞"	3⅜"	3⅞"	4⅜"	4⅞"
	E: 2 ◻	2"	2½"	3"	3½"	4"	4½"

Try this: Use a dark instead of a medium for C.

DENALI

8-Unit Grid

Color Illustration: page 15

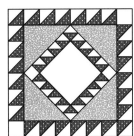 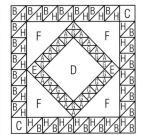 

FOR 2 BLOCKS:		FINISHED BLOCK SIZE Single dimensions in the cutting chart indicate the size of the cut square (3" = 3" x 3").					
		6"	**8"**	**9"**	**10"**	**12"**	**14"**
Light	A: 9 ⊠→⊠	2"	2¼"	2⅜"	2½"	2¾"	3"
	B: 26 ◻→◻	1⅝"	1⅞"	2"	2⅛"	2⅜"	2⅝"
	C: 4 ◻	1¼"	1½"	1⅝"	1¾"	2"	2¼"
	D: 2 ◇	T11	T14	T15	T16	T19	T21
	E: 4 ◇	T1	T2	T3	T4	T5	T6
Medium	F: 4 ◻→◻	3⅛"	3⅞"	4¼"	4⅝"	5⅜"	6⅛"
Dark	G: 9 ⊠→⊠	2"	2¼"	2⅜"	2½"	2¾"	3"
	H: 26 ◻→◻	1⅝"	1⅞"	2"	2⅛"	2⅜"	2⅝"

Try this: Use many different darks for G and H.

DEVIL'S CLAWS

4-Unit Grid

Color Illustration: page 15

 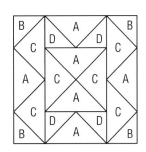 

FOR 2 BLOCKS:		FINISHED BLOCK SIZE Single dimensions in the cutting chart indicate the size of the cut square (3" = 3" x 3").					
		4"	**6"**	**8"**	**9"**	**10"**	**12"**
Light	A: 3 ⊠→⊠	3¼"	4¼"	5¼"	5¾"	6¼"	7¼"
	B: 4 ◻→◻	1⅞"	2⅜"	2⅞"	3⅛"	3⅜"	3⅞"
Dark	C: 3 ⊠→⊠	3¼"	4¼"	5¼"	5¾"	6¼"	7¼"
	D: 4 ◻→◻	1⅞"	2⅜"	2⅞"	3⅛"	3⅜"	3⅞"

Try this: Reverse the lights and darks in every other block.

DEWEY DREAM QUILT

5-Unit Grid
Color Illustration: page 15

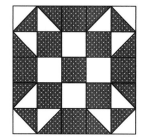 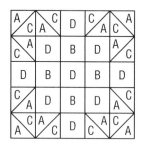 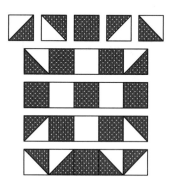

FOR 1 BLOCK:		FINISHED BLOCK SIZE Single dimensions in the cutting chart indicate the size of the cut square (3" = 3" x 3").					
		5"	6¼"	7½"	8¾"	10"	12½"
Light	A: 6 ◻→◸	1⅞"	2⅛"	2⅜"	2⅝"	2⅞"	3⅜"
	B: 4 ◻	1½"	1¾"	2"	2¼"	2½"	3"
Dark	C: 6 ◻→◸	1⅞"	2⅛"	2⅜"	2⅝"	2⅞"	3⅜"
	D: 9 ◻	1½"	1¾"	2"	2¼"	2½"	3"
Try this:	Use a medium instead of a dark for C.						

DIAGONAL SQUARE

4-Unit Grid
Color Illustration: page 15

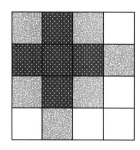 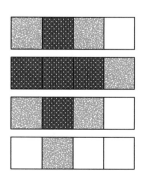

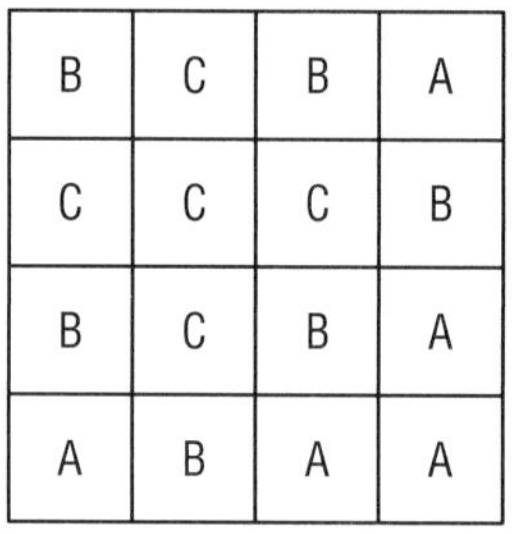

FOR 1 BLOCK:		FINISHED BLOCK SIZE Single dimensions in the cutting chart indicate the size of the cut square (3" = 3" x 3").					
		4"	6"	8"	9"	10"	12"
Light	A: 5 ◻	1½"	2"	2½"	2¾"	3"	3½"
Medium	B: 6 ◻	1½"	2"	2½"	2¾"	3"	3½"
Dark	C: 5 ◻	1½"	2"	2½"	2¾"	3"	3½"
Try this:	Use a different dark in every block.						

DIAMOND PANES

7-Unit Grid

Color Illustration: page 15

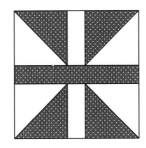
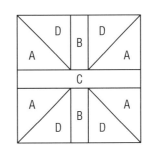
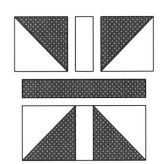

FINISHED BLOCK SIZE						
Single dimensions in the cutting chart indicate the size of the cut square (3" = 3" x 3").						
FOR 1 BLOCK:	**5¼"**	**7"**	**8¾"**	**10½"**	**12¼"**	**14"**
Light A: 2 �«→�«ı	3⅛"	3⅞"	4⅝"	5⅜"	6⅛"	6⅞"
B: 2 ▭	1¼" x 2¾"	1½" x 3½"	1¾" x 4¼"	2" x 5"	2¼" x 5¾"	2½" x 6½"
Dark C: 1 ▭	1¼" x 5¾"	1½" x 7½"	1¾" x 9¼"	2" x 11"	2¼" x 12¾"	2½" x 14½"
D: 2 �«→�«ı	3⅛"	3⅞"	4⅝"	5⅜"	6⅛"	6⅞"

Try this: Use one light for A and a different light for B.

DIAMOND PLAID BLOCK

9-Unit Grid

Color Illustration: page 15

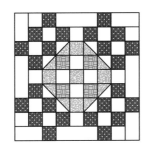
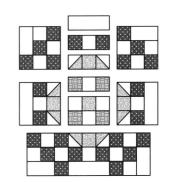

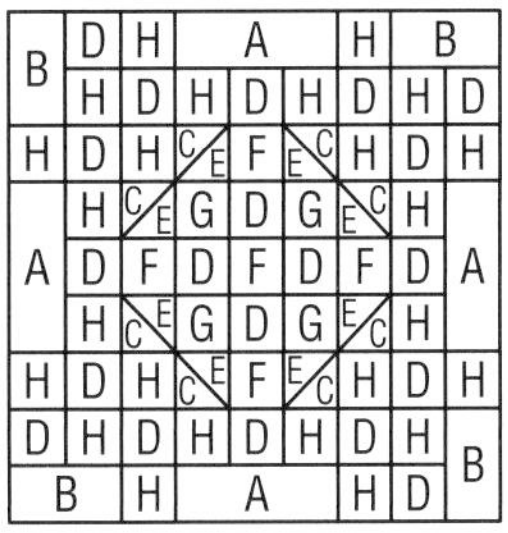

FINISHED BLOCK SIZE						
Single dimensions in the cutting chart indicate the size of the cut square (3" = 3" x 3").						
FOR 1 BLOCK:	**6¾"**	**9"**	**10⅛"**	**11¼"**	**12⅜"**	**13½"**
Light A: 4 ▭	1¼" x 2¾"	1½" x 3½"	1⅝" x 3⅞"	1¾" x 4¼"	1⅞" x 4⅝"	2" x 5"
B: 4 ▭	1¼" x 2"	1½" x 2½"	1⅝" x 2¾"	1¾" x 3"	1⅞" x 3¼"	2" x 3½"
C: 4 �«→�«ı	1⅝"	1⅞"	2"	2⅛"	2¼"	2⅜"
D: 20 ▢	1¼"	1½"	1⅝"	1¾"	1⅞"	2"
Medium E: 4 �«→�«ı	1⅝"	1⅞"	2"	2⅛"	2¼"	2⅜"
F: 5 ▢	1¼"	1½"	1⅝"	1¾"	1⅞"	2"
Medium 2 G: 4 ▢	1¼"	1½"	1⅝"	1¾"	1⅞"	2"
Dark H: 24 ▢	1¼"	1½"	1⅝"	1¾"	1⅞"	2"

Try this: Use a different medium in every block.

DOES DOUBLE DUTY

5-Unit Grid

Color Illustration: page 15

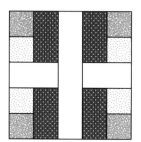
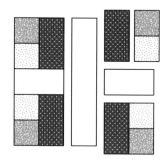

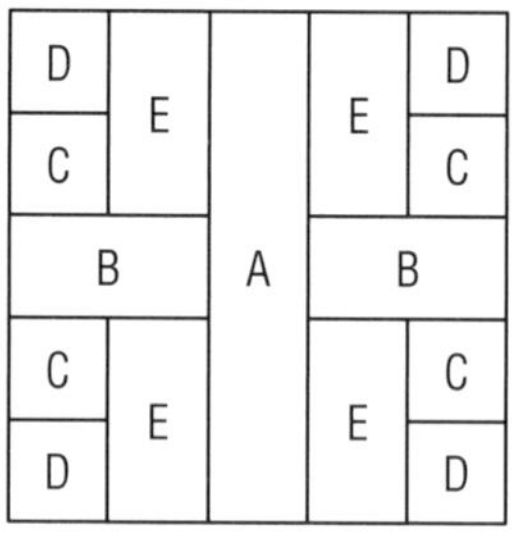

FOR 1 BLOCK:		**FINISHED BLOCK SIZE** Single dimensions in the cutting chart indicate the size of the cut square (3" = 3" x 3").					
		5"	**6¼"**	**7½"**	**8¾"**	**10"**	**12½"**
Light	A: 1	1½" x 5½"	1¾" x 6¾"	2" x 8"	2¼" x 9¼"	2½" x 10½"	3" x 13"
	B: 2	1½" x 2½"	1¾" x 3"	2" x 3½"	2¼" x 4"	2½" x 4½"	3" x 5½"
Light 2	C: 4	1½"	1¾"	2"	2¼"	2½"	3"
Medium	D: 4	1½"	1¾"	2"	2¼"	2½"	3"
Dark	E: 4	1½" x 2½"	1¾" x 3"	2" x 3½"	2¼" x 4"	2½" x 4½"	3" x 5½"

Try this: Reverse the lights and darks in every other block.

DOMINO AND SQUARE

5-Unit Grid

Color Illustration: page 15

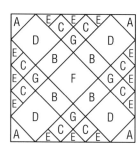

FOR 1 BLOCK:		**FINISHED BLOCK SIZE** Single dimensions in the cutting chart indicate the size of the cut square (3" = 3" x 3").					
		5"	**6¼"**	**7½"**	**8¾"**	**10"**	**12½"**
Light	A: 2	1⅞"	2⅛"	2⅜"	2⅝"	2⅞"	3⅜"
	B: 4	T32	T36	T41	T46	T51	T59
	C: 8	T2	T4	T5	T6	T7	T9
Medium	D: 4	T7	T9	T11	T12	T14	T16
Dark	E: 3	2¼"	2½"	2¾"	3"	3¼"	3¾"
	F: 1	T7	T9	T11	T12	T14	T16
	G: 4	T2	T4	T5	T6	T7	T9

Try this: Reverse the darks and mediums.

DOMINO NET

6-Unit Grid
Color Illustration: page 15

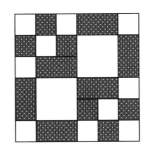

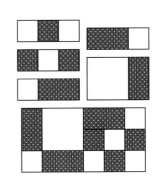

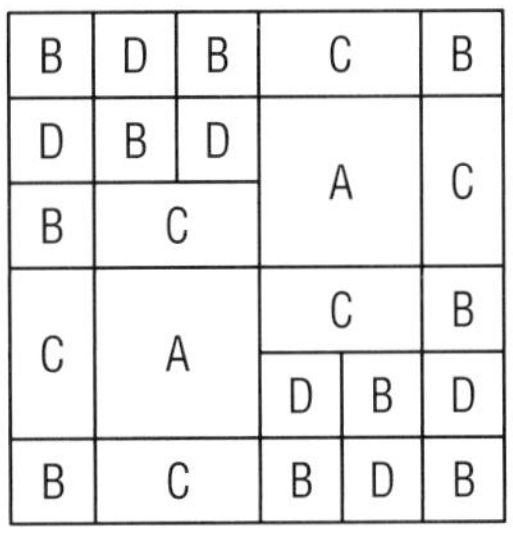

FOR 1 BLOCK:		FINISHED BLOCK SIZE *Single dimensions in the cutting chart indicate the size of the cut square (3" = 3" x 3").*					
		4½"	**6"**	**7½"**	**9"**	**10½"**	**12"**
Light	A: 2 ☐	2"	2½"	3"	3½"	4"	4½"
	B: 10 ☐	1¼"	1½"	1¾"	2"	2¼"	2½"
Dark	C: 6 ▭	1¼" x 2"	1½" x 2½"	1¾" x 3"	2" x 3½"	2¼" x 4"	2½" x 4½"
	D: 6 ☐	1¼"	1½"	1¾"	2"	2¼"	2½"

Try this: Use a medium instead of a light for A.

DOUBLE SAWTOOTH

5-Unit Grid
Color Illustration: page 15

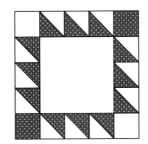

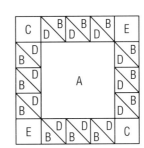

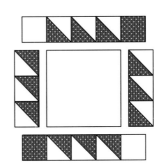

FOR 1 BLOCK:		FINISHED BLOCK SIZE *Single dimensions in the cutting chart indicate the size of the cut square (3" = 3" x 3").*					
		5"	**6¼"**	**7½"**	**8¾"**	**10"**	**12½"**
Light	A: 1 ☐	3½"	4¼"	5"	5¾"	6½"	8"
	B: 6 ◲ → ◳	1⅞"	2⅛"	2⅜"	2⅝"	2⅞"	3⅜"
	C: 2 ☐	1½"	1¾"	2"	2¼"	2½"	3"
Dark	D: 6 ◲ → ◳	1⅞"	2⅛"	2⅜"	2⅝"	2⅞"	3⅜"
	E: 2 ☐	1½"	1¾"	2"	2¼"	2½"	3"

Try this: Use a large-scale print for A.

☐ *Light*   ▨ *Light 2*   ▨ *Medium*   ▦ *Medium 2*   ▩ *Dark*

THE DOUBLE SQUARE

10-Unit Grid
Color Illustration: page 15

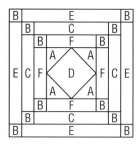
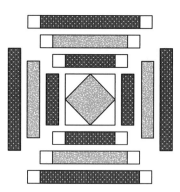

FOR 1 BLOCK:		**FINISHED BLOCK SIZE** *Single dimensions in the cutting chart indicate the size of the cut square (3" = 3" x 3").*					
		6¼"	**7½"**	**8¾"**	**10"**	**12½"**	**13¾"**
Light	A: 2 ◻→◪	2⅛"	2⅜"	2⅝"	2⅞"	3⅜"	3⅝"
	B: 12 ◻	1⅛"	1¼"	1⅜"	1½"	1¾"	1⅞"
Medium	C: 4 ▭	1⅛" x 4¼"	1¼" x 5"	1⅜" x 5¾"	1½" x 6½"	1¾" x 8"	1⅞" x 8¾"
	D: 1 ◇	T9	T11	T12	T14	T16	T18
Dark	E: 4 ▭	1⅛" x 5½"	1¼" x 6½"	1⅜" x 7½"	1½" x 8½"	1¾" x 10½"	1⅞" x 11½"
	F: 4 ▭	1⅛" x 3"	1¼" x 3½"	1⅜" x 4"	1½" x 4½"	1¾" x 5½"	1⅞" x 6"

Try this: Reverse the mediums and darks in every other block.

THE DOUBLE V

5-Unit Grid
Color Illustration: page 15

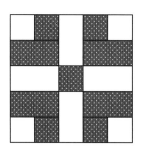
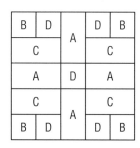
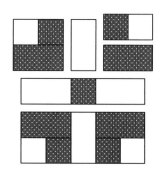

FOR 1 BLOCK:		**FINISHED BLOCK SIZE** *Single dimensions in the cutting chart indicate the size of the cut square (3" = 3" x 3").*					
		5"	**6¼"**	**7½"**	**8¾"**	**10"**	**12½"**
Light	A: 4 ▭	1½" x 2½"	1¾" x 3"	2" x 3½"	2¼" x 4"	2½" x 4½"	3" x 5½"
	B: 4 ◻	1½"	1¾"	2"	2¼"	2½"	3"
Dark	C: 4 ▭	1½" x 2½"	1¾" x 3"	2" x 3½"	2¼" x 4"	2½" x 4½"	3" x 5½"
	D: 5 ◻	1½"	1¾"	2"	2¼"	2½"	3"

Try this: Use a medium instead of a light for A.

DOUBLE X

4-Unit Grid

Color Illustration: page 15

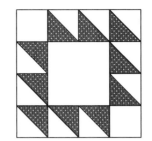 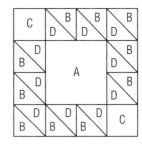 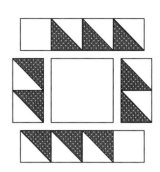

FOR 1 BLOCK:		**FINISHED BLOCK SIZE** *Single dimensions in the cutting chart indicate the size of the cut square (3" = 3" x 3").*					
		4"	**6"**	**8"**	**9"**	**10"**	**12"**
Light	A: 1 ☐	2½"	3½"	4½"	5"	5½"	6½"
	B: 5 ◩ → ◩	1⅞"	2⅜"	2⅞"	3⅛"	3⅜"	3⅞"
	C: 2 ☐	1½"	2"	2½"	2¾"	3"	3½"
Dark	D: 5 ◩ → ◩	1⅞"	2⅜"	2⅞"	3⅛"	3⅜"	3⅞"
Try this:	Use a large-scale print for A.						

DOUBLE X #3

4-Unit Grid

Color Illustration: page 15

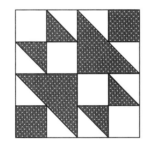 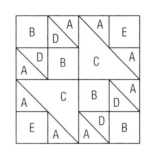 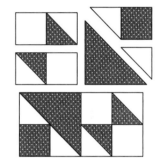

FOR 1 BLOCK:		**FINISHED BLOCK SIZE** *Single dimensions in the cutting chart indicate the size of the cut square (3" = 3" x 3").*					
		4"	**6"**	**8"**	**9"**	**10"**	**12"**
Light	A: 4 ◩ → ◩	1⅞"	2⅜"	2⅞"	3⅛"	3⅜"	3⅞"
	B: 4 ☐	1½"	2"	2½"	2¾"	3"	3½"
Dark	C: 1 ◩ → ◩	2⅞"	3⅞"	4⅞"	5⅜"	5⅞"	6⅞"
	D: 2 ◩ → ◩	1⅞"	2⅜"	2⅞"	3⅛"	3⅜"	3⅞"
	E: 2 ☐	1½"	2"	2½"	2¾"	3"	3½"
Try this:	Use a medium instead of a dark for D and E.						

☐ Light ▫ Light 2 ▦ Medium ▥ Medium 2 ■ Dark

DOUBLE X #4

6-Unit Grid

Color Illustration: page 15

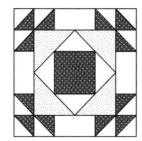
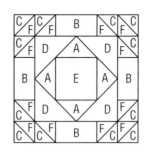

		FINISHED BLOCK SIZE Single dimensions in the cutting chart indicate the size of the cut square (3" = 3" x 3").					
FOR 1 BLOCK:		**4½"**	**6"**	**7½"**	**9"**	**10½"**	**12"**
Light	A: 1 ⊠ → ⊠	2¾"	3¼"	3¾"	4¼"	4¾"	5¼"
	B: 4 ▭	1¼" x 2"	1½" x 2½"	1¾" x 3"	2" x 3½"	2¼" x 4"	2½" x 4½"
	C: 6 ◻ → ◻	1⅝"	1⅞"	2⅛"	2⅜"	2⅝"	2⅞"
Light 2	D: 2 ◻ → ◻	2⅜"	2⅞"	3⅜"	3⅞"	4⅜"	4⅞"
Dark	E: 1 ◻	2"	2½"	3"	3½"	4"	4½"
	F: 6 ◻ → ◻	1⅝"	1⅞"	2⅛"	2⅜"	2⅝"	2⅞"
Try this:	Use several different darks for F.						

DOVES IN THE WINDOW

7-Unit Grid

Color Illustration: page 15

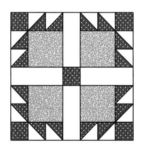
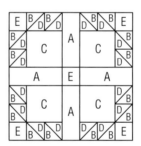
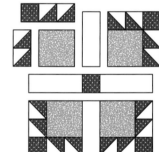

		FINISHED BLOCK SIZE Single dimensions in the cutting chart indicate the size of the cut square (3" = 3" x 3").					
FOR 1 BLOCK:		**5¼"**	**7"**	**8¾"**	**10½"**	**12¼"**	**14"**
Light	A: 4 ▭	1¼ " x 2¾"	1½" x 3½"	1¾" x 4¼"	2" x 5"	2¼" x 5¾"	2½" x 6½"
	B: 8 ◻ → ◻	1⅝"	1⅞"	2⅛"	2⅜"	2⅝"	2⅞"
Medium	C: 4 ◻	2"	2½"	3"	3½"	4"	4½"
Dark	D: 8 ◻ → ◻	1⅝"	1⅞"	2⅛"	2⅜"	2⅝"	2⅞"
	E: 5 ◻	1¼"	1½"	1¾"	2"	2¼"	2½"
Try this:	Use a dark instead of a medium for C.						

DUCK AND DUCKLINGS

8-Unit Grid

Color Illustration: page 15

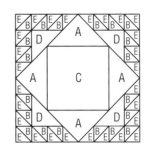

	FINISHED BLOCK SIZE Single dimensions in the cutting chart indicate the size of the cut square (3" = 3" x 3").					
FOR 1 BLOCK:	**6"**	**8"**	**9"**	**10"**	**12"**	**14"**
Light A: 1 ⊠ → ⊠	4¼"	5¼"	5¾"	6¼"	7¼"	8¼"
B: 10 ◺ → ◲	1⅝"	1⅞"	2"	2⅛"	2⅜"	2⅝"
Medium C: 1 ☐	3½"	4½"	5"	5½"	6½"	7½"
Dark D: 2 ◺ → ◲	2⅜"	2⅞"	3⅛"	3⅜"	3⅞"	4⅜"
E: 14 ◺ → ◲	1⅝"	1⅞"	2"	2⅛"	2⅜"	2⅝"

Try this: Use a large-scale print for C.

DUCK'S FOOT

5-Unit Grid

Color Illustration: page 15

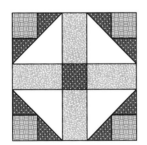
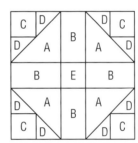
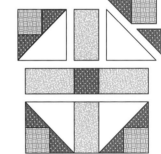

	FINISHED BLOCK SIZE Single dimensions in the cutting chart indicate the size of the cut square (3" = 3" x 3").					
FOR 1 BLOCK:	**5"**	**6¼"**	**7½"**	**8¾"**	**10"**	**12½"**
Light A: 2 ◺ → ◲	2⅞"	3⅜"	3⅞"	4⅜"	4⅞"	5⅞"
Medium B: 4 ▭	1½" x 2½"	1¾" x 3"	2" x 3½"	2¼" x 4"	2½" x 4½"	3" x 5½"
Medium 2 C: 4 ☐	1½"	1¾"	2"	2¼"	2½"	3"
Dark D: 4 ◺ → ◲	1⅞"	2⅛"	2⅜"	2⅝"	2⅞"	3⅜"
E: 1 ☐	1½"	1¾"	2"	2¼"	2½"	3"

Try this: Use a light instead of medium 2 for C.

Light   Light 2   Medium   Medium 2   Dark

DUTCHMAN'S PUZZLE

4-Unit Grid
Color Illustration: page 15

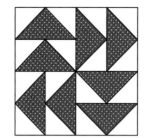 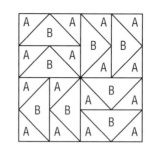 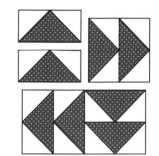

		FINISHED BLOCK SIZE *Single dimensions in the cutting chart indicate the size of the cut square (3" = 3" x 3").*					
FOR 1 BLOCK:		**4"**	**6"**	**8"**	**9"**	**10"**	**12"**
Light	A: 8 ☐→◺	1⅞"	2⅜"	2⅞"	3⅛"	3⅜"	3⅞"
Dark	B: 2 ⊠→⧗	3¼"	4¼"	5¼"	5¾"	6¼"	7¼"

Try this: Use a medium instead of a dark for one of the B squares.

EAGLE'S NEST

8-Unit Grid
Color Illustration: page 15

 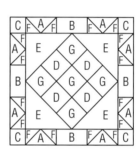 

		FINISHED BLOCK SIZE *Single dimensions in the cutting chart indicate the size of the cut square (3" = 3" x 3").*					
FOR 1 BLOCK:		**6"**	**8"**	**9"**	**10"**	**12"**	**14"**
Light	A: 2 ⊠→⧗	2¾"	3¼"	3½"	3¾"	4¼"	4¾"
	B: 4 ▭	1¼" x 2"	1½" x 2½"	1⅝" x 2¾"	1¾" x 3"	2" x 3½"	2¼" x 4"
	C: 4 ☐	1¼"	1½"	1⅝"	1¾"	2"	2¼"
	D: 4 ◇	T5	T7	T8	T9	T11	T12
Medium	E: 2 ☐→◺	3⅛"	3⅞"	4¼"	4⅝"	5⅜"	6⅛"
Dark	F: 8 ☐→◺	1⅝"	1⅞"	2"	2⅛"	2⅜"	2⅝"
	G: 5 ◇	T5	T7	T8	T9	T11	T12

Try this: Use one light for A, B, and C and a different light for D.

ECCENTRIC STAR

3-Unit Grid

Color Illustration: page 15

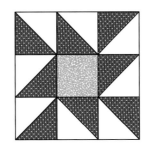
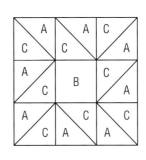
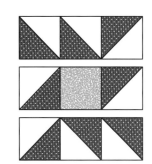

		FINISHED BLOCK SIZE					
FOR 1 BLOCK:		Single dimensions in the cutting chart indicate the size of the cut square (3" = 3" x 3").					
		4½"	**6"**	**7½"**	**9"**	**10½"**	**12"**
Light	A: 4 ◻→◺	2⅜"	2⅞"	3⅜"	3⅞"	4⅜"	4⅞"
Medium	B: 1 ◻	2"	2½"	3"	3½"	4"	4½"
Dark	C: 4 ◻→◺	2⅜"	2⅞"	3⅜"	3⅞"	4⅜"	4⅞"
Try this:	Use several different lights for A.						

ECONOMY

4-Unit Grid

Color Illustration: page 15

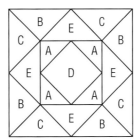

		FINISHED BLOCK SIZE					
FOR 1 BLOCK:		Single dimensions in the cutting chart indicate the size of the cut square (3" = 3" x 3").					
		4"	**6"**	**8"**	**9"**	**10"**	**12"**
Light	A: 2 ◻→◺	1⅞"	2⅜"	2⅞"	3⅛"	3⅜"	3⅞"
Light 2	B: 1 ⊠→⊠	3¼"	4¼"	5¼"	5¾"	6¼"	7¼"
Medium	C: 1 ⊠→⊠	3¼"	4¼"	5¼"	5¾"	6¼"	7¼"
Medium 2	D: 1 ◇	T7	T11	T14	T15	T16	T19
Dark	E: 1 ⊠→⊠	3¼"	4¼"	5¼"	5¾"	6¼"	7¼"
Try this:	Use several different fabrics for B and C.						

☐ Light ▢ Light 2 ▨ Medium ▦ Medium 2 ▦ Dark

ECONOMY PATCH

4-Unit Grid
Color Illustration: page 15

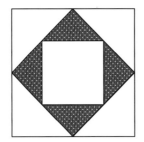 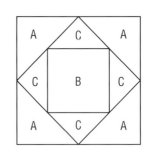 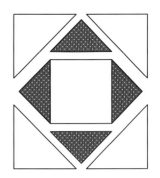

FOR 1 BLOCK:	FINISHED BLOCK SIZE *Single dimensions in the cutting chart indicate the size of the cut square (3" = 3" x 3").*					
	4"	**6"**	**8"**	**9"**	**10"**	**12"**
Light A: 2 ◻→◺	2⅞"	3⅞"	4⅞"	5⅜"	5⅞"	6⅞"
B: 1 ◻	2½"	3½"	4½"	5"	5½"	6½"
Dark C: 1 ⊠→⧖	3¼"	4¼"	5¼"	5¾"	6¼"	7¼"

Try this: Reverse the lights and darks in every other block.

EDDYSTONE LIGHT

6-Unit Grid
Color Illustration: page 15

 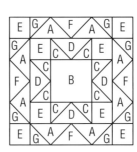 

FOR 1 BLOCK:	FINISHED BLOCK SIZE *Single dimensions in the cutting chart indicate the size of the cut square (3" = 3" x 3").*					
	4½"	**6"**	**7½"**	**9"**	**10½"**	**12"**
Light A: 2 ⊠→⧖	2¾"	3¼"	3¾"	4¼"	4¾"	5¼"
B: 1 ◻	2"	2½"	3"	3½"	4"	4½"
C: 4 ◻→◺	1⅝"	1⅞"	2⅛"	2⅜"	2⅝"	2⅞"
Medium D: 1 ⊠→⧖	2¾"	3¼"	3¾"	4¼"	4¾"	5¼"
E: 8 ◻	1¼"	1½"	1¾"	2"	2¼"	2½"
Dark F: 1 ⊠→⧖	2¾"	3¼"	3¾"	4¼"	4¾"	5¼"
G: 4 ◻→◺	1⅝"	1⅞"	2⅛"	2⅜"	2⅝"	2⅞"

Try this: Reverse the mediums and darks.

EIGHT HANDS AROUND

8-Unit Grid
Color Illustration: page 16

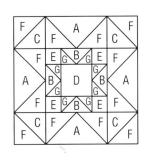
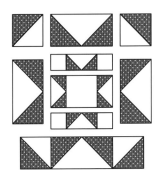

		FINISHED BLOCK SIZE					
		Single dimensions in the cutting chart indicate the size of the cut square (3" = 3" x 3").					
FOR 1 BLOCK:		**6"**	**8"**	**9"**	**10"**	**12"**	**14"**
Light	A: 1 ⊠ → ⊠	4¼"	5¼"	5¾"	6¼"	7¼"	8¼"
	B: 1 ⊠ → ⊠	2¾"	3¼"	3½"	3¾"	4¼"	4¾"
	C: 2 ◻ → ◻	2⅜"	2⅞"	3⅛"	3⅜"	3⅞"	4⅜"
	D: 1 ◻	2"	2½"	2¾"	3"	3½"	4"
	E: 4 ◻	1¼"	1½"	1⅝"	1¾"	2"	2¼"
Dark	F: 6 ◻ → ◻	2⅜"	2⅞"	3⅛"	3⅜"	3⅞"	4⅜"
	G: 4 ◻ → ◻	1⅝"	1⅞"	2"	2⅛"	2⅜"	2⅝"

Try this: Use one dark for F and a different dark for G.

ELECTRIC FAN

2-Unit Grid
Color Illustration: page 16

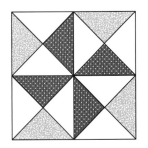
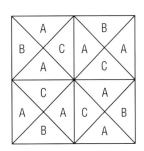
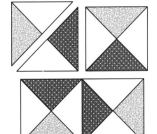

		FINISHED BLOCK SIZE					
		Single dimensions in the cutting chart indicate the size of the cut square (3" = 3" x 3").					
FOR 1 BLOCK:		**4"**	**6"**	**8"**	**9"**	**10"**	**12"**
Light	A: 2 ⊠ → ⊠	3¼"	4¼"	5¼"	5¾"	6¼"	7¼"
Medium	B: 1 ⊠ → ⊠	3¼"	4¼"	5¼"	5¾"	6¼"	7¼"
Dark	C: 1 ⊠ → ⊠	3¼"	4¼"	5¼"	5¾"	6¼"	7¼"

Try this: Use a different light for one of the A squares.

◻ Light   ◻ Light 2   ▨ Medium   ▦ Medium 2   ■ Dark

ENVELOPE

4-Unit Grid
Color Illustration: page 16

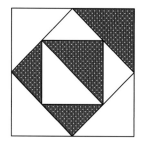
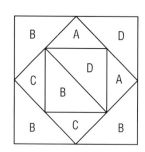
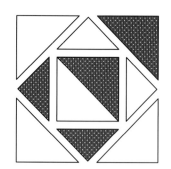

FOR 2 BLOCKS:		**FINISHED BLOCK SIZE** *Single dimensions in the cutting chart indicate the size of the cut square (3" = 3" x 3").*					
		4"	**6"**	**8"**	**9"**	**10"**	**12"**
Light	A: 1 ⊠ → ⊠	3¼"	4¼"	5¼"	5¾"	6¼"	7¼"
	B: 4 ◻ → ◹	2⅞"	3⅞"	4⅞"	5⅜"	5⅞"	6⅞"
Dark	C: 1 ⊠ → ⊠	3¼"	4¼"	5¼"	5¾"	6¼"	7¼"
	D: 2 ◻ → ◹	2⅞"	3⅞"	4⅞"	5⅜"	5⅞"	6⅞"

Try this: Reverse the lights and darks.

EQUINOX

8-Unit Grid
Color Illustration: page 16

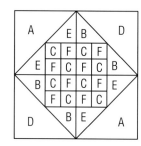
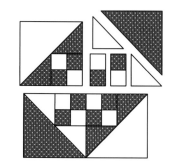

FOR 1 BLOCK:		**FINISHED BLOCK SIZE** *Single dimensions in the cutting chart indicate the size of the cut square (3" = 3" x 3").*					
		6"	**8"**	**9"**	**10"**	**12"**	**14"**
Light	A: 1 ◻ → ◹	3⅞"	4⅞"	5⅜"	5⅞"	6⅞"	7⅞"
	B: 2 ◻ → ◹	2⅜"	2⅞"	3⅛"	3⅜"	3⅞"	4⅜"
	C: 8 ◻	1¼"	1½"	1⅝"	1¾"	2"	2¼"
Dark	D: 1 ◻ → ◹	3⅞"	4⅞"	5⅜"	5⅞"	6⅞"	7⅞"
	E: 2 ◻ → ◹	2⅜"	2⅞"	3⅛"	3⅜"	3⅞"	4⅜"
	F: 8 ◻	1¼"	1½"	1⅝"	1¾"	2"	2¼"

Try this: Use a different combination of lights and darks in each quadrant of the block.

EVA'S DELIGHT

6-Unit Grid

Color Illustration: page 16

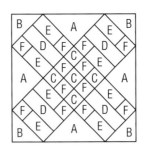
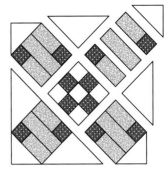

FOR 1 BLOCK:		FINISHED BLOCK SIZE *Single dimensions in the cutting chart indicate the size of the cut square (3" = 3" x 3").*					
		4½"	**6"**	**7½"**	**9"**	**10½"**	**12"**
Light	A: 1 ⊠ → ⊠	3½"	4¼"	5"	5¾"	6½"	7¼"
	B: 2 ◻ → ◹	2"	2⅜"	2¾"	3⅛"	3½"	3⅞"
	C: 5 ◇	T1	T2	T4	T5	T6	T7
Medium	D: 4 ▱	T29	T33	T37	T42	T47	T52
	E: 8 ▱	T28	T32	T36	T41	T46	T51
Dark	F: 12 ◇	T1	T2	T4	T5	T6	T7

Try this: Use one medium for D and a different medium for E.

FAIR AND SQUARE

4-Unit Grid

Color Illustration: page 16

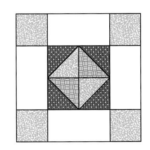
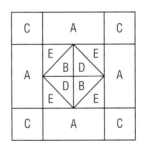
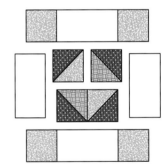

FOR 1 BLOCK:		FINISHED BLOCK SIZE *Single dimensions in the cutting chart indicate the size of the cut square (3" = 3" x 3").*					
		4"	**6"**	**8"**	**9"**	**10"**	**12"**
Light	A: 4 ▭	1½" x 2½"	2" x 3½"	2½" x 4½"	2¾" x 5"	3" x 5½"	3½" x 6½"
Medium	B: 1 ◻ → ◹	1⅞"	2⅜"	2⅞"	3⅛"	3⅜"	3⅞"
	C: 4 ◻	1½"	2"	2½"	2¾"	3"	3½"
Medium 2	D: 1 ◻ → ◹	1⅞"	2⅜"	2⅞"	3⅛"	3⅜"	3⅞"
Dark	E: 2 ◻ → ◹	1⅞"	2⅜"	2⅞"	3⅛"	3⅜"	3⅞"

Try this: Reverse the light and dark in every other block.

Light ▢   Light 2 ▢   Medium ▨   Medium 2 ▨   Dark ▨

FARM FRIENDLINESS

6-Unit Grid
Color Illustration: page 16

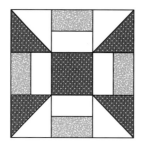

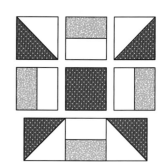

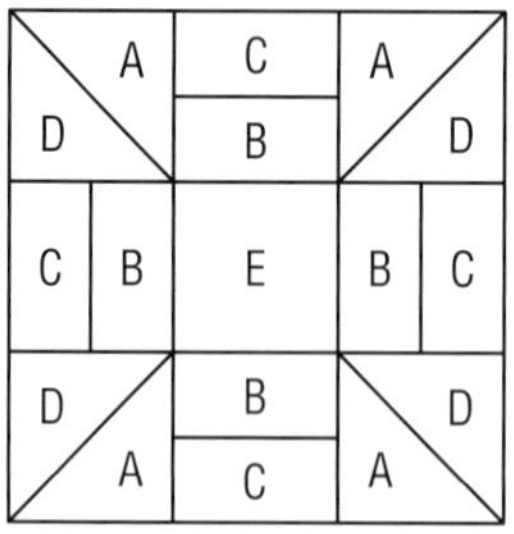

FOR 1 BLOCK:	FINISHED BLOCK SIZE Single dimensions in the cutting chart indicate the size of the cut square (3" = 3" x 3").					
	4½"	**6"**	**7½"**	**9"**	**10½"**	**12"**
Light A: 2 ◻→◹	2⅜"	2⅞"	3⅜"	3⅞"	4⅜"	4⅞"
B: 4 ▭	1¼" x 2"	1½" x 2½"	1¾" x 3"	2" x 3½"	2¼" x 4"	2½" x 4½"
Medium C: 4 ▭	1¼" x 2"	1½" x 2½"	1¾" x 3"	2" x 3½"	2¼" x 4"	2½" x 4½"
Dark D: 2 ◻→◹	2⅜"	2⅞"	3⅜"	3⅞"	4⅜"	4⅞"
E: 1 ◻	2"	2½"	3"	3½"	4"	4½"

Try this: Use one light for A and a different light for B.

FATHER'S CHOICE

5-Unit Grid
Color Illustration: page 16

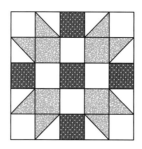

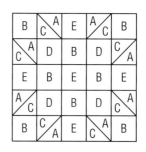

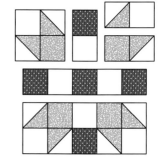

FOR 1 BLOCK:	FINISHED BLOCK SIZE Single dimensions in the cutting chart indicate the size of the cut square (3" = 3" x 3").					
	5"	**6¼"**	**7½"**	**8¾"**	**10"**	**12½"**
Light A: 4 ◻→◹	1⅞"	2⅛"	2⅜"	2⅝"	2⅞"	3⅜"
B: 8 ◻	1½"	1¾"	2"	2¼"	2½"	3"
Medium C: 4 ◻→◹	1⅞"	2⅛"	2⅜"	2⅝"	2⅞"	3⅜"
D: 4 ◻	1½"	1¾"	2"	2¼"	2½"	3"
Dark E: 5 ◻	1½"	1¾"	2"	2¼"	2½"	3"

Try this: Reverse the mediums and darks.

FEDERAL SQUARE

4-Unit Grid
Color Illustration: page 16

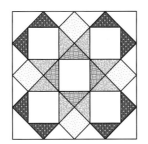
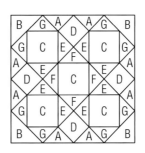

			FINISHED BLOCK SIZE				
			Single dimensions in the cutting chart indicate the size of the cut square (3" = 3" x 3").				
FOR 1 BLOCK:			**4"**	**6"**	**8"**	**9"**	**10"**	**12"**
Light	A: 2 ⊠ → ⊠		2¼"	2¾"	3¼"	3½"	3¾"	4¼"
	B: 2 ◻ → ◺		1⅞"	2⅜"	2⅞"	3⅛"	3⅜"	3⅞"
	C: 5 ◻		1½"	2"	2½"	2¾"	3"	3½"
Light 2	D: 4 ◇		T2	T5	T7	T8	T9	T11
Medium	E: 2 ⊠ → ⊠		2¼"	2¾"	3¼"	3½"	3¾"	4¼"
Medium 2	F: 1 ⊠ → ⊠		2¼"	2¾"	3¼"	3½"	3¾"	4¼"
Dark	G: 2 ⊠ → ⊠		2¼"	2¾"	3¼"	3½"	3¾"	4¼"

Try this: Use a dark instead of a light for the center square.

FIELDS AND FENCES

11-Unit Grid
Color Illustration: page 16

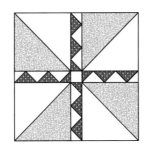
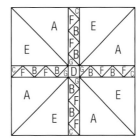
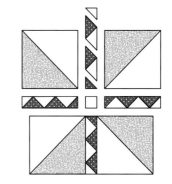

			FINISHED BLOCK SIZE				
			Single dimensions in the cutting chart indicate the size of the cut square (3" = 3" x 3").				
FOR 1 BLOCK:			**6⅞"**	**8¼"**	**9⅝"**	**11"**	**12⅜"**	**15⅛"**
Light	A: 2 ◻ → ◺		4"	4⅝"	5¼"	5⅞"	6½"	7¾"
	B: 2 ⊠ → ⊠		2½"	2¾"	3"	3¼"	3½"	4"
	C: 2 ◻ → ◺		1½"	1⅝"	1¾"	1⅞"	2"	2¼"
	D: 1 ◻		1⅛"	1¼"	1⅜"	1½"	1⅝"	1⅞"
Medium	E: 2 ◻ → ◺		4"	4⅝"	5¼"	5⅞"	6½"	7¾"
Dark	F: 2 ⊠ → ⊠		2½"	2¾"	3"	3¼"	3½"	4"
	G: 2 ◻ → ◺		1½"	1⅝"	1¾"	1⅞"	2"	2¼"

Try this: Use a different medium in every block.

FIREFLIES

4-Unit Grid

Color Illustration: page 16

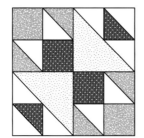
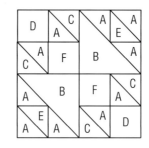
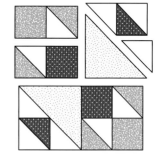

	FINISHED BLOCK SIZE Single dimensions in the cutting chart indicate the size of the cut square (3" = 3" x 3").					
FOR 1 BLOCK:	**4"**	**6"**	**8"**	**9"**	**10"**	**12"**
Light A: 5 ◻ → ◹	1⅞"	2⅜"	2⅞"	3⅛"	3⅜"	3⅞"
Light 2 B: 1 ◻ → ◹	2⅞"	3⅞"	4⅞"	5⅜"	5⅞"	6⅞"
Medium C: 2 ◻ → ◹	1⅞"	2⅜"	2⅞"	3⅛"	3⅜"	3⅞"
D: 2 ◻	1½"	2"	2½"	2¾"	3"	3½"
Dark E: 1 ◻ → ◹	1⅞"	2⅜"	2⅞"	3⅛"	3⅜"	3⅞"
F: 2 ◻	1½"	2"	2½"	2¾"	3"	3½"

Try this: Use a different combination of fabrics in every block.

FIVE CROSSES

8-Unit Grid

Color Illustration: page 16

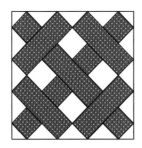

	FINISHED BLOCK SIZE Single dimensions in the cutting chart indicate the size of the cut square (3" = 3" x 3").					
FOR 1 BLOCK:	**6"**	**8"**	**9"**	**10"**	**12"**	**14"**
Light A: 3 ⊠ → ⊠	2¾"	3¼"	3½"	3¾"	4¼"	4¾"
B: 2 ◻ → ◹	1⅝"	1⅞"	2"	2⅛"	2⅜"	2⅝"
C: 4 ◇	T5	T7	T8	T9	T11	T12
Dark D: 5 ◇	T42	T52	T57	T60	T68	T71
E: 6 ◇	T5	T7	T8	T9	T11	T12

Try this: Reverse the lights and darks in every other block.

Five Diamonds

6-Unit Grid
Color Illustration: page 16

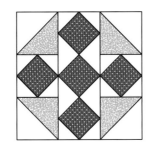 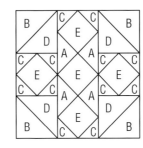 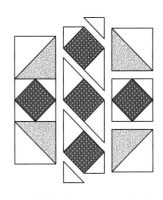

FOR 1 BLOCK:	FINISHED BLOCK SIZE *Single dimensions in the cutting chart indicate the size of the cut square (3" = 3" x 3").*					
	4½"	**6"**	**7½"**	**9"**	**10½"**	**12"**
Light A: 1 ⊠ → ⊠	2¾"	3¼"	3¾"	4¼"	4¾"	5¼"
B: 2 ◻ → ◻	2⅜"	2⅞"	3⅜"	3⅞"	4⅜"	4⅞"
C: 6 ◻ → ◻	1⅝"	1⅞"	2⅛"	2⅜"	2⅝"	2⅞"
Medium D: 2 ◻ → ◻	2⅜"	2⅞"	3⅜"	3⅞"	4⅜"	4⅞"
Dark E: 5 ◇	T5	T7	T9	T11	T12	T14

Try this: Use one light for A and C and a different light for B.

Five Spot

6-Unit Grid
Color Illustration: page 16

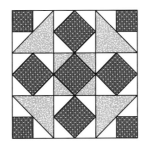 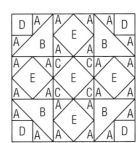 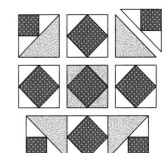

FOR 1 BLOCK:	FINISHED BLOCK SIZE *Single dimensions in the cutting chart indicate the size of the cut square (3" = 3" x 3").*					
	4½"	**6"**	**7½"**	**9"**	**10½"**	**12"**
Light A: 12 ◻ → ◻	1⅝"	1⅞"	2⅛"	2⅜"	2⅝"	2⅞"
Medium B: 2 ◻ → ◻	2⅜"	2⅞"	3⅜"	3⅞"	4⅜"	4⅞"
C: 2 ◻ → ◻	1⅝"	1⅞"	2⅛"	2⅜"	2⅝"	2⅞"
Dark D: 4 ◻	1¼"	1½"	1¾"	2"	2¼"	2½"
E: 5 ◇	T5	T7	T9	T11	T12	T14

Try this: Use one dark for D and a different dark for E.

FLOCK OF BIRDS

6-Unit Grid

Color Illustration: page 16

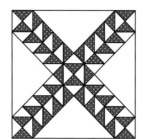 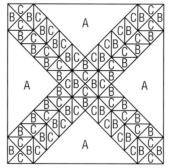 

FOR 1 BLOCK:	**FINISHED BLOCK SIZE** Single dimensions in the cutting chart indicate the size of the cut square (3" = 3" x 3").					
	4½"	**6"**	**7½"**	**9"**	**10½"**	**12"**
Light A: 1 ⊠ → ⊠	4¼"	5¼"	6¼"	7¼"	8¼"	9¼"
B: 10 ⊠ → ⊠	2"	2¼"	2½"	2¾"	3"	3¼"
Dark C: 10 ⊠ → ⊠	2"	2¼"	2½"	2¾"	3"	3¼"

Try this: Use many different darks for C.

FLOCK OF GEESE

4-Unit Grid

Color Illustration: page 16

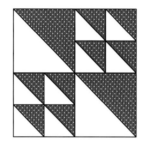 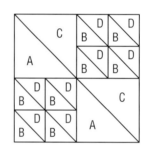 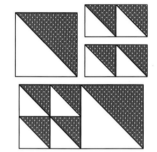

FOR 1 BLOCK:	**FINISHED BLOCK SIZE** Single dimensions in the cutting chart indicate the size of the cut square (3" = 3" x 3").					
	4"	**6"**	**8"**	**9"**	**10"**	**12"**
Light A: 1 ◻ → ◻	2⅞"	3⅞"	4⅞"	5⅜"	5⅞"	6⅞"
B: 4 ◻ → ◻	1⅞"	2⅜"	2⅞"	3⅛"	3⅜"	3⅞"
Dark C: 1 ◻ → ◻	2⅞"	3⅞"	4⅞"	5⅜"	5⅞"	6⅞"
D: 4 ◻ → ◻	1⅞"	2⅜"	2⅞"	3⅛"	3⅜"	3⅞"

Try this: Use several different darks for D.

Light | Light 2 | Medium | Medium 2 | Dark

FLOWER BASKET

4-Unit Grid
Color Illustration: page 16

 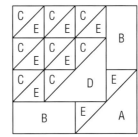 

	FINISHED BLOCK SIZE *Single dimensions in the cutting chart indicate the size of the cut square (3" = 3" x 3").*					
FOR 2 BLOCKS:	**4"**	**6"**	**8"**	**9"**	**10"**	**12"**
Light A: 1 ▢→◩	2⅞"	3⅞"	4⅞"	5⅜"	5⅞"	6⅞"
B: 4 ▭	1½" x 2½"	2" x 3½"	2½" x 4½"	2¾" x 5"	3" x 5½"	3½" x 6½"
C: 8 ▢→◩	1⅞"	2⅜"	2⅞"	3⅛"	3⅜"	3⅞"
Dark D: 1 ▢→◩	2⅞"	3⅞"	4⅞"	5⅜"	5⅞"	6⅞"
E: 8 ▢→◩	1⅞"	2⅜"	2⅞"	3⅛"	3⅜"	3⅞"

Try this: Use a medium instead of a dark for D and E.

FLOWER POT

5-Unit Grid
Color Illustration: page 16

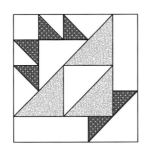 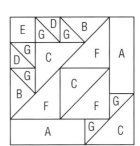 

	FINISHED BLOCK SIZE *Single dimensions in the cutting chart indicate the size of the cut square (3" = 3" x 3").*					
FOR 2 BLOCKS:	**5"**	**6¼"**	**7½"**	**8¾"**	**10"**	**12½"**
Light A: 4 ▭	1½" x 3½"	1¾" x 4¼"	2" x 5"	2¼" x 5¾"	2½" x 6½"	3" x 8"
B: 1 ⊠→⊠	3¼"	3¾"	4¼"	4¾"	5¼"	6¼"
C: 3 ▢→◩	2⅞"	3⅜"	3⅞"	4⅜"	4⅞"	5⅞"
D: 2 ▢→◩	1⅞"	2⅛"	2⅜"	2⅝"	2⅞"	3⅜"
E: 2 ▢	1½"	1¾"	2"	2¼"	2½"	3"
Medium F: 3 ▢→◩	2⅞"	3⅜"	3⅞"	4⅜"	4⅞"	5⅞"
Dark G: 6 ▢→◩	1⅞"	2⅛"	2⅜"	2⅝"	2⅞"	3⅜"

Try this: Use a different light for one of the C squares.

FLOWER POT II

4-Unit Grid

Color Illustration: page 16

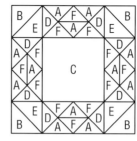

| | | | FINISHED BLOCK SIZE | | | | |
| | | | *Single dimensions in the cutting chart indicate the size of the cut square (3" = 3" x 3").* | | | | |
FOR 1 BLOCK:		**4"**	**6"**	**8"**	**9"**	**10"**	**12"**
Light	A: 3 ⊠→⊠	2¼"	2¾"	3¼"	3½"	3¾"	4¼"
	B: 2 ◻→◺	1⅞"	2⅜"	2⅞"	3⅛"	3⅜"	3⅞"
Light 2	C: 1 ◻	2½"	3½"	4½"	5"	5½"	6½"
	D: 2 ⊠→⊠	2¼"	2¾"	3¼"	3½"	3¾"	4¼"
Medium	E: 2 ◻→◺	1⅞"	2⅜"	2⅞"	3⅛"	3⅜"	3⅞"
Dark	F: 3 ⊠→⊠	2¼"	2¾"	3¼"	3½"	3¾"	4¼"

Try this: Use a different dark in every block.

FLYING BIRDS

3-Unit Grid

Color Illustration: page 16

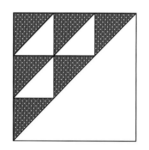
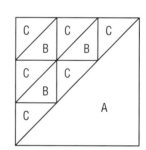

| | | | FINISHED BLOCK SIZE | | | | |
| | | | *Single dimensions in the cutting chart indicate the size of the cut square (3" = 3" x 3").* | | | | |
FOR 2 BLOCKS:		**4½"**	**6"**	**7½"**	**9"**	**10½"**	**12"**
Light	A: 1 ◻→◺	5⅜"	6⅞"	8⅜"	9⅞"	11⅜"	12⅞"
	B: 3 ◻→◺	2⅜"	2⅞"	3⅜"	3⅞"	4⅜"	4⅞"
Dark	C: 6 ◻→◺	2⅜"	2⅞"	3⅜"	3⅞"	4⅜"	4⅞"

Try this: Use several different darks for C.

FLYING CLOUD

4-Unit Grid
Color Illustration: page 16

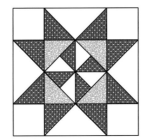 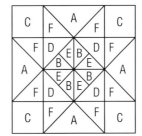 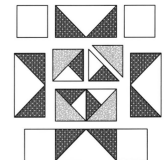

FOR 1 BLOCK:		**FINISHED BLOCK SIZE** *Single dimensions in the cutting chart indicate the size of the cut square (3" = 3" x 3").*					
		4"	**6"**	**8"**	**9"**	**10"**	**12"**
Light	A: 1 ⊠ → ⊠	3¼"	4¼"	5¼"	5¾"	6¼"	7¼"
	B: 1 ⊠ → ⊠	2¼"	2¾"	3¼"	3½"	3¾"	4¼"
	C: 4 ☐	1½"	2"	2½"	2¾"	3"	3½"
Medium	D: 2 ◻ → ◺	1⅞"	2⅜"	2⅞"	3⅛"	3⅜"	3⅞"
Dark	E: 1 ⊠ → ⊠	2¼"	2¾"	3¼"	3½"	3¾"	4¼"
	F: 4 ◻ → ◺	1⅞"	2⅜"	2⅞"	3⅛"	3⅜"	3⅞"

Try this: Reverse the lights and mediums in every other block.

FLYING GEESE

5-Unit Grid
Color Illustration: page 16

 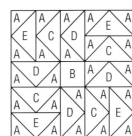 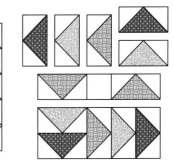

FOR 1 BLOCK:		**FINISHED BLOCK SIZE** *Single dimensions in the cutting chart indicate the size of the cut square (3" = 3" x 3").*					
		5"	**6¼"**	**7½"**	**8¾"**	**10"**	**12½"**
Light	A: 12 ◻ → ◺	1⅞"	2⅛"	2⅜"	2⅝"	2⅞"	3⅜"
	B: 1 ☐	1½"	1¾"	2"	2¼"	2½"	3"
Medium	C: 1 ⊠ → ⊠	3¼"	3¾"	4¼"	4¾"	5¼"	6¼"
Medium 2	D: 1 ⊠ → ⊠	3¼"	3¾"	4¼"	4¾"	5¼"	6¼"
Dark	E: 1 ⊠ → ⊠	3¼"	3¾"	4¼"	4¾"	5¼"	6¼"

Try this: Change the position of the dark triangles in every other block.

☐ Light   ▢ Light 2   ▨ Medium   ▦ Medium 2   ■ Dark

FLYING GEESE II

4-Unit Grid
Color Illustration: page 16

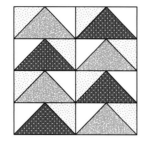 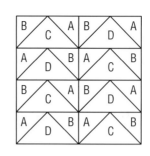 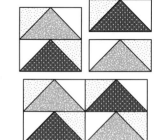

			FINISHED BLOCK SIZE					
			Single dimensions in the cutting chart indicate the size of the cut square (3" = 3" x 3").					
FOR 1 BLOCK:			4"	6"	8"	9"	10"	12"
Light	A: 4 ▱ → ◺		1⅞"	2⅜"	2⅞"	3⅛"	3⅜"	3⅞"
Light 2	B: 4 ▱ → ◺		1⅞"	2⅜"	2⅞"	3⅛"	3⅜"	3⅞"
Medium	C: 1 ⊠ → ◹		3¼"	4¼"	5¼"	5¾"	6¼"	7¼"
Dark	D: 1 ⊠ → ◹		3¼"	4¼"	5¼"	5¾"	6¼"	7¼"
Try this:	Use a scrappy assortment of lights for A and B.							

FLYING GOOSE

2-Unit Grid
Color Illustration: page 16

 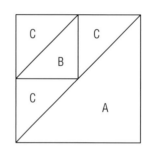 

			FINISHED BLOCK SIZE					
			Single dimensions in the cutting chart indicate the size of the cut square (3" = 3" x 3").					
FOR 2 BLOCKS:			4"	6"	8"	9"	10"	12"
Light	A: 1 ▱ → ◺		4⅞"	6⅞"	8⅞"	9⅞"	10⅞"	12⅞"
	B: 1 ▱ → ◺		2⅞"	3⅞"	4⅞"	5⅜"	5⅞"	6⅞"
Dark	C: 3 ▱ → ◺		2⅞"	3⅞"	4⅞"	5⅜"	5⅞"	6⅞"
Try this:	Use several different darks for C.							

FLYING SHUTTLES

6-Unit Grid
Color Illustration: page 16

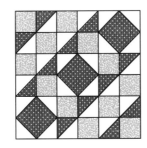 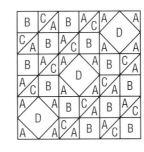 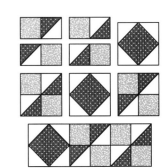

FOR 1 BLOCK:		FINISHED BLOCK SIZE *Single dimensions in the cutting chart indicate the size of the cut square (3" = 3" x 3").*					
		4½"	**6"**	**7½"**	**9"**	**10½"**	**12"**
Light	A: 12 ☐→◩	1⅝"	1⅞"	2⅛"	2⅜"	2⅝"	2⅞"
Medium	B: 12 ☐	1¼"	1½"	1¾"	2"	2¼"	2½"
Dark	C: 6 ☐→◩	1⅝"	1⅞"	2⅛"	2⅜"	2⅝"	2⅞"
	D: 3 ◇	T5	T7	T9	T11	T12	T14
Try this:	Use many different lights and mediums.						

FOGGY MOUNTAIN BREAKDOWN

8-Unit Grid
Color Illustration: page 16

 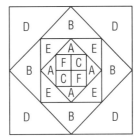 

FOR 1 BLOCK:		FINISHED BLOCK SIZE *Single dimensions in the cutting chart indicate the size of the cut square (3" = 3" x 3").*					
		6"	**8"**	**9"**	**10"**	**12"**	**14"**
Light	A: 1 ⊠→⧯	2¾"	3¼"	3½"	3¾"	4¼"	4¾"
Light 2	B: 1 ⊠→⧯	4¼"	5¼"	5¾"	6¼"	7¼"	8¼"
Medium	C: 2 ☐	1¼"	1½"	1⅝"	1¾"	2"	2¼"
Dark	D: 2 ☐→◩	3⅞"	4⅞"	5⅜"	5⅞"	6⅞"	7⅞"
	E: 2 ☐→◩	2⅜"	2⅞"	3⅛"	3⅜"	3⅞"	4⅜"
	F: 2 ☐	1¼"	1½"	1⅝"	1¾"	2"	2¼"
Try this:	Use a different combination of lights in every block.						

Light · Light 2 · Medium · Medium 2 · Dark

FOOT STOOL

5-Unit Grid

Color Illustration: page 16

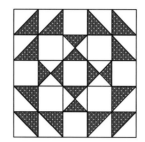
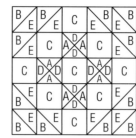
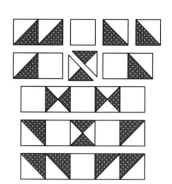

		FINISHED BLOCK SIZE Single dimensions in the cutting chart indicate the size of the cut square (3" = 3" x 3").					
FOR 1 BLOCK:		**5"**	**6¼"**	**7½"**	**8¾"**	**10"**	**12½"**
Light	A: 2 ⊠ → ⊠	2¼"	2½"	2¾"	3"	3¼"	3¾"
	B: 6 ◺ → ◺	1⅞"	2⅛"	2⅜"	2⅝"	2⅞"	3⅜"
	C: 9 ☐	1½"	1¾"	2"	2¼"	2½"	3"
Dark	D: 2 ⊠ → ⊠	2¼"	2½"	2¾"	3"	3¼"	3¾"
	E: 6 ◺ → ◺	1⅞"	2⅛"	2⅜"	2⅝"	2⅞"	3⅜"
Try this:	Use a medium instead of a dark for D.						

FOREST PATH

8-Unit Grid

Color Illustration: page 16

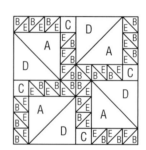

		FINISHED BLOCK SIZE Single dimensions in the cutting chart indicate the size of the cut square (3" = 3" x 3").					
FOR 1 BLOCK:		**6"**	**8"**	**9"**	**10"**	**12"**	**14"**
Light	A: 2 ◺ → ◺	3⅛"	3⅞"	4¼"	4⅝"	5⅜"	6⅛"
	B: 12 ◺ → ◺	1⅝"	1⅞"	2"	2⅛"	2⅜"	2⅝"
	C: 4 ☐	1¼"	1½"	1⅝"	1¾"	2"	2¼"
Dark	D: 2 ◺ → ◺	3⅛"	3⅞"	4¼"	4⅝"	5⅜"	6⅛"
	E: 12 ◺ → ◺	1⅝"	1⅞"	2"	2⅛"	2⅜"	2⅝"
Try this:	Use a large-scale print for D.						

FOREST PATHS

6-Unit Grid
Color Illustration: page 16

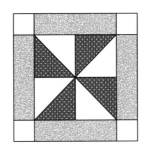 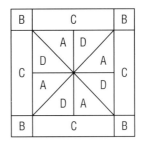 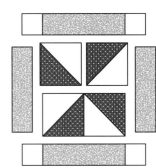

		FINISHED BLOCK SIZE *Single dimensions in the cutting chart indicate the size of the cut square (3" = 3" x 3").*					
FOR 1 BLOCK:		**4½"**	**6"**	**7½"**	**9"**	**10½"**	**12"**
Light	A: 2 ◻→◺	2⅜"	2⅞"	3⅜"	3⅞"	4⅜"	4⅞"
	B: 4 ◻	1¼"	1½"	1¾"	2"	2¼"	2½"
Medium	C: 4 ▭	1¼" x 3½"	1½" x 4½"	1¾" x 5½"	2" x 6½"	2¼" x 7½"	2½" x 8½"
Dark	D: 2 ◻→◺	2⅜"	2⅞"	3⅜"	3⅞"	4⅜"	4⅞"
Try this:	Reverse the lights and mediums in every other block.						

FOUR CORNERS

6-Unit Grid
Color Illustration: page 16

 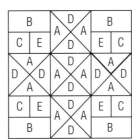 

		FINISHED BLOCK SIZE *Single dimensions in the cutting chart indicate the size of the cut square (3" = 3" x 3").*					
FOR 2 BLOCKS:		**4½"**	**6"**	**7½"**	**9"**	**10½"**	**12"**
Light	A: 5 ⊠→⧅	2¾"	3¼"	3¾"	4¼"	4¾"	5¼"
	B: 8 ▭	1¼" x 2"	1½" x 2½"	1¾" x 3"	2" x 3½"	2¼" x 4"	2½" x 4½"
	C: 8 ◻	1¼"	1½"	1¾"	2"	2¼"	2½"
Dark	D: 5 ⊠→⧅	2¾"	3¼"	3¾"	4¼"	4¾"	5¼"
	E: 8 ◻	1¼"	1½"	1¾"	2"	2¼"	2½"
Try this:	Use a medium instead of a light for B and C.						

FOUR KNAVES

4-Unit Grid
Color Illustration: page 17

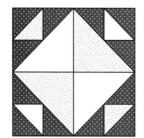
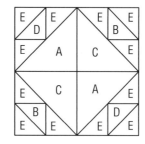

		FINISHED BLOCK SIZE *Single dimensions in the cutting chart indicate the size of the cut square (3" = 3" x 3").*					
FOR 1 BLOCK:		**4"**	**6"**	**8"**	**9"**	**10"**	**12"**
Light	A: 1 ☐ ➔ ◩	2⅞"	3⅞"	4⅞"	5⅜"	5⅞"	6⅞"
	B: 1 ☐ ➔ ◩	1⅞"	2⅜"	2⅞"	3⅛"	3⅜"	3⅞"
Light 2	C: 1 ☐ ➔ ◩	2⅞"	3⅞"	4⅞"	5⅜"	5⅞"	6⅞"
	D: 1 ☐ ➔ ◩	1⅞"	2⅜"	2⅞"	3⅛"	3⅜"	3⅞"
Dark	E: 6 ☐ ➔ ◩	1⅞"	2⅜"	2⅞"	3⅛"	3⅜"	3⅞"

Try this: Use a medium instead of a light for C and D.

FOUR PATCH

4-Unit Grid
Color Illustration: page 17

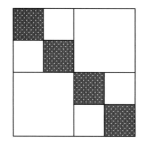
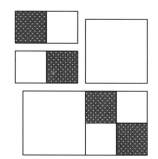

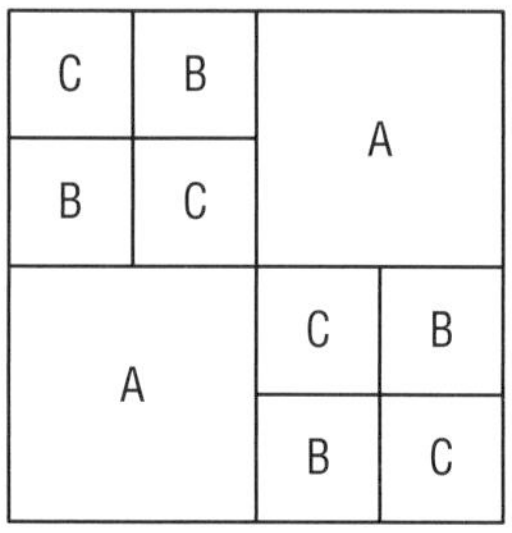

		FINISHED BLOCK SIZE *Single dimensions in the cutting chart indicate the size of the cut square (3" = 3" x 3").*					
FOR 1 BLOCK:		**4"**	**6"**	**8"**	**9"**	**10"**	**12"**
Light	A: 2 ☐	2½"	3½"	4½"	5"	5½"	6½"
	B: 4 ☐	1½"	2"	2½"	2¾"	3"	3½"
Dark	C: 4 ☐	1½"	2"	2½"	2¾"	3"	3 ½"

Try this: Use a medium instead of a light for A.

☐ *Light* ▤ *Light 2* ▥ *Medium* ▦ *Medium 2* ▧ *Dark*

FOUR SQUARES

6-Unit Grid

Color Illustration: page 17

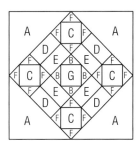

		FINISHED BLOCK SIZE Single dimensions in the cutting chart indicate the size of the cut square (3" = 3" x 3").					
FOR 1 BLOCK:		**4½"**	**6"**	**7½"**	**9"**	**10½"**	**12"**
Light	A: 2 ☐ → ◩	3⅛"	3⅞"	4⅝"	5⅜"	6⅛"	6⅞"
	B: 1 ⊠ → ⊠	2"	2¼"	2½"	2¾"	3"	3¼"
	C: 4 ☐	1¼"	1½"	1¾"	2"	2¼"	2½"
	D: 4 ◇	T28	T32	T36	T41	T46	T51
Medium	E: 4 ◇	T28	T32	T36	T41	T46	T51
Dark	F: 4 ⊠ → ⊠	2"	2¼"	2½"	2¾"	3"	3¼"
	G: 1 ☐	1¼"	1½"	1¾"	2"	2¼"	2½"

Try this: Use a medium instead of a light for A.

FOUR-FOUR TIME

4-Unit Grid

Color Illustration: page 17

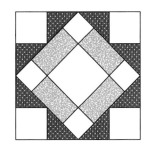
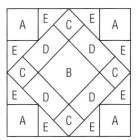
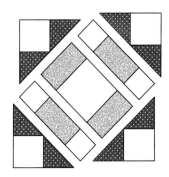

		FINISHED BLOCK SIZE Single dimensions in the cutting chart indicate the size of the cut square (3" = 3" x 3").					
FOR 1 BLOCK:		**4"**	**6"**	**8"**	**9"**	**10"**	**12"**
Light	A: 4 ☐	1½"	2"	2½"	2¾"	3"	3½"
	B: 1 ◇	T7	T11	T14	T15	T16	T19
	C: 4 ◇	T2	T5	T7	T8	T9	T11
Medium	D: 4 ◇	T32	T41	T51	T56	T59	T67
Dark	E: 4 ☐ → ◩	1⅞"	2⅜"	2⅞"	3⅛"	3⅜"	3⅞"

Try this: Use one light for A and B and a different light for C.

FOX AND GEESE

8-Unit Grid

Color Illustration: page 17

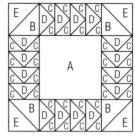

FOR 1 BLOCK:		FINISHED BLOCK SIZE *Single dimensions in the cutting chart indicate the size of the cut square (3" = 3" x 3").*					
		6"	**8"**	**9"**	**10"**	**12"**	**14"**
Light	A: 1 □	3½"	4½"	5"	5½"	6½"	7½"
	B: 2 ◹ → ◺	2⅜"	2⅞"	3⅛"	3⅜"	3⅞"	4⅜"
	C: 16 ◹ → ◺	1⅝"	1⅞"	2"	2⅛"	2⅜"	2⅝"
Dark	D: 4 ⊠ → ⧄	2¾"	3¼"	3½"	3¾"	4¼"	4¾"
	E: 2 ◹ → ◺	2⅜"	2⅞"	3⅛"	3⅜"	3⅞"	4⅜"

Try this: Use several different darks for D.

FOX PAWS

8-Unit Grid

Color Illustration: page 17

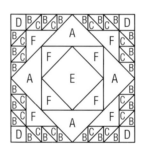

FOR 1 BLOCK:		FINISHED BLOCK SIZE *Single dimensions in the cutting chart indicate the size of the cut square (3" = 3" x 3").*					
		6"	**8"**	**9"**	**10"**	**12"**	**14 "**
Light	A: 1 ⊠ → ⧄	4¼"	5¼"	5¾"	6¼"	7¼"	8¼"
	B: 12 ◹ → ◺	1⅝"	1⅞"	2"	2⅛"	2⅜"	2⅝"
Medium	C: 8 ◹ → ◺	1⅝"	1⅞"	2"	2⅛"	2⅜"	2⅝"
	D: 4 □	1¼"	1½"	1⅝"	1¾"	2"	2¼"
	E: 1 ◇	T11	T14	T15	T16	T19	T21
Dark	F: 4 ◹ → ◺	2⅜"	2⅞"	3⅛"	3⅜"	3⅞"	4⅜"

Try this: Use a medium instead of a light for A.

Note: This block is listed as "Unnamed" in Barbara Brackman's *Encyclopedia of Pieced Quilt Patterns*; the source given is Robert Bishop and Elizabeth Safanda's book *A Gallery of Amish Quilts: Design Diversity from a Plain People*, published in 1976. For this book, I've chosen to call the block "Fox Paws."

FOXY GRANDPA

6-Unit Grid

Color Illustration: page 17

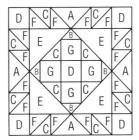

| FOR 1 BLOCK: | | | FINISHED BLOCK SIZE | | | | | |
| | | | Single dimensions in the cutting chart indicate the size of the cut square (3" = 3" x 3"). | | | | | |
			4½"	6"	7½"	9"	10½"	12"
Light	A: 1 ⊠ → ⊠		2¾"	3¼"	3¾"	4¼"	4¾"	5¼"
	B: 1 ⊠ → ⊠		2"	2¼"	2½"	2¾"	3"	3¼"
	C: 6 ◺ → ◺		1⅝"	1⅞"	2⅛"	2⅜"	2⅝"	2⅞"
	D: 5 ☐		1¼"	1½"	1¾"	2"	2¼"	2½"
Dark	E: 2 ◺ → ◺		2⅜"	2⅞"	3⅜"	3⅞"	4⅜"	4⅞"
	F: 8 ◺ → ◺		1⅝"	1⅞"	2⅛"	2⅜"	2⅝"	2⅞"
	G: 4 ☐		1¼"	1½"	1¾"	2"	2¼"	2½"

Try this: Use a medium instead of a dark for G.

FRAMED SQUARES

6-Unit Grid

Color Illustration: page 17

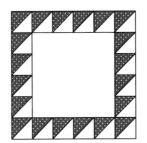
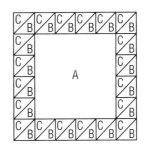
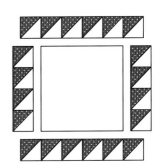

| FOR 1 BLOCK: | | | FINISHED BLOCK SIZE | | | | | |
| | | | Single dimensions in the cutting chart indicate the size of the cut square (3" = 3" x 3"). | | | | | |
			4½"	6"	7½"	9"	10½"	12"
Light	A: 1 ☐		3½"	4½"	5½"	6½"	7½"	8½"
	B: 10 ◺ → ◺		1⅝"	1⅞"	2⅛"	2⅜"	2⅝"	2⅞"
Dark	C: 10 ◺ → ◺		1⅝"	1⅞"	2⅛"	2⅜"	2⅝"	2⅞"

Try this: Use a large-scale print or an autographed square for A.

Light   Light 2   Medium   Medium 2   Dark

Free Trade

4-Unit Grid
Color Illustration: page 17

 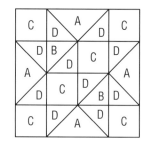 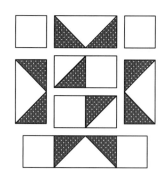

FOR 1 BLOCK:		FINISHED BLOCK SIZE *Single dimensions in the cutting chart indicate the size of the cut square (3" = 3" x 3").*					
		4"	**6"**	**8"**	**9"**	**10"**	**12"**
Light	A: 1 ⊠ → ⊠	3¼"	4¼"	5¼"	5¾"	6¼"	7¼"
	B: 1 ◩ → ◪	1⅞"	2⅜"	2⅞"	3⅛"	3⅜"	3⅞"
	C: 6 ☐	1½"	2"	2½"	2¾"	3"	3½"
Dark	D: 5 ◩ → ◪	1⅞"	2⅜"	2⅞"	3⅛"	3⅜"	3⅞"

Try this: Reverse the lights and darks.

Friendship Chain

8-Unit Grid
Color Illustration: page 17

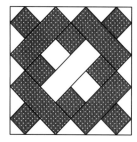  

FOR 1 BLOCK:		FINISHED BLOCK SIZE *Single dimensions in the cutting chart indicate the size of the cut square (3" = 3" x 3").*					
		6"	**8"**	**9"**	**10"**	**12"**	**14"**
Light	A: 3 ⊠ → ⊠	2¾"	3¼"	3½"	3¾"	4¼"	4¾"
	B: 2 ◩ → ◪	1⅝"	1⅞"	2"	2⅛"	2⅜"	2⅝"
	C: 1 ◇	T42	T52	T57	T60	T68	T71
	D: 2 ◇	T5	T7	T8	T9	T11	T12
Dark	E: 4 ◇	T42	T52	T57	T60	T68	T71
	F: 8 ◇	T5	T7	T8	T9	T11	T12

Try this: Use a light and a medium instead of a light and a dark for every other block.

FRIENDSHIP QUILT

9-Unit Grid

Color Illustration: page 17

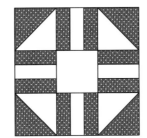 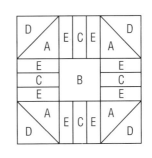 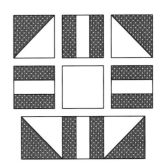

		FINISHED BLOCK SIZE Single dimensions in the cutting chart indicate the size of the cut square (3" = 3" x 3").					
FOR 1 BLOCK:		**6¾"**	**9"**	**10⅛"**	**11¼"**	**12⅜"**	**13½"**
Light	A: 2 ◻ → ◻	3⅛"	3⅞"	4¼"	4⅝"	5"	5⅜"
	B: 1 ◻	2¾"	3½"	3⅞"	4¼"	4⅝"	5"
	C: 4 ▭	1¼" x 2¾"	1½" x 3½"	1⅝" x 3⅞"	1¾" x 4¼"	1⅞" x 4⅝"	2" x 5"
Dark	D: 2 ◻ → ◻	3⅛"	3⅞"	4¼"	4⅝"	5"	5⅜"
	E: 8 ▭	1¼" x 2¾"	1½" x 3½"	1⅝" x 3⅞"	1¾" x 4¼"	1⅞" x 4⅝"	2" x 5"

Try this: Use autographed rectangles for C.

FRIENDSHIP QUILT II

10-Unit Grid

Color Illustration: page 17

 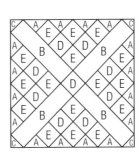 

		FINISHED BLOCK SIZE Single dimensions in the cutting chart indicate the size of the cut square (3" = 3" x 3").					
FOR 1 BLOCK:		**6¼"**	**7½"**	**8¾"**	**10"**	**12½"**	**13¾"**
Light	A: 4 ⊠ → ⊠	2½"	2¾"	3"	3¼"	3¾"	4"
	B: 4 ◇	T38	T43	T48	T53	T61	T65
Medium	C: 2 ◻ → ◻	1½"	1⅝"	1¾"	1⅞"	2⅛"	2¼"
	D: 9 ◇	T4	T5	T6	T7	T9	T10
Dark	E: 16 ◇	T4	T5	T6	T7	T9	T10

Try this: Use many different fabrics for D and E.

Light | Light 2 | Medium | Medium 2 | Dark

FRUIT BASKET

5-Unit Grid
Color Illustration: page 17

 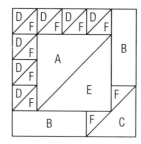 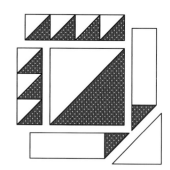

		FINISHED BLOCK SIZE *Single dimensions in the cutting chart indicate the size of the cut square (3" = 3" x 3").*					
FOR 2 BLOCKS:		**5"**	**6¼"**	**7½"**	**8¾"**	**10"**	**12½"**
Light	A: 1 ◻→◺	3⅞"	4⅝"	5⅜"	6⅛"	6⅞"	8⅜"
	B: 4 ▭	1½" x 3½"	1¾" x 4¼"	2" x 5"	2¼" x 5¾"	2½" x 6½"	3" x 8"
	C: 1 ◻→◺	2⅞"	3⅜"	3⅞"	4⅜"	4⅞"	5⅞"
	D: 7 ◻→◺	1⅞"	2⅛"	2⅜"	2⅝"	2⅞"	3⅜"
Dark	E: 1 ◻→◺	3⅞"	4⅝"	5⅜"	6⅛"	6⅞"	8⅜"
	F: 9 ◻→◺	1⅞"	2⅛"	2⅜"	2⅝"	2⅞"	3⅜"

Try this: Use several different mediums instead of a dark for F.

GAGGLE OF GEESE

6-Unit Grid
Color Illustration: page 17

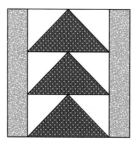 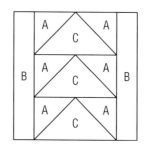 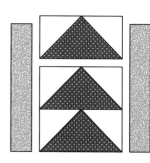

		FINISHED BLOCK SIZE *Single dimensions in the cutting chart indicate the size of the cut square (3" = 3" x 3").*					
FOR 4 BLOCKS:		**4½"**	**6"**	**7½"**	**9"**	**10½"**	**12"**
Light	A: 12 ◻→◺	2⅜"	2⅞"	3⅜"	3⅞"	4⅜"	4⅞"
Medium	B: 8 ▭	1¼" x 5"	1½" x 6½"	1¾" x 8"	2" x 9½"	2¼" x 11"	2½" x 12½"
Dark	C: 3 ⊠→⧇	4¼"	5¼"	6¼"	7¼"	8¼"	9¼"

Try this: Use several different darks for C.

GARDEN OF EDEN

5-Unit Grid
Color Illustration: page 17

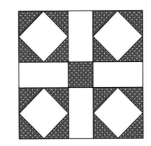 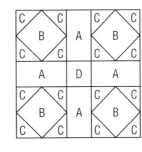 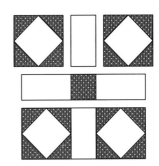

FOR 1 BLOCK:		FINISHED BLOCK SIZE					
		Single dimensions in the cutting chart indicate the size of the cut square (3" = 3" x 3").					
		5"	6¼"	7½"	8¾"	10"	12½"
Light	A: 4 ▭	1½" x 2½"	1¾" x 3"	2" x 3½"	2¼" x 4"	2½" x 4½"	3" x 5½"
	B: 4 ◇	T7	T9	T11	T12	T14	T16
Dark	C: 8 ◻→◰	1⅞"	2⅛"	2⅜"	2⅝"	2⅞"	3⅜"
	D: 1 ▢	1½"	1¾"	2"	2¼"	2½"	3"

Try this: Reverse the lights and darks in every other block.

GEM BLOCK

6-Unit Grid
Color Illustration: page 17

 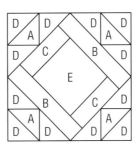 

FOR 1 BLOCK:		FINISHED BLOCK SIZE					
		Single dimensions in the cutting chart indicate the size of the cut square (3" = 3" x 3").					
		4½"	6"	7½"	9"	10½"	12"
Light	A: 2 ◻→◰	2"	2⅜"	2¾"	3⅛"	3½"	3⅞"
	B: 2 ◇	T31	T35	T40	T45	T50	T55
	C: 2 ◇	T30	T34	T38	T43	T48	T53
Dark	D: 6 ◻→◰	2"	2⅜"	2¾"	3⅛"	3½"	3⅞"
	E: 1 ◇	T11	T14	T16	T19	T21	T23

Try this: Use a large-scale print for E.

□ Light   ▦ Light 2   ▦ Medium   ▦ Medium 2   ▦ Dark

GENTLEMAN'S FANCY

6-Unit Grid

Color Illustration: page 17

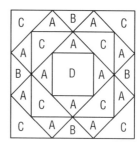

FOR 1 BLOCK:	**FINISHED BLOCK SIZE** Single dimensions in the cutting chart indicate the size of the cut square (3" = 3" x 3").					
	4½"	**6"**	**7½"**	**9"**	**10½"**	**12"**
Light A: 3 ⊠ → ⊠	2¾"	3¼"	3¾"	4¼"	4¾"	5¼"
Dark B: 1 ⊠ → ⊠	2¾"	3¼"	3¾"	4¼"	4¾"	5¼"
C: 4 ◱ → ◲	2⅜"	2⅞"	3⅜"	3⅞"	4⅜"	4⅞"
D: 1 □	2"	2½"	3"	3½"	4"	4½"

Try this: Use a medium for B and D and two different darks for C.

GEORGETOWN CIRCLE

4-Unit Grid

Color Illustration: page 17

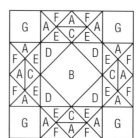

FOR 1 BLOCK:	**FINISHED BLOCK SIZE** Single dimensions in the cutting chart indicate the size of the cut square (3" = 3" x 3").					
	4"	**6"**	**8"**	**9"**	**10"**	**12"**
Light A: 3 ⊠ → ⊠	2¼"	2¾"	3¼"	3½"	3¾"	4¼"
B: 1 ◇	T7	T11	T14	T15	T16	T19
Medium C: 1 ⊠ → ⊠	2¼"	2¾"	3¼"	3½"	3¾"	4¼"
D: 2 ◱ → ◲	1⅞"	2⅜"	2⅞"	3⅛"	3⅜"	3⅞"
Medium 2 E: 2 ⊠ → ⊠	2¼"	2¾"	3¼"	3½"	3¾"	4¼"
Dark F: 2 ⊠ → ⊠	2¼"	2¾"	3¼"	3½"	3¾"	4¼"
G: 4 □	1½"	2"	2½"	2¾"	3"	3½"

Try this: Use one light for A and a different light for B.

GLORIFIED NINE PATCH

9-Unit Grid

Color Illustration: page 17

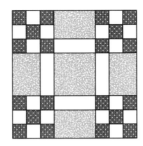

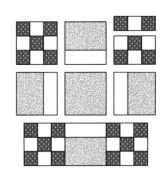

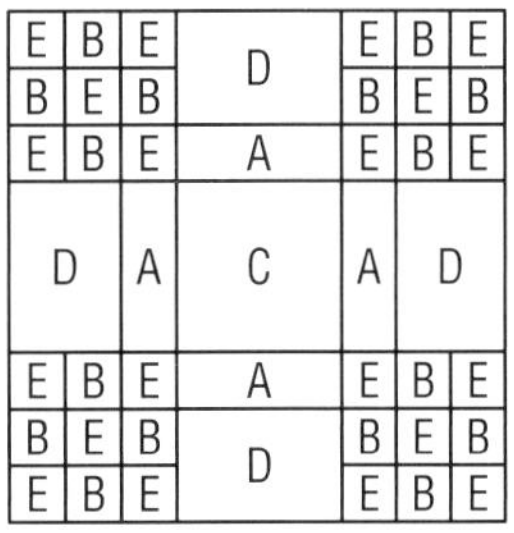

		FINISHED BLOCK SIZE					
		Single dimensions in the cutting chart indicate the size of the cut square (3" = 3" x 3").					
FOR 1 BLOCK:		**6¾"**	**9"**	**10⅛"**	**11¼"**	**12⅜"**	**13½"**
Light	A: 4 ▭	1¼" x 2¾"	1½" x 3½"	1⅝" x 3⅞"	1¾" x 4¼"	1⅞" x 4⅝"	2" x 5"
	B: 16 □	1¼"	1½"	1⅝"	1¾"	1⅞"	2"
Medium	C: 1 □	2¾"	3½"	3⅞"	4¼"	4⅝"	5"
	D: 4 ▭	2" x 2¾"	2½" x 3½"	2¾" x 3⅞"	3" x 4¼"	3¼" x 4⅝"	3½" x 5"
Dark	E: 20 □	1¼"	1½"	1⅝"	1¾"	1⅞"	2"

Try this: Reverse the lights and mediums.

GOOD FORTUNE

6-Unit Grid

Color Illustration: page 17

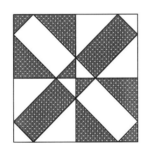

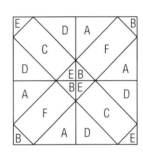

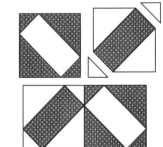

		FINISHED BLOCK SIZE					
		Single dimensions in the cutting chart indicate the size of the cut square (3" = 3" x 3").					
FOR 1 BLOCK:		**4½"**	**6"**	**7½"**	**9"**	**10½"**	**12"**
Light	A: 2 ◻→◺	2⅜"	2⅞"	3⅜"	3⅞"	4⅜"	4⅞"
	B: 2 ◻→◺	1⅝"	1⅞"	2⅛"	2⅜"	2⅝"	2⅞"
	C: 2 ◇	T41	T51	T59	T67	T70	T72
Dark	D: 2 ◻→◺	2⅜"	2⅞"	3⅜"	3⅞"	4⅜"	4⅞"
	E: 2 ◻→◺	1⅝"	1⅞"	2⅛"	2⅜"	2⅝"	2⅞"
	F: 2 ◇	T41	T51	T59	T67	T70	T72

Try this: Use a different combination of light and dark fabrics in each quadrant of the block.

126

GOOSE IN THE POND

5-Unit Grid

Color Illustration: page 17

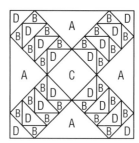

| FOR 1 BLOCK: | FINISHED BLOCK SIZE | | | | | |
| | Single dimensions in the cutting chart indicate the size of the cut square (3" = 3" x 3"). | | | | | |
	5"	6¼"	7½"	8¾"	10"	12½"
Light A: 1 ⊠ → ⊠	4¼"	5"	5¾"	6½"	7¼"	8¾"
B: 6 ⊠ → ⊠	2¼"	2½"	2¾"	3"	3¼"	3¾"
C: 1 ◇	T7	T9	T11	T12	T14	T16
Dark D: 8 ◻ → ◻	1⅞"	2⅛"	2⅜"	2⅝"	2⅞"	3⅜"

Try this: Use one light for A and a different light for B and C.

GOOSE TRACKS

5-Unit Grid

Color Illustration: page 17

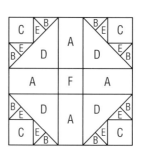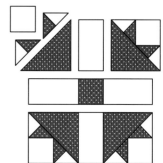

| FOR 1 BLOCK: | FINISHED BLOCK SIZE | | | | | |
| | Single dimensions in the cutting chart indicate the size of the cut square (3" = 3" x 3"). | | | | | |
	5"	6¼"	7½"	8¾"	10"	12½"
Light A: 4 ▭	1½" x 2½"	1¾" x 3"	2" x 3½"	2¼" x 4"	2½" x 4½"	3" x 5½"
B: 2 ⊠ → ⊠	2¼"	2½"	2¾"	3"	3¼"	3¾"
C: 4 ◻	1½"	1¾"	2"	2¼"	2½"	3"
Dark D: 2 ◻ → ◻	2⅞"	3⅜"	3⅞"	4⅜"	4⅞"	5⅞"
E: 2 ⊠ → ⊠	2¼"	2½"	2¾"	3"	3¼"	3¾"
F: 1 ◻	1½"	1¾"	2"	2¼"	2½"	3"

Try this: Use one dark for D and a different dark for E and F.

GRAND RIGHT AND LEFT

8-Unit Grid
Color Illustration: page 17

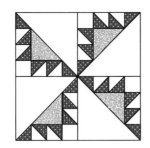
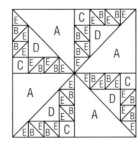

FOR 1 BLOCK:			FINISHED BLOCK SIZE *Single dimensions in the cutting chart indicate the size of the cut square (3" = 3" x 3").*					
			6"	**8"**	**9"**	**10"**	**12"**	**14"**
Light	A: 2 □→◩		3⅞"	4⅞"	5⅜"	5⅞"	6⅞"	7⅞"
	B: 8 □→◩		1⅝"	1⅞"	2"	2⅛"	2⅜"	2⅝"
	C: 4 □		1¼"	1½"	1⅝"	1¾"	2"	2¼"
Medium	D: 2 □→◩		2⅜"	2⅞"	3⅛"	3⅜"	3⅞"	4⅜"
Dark	E: 12 □→◩		1⅝"	1⅞"	2"	2⅛"	2⅜"	2⅝"

Try this: Use several different darks for E.

GRANDMA'S FAVORITE

5-Unit Grid
Color Illustration: page 17

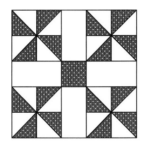
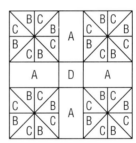

FOR 1 BLOCK:			FINISHED BLOCK SIZE *Single dimensions in the cutting chart indicate the size of the cut square (3" = 3" x 3").*					
			5"	**6¼"**	**7½"**	**8¾"**	**10"**	**12½"**
Light	A: 4 ▭		1½" x 2½"	1¾" x 3"	2" x 3½"	2¼" x 4"	2½" x 4½"	3" x 5½"
	B: 8 □→◩		1⅞"	2⅛"	2⅜"	2⅝"	2⅞"	3⅜"
Dark	C: 8 □→◩		1⅞"	2⅛"	2⅜"	2⅝"	2⅞"	3⅜"
	D: 1 □		1½"	1¾"	2"	2¼"	2½"	3"

Try this: Use a medium instead of a light for A.

□ Light   ▨ Light 2   ▨ Medium   ▥ Medium 2   ■ Dark

GRANDMOTHER'S CHOICE

5-Unit Grid
Color Illustration: page 17

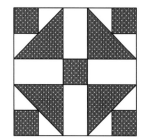 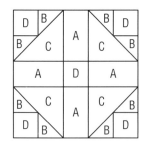 

FOR 1 BLOCK:		FINISHED BLOCK SIZE *Single dimensions in the cutting chart indicate the size of the cut square (3" = 3" x 3").*					
		5"	**6¼"**	**7½"**	**8¾"**	**10"**	**12½"**
Light	A: 4 ▭	1½" x 2½"	1¾" x 3"	2" x 3½"	2¼" x 4"	2½" x 4½"	3" x 5½"
	B: 4 ◰ → ◸	1⅞"	2⅛"	2⅜"	2⅝"	2⅞"	3⅜"
Dark	C: 2 ◰ → ◸	2⅞"	3⅜"	3⅞"	4⅜"	4⅞"	5⅞"
	D: 5 □	1½"	1¾"	2"	2¼"	2½"	3"

Try this: Reverse the lights and darks in every other block.

GRANDMOTHER'S CHOICE II

5-Unit Grid
Color Illustration: page 17

 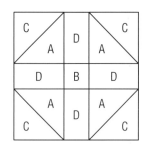 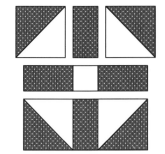

FOR 1 BLOCK:		FINISHED BLOCK SIZE *Single dimensions in the cutting chart indicate the size of the cut square (3" = 3" x 3").*					
		5"	**6¼"**	**7½"**	**8¾"**	**10"**	**12½"**
Light	A: 2 ◰ → ◸	2⅞"	3⅜"	3⅞"	4⅜"	4⅞"	5⅞"
	B: 1 □	1½"	1¾"	2"	2¼"	2½"	3"
Dark	C: 2 ◰ → ◸	2⅞"	3⅜"	3⅞"	4⅜"	4⅞"	5⅞"
	D: 4 ▭	1½" x 2½"	1¾" x 3"	2" x 3½"	2¼" x 4"	2½" x 4½"	3" x 5½"

Try this: Use a different combination of lights and darks in every block.

GRANDMOTHER'S CROSS

4-Unit Grid

Color Illustration: page 17

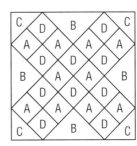

FOR 1 BLOCK:		FINISHED BLOCK SIZE					
		Single dimensions in the cutting chart indicate the size of the cut square (3" = 3" x 3").					
		4"	6"	8"	9"	10"	12"
Light	A: 10 ◇	T2	T5	T7	T8	T9	T11
Medium	B: 1 ⊠→⊠	3¼"	4¼"	5¼"	5¾"	6¼"	7¼"
Medium 2	C: 2 ◺→◺	1⅞"	2⅜"	2⅞"	3⅛"	3⅜"	3⅞"
Dark	D: 10 ◇	T2	T5	T7	T8	T9	T11

Try this: Use several different darks for D.

GRANDMOTHER'S FAVORITE

8-Unit Grid

Color Illustration: page 17

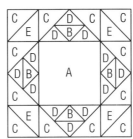

FOR 1 BLOCK:		FINISHED BLOCK SIZE					
		Single dimensions in the cutting chart indicate the size of the cut square (3" = 3" x 3").					
		4"	6"	8"	9"	10"	12"
Light	A: 1 □	2½"	3½"	4½"	5"	5½"	6½"
	B: 1 ⊠→⊠	2¼"	2¾"	3¼"	3½"	3¾"	4¼"
	C: 6 ◺→◺	1⅞"	2⅜"	2⅞"	3⅛"	3⅜"	3⅞"
Dark	D: 3 ⊠→⊠	2¼"	2¾"	3¼"	3½"	3¾"	4¼"
	E: 2 ◺→◺	1⅞"	2⅜"	2⅞"	3⅛"	3⅜"	3⅞"

Try this: Use a medium instead of a dark for E.

GRANDMOTHER'S PINWHEEL

10-Unit Grid

Color Illustration: page 17

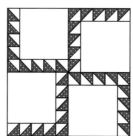
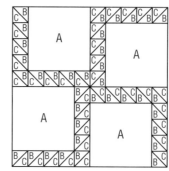
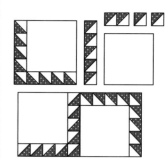

FOR 1 BLOCK:	FINISHED BLOCK SIZE *Single dimensions in the cutting chart indicate the size of the cut square (3" = 3" x 3").*					
	6¼"	**7½"**	**8¾"**	**10"**	**12½"**	**13¾"**
Light A: 4 ☐	3"	3½"	4"	4½"	5½"	6"
B: 18 ◺ → ◹	1½"	1⅝"	1¾"	1⅞"	2⅛"	2¼"
Dark C: 18 ◺ → ◹	1½"	1⅝"	1¾"	1⅞"	2⅛"	2¼"

Try this: Use many different darks for C.

GRANDMOTHER'S PRIDE

6-Unit Grid

Color Illustration: page 17

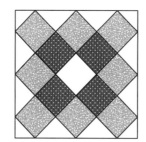
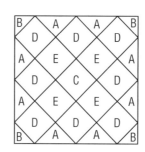
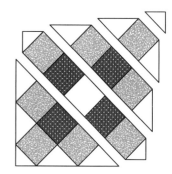

FOR 1 BLOCK:	FINISHED BLOCK SIZE *Single dimensions in the cutting chart indicate the size of the cut square (3" = 3" x 3").*					
	4½"	**6"**	**7½"**	**9"**	**10½"**	**12"**
Light A: 2 ⊠ → ⬔	2¾"	3¼"	3¾"	4¼"	4¾"	5¼"
B: 2 ◺ → ◹	1⅝"	1⅞"	2⅛"	2⅜"	2⅝"	2⅞"
C: 1 ◇	T5	T7	T9	T11	T12	T14
Medium D: 8 ◇	T5	T7	T9	T11	T12	T14
Dark E: 4 ◇	T5	T7	T9	T11	T12	T14

Try this: Reverse the lights and mediums in every other block.

☐ *Light*   ▨ *Light 2*   ▨ *Medium*   ▨ *Medium 2*   ▨ *Dark*

GRAPE BASKET

5-Unit Grid

Color Illustration: page 18

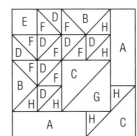

		FINISHED BLOCK SIZE Single dimensions in the cutting chart indicate the size of the cut square (3" = 3" x 3").					
FOR 2 BLOCKS:		**5"**	**6¼"**	**7½"**	**8¾"**	**10"**	**12½"**
Light	A: 4 ▭	1½" x 3½"	1¾" x 4¼"	2" x 5"	2¼" x 5¾"	2½" x 6½"	3" x 8"
	B: 1 ⊠ → ⊠	3¼"	3¾"	4¼"	4¾"	5¼"	6¼"
	C: 2 ◻ → ◹	2⅞"	3⅜"	3⅞"	4⅜"	4⅞"	5⅞"
	D: 7 ◻ → ◹	1⅞"	2⅛"	2⅜"	2⅝"	2⅞"	3⅜"
	E: 2 ☐	1½"	1¾"	2"	2¼"	2½"	3"
Medium	F: 7 ◻ → ◹	1⅞"	2⅛"	2⅜"	2⅝"	2⅞"	3⅜"
Dark	G: 1 ◻ → ◹	2⅞"	3⅜"	3⅞"	4⅜"	4⅞"	5⅞"
	H: 6 ◻ → ◹	1⅞"	2⅛"	2⅜"	2⅝"	2⅞"	3⅜"

Try this: Use several different mediums for F.

GREAT BLUE HERON

3-Unit Grid

Color Illustration: page 18

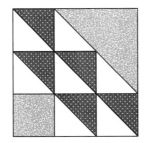
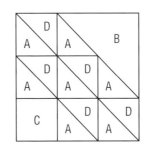
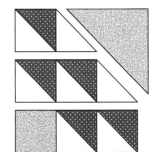

		FINISHED BLOCK SIZE Single dimensions in the cutting chart indicate the size of the cut square (3" = 3" x 3").					
FOR 2 BLOCKS:		**4½"**	**6"**	**7½"**	**9"**	**10½"**	**12"**
Light	A: 7 ◻ → ◹	2⅜"	2⅞"	3⅜"	3⅞"	4⅜"	4⅞"
Medium	B: 1 ◻ → ◹	3⅞"	4⅞"	5⅞"	6⅞"	7⅞"	8⅞"
	C: 2 ☐	2"	2½"	3"	3½"	4"	4½"
Dark	D: 5 ◻ → ◹	2⅜"	2⅞"	3⅜"	3⅞"	4⅜"	4⅞"

Try this: Use a different medium in every block.

THE H SQUARE QUILT

6-Unit Grid

Color Illustration: page 18

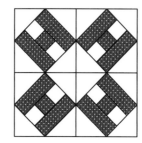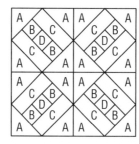

	FINISHED BLOCK SIZE					
	Single dimensions in the cutting chart indicate the size of the cut square (3" = 3" x 3").					
FOR 1 BLOCK:	**4½"**	**6"**	**7½"**	**9"**	**10½"**	**12"**
Light A: 8 ◻→◪	2"	2⅜"	2¾"	3⅛"	3½"	3⅞"
B: 8 ◇	T1	T2	T4	T5	T6	T7
Dark C: 8 ◇	T29	T33	T37	T42	T47	T52
D: 4 ◇	T1	T2	T4	T5	T6	T7

Try this: Use a different combination of light and dark fabrics for each "H."

HANDY ANDY

5-Unit Grid

Color Illustration: page 18

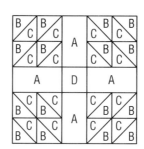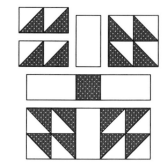

	FINISHED BLOCK SIZE					
	Single dimensions in the cutting chart indicate the size of the cut square (3" = 3" x 3").					
FOR 1 BLOCK:	**5"**	**6¼"**	**7½"**	**8¾"**	**10"**	**12½"**
Light A: 4 ▭	1½" x 2½"	1¾" x 3"	2" x 3½"	2¼" x 4"	2½" x 4½"	3" x 5½"
B: 8 ◻→◪	1⅞"	2⅛"	2⅜"	2⅝"	2⅞"	3⅜"
Dark C: 8 ◻→◪	1⅞"	2⅛"	2⅜"	2⅝"	2⅞"	3⅜"
D: 1 ◻	1½"	1¾"	2"	2¼"	2½"	3"

Try this: Use several different darks for C.

HANGING BASKET

12-Unit Grid

Color Illustration: page 18

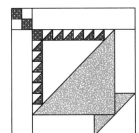
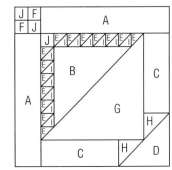
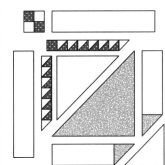

		FINISHED BLOCK SIZE					
		Single dimensions in the cutting chart indicate the size of the cut square (3" = 3" x 3").					
FOR 2 BLOCKS:		**6"**	**7½"**	**9"**	**12"**	**13½"**	**15"**
Light	A: 4 ▭	1½" x 5½"	1¾" x 6¾"	2" x 8"	2½" x 10½"	2¾" x 11¾"	3" x 13"
	B: 1 ◻→◺	3⅞"	4⅝"	5⅜"	6⅞"	7⅝"	8⅜"
	C: 4 ▭	1½" x 3½"	1¾" x 4¼"	2" x 5"	2½" x 6½"	2¾" x 7¼ "	3" x 8"
	D: 1 ◻→◺	2⅞"	3⅜"	3⅞"	4⅞"	5⅜"	5⅞"
	E: 14 ◻→◺	1⅜"	1½"	1⅝"	1⅞"	2"	2⅛"
	F: 4 ◻	1"	1⅛"	1¼"	1½"	1⅝"	1¾"
Medium	G: 1 ◻→◺	4⅞"	5⅞"	6⅞"	8⅞"	9⅞"	10⅞"
	H: 2 ◻→◺	1⅞"	2⅛"	2⅜"	2⅞"	3⅛"	3⅜"
Dark	I: 12 ◻→◺	1⅜"	1½"	1⅝"	1⅞"	2"	2⅛"
	J: 6 ◻	1"	1⅛"	1¼"	1½"	1⅝"	1¾"
Try this:	Use a different combination of fabrics in every block.						

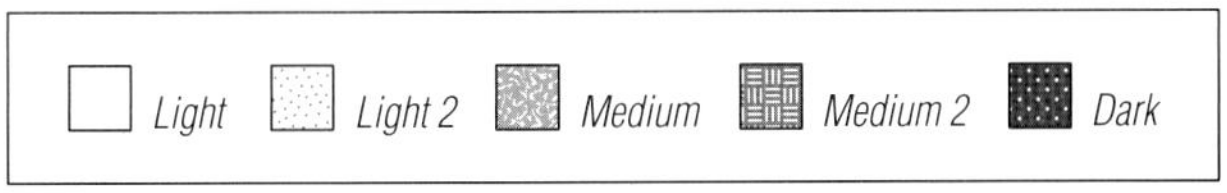

☐ Light ▦ Light 2 ▨ Medium ▦ Medium 2 ▪ Dark

HARMONY SQUARE

10-Unit Grid

Color Illustration: page 18

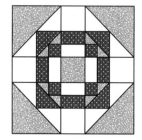
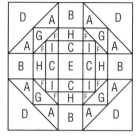
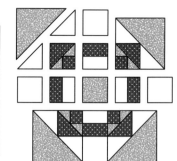

		FINISHED BLOCK SIZE					
		Single dimensions in the cutting chart indicate the size of the cut square (3" = 3" x 3").					
FOR 1 BLOCK:		**5"**	**7½"**	**10"**	**11¼"**	**12½"**	**15"**
Light	A: 4 ◻→◩	1⅞"	2⅜"	2⅞"	3⅛"	3⅜"	3⅞"
	B: 4 ◻	1½"	2"	2½"	2¾"	3"	3½"
	C: 4 ▭	1" x 1½"	1¼" x 2"	1½" x 2½"	1⅝" x 2¾"	1¾" x 3"	2" x 3½"
Medium	D: 2 ◻→◩	2⅞"	3⅞"	4⅞"	5⅜"	5⅞"	6⅞"
	E: 1 ◻	1½"	2"	2½"	2¾"	3"	3½"
	F: 4 ◻→◩	1⅜"	1⅝"	1⅞"	2"	2⅛"	2⅜"
Dark	G: 2 ◻→◩	1⅞"	2⅜"	2⅞"	3⅛"	3⅜"	3⅞"
	H: 4 ▭	1" x 1½"	1¼" x 2"	1½" x 2½"	1⅝" x 2¾"	1¾" x 3"	2" x 3½"
	I: 4 ◻	1"	1¼"	1½"	1⅝"	1¾"	2"

Try this: Reverse the mediums and darks in every other block.

HAYES CORNER

6-Unit Grid

Color Illustration: page 18

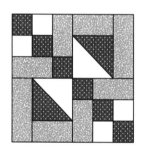
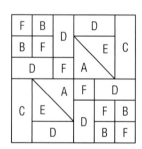
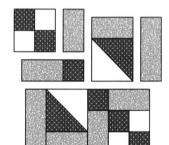

		FINISHED BLOCK SIZE					
		Single dimensions in the cutting chart indicate the size of the cut square (3" = 3" x 3").					
FOR 1 BLOCK:		**4½"**	**6"**	**7½"**	**9"**	**10½"**	**12"**
Light	A: 1 ◻→◩	2⅜"	2⅞"	3⅜"	3⅞"	4⅜"	4⅞"
	B: 4 ◻	1¼"	1½"	1¾"	2"	2 ¼"	2½"
Medium	C: 2 ▭	1¼" x 2¾"	1½" x 3½"	1¾" x 4¼"	2" x 5"	2¼" x 5¾"	2½" x 6½"
	D: 6 ▭	1¼" x 2"	1½" x 2½"	1¾" x 3"	2" x 3½"	2¼" x 4"	2½" x 4½"
Dark	E: 1 ◻→◩	2⅜"	2 ⅞"	3⅜"	3⅞"	4⅜"	4⅞"
	F: 6 ◻	1¼"	1½"	1¾"	2"	2¼"	2½"

Try this: Use a different medium in every block.

HAZY DAISY

4-Unit Grid

Color Illustration: page 18

 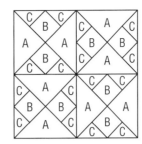 

FOR 1 BLOCK:	FINISHED BLOCK SIZE *Single dimensions in the cutting chart indicate the size of the cut square (3" = 3" x 3").*					
	4"	**6"**	**8"**	**9"**	**10"**	**12"**
Light A: 2 ⊠ → ⊠	3¼"	4¼"	5¼"	5¾"	6¼"	7¼"
Medium B: 8 ◇		T2	T5	T7	T8	T9	T11
Dark C: 4 ⊠ → ⊠	2¼"	2¾"	3¼"	3½"	3¾"	4¼"

Try this: Use different light, medium, and dark fabrics in each quadrant of the block.

HEARTH AND HOME

5-Unit Grid

Color Illustration: page 18

 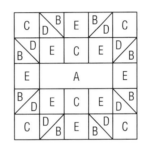 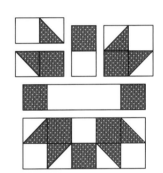

FOR 1 BLOCK:	FINISHED BLOCK SIZE *Single dimensions in the cutting chart indicate the size of the cut square (3" = 3" x 3").*					
	5"	**6¼"**	**7½"**	**8¾"**	**10"**	**12½"**
Light A: 1 ▭	1½" x 3½"	1¾" x 4¼"	2" x 5"	2¼" x 5¾"	2½" x 6½"	3" x 8"
B: 4 ◲ → ◺	1⅞"	2⅛"	2⅜"	2⅝"	2⅞"	3⅜"
C: 6 □	1½"	1¾"	2"	2¼"	2½"	3"
Dark D: 4 ◲ → ◺	1⅞"	2⅛"	2⅜"	2⅝"	2⅞"	3⅜"
E: 8 □	1½"	1¾"	2"	2¼"	2½"	3"

Try this: Use an autographed rectangle for A.

HEN AND CHICKENS

5-Unit Grid
Color Illustration: page 18

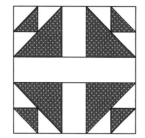 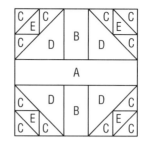 

| FOR 1 BLOCK: | | FINISHED BLOCK SIZE | | | | | |
| | | *Single dimensions in the cutting chart indicate the size of the cut square (3" = 3" x 3").* | | | | | |
		5"	**6¼"**	**7½"**	**8¾"**	**10"**	**12½"**
Light	A: 1 ▭	1½" x 5½"	1¾" x 6¾"	2" x 8"	2¼" x 9¼"	2½" x 10½"	3" x 13"
	B: 2 ▭	1½" x 2½"	1¾" x 3"	2" x 3½"	2¼" x 4"	2½" x 4½"	3" x 5½"
	C: 6 ◱ → ◺	1⅞"	2⅛"	2⅜"	2⅝"	2⅞"	3⅜"
Dark	D: 2 ◱ → ◺	2⅞"	3⅜"	3⅞"	4⅜"	4⅞"	5⅞"
	E: 2 ◱ → ◺	1⅞"	2⅛"	2⅜"	2⅝"	2⅞"	3⅜"

Try this: Use a medium instead of a dark for E.

THE HEN AND HER CHICKS

8-Unit Grid
Color Illustration: page 18

 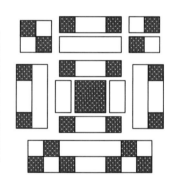

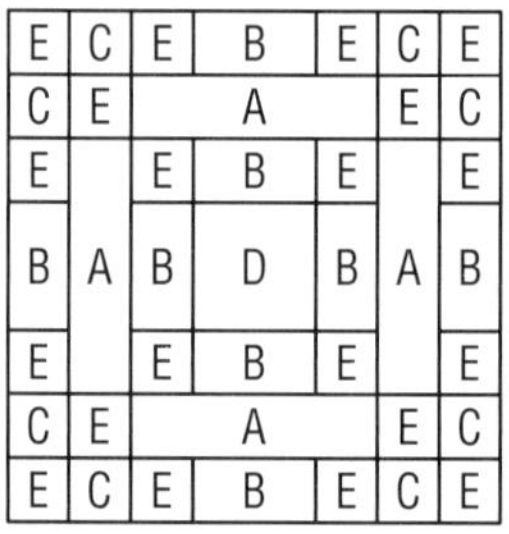

| FOR 1 BLOCK: | | FINISHED BLOCK SIZE | | | | | |
| | | *Single dimensions in the cutting chart indicate the size of the cut square (3" = 3" x 3").* | | | | | |
		6"	**8"**	**9"**	**10"**	**12"**	**14"**
Light	A: 4 ▭	1¼" x 3½"	1½" x 4½"	1⅝" x 5"	1¾" x 5½"	2" x 6½"	2¼" x 7½"
	B: 8 ▭	1¼" x 2"	1½" x 2½"	1⅝" x 2¾"	1¾" x 3"	2" x 3½"	2¼" x 4"
	C: 8 □	1¼"	1½"	1⅝"	1¾"	2"	2¼"
Dark	D: 1 □	2"	2½"	2¾"	3"	3½"	4"
	E: 20 □	1¼"	1½"	1⅝"	1¾"	2"	2¼"

Try this: Use a medium instead of a light for B.

HERM'S SHIRT

4-Unit Grid

Color Illustration: page 18

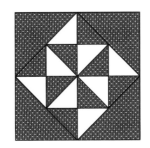
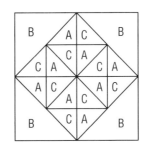

		FINISHED BLOCK SIZE *Single dimensions in the cutting chart indicate the size of the cut square (3" = 3" x 3").*					
FOR 1 BLOCK:		**4"**	**6"**	**8"**	**9"**	**10"**	**12"**
Light	A: 4 ⬚→◨	1⅞"	2⅜"	2⅞"	3⅛"	3⅜"	3⅞"
Dark	B: 2 ⬚→◨	2⅞"	3⅞"	4⅞"	5⅜"	5⅞"	6⅞"
	C: 4 ⬚→◨	1⅞"	2⅜"	2⅞"	3⅛"	3⅜"	3⅞"

Try this: Reverse the lights and darks in every other block.

HILL AND CRAG

5-Unit Grid

Color Illustration: page 18

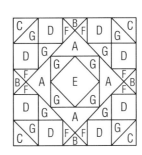

		FINISHED BLOCK SIZE *Single dimensions in the cutting chart indicate the size of the cut square (3" = 3" x 3").*					
FOR 1 BLOCK:		**5"**	**6¼"**	**7½"**	**8¾"**	**10"**	**12½"**
Light	A: 1 ⊠→⧖	3¼"	3¾"	4¼"	4¾"	5¼"	6¼"
	B: 1 ⊠→⧖	2¼"	2½"	2¾"	3"	3¼"	3¾"
	C: 2 ⬚→◨	1⅞"	2⅛"	2⅜"	2⅝"	2⅞"	3⅜"
	D: 8 ☐	1½"	1¾"	2"	2¼"	2½"	3"
	E: 1 ◇	T7	T9	T11	T12	T14	T16
Dark	F: 2 ⊠→⧖	2¼"	2½"	2¾"	3"	3¼"	3¾"
	G: 6 ⬚→◨	1⅞"	2⅛"	2⅜"	2⅝"	2⅞"	3⅜"

Try this: Use a medium instead of a light for A and C.

☐ *Light*   ░ *Light 2*   ▦ *Medium*   ▤ *Medium 2*   ▓ *Dark*

HILL AND VALLEY

6-Unit Grid
Color Illustration: page 18

 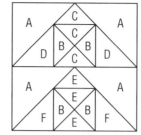 

			FINISHED BLOCK SIZE				
			Single dimensions in the cutting chart indicate the size of the cut square (3" = 3" x 3").				
FOR 4 BLOCKS:		**4½"**	**6"**	**7½"**	**9"**	**10½"**	**12"**
Light	A: 8 ◻→◺	3⅛"	3⅞"	4⅝"	5⅜"	6⅛"	6⅞"
	B: 4 ⊠→⧖	2¾"	3¼"	3¾"	4¼"	4¾"	5¼"
Medium	C: 3 ⊠→⧖	2¾"	3¼"	3¾"	4¼"	4¾"	5¼"
	D: 4 ◻→◺	2⅜"	2⅞"	3⅜"	3⅞"	4⅜"	4⅞"
Dark	E: 3 ⊠→⧖	2¾"	3¼"	3¾"	4¼"	4¾"	5¼"
	F: 4 ◻→◺	2⅜"	2⅞"	3⅜"	3⅞"	4⅜"	4⅞"

Try this: Use a different combination of mediums and darks in every block.

HITHER AND YON

4-Unit Grid
Color Illustration: page 18

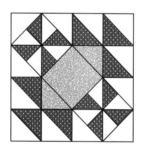 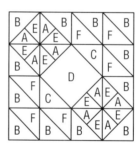 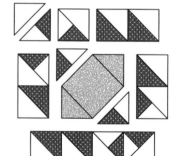

			FINISHED BLOCK SIZE				
			Single dimensions in the cutting chart indicate the size of the cut square (3" = 3" x 3").				
FOR 1 BLOCK:		**4"**	**6"**	**8"**	**9"**	**10"**	**12"**
Light	A: 2 ⊠→⧖	2¼"	2¾"	3¼"	3½"	3¾"	4¼"
	B: 6 ◻→◺	1⅞"	2⅜"	2⅞"	3⅛"	3⅜"	3⅞"
Medium	C: 1 ◻→◺	1⅞"	2⅜"	2⅞"	3⅛"	3⅜"	3⅞"
	D: 1 ◇	T7	T11	T14	T15	T16	T19
Dark	E: 2 ⊠→⧖	2¼"	2¾"	3¼"	3½"	3¾"	4¼"
	F: 3 ◻→◺	1⅞"	2⅜"	2⅞"	3⅛"	3⅜"	3⅞"

Try this: Use one dark for E and a different dark for F.

HOBSON'S KISS

8-Unit Grid
Color Illustration: page 18

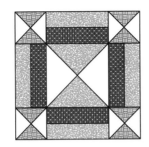 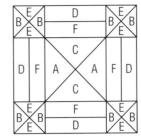 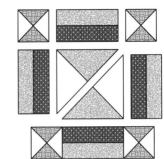

		FINISHED BLOCK SIZE *Single dimensions in the cutting chart indicate the size of the cut square (3" = 3" x 3").*					
FOR 2 BLOCKS:		**6"**	**8"**	**9"**	**10"**	**12"**	**14"**
Light	A: 1 ⊠ → ⊠	4¼"	5¼"	5¾"	6¼"	7¼"	8¼"
	B: 4 ⊠ → ⊠	2¾"	3¼"	3½"	3¾"	4¼"	4¾"
Medium	C: 1 ⊠ → ⊠	4¼"	5¼"	5¾"	6¼"	7¼"	8¼"
	D: 8 ▭	1¼" x 3½"	1½" x 4½"	1⅝" x 5"	1¾" x 5½"	2" x 6½"	2¼" x 7½"
Medium 2	E: 4 ⊠ → ⊠	2¾"	3¼"	3½"	3¾"	4¼"	4¾"
Dark	F: 8 ▭	1¼" x 3½"	1½" x 4½"	1⅝" x 5"	1¾" x 5½"	2" x 6½"	2¼" x 7½"

Try this: Reverse the mediums and darks in every other block.

HOME CIRCLE

5-Unit Grid
Color Illustration: page 18

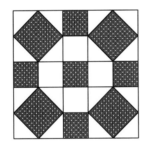 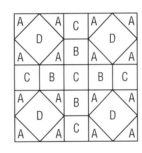 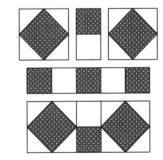

		FINISHED BLOCK SIZE *Single dimensions in the cutting chart indicate the size of the cut square (3" = 3" x 3").*					
FOR 1 BLOCK:		**5"**	**6¼"**	**7½"**	**8¾"**	**10"**	**12½"**
Light	A: 8 ◻ → ◺	1⅞"	2⅛"	2⅜"	2⅝"	2⅞"	3⅜"
	B: 4 ◻	1½"	1¾"	2"	2¼"	2½"	3"
Dark	C: 5 ◻	1½"	1¾"	2"	2¼"	2½"	3"
	D: 4 ◇	T7	T9	T11	T12	T14	T16

Try this: Reverse the lights and darks.

Light Light 2 Medium Medium 2 Dark

HOME TREASURE

8-Unit Grid

Color Illustration: page 18

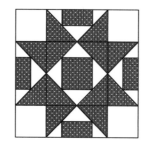 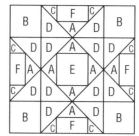 

FOR 1 BLOCK:		**FINISHED BLOCK SIZE** Single dimensions in the cutting chart indicate the size of the cut square (3" = 3" x 3").					
		6"	**8"**	**9"**	**10"**	**12"**	**14"**
Light	A: 2 ⊠→⊠	2¾"	3¼"	3½"	3¾"	4¼"	4¾"
	B: 4 ☐	2"	2½"	2¾"	3"	3½"	4"
	C: 4 ◻→◹	1⅝"	1⅞"	2"	2⅛"	2⅜"	2⅝"
Dark	D: 6 ◻→◹	2⅜"	2⅞"	3⅛"	3⅜"	3⅞"	4⅜"
	E: 1 ☐	2"	2½"	2¾"	3"	3½"	4"
	F: 4 ▭	1¼" x 2"	1½" x 2½"	1⅝" x 2¾"	1¾" x 3"	2" x 3½"	2¼" x 4"
Try this:	Use a medium instead of a dark for E and F.						

HOMEWARD BOUND

2-Unit Grid

Color Illustration: page 18

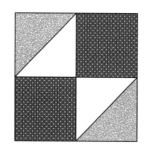 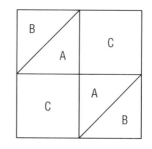 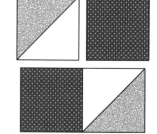

FOR 1 BLOCK:		**FINISHED BLOCK SIZE** Single dimensions in the cutting chart indicate the size of the cut square (3" = 3" x 3").					
		4"	**6"**	**8"**	**9"**	**10"**	**12"**
Light	A: 1 ◻→◹	2⅞"	3⅞"	4⅞"	5⅜"	5⅞"	6⅞"
Medium	B: 1 ◻→◹	2⅞"	3⅞"	4⅞"	5⅜"	5⅞"	6⅞"
Dark	C: 2 ☐	2½"	3½"	4½"	5"	5½"	6½"
Try this:	Reverse the lights and mediums in every other block.						

HOPKINS SQUARE

4-Unit Grid

Color Illustration: page 18

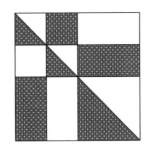
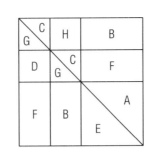
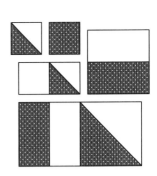

		FINISHED BLOCK SIZE *Single dimensions in the cutting chart indicate the size of the cut square (3" = 3" x 3").*					
FOR 2 BLOCKS:		**4"**	**6"**	**8"**	**9"**	**10"**	**12"**
Light	A: 1 ◻→◻	2⅞"	3⅞"	4⅞"	5⅜"	5⅞"	6⅞"
	B: 4 ▭	1½" x 2½"	2" x 3½"	2½" x 4½"	2¾" x 5"	3" x 5½"	3½" x 6½"
	C: 2 ◻→◻	1⅞"	2⅜"	2⅞"	3⅛"	3⅜"	3⅞"
	D: 2 ◻	1½"	2"	2½"	2¾"	3"	3½"
Dark	E: 1 ◻→◻	2⅞"	3⅞"	4⅞"	5⅜"	5⅞"	6⅞"
	F: 4 ▭	1½" x 2½"	2" x 3½"	2½" x 4½"	2¾" x 5"	3" x 5½"	3½" x 6½"
	G: 2 ◻→◻	1⅞"	2⅜"	2⅞"	3⅛"	3⅜"	3⅞"
	H: 2 ◻	1½"	2"	2½"	2¾"	3"	3½"

Try this: Use one light for A and C and a different light for B and D.

HOPSCOTCH

4-Unit Grid

Color Illustration: page 18

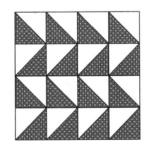
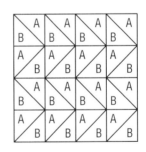
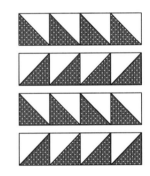

		FINISHED BLOCK SIZE *Single dimensions in the cutting chart indicate the size of the cut square (3" = 3" x 3").*					
FOR 1 BLOCK:		**4"**	**6"**	**8"**	**9"**	**10"**	**12"**
Light	A: 8 ◻→◻	1⅞"	2⅜"	2⅞"	3⅛"	3⅜"	3⅞"
Dark	B: 8 ◻→◻	1⅞"	2⅜"	2⅞"	3⅛"	3⅜"	3⅞"

Try this: Use several different lights and darks.

HOUR GLASS

3-Unit Grid
Color Illustration: page 18

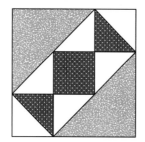
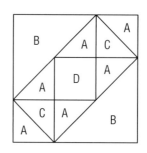
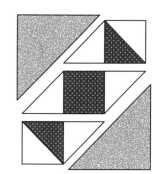

		FINISHED BLOCK SIZE *Single dimensions in the cutting chart indicate the size of the cut square (3" = 3" x 3").*					
FOR 1 BLOCK:		**4½"**	**6"**	**7½"**	**9"**	**10½"**	**12"**
Light	A: 3 ◻ → ◻	2⅜"	2⅞"	3⅜"	3⅞"	4⅜"	4⅞"
Medium	B: 1 ◻ → ◻	3⅞"	4⅞"	5⅞"	6⅞"	7⅞"	8⅞"
Dark	C: 1 ◻ → ◻	2⅜"	2⅞"	3⅜"	3⅞"	4⅜"	4⅞"
	D: 1 ◻	2"	2½"	3"	3½"	4"	4½"
Try this:	Use several different lights for A.						

HOUR GLASS II

4-Unit Grid
Color Illustration: page 18

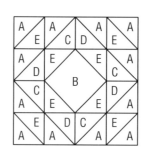
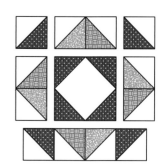

		FINISHED BLOCK SIZE *Single dimensions in the cutting chart indicate the size of the cut square (3" = 3" x 3").*					
FOR 1 BLOCK:		**4"**	**6"**	**8"**	**9"**	**10"**	**12"**
Light	A: 6 ◻ → ◻	1⅞"	2⅜"	2⅞"	3⅛"	3⅜"	3⅞"
	B: 1 ◇	T7	T11	T14	T15	T16	T19
Medium	C: 2 ◻ → ◻	1⅞"	2⅜"	2⅞"	3⅛"	3⅜"	3⅞"
Medium 2	D: 2 ◻ → ◻	1⅞"	2⅜"	2⅞"	3⅛"	3⅜"	3⅞"
Dark	E: 4 ◻ → ◻	1⅞"	2⅜"	2⅞"	3⅛"	3⅜"	3⅞"
Try this:	Use several different mediums for C and D.						

HOUR GLASS III

3-Unit Grid

Color Illustration: page 18

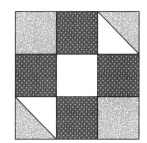

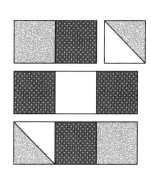

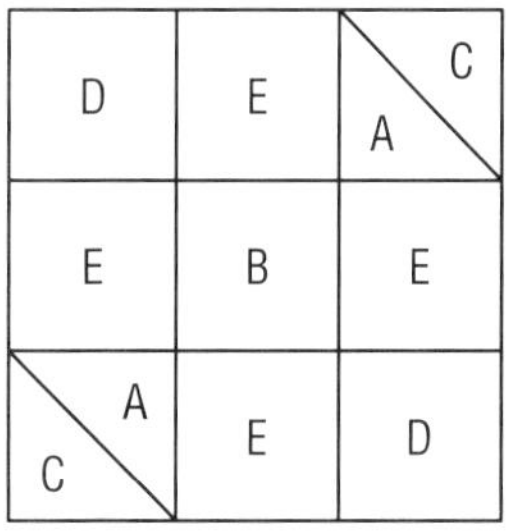

FOR 1 BLOCK:			FINISHED BLOCK SIZE *Single dimensions in the cutting chart indicate the size of the cut square (3" = 3" x 3").*					
			4½"	**6"**	**7½"**	**9"**	**10½"**	**12"**
Light	A: 1 ◻→◺		2⅜"	2⅞"	3⅜"	3⅞"	4⅜"	4⅞"
	B: 1 ◻		2"	2½"	3"	3½"	4"	4½"
Medium	C: 1 ◻→◺		2⅜"	2⅞"	3⅜"	3⅞"	4⅜"	4⅞"
	D: 2 ◻		2"	2½"	3"	3½"	4"	4½"
Dark	E: 4 ◻		2"	2½"	3"	3½"	4"	4½"

Try this: Use a different combination of fabrics in every block.

HOUR GLASS IV

6-Unit Grid

Color Illustration: page 18

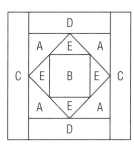

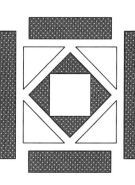

FOR 1 BLOCK:			FINISHED BLOCK SIZE *Single dimensions in the cutting chart indicate the size of the cut square (3" = 3" x 3").*					
			4½"	**6"**	**7½"**	**9"**	**10½"**	**12"**
Light	A: 2 ◻→◺		2⅜"	2⅞"	3⅜"	3⅞"	4⅜"	4⅞"
	B: 1 ◻		2"	2½"	3"	3½"	4"	4½"
Dark	C: 2 ▭		1¼" x 5"	1½" x 6½"	1¾" x 8"	2" x 9½"	2¼" x 11"	2½" x 12½"
	D: 2 ▭		1¼" x 3½"	1½" x 4½"	1¾" x 5½"	2" x 6½"	2¼" x 7½"	2½" x 8½"
	E: 1 ⊠→⊠		2¾"	3¼"	3¾"	4¼"	4¾"	5¼"

Try this: Reverse the lights and darks in every other block.

◻ Light   ▦ Light 2   ▩ Medium   ▤ Medium 2   ▦ Dark

THE HOUSE JACK BUILT

6-Unit Grid
Color Illustration: page 18

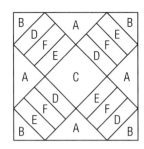
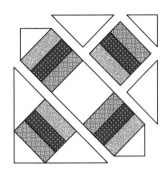

		FINISHED BLOCK SIZE *Single dimensions in the cutting chart indicate the size of the cut square (3" = 3" x 3").*					
FOR 1 BLOCK:		**4½"**	**6"**	**7½"**	**9"**	**10½"**	**12"**
Light	A: 1 ⊠ → ⊠	3½"	4¼"	5"	5¾"	6½"	7¼"
	B: 2 �«◻ → ◻	2"	2⅜"	2¾"	3⅛"	3½"	3⅞"
	C: 1 ◇	T8	T11	T13	T15	T17	T19
Medium	D: 4 ◇	T29	T33	T37	T42	T47	T52
Medium 2	E: 4 ◇	T29	T33	T37	T42	T47	T52
Dark	F: 4 ◇	T29	T33	T37	T42	T47	T52

Try this: Use one light for A and B and a different light for C.

HOVERING HAWKS

4-Unit Grid
Color Illustration: page 18

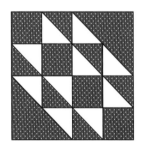
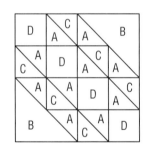
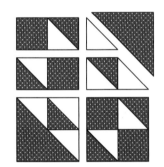

		FINISHED BLOCK SIZE *Single dimensions in the cutting chart indicate the size of the cut square (3" = 3" x 3").*					
FOR 1 BLOCK:		**4"**	**6"**	**8"**	**9"**	**10"**	**12"**
Light	A: 5 ◻ → ◻	1⅞"	2⅜"	2⅞"	3⅛"	3⅜"	3⅞"
Dark	B: 1 ◻ → ◻	2⅞"	3⅞"	4⅞"	5⅜"	5⅞"	6⅞"
	C: 3 ◻ → ◻	1⅞"	2⅜"	2⅞"	3⅛"	3⅜"	3⅞"
	D: 4 ◻	1½"	2"	2½"	2¾"	3"	3½"

Try this: Reverse the lights and darks in every other block.

IDITAROD TRAIL

10-Unit Grid
Color Illustration: page 18

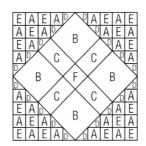

	FINISHED BLOCK SIZE					
	Single dimensions in the cutting chart indicate the size of the cut square (3" = 3" x 3").					
FOR 1 BLOCK:	**6¼"**	**7½"**	**8¾"**	**10"**	**12½"**	**13¾"**
Light A: 24 ▢	1⅛"	1¼"	1⅜"	1½"	1¾"	1⅞"
B: 4 ◇	T9	T11	T12	T14	T16	T18
Medium C: 4 ◇	T36	T41	T46	T51	T59	T63
Dark D: 10 ▢→◹	1½"	1⅝"	1¾"	1⅞"	2⅛"	2¼"
E: 16 ▢	1⅛"	1¼"	1⅜"	1½"	1¾"	1⅞"
F: 1 ◇	T4	T5	T6	T7	T9	T10

Try this: Use many different darks for E.

IMPERIAL T

6-Unit Grid
Color Illustration: page 18

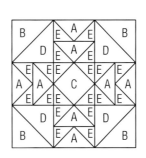

	FINISHED BLOCK SIZE					
	Single dimensions in the cutting chart indicate the size of the cut square (3" = 3" x 3").					
FOR 1 BLOCK:	**4½"**	**6"**	**7½"**	**9"**	**10½"**	**12"**
Light A: 2 ⊠→⧖	2¾"	3¼"	3¾"	4¼"	4¾"	5¼"
B: 2 ▢→◹	2⅜"	2⅞"	3⅜"	3⅞"	4⅜"	4⅞"
C: 1 ◇	T5	T7	T9	T11	T12	T14
Dark D: 2 ▢→◹	2⅜"	2⅞"	3⅜"	3⅞"	4⅜"	4⅞"
E: 10 ▢→◹	1⅝"	1⅞"	2⅛"	2⅜"	2⅝"	2⅞"

Try this: Reverse the lights and darks in every other block.

IMPROVED FOUR PATCH

4-Unit Grid

Color Illustration: page 18

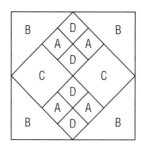

		FINISHED BLOCK SIZE					
		Single dimensions in the cutting chart indicate the size of the cut square (3" = 3" x 3").					
FOR 1 BLOCK:		**4"**	**6"**	**8"**	**9"**	**10"**	**12"**
Light	A: 4 ◇	T2	T5	T7	T8	T9	T11
Light 2	B: 2 ◻→◲	2⅞"	3⅞"	4⅞"	5⅜"	5⅞"	6⅞"
Medium	C: 2 ◇	T7	T11	T14	T15	T16	T19
Dark	D: 4 ◇	T2	T5	T7	T8	T9	T11

Try this: Reverse the dark and medium in every other block.

INDIAN

4-Unit Grid

Color Illustration: page 19

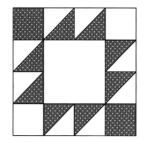
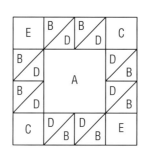
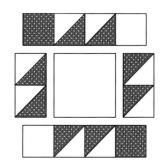

		FINISHED BLOCK SIZE					
		Single dimensions in the cutting chart indicate the size of the cut square (3" = 3" x 3").					
FOR 1 BLOCK:		**4"**	**6"**	**8"**	**9"**	**10"**	**12"**
Light	A: 1 ◻	2½"	3½"	4½"	5"	5½"	6½"
	B: 4 ◻→◲	1⅞"	2⅜"	2⅞"	3⅛"	3⅜"	3⅞"
	C: 2 ◻	1½"	2"	2½"	2¾"	3"	3½"
Dark	D: 4 ◻→◲	1⅞"	2⅜"	2⅞"	3⅛"	3⅜"	3⅞"
	E: 2 ◻	1½"	2"	2½"	2¾"	3"	3½"

Try this: Use a medium instead of a light for A.

INDIAN PLUMES

8-Unit Grid
Color Illustration: page 19

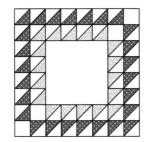 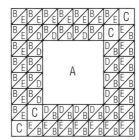 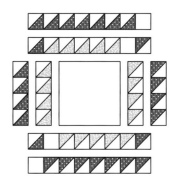

		FINISHED BLOCK SIZE					
		Single dimensions in the cutting chart indicate the size of the cut square (3" = 3" x 3").					
FOR 1 BLOCK:		**6"**	**8"**	**9"**	**10"**	**12"**	**14"**
Light	A: 1 ▢	3½"	4½"	5"	5½"	6½"	7½"
	B: 22 ◨ → ◨	1⅝"	1⅞"	2"	2⅛"	2⅜"	2⅝"
	C: 4 ▢	1¼"	1½"	1⅝"	1¾"	2"	2¼"
Medium	D: 9 ◨ → ◨	1⅝"	1⅞"	2"	2⅛"	2⅜"	2⅝"
Dark	E: 13 ◨ → ◨	1⅝"	1⅞"	2"	2⅛"	2⅜"	2⅝"

Try this: Use several different lights for B and C.

INDIAN STAR

4-Unit Grid
Color Illustration: page 19

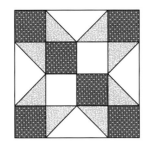 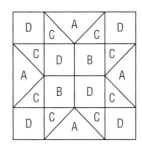 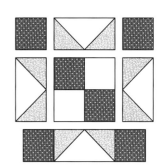

		FINISHED BLOCK SIZE					
		Single dimensions in the cutting chart indicate the size of the cut square (3" = 3" x 3").					
FOR 1 BLOCK:		**4"**	**6"**	**8"**	**9"**	**10"**	**12"**
Light	A: 1 ⊠ → ⊠	3¼"	4¼"	5¼"	5¾"	6¼"	7¼"
	B: 2 ▢	1½"	2"	2½"	2¾"	3"	3½"
Medium	C: 4 ◨ → ◨	1⅞"	2⅜"	2⅞"	3⅛"	3⅜"	3⅞"
Dark	D: 6 ▢	1½"	2"	2½"	2¾"	3"	3½"

Try this: Reverse the mediums and darks in every other block.

INDIANA PUZZLE

6-Unit Grid
Color Illustration: page 19

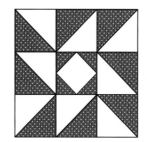
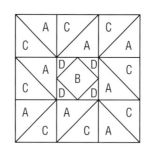
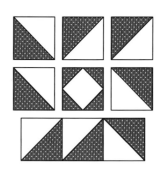

		FINISHED BLOCK SIZE *Single dimensions in the cutting chart indicate the size of the cut square (3" = 3" x 3").*					
FOR 1 BLOCK:		**4½"**	**6"**	**7½"**	**9"**	**10½"**	**12"**
Light	A: 4 ▢→◩	2⅜"	2⅞"	3⅜"	3⅞"	4⅜"	4⅞"
	B: 1 ◇	T5	T7	T9	T11	T12	T14
Dark	C: 4 ▢→◩	2⅜"	2⅞"	3⅜"	3⅞"	4⅜"	4⅞"
	D: 2 ▢→◩	1⅝"	1⅞"	2⅛"	2⅜"	2⅝"	2⅞"

Try this: Reverse the lights and darks in every other block.

INDIANA PUZZLE II

4-Unit Grid
Color Illustration: page 19

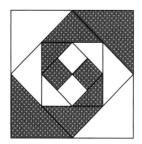
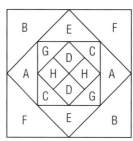

		FINISHED BLOCK SIZE *Single dimensions in the cutting chart indicate the size of the cut square (3" = 3" x 3").*					
FOR 2 BLOCKS:		**4"**	**6"**	**8"**	**9"**	**10"**	**12"**
Light	A: 1 ⊠→⊠	3¼"	4¼"	5¼"	5¾"	6¼"	7¼"
	B: 2 ▢→◩	2⅞"	3⅞"	4⅞"	5⅜"	5⅞"	6⅞"
	C: 2 ▢→◩	1⅞"	2⅜"	2⅞"	3⅛"	3⅜"	3⅞"
	D: 4 ◇	T2	T5	T7	T8	T9	T11
Dark	E: 1 ⊠→⊠	3¼"	4¼"	5¼"	5¾"	6¼"	7¼"
	F: 2 ▢→◩	2⅞"	3⅞"	4⅞"	5⅜"	5⅞"	6⅞"
	G: 2 ▢→◩	1⅞"	2⅜"	2⅞"	3⅛"	3⅜"	3⅞"
	H: 4 ◇	T2	T5	T7	T8	T9	T11

Try this: Use a different dark for each "curl."

	Light		Light 2		Medium		Medium 2		Dark

IRISH CHAIN

8-Unit Grid

Color Illustration: page 19

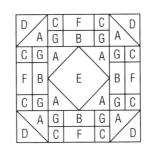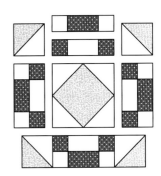

		FINISHED BLOCK SIZE Single dimensions in the cutting chart indicate the size of the cut square (3" = 3" x 3").					
FOR 1 BLOCK:		**6"**	**8"**	**9"**	**10"**	**12"**	**14"**
Light	A: 4 ◻→◺	2⅜"	2⅞"	3⅛"	3⅜"	3⅞"	4⅜"
	B: 4 ▭	1¼" x 2"	1½" x 2½"	1⅝" x 2¾"	1¾" x 3"	2" x 3½"	2¼" x 4"
	C: 8 ◻	1¼"	1½"	1⅝"	1¾"	2"	2¼"
Medium	D: 2 ◻→◺	2⅜"	2⅞"	3⅛"	3⅜"	3⅞"	4⅜"
	E: 1 ◇	T11	T14	T15	T16	T19	T21
Dark	F: 4 ▭	1¼" x 2"	1½" x 2½"	1⅝" x 2¾"	1¾" x 3"	2" x 3½"	2¼" x 4"
	G: 8 ◻	1¼"	1½"	1⅝"	1¾"	2"	2¼"

Try this: Use one medium for D and a different medium for E.

JACK IN THE BOX

5-Unit Grid

Color Illustration: page 19

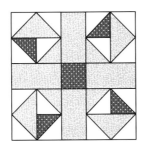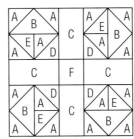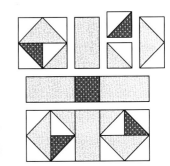

		FINISHED BLOCK SIZE Single dimensions in the cutting chart indicate the size of the cut square (3" = 3" x 3").					
FOR 1 BLOCK:		**5"**	**6¼"**	**7½"**	**8¾"**	**10"**	**12½"**
Light	A: 8 ◻→◺	1⅞"	2⅛"	2⅜"	2⅝"	2⅞"	3⅜"
Medium	B: 1 ⊠→⧇	3¼"	3¾"	4¼"	4¾"	5¼"	6¼"
	C: 4 ▭	1½" x 2½"	1¾" x 3"	2" x 3½"	2¼" x 4"	2½" x 4½"	3" x 5½"
	D: 2 ◻→◺	1⅞"	2⅛"	2⅜"	2⅝"	2⅞"	3⅜"
Dark	E: 2 ◻→◺	1⅞"	2⅛"	2⅜"	2⅝"	2⅞"	3⅜"
	F: 1 ◻	1½"	1¾"	2"	2¼"	2½"	3"

Try this: Use one medium for C and a different medium for B and D.

JACK IN THE PULPIT

4-Unit Grid
Color Illustration: page 19

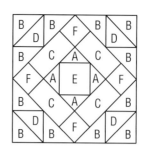

FOR 1 BLOCK:		**FINISHED BLOCK SIZE** Single dimensions in the cutting chart indicate the size of the cut square (3" = 3" x 3").					
		4"	**6"**	**8"**	**9"**	**10"**	**12"**
Light	A: 1 ⊠→⊠	2¼"	2¾"	3¼"	3½"	3¾"	4¼"
	B: 6 ◺→◺	1⅞"	2⅜"	2⅞"	3⅛"	3⅜"	3⅞"
	C: 4 ◇	T32	T41	T51	T56	T59	T67
Dark	D: 2 ◺→◺	1⅞"	2⅜"	2⅞"	3⅛"	3⅜"	3⅞"
	E: 1 ☐	1½"	2"	2½"	2¾"	3"	3½"
	F: 4 ◇	T2	T5	T7	T8	T9	T11

Try this: Use a medium instead of a light for C.

JACK'S DELIGHT

3-Unit Grid
Color Illustration: page 19

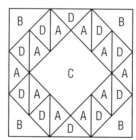

FOR 2 BLOCKS:		**FINISHED BLOCK SIZE** Single dimensions in the cutting chart indicate the size of the cut square (3" = 3" x 3").					
		4½"	**6"**	**7½"**	**9"**	**10½"**	**12"**
Light	A: 5 ⊠→⊠	2¾"	3¼"	3¾"	4¼"	4¾"	5¼"
	B: 4 ◺→◺	2⅜"	2⅞"	3⅜"	3⅞"	4⅜"	4⅞"
Medium	C: 2 ◇	T11	T14	T16	T19	T21	T23
Dark	D: 5 ⊠→⊠	2¾"	3¼"	3¾"	4¼"	4¾"	5¼"

Try this: Reverse the lights and darks in every other block.

JACOB'S LADDER

8-Unit Grid
Color Illustration: page 19

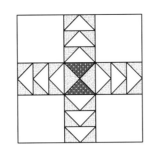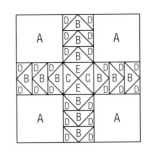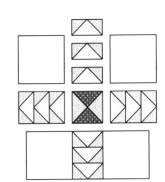

		FINISHED BLOCK SIZE *Single dimensions in the cutting chart indicate the size of the cut square (3" = 3" x 3").*					
FOR 2 BLOCKS:		**6"**	**8"**	**9"**	**10"**	**12"**	**14"**
Light	A: 8 ☐	2¾"	3½"	3⅞"	4¼"	5"	5¾"
	B: 6 ⊠→⊠	2¾"	3¼"	3½"	3¾"	4¼"	4¾"
Medium	C: 1 ⊠→⊠	2¾"	3¼"	3½"	3¾"	4¼"	4¾"
	D: 24 ◻→◺	1⅝"	1⅞"	2"	2⅛"	2⅜"	2⅝"
Dark	E: 1 ⊠→⊠	2¾"	3¼"	3½"	3¾"	4¼"	4¾"

Try this: Use several different mediums for D.

JANET'S STAR

6-Unit Grid
Color Illustration: page 19

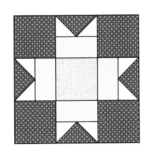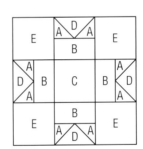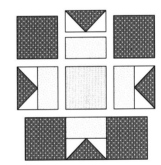

		FINISHED BLOCK SIZE *Single dimensions in the cutting chart indicate the size of the cut square (3" = 3" x 3").*					
FOR 1 BLOCK:		**4½"**	**6"**	**7½"**	**9"**	**10½"**	**12"**
Light	A: 4 ◻→◺	1⅝"	1⅞"	2⅛"	2⅜"	2⅝"	2⅞"
Light 2	B: 4 ▭	1¼" x 2"	1½" x 2½"	1¾" x 3"	2" x 3½"	2¼" x 4"	2½" x 4½"
Medium	C: 1 ☐	2"	2½"	3"	3½"	4"	4½"
Dark	D: 1 ⊠→⊠	2¾"	3¼"	3¾"	4¼"	4¾"	5¼"
	E: 4 ☐	2"	2½"	3"	3½"	4"	4½"

Try this: Use a different dark in every block.

JEFFERSON CITY

3-Unit Grid
Color Illustration: page 19

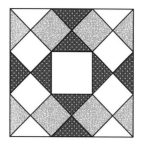
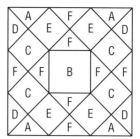

| | | **FINISHED BLOCK SIZE** | | | | | |
| | | *Single dimensions in the cutting chart indicate the size of the cut square (3" = 3" x 3").* | | | | | |
FOR 1 BLOCK:		**4½"**	**6"**	**7½"**	**9"**	**10½"**	**12"**
Light	A: 1 ⊠ → ⧖	2¾"	3¼"	3¾"	4¼"	4¾"	5¼"
	B: 1 ☐	2"	2½"	3"	3½"	4"	4½"
	C: 4 ◇	T5	T7	T9	T11	T12	T14
Medium	D: 1 ⊠ → ⧖	2¾"	3¼"	3¾"	4¼"	4¾"	5 ¼"
	E: 4 ◇	T5	T7	T9	T11	T12	T14
Dark	F: 2 ⊠ → ⧖	2¾"	3¼"	3¾"	4¼"	4¾"	5¼"
Try this:	Use several different mediums for D and E.						

JOSEPH'S COAT

5-Unit Grid
Color Illustration: page 19

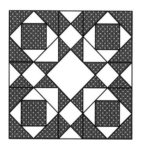
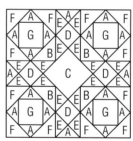

| | | **FINISHED BLOCK SIZE** | | | | | |
| | | *Single dimensions in the cutting chart indicate the size of the cut square (3" = 3" x 3").* | | | | | |
FOR 1 BLOCK:		**5"**	**6¼"**	**7½"**	**8¾"**	**10"**	**12½"**
Light	A: 5 ⊠ → ⧖	2¼"	2½"	2¾"	3"	3¼"	3¾"
	B: 2 ◺ → ◹	1⅞"	2⅛"	2⅜"	2⅝"	2⅞"	3⅜"
	C: 1 ◇	T7	T9	T11	T12	T14	T16
	D: 4 ◇	T2	T4	T5	T6	T7	T9
Dark	E: 4 ⊠ → ⧖	2¼"	2½"	2¾"	3"	3¼"	3¾"
	F: 6 ◺ → ◹	1⅞"	2⅛"	2⅜"	2⅝"	2⅞"	3⅜"
	G: 4 ☐	1½"	1¾"	2"	2¼"	2½"	3"
Try this:	Use one light for A and a different light or a medium for B, C, and D.						

July Fourth

4-Unit Grid
Color Illustration: page 19

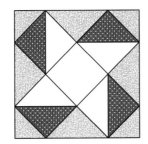 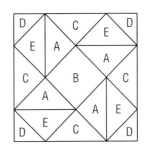 

FOR 1 BLOCK:		FINISHED BLOCK SIZE *Single dimensions in the cutting chart indicate the size of the cut square (3" = 3" x 3").*					
		4"	**6"**	**8"**	**9"**	**10"**	**12"**
Light	A: 1 ⊠ → ⊠	3¼"	4¼"	5¼"	5¾"	6¼"	7¼"
	B: 1 ◇	T7	T11	T14	T15	T16	T19
Medium	C: 1 ⊠ → ⊠	3¼"	4¼"	5¼"	5¾"	6¼"	7¼"
	D: 2 ◻ → ◻	1⅞"	2⅜"	2⅞"	3⅛"	3⅜"	3⅞"
Dark	E: 1 ⊠ → ⊠	3¼"	4¼"	5¼"	5¾"	6¼"	7¼"

Try this: Use a different combination of mediums and darks in every block.

Juneau

8-Unit Grid
Color Illustration: page 19

 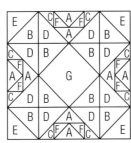 

FOR 1 BLOCK:		FINISHED BLOCK SIZE *Single dimensions in the cutting chart indicate the size of the cut square (3" = 3" x 3").*					
		6"	**8"**	**9"**	**10"**	**12"**	**14"**
Light	A: 2 ⊠ → ⊠	2¾"	3¼"	3½"	3¾"	4¼"	4¾"
	B: 4 ◻ → ◻	2⅜"	2⅞"	3⅛"	3⅜"	3⅞"	4⅜"
	C: 4 ◻ → ◻	1⅝"	1⅞"	2"	2⅛"	2⅜"	2⅝"
Medium	D: 4 ◻ → ◻	2⅜"	2⅞"	3⅛"	3⅜"	3⅞"	4⅜"
Dark	E: 2 ◻ → ◻	2⅜"	2⅞"	3⅛"	3⅜"	3⅞"	4⅜"
	F: 4 ◻ → ◻	1⅝"	1⅞"	2"	2⅛"	2⅜"	2⅝"
	G: 1 ◇	T11	T14	T15	T16	T19	T21

Try this: Reverse the mediums and darks.

KALEIDOSCOPE

12-Unit Grid
Color Illustration: page 19

 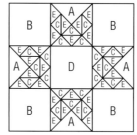 

FOR 1 BLOCK:	FINISHED BLOCK SIZE *Single dimensions in the cutting chart indicate the size of the cut square (3" = 3" x 3").*					
	4½"	**6"**	**7½"**	**9"**	**10½"**	**12"**
Light A: 1 ⊠ → ⊠	2¾"	3¼"	3¾"	4¼"	4¾"	5¼"
B: 4 □	2"	2½"	3"	3½"	4"	4½"
C: 5 ⊠ → ⊠	2"	2¼"	2½"	2¾"	3"	3¼"
Medium D: 1 □	2"	2½"	3"	3½"	4"	4½"
Dark E: 7 ⊠ → ⊠	2"	2¼"	2½"	2¾"	3"	3¼"
Try this:	Use several different lights for C.					

KANSAS STAR

6-Unit Grid
Color Illustration: page 19

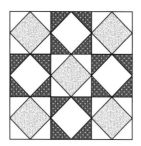 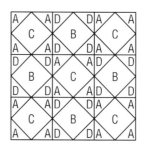 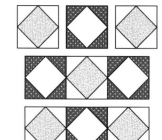

FOR 1 BLOCK:	FINISHED BLOCK SIZE *Single dimensions in the cutting chart indicate the size of the cut square (3" = 3" x 3").*					
	4½"	**6"**	**7½"**	**9"**	**10½"**	**12"**
Light A: 10 □ → ◺	1⅝"	1⅞"	2⅛"	2⅜"	2⅝"	2⅞"
B: 4 ◇	T5	T7	T9	T11	T12	T14
Medium C: 5 ◇	T5	T7	T9	T11	T12	T14
Dark D: 8 □ → ◺	1⅝"	1⅞"	2⅛"	2⅜"	2⅝"	2⅞"
Try this:	Reverse the lights and mediums in every other block.					

KANSAS TROUBLES

6-Unit Grid
Color Illustration: page 19

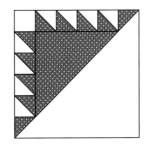
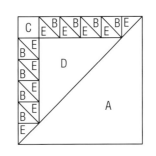
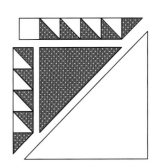

	FINISHED BLOCK SIZE					
	Single dimensions in the cutting chart indicate the size of the cut square (3" = 3" x 3").					
FOR 2 BLOCKS:	**4½"**	**6"**	**7½"**	**9"**	**10½"**	**12"**
Light A: 1 ◻→◹	5⅜"	6⅞"	8⅜"	9⅞"	11⅜"	12⅞"
B: 8 ◻→◹	1⅝"	1⅞"	2⅛"	2⅜"	2⅝"	2⅞"
C: 2 ◻	1¼"	1½"	1¾"	2"	2¼"	2½"
Dark D: 1 ◻→◹	3⅞"	4⅞"	5⅞"	6⅞"	7⅞"	8⅞"
E: 10 ◻→◹	1⅝"	1⅞"	2⅛"	2⅜"	2⅝"	2⅞"

Try this: Use a large-scale print for A.

KENTUCKY CROSSROADS

6-Unit Grid
Color Illustration: page 19

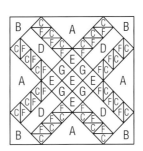

	FINISHED BLOCK SIZE					
	Single dimensions in the cutting chart indicate the size of the cut square (3" = 3" x 3").					
FOR 1 BLOCK:	**4½"**	**6"**	**7½"**	**9"**	**10½"**	**12"**
Light A: 1 ⊠→⊠	3½"	4¼"	5"	5¾"	6½"	7¼"
B: 2 ◻→◹	2"	2⅜"	2¾"	3⅛"	3½"	3⅞"
C: 6 ⊠→⊠	2"	2¼"	2½"	2¾"	3"	3¼"
D: 4 ◇	T29	T33	T37	T42	T47	T52
E: 5 ◇	T1	T2	T4	T5	T6	T7
Dark F: 6 ⊠→⊠	2"	2¼"	2½"	2¾"	3"	3¼"
G: 4 ◇	T1	T2	T4	T5	T6	T7

Try this: Use several different darks for F.

Light   Light 2   Medium   Medium 2   Dark

KING'S CROWN

4-Unit Grid

Color Illustration: page 19

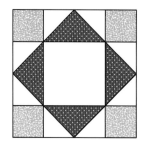

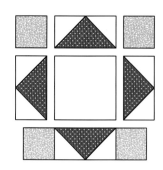

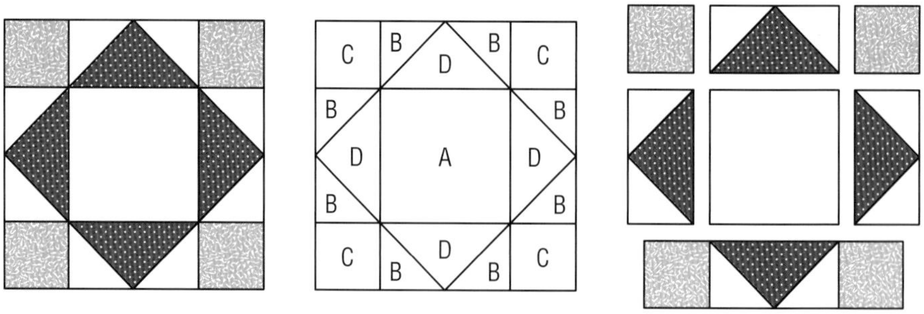

FOR 1 BLOCK:		**FINISHED BLOCK SIZE** *Single dimensions in the cutting chart indicate the size of the cut square (3" = 3" x 3").*					
		4"	**6"**	**8"**	**9"**	**10"**	**12"**
Light	A: 1 ☐	2½"	3½"	4½"	5"	5½"	6½"
	B: 4 ◺ → ◹	1⅞"	2⅜"	2⅞"	3⅛"	3⅜"	3⅞"
Medium	C: 4 ☐	1½"	2"	2½"	2¾"	3"	3½"
Dark	D: 1 ⊠ → ⊠	3¼"	4¼"	5¼"	5¾"	6¼"	7¼"

Try this: Reverse the mediums and darks in every other block.

KING'S CROWN II

5-Unit Grid

Color Illustration: page 19

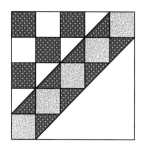

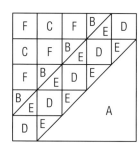

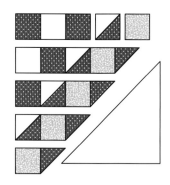

FOR 2 BLOCKS:		**FINISHED BLOCK SIZE** *Single dimensions in the cutting chart indicate the size of the cut square (3" = 3" x 3").*					
		5"	**6¼"**	**7½"**	**8¾"**	**10"**	**12½"**
Light	A: 1 ◺ → ◹	4⅞"	5⅞"	6⅞"	7⅞"	8⅞"	10⅞"
	B: 4 ◺ → ◹	1⅞"	2⅛"	2⅜"	2⅝"	2⅞"	3⅜"
	C: 4 ☐	1½"	1¾"	2"	2¼"	2½"	3"
Medium	D: 10 ☐	1½"	1¾"	2"	2¼"	2½"	3"
Dark	E: 8 ◺ → ◹	1⅞"	2⅛"	2⅜"	2⅝"	2⅞"	3⅜"
	F: 8 ☐	1½"	1¾"	2"	2¼"	2½"	3"

Try this: Use a large-scale print for A.

☐ Light ☐ Light 2 ☐ Medium ☐ Medium 2 ☐ Dark

Ladies' Aid Album

6-Unit Grid
Color Illustration: page 19

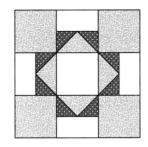 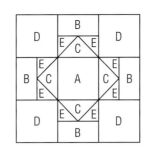 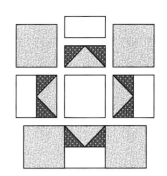

FOR 1 BLOCK:	FINISHED BLOCK SIZE Single dimensions in the cutting chart indicate the size of the cut square (3" = 3" x 3").					
	4½"	6"	7½"	9"	10½"	12"
Light A: 1 ☐	2"	2½"	3"	3½"	4"	4½"
B: 4 ▭	1¼" x 2"	1½" x 2½"	1¾" x 3"	2" x 3½"	2¼" x 4"	2½" x 4½"
Medium C: 1 ⊠ → ⊠	2¾"	3¼"	3¾"	4¼"	4¾"	5¼"
D: 4 ☐	2"	2½"	3"	3½"	4"	4½"
Dark E: 4 ◺ → ◺	1⅝"	1⅞"	2⅛"	2⅜"	2⅝"	2⅞"

Try this: Reverse the mediums and darks.

Ladies' Aid Block

6-Unit Grid
Color Illustration: page 19

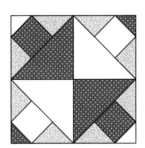 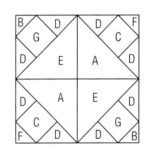 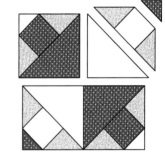

FOR 1 BLOCK:	FINISHED BLOCK SIZE Single dimensions in the cutting chart indicate the size of the cut square (3" = 3" x 3").					
	4½"	6"	7½"	9"	10½"	12"
Light A: 1 ◺ → ◺	3⅛"	3⅞"	4⅝"	5⅜"	6⅛"	6⅞"
B: 1 ◺ → ◺	1⅝"	1⅞"	2⅛"	2⅜"	2⅝"	2⅞"
C: 2 ◇	T5	T7	T9	T11	T12	T14
Medium D: 2 ⊠ → ⊠	2¾"	3¼"	3¾"	4¼"	4¾"	5¼"
Dark E: 1 ◺ → ◺	3⅛"	3⅞"	4⅝"	5⅜"	6⅛"	6⅞"
F: 1 ◺ → ◺	1⅝"	1⅞"	2⅛"	2⅜"	2⅝"	2⅞"
G: 2 ◇	T5	T7	T9	T11	T12	T14

Try this: Use a different combination of lights, mediums and darks in each quadrant of the block.

LADIES' WREATH

4-Unit Grid
Color Illustration: page 19

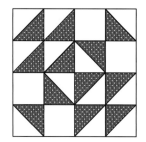
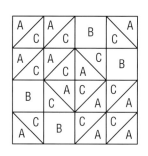
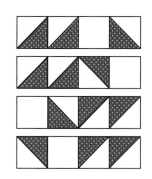

FOR 1 BLOCK:		**FINISHED BLOCK SIZE** *Single dimensions in the cutting chart indicate the size of the cut square (3" = 3" x 3").*					
		4"	**6"**	**8"**	**9"**	**10"**	**12"**
Light	A: 6 ◻→◲	1⅞"	2⅜"	2⅞"	3⅛"	3⅜"	3⅞"
	B: 4 ◻	1½"	2"	2½"	2¾"	3"	3½"
Dark	C: 6 ◻→◲	1⅞"	2⅜"	2⅞"	3⅛"	3⅜"	3⅞"
Try this:	Use several different darks for C.						

LADY OF THE LAKE

5-Unit Grid
Color Illustration: page 19

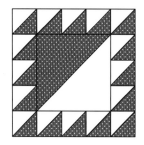
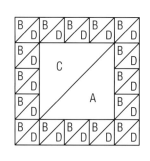
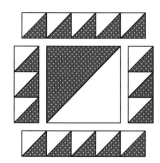

FOR 2 BLOCKS:		**FINISHED BLOCK SIZE** *Single dimensions in the cutting chart indicate the size of the cut square (3" = 3" x 3").*					
		5"	**6¼"**	**7½"**	**8¾"**	**10"**	**12½"**
Light	A: 1 ◻→◲	3⅞"	4⅝"	5⅜"	6⅛"	6⅞"	8⅜"
	B: 16 ◻→◲	1⅞"	2⅛"	2⅜"	2⅝"	2⅞"	3⅜"
Dark	C: 1 ◻→◲	3⅞"	4⅝"	5⅜"	6⅛"	6⅞"	8⅜"
	D: 16 ◻→◲	1⅞"	2⅛"	2⅜"	2⅝"	2⅞"	3⅜"
Try this:	Use several different darks for D.						

LAWYER'S PUZZLE

8-Unit Grid
Color Illustration: page 19

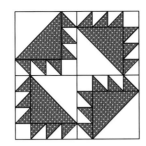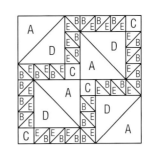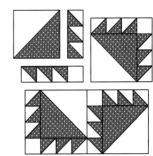

	FINISHED BLOCK SIZE					
	Single dimensions in the cutting chart indicate the size of the cut square (3" = 3" x 3").					
FOR 1 BLOCK:	**6"**	**8"**	**9"**	**10"**	**12"**	**14"**
Light A: 2 ☐→◩	3⅛"	3⅞"	4¼"	4⅝"	5⅜"	6⅛"
B: 12 ☐→◩	1⅝"	1⅞"	2"	2⅛"	2⅜"	2⅝"
C: 4 ☐	1¼"	1½"	1⅝"	1¾"	2"	2¼"
Dark D: 2 ☐→◩	3⅛"	3⅞"	4¼"	4⅝"	5⅜"	6⅛"
E: 12 ☐→◩	1⅝"	1⅞"	2"	2⅛"	2⅜"	2⅝"

Try this: Use a large-scale print for D.

THE LETTER X

3-Unit Grid
Color Illustration: page 19

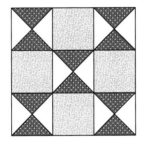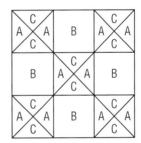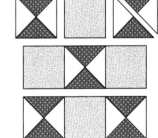

	FINISHED BLOCK SIZE					
	Single dimensions in the cutting chart indicate the size of the cut square (3" = 3" x 3").					
FOR 2 BLOCKS:	**4½"**	**6"**	**7½"**	**9"**	**10½"**	**12"**
Light A: 5 ⊠→⧅	2¾"	3¼"	3¾"	4¼"	4¾"	5¼"
Medium B: 8 ☐	2"	2½"	3"	3½"	4"	4½"
Dark C: 5 ⊠→⧅	2¾"	3¼"	3¾"	4¼"	4¾"	5¼"

Try this: Reverse the mediums and darks in every other block.

☐ *Light*	▦ *Light 2*	▥ *Medium*	▤ *Medium 2*	■ *Dark*

LIGHT AND SHADOWS

4-Unit Grid
Color Illustration: page 19

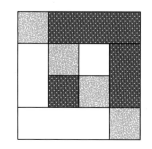

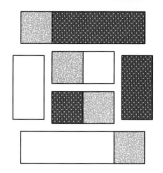

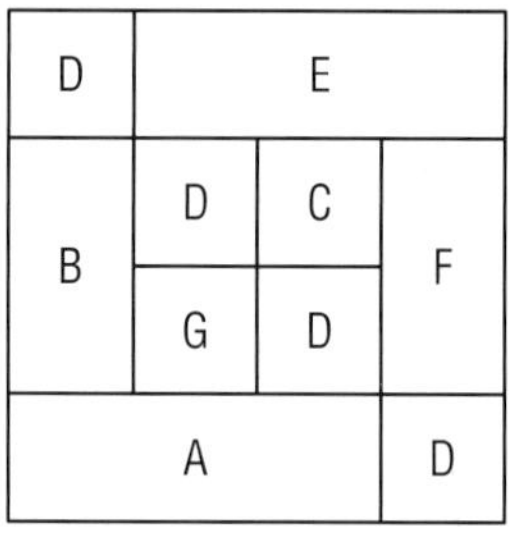

		FINISHED BLOCK SIZE					
		Single dimensions in the cutting chart indicate the size of the cut square (3" = 3" x 3").					
FOR 1 BLOCK:		**4"**	**6"**	**8"**	**9"**	**10"**	**12"**
Light	A: 1 ▭	1½" x 3½"	2" x 5"	2½" x 6½"	2¾" x 7¼"	3" x 8"	3½" x 9½"
	B: 1 ▭	1½" x 2½"	2" x 3½"	2½" x 4½"	2¾" x 5"	3" x 5½"	3½" x 6½"
	C: 1 ☐	1½"	2"	2½"	2¾"	3"	3½"
Medium	D: 4 ☐	1½"	2"	2½"	2¾"	3"	3½"
Dark	E: 1 ▭	1½" x 3½"	2" x 5"	2½" x 6½"	2¾" x 7¼"	3" x 8"	3½" x 9½"
	F: 1 ▭	1½" x 2½"	2" x 3½"	2½" x 4½"	2¾" x 5"	3" x 5½"	3½" x 6½"
	G: 1 ☐	1½"	2"	2½"	2¾"	3"	3½"

Try this: Use a different combination of lights and darks in every block.

LIGHTHOUSE

10-Unit Grid
Color Illustration: page 19

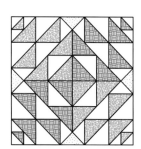

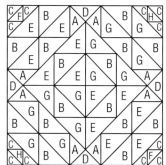

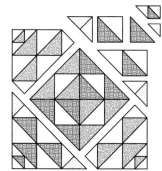

		FINISHED BLOCK SIZE					
		Single dimensions in the cutting chart indicate the size of the cut square (3" = 3" x 3").					
FOR 1 BLOCK:		**6¼"**	**7½"**	**8¾"**	**10"**	**12½"**	**13¾"**
Light	A: 2 ⊠ → ⊠	2½"	2¾"	3"	3¼"	3¾"	4"
	B: 8 ◨ → ◺	2⅛"	2⅜"	2⅝"	2⅞"	3⅜"	3⅝"
	C: 6 ◨ → ◺	1½"	1⅝"	1¾"	1⅞"	2⅛"	2¼"
Light 2	D: 1 ⊠ → ⊠	2½"	2¾"	3"	3¼"	3¾"	4"
Medium	E: 6 ◨ → ◺	2⅛"	2⅜"	2⅝"	2⅞"	3⅜"	3⅝"
	F: 1 ◨ → ◺	1½"	1⅝"	1¾"	1⅞"	2⅛"	2¼"
Medium 2	G: 6 ◨ → ◺	2⅛"	2⅜"	2⅝"	2⅞"	3⅜"	3⅝"
	H: 1 ◨ → ◺	1½"	1⅝"	1¾"	1⅞"	2⅛"	2¼"

Try this: Use a dark instead of medium 2 for G and H.

LINCOLN

5-Unit Grid

Color Illustration: page 19

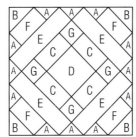

FOR 1 BLOCK:		FINISHED BLOCK SIZE *Single dimensions in the cutting chart indicate the size of the cut square (3" = 3" x 3").*					
		5"	**6¼"**	**7½"**	**8¾"**	**10"**	**12½"**
Light	A: 3 ⊠ → ⊠	2¼"	2½"	2¾"	3"	3¼"	3¾"
	B: 2 ⧄ → ⧄	1⅞"	2⅛"	2⅜"	2⅝"	2⅞"	3⅜"
	C: 4 ▱	T32	T36	T41	T46	T51	T59
Dark	D: 1 ◇	T7	T9	T11	T12	T14	T16
	E: 4 ▱	T34	T38	T43	T48	T53	T61
	F: 4 ▱	T32	T36	T41	T46	T51	T59
	G: 4 ◇	T2	T4	T5	T6	T7	T9
Try this:	Use a light and a medium instead of a light and a dark in every other block.						

LINCOLN'S PLATFORM

7-Unit Grid

Color Illustration: page 20

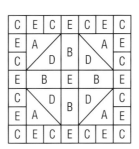

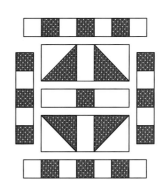

FOR 1 BLOCK:		FINISHED BLOCK SIZE *Single dimensions in the cutting chart indicate the size of the cut square (3" = 3" x 3").*					
		5¼"	**7"**	**8¾"**	**10½"**	**12¼"**	**14"**
Light	A: 2 ⧄ → ⧄	2⅜"	2⅞"	3⅜"	3⅞"	4⅜"	4⅞"
	B: 4 ▭	1¼" x 2"	1½" x 2½"	1¾" x 3"	2" x 3½"	2¼" x 4"	2½" x 4½"
	C: 12 □	1¼"	1½"	1¾"	2"	2¼"	2½"
Dark	D: 2 ⧄ → ⧄	2⅜"	2⅞"	3⅜"	3⅞"	4⅜"	4⅞"
	E: 13 □	1¼"	1½"	1¾"	2"	2¼"	2½"
Try this:	Use one dark for D and a different dark for E.						

Light *Light 2* *Medium* *Medium 2* *Dark*

LOIS' STAR

11-Unit Grid

Color Illustration: page 20

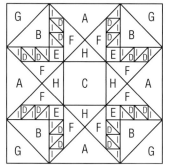

FOR 1 BLOCK:		FINISHED BLOCK SIZE *Single dimensions in the cutting chart indicate the size of the cut square (3" = 3" x 3").*					
		6⅞"	8¼"	9⅝"	11"	12⅜"	15⅛"
Light	A: 1 ⊠ → ⊠	4⅜"	5"	5⅝"	6¼"	6⅞"	8⅛"
	B: 2 ◺ → ◺	2¾"	3⅛"	3½"	3⅞"	4¼"	5"
	C: 1 ▢	2⅜"	2¾"	3⅛"	3½"	3⅞"	4⅝"
	D: 8 ◺ → ◺	1½"	1⅝"	1¾"	1⅞"	2"	2¼"
	E: 4 ▢	1⅛"	1¼"	1⅜"	1½"	1⅝"	1⅞"
Medium	F: 2 ⊠ → ⊠	3⅛"	3½"	3⅞"	4¼"	4⅝"	5⅜"
	G: 2 ◺ → ◺	2¾"	3⅛"	3½"	3⅞"	4¼"	5"
Dark	H: 1 ⊠ → ⊠	3⅛"	3½"	3⅞"	4¼"	4⅝"	5⅜"
	I: 12 ◺ → ◺	1½"	1⅝"	1¾"	1⅞"	2"	2¼"

Try this: Use a different medium in every block.

LOLA

4-Unit Grid

Color Illustration: page 20

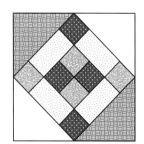
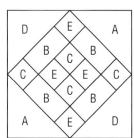
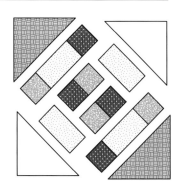

FOR 1 BLOCK:		FINISHED BLOCK SIZE *Single dimensions in the cutting chart indicate the size of the cut square (3" = 3" x 3").*					
		4"	6"	8"	9"	10"	12"
Light	A: 1 ◺ → ◺	2⅞"	3⅞"	4⅞"	5⅜"	5⅞"	6⅞"
Light 2	B: 4 ◇	T32	T41	T51	T56	T59	T67
Medium	C: 4 ◇	T2	T5	T7	T8	T9	T11
Medium 2	D: 1 ◺ → ◺	2⅞"	3⅞"	4⅞"	5⅜"	5⅞"	6⅞"
Dark	E: 4 ◇	T2	T5	T7	T8	T9	T11

Try this: Use different fabrics for A and D in every block.

LONDON ROADS

9-Unit Grid

Color Illustration: page 20

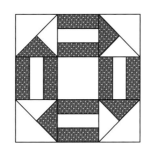
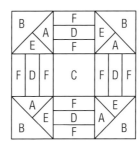

		FINISHED BLOCK SIZE					
		Single dimensions in the cutting chart indicate the size of the cut square (3" = 3" x 3").					
FOR 1 BLOCK:		**6¾"**	**9"**	**10⅛"**	**11¼"**	**12⅜"**	**13½"**
Light	A: 1 ⊠→⊠	3½"	4¼"	4⅝"	5"	5⅜"	5¾"
	B: 2 ◻→◹	3⅛"	3⅞"	4¼"	4⅝"	5"	5⅜"
	C: 1 ☐	2¾"	3½"	3⅞"	4¼"	4⅝"	5"
	D: 4 ▭	1¼" x 2¾"	1½" x 3½"	1⅝" x 3⅞"	1¾" x 4¼"	1⅞" x 4⅝"	2" x 5"
Dark	E: 1 ⊠→⊠	3½"	4¼"	4⅝"	5"	5⅜"	5¾"
	F: 8 ▭	1¼" x 2¾"	1½" x 3½"	1⅝" x 3⅞"	1¾" x 4¼"	1⅞" x 4⅝"	2" x 5"

Try this: Reverse the lights and darks in every other block.

LONDON SQUARE

6-Unit Grid

Color Illustration: page 20

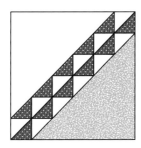
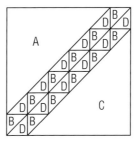
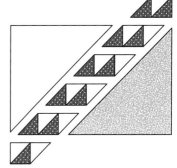

		FINISHED BLOCK SIZE					
		Single dimensions in the cutting chart indicate the size of the cut square (3" = 3" x 3").					
FOR 2 BLOCKS:		**4½"**	**6"**	**7½"**	**9"**	**10½"**	**12"**
Light	A: 1 ◻→◹	4⅝"	5⅞"	7⅛"	8⅜"	9⅝"	10⅞"
	B: 11 ◻→◹	1⅝"	1⅞"	2⅛"	2⅜"	2⅝"	2⅞"
Medium	C: 1 ◻→◹	4⅝"	5⅞"	7⅛"	8⅜"	9⅝"	10⅞"
Dark	D: 11 ◻→◹	1⅝"	1⅞"	2⅛"	2⅜"	2⅝"	2⅞"

Try this: Use a large-scale print for C.

Lost Ship

6-Unit Grid
Color Illustration: page 20

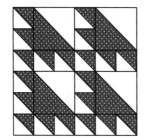
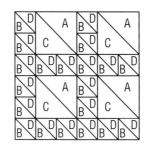
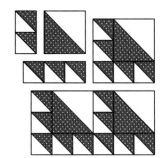

FOR 1 BLOCK:		FINISHED BLOCK SIZE *Single dimensions in the cutting chart indicate the size of the cut square (3" = 3" x 3").*					
		4½"	**6"**	**7½"**	**9"**	**10½"**	**12"**
Light	A: 2 ◻→◹	2⅜"	2⅞"	3⅜"	3⅞"	4⅜"	4⅞"
	B: 10 ◻→◹	1⅝"	1⅞"	2⅛"	2⅜"	2⅝"	2⅞"
Dark	C: 2 ◻→◹	2⅜"	2⅞"	3⅜"	3⅞"	4⅜"	4⅞"
	D: 10 ◻→◹	1⅝"	1⅞"	2⅛"	2⅜"	2⅝"	2⅞"

Try this: Use several different darks for D.

Louisiana

4-Unit Grid
Color Illustration: page 20

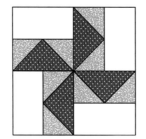
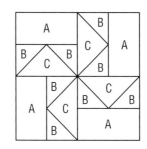
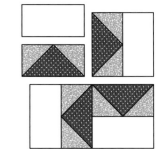

FOR 1 BLOCK:		FINISHED BLOCK SIZE *Single dimensions in the cutting chart indicate the size of the cut square (3" = 3" x 3").*					
		4"	**6"**	**8"**	**9"**	**10"**	**12"**
Light	A: 4 ▭	1½" x 2½"	2" x 3½"	2½" x 4½"	2¾" x 5"	3" x 5½"	3½" x 6½"
Medium	B: 4 ◻→◹	1⅞"	2⅜"	2⅞"	3⅛"	3⅜"	3⅞"
Dark	C: 1 ⊠→⧅	3¼"	4¼"	5¼"	5¾"	6¼"	7¼"

Try this: Reverse the lights and mediums.

LOVER'S LANE

6-Unit Grid
Color Illustration: page 20

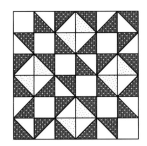
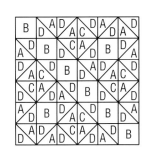
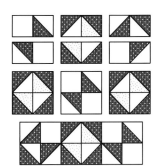

FOR 1 BLOCK:		FINISHED BLOCK SIZE Single dimensions in the cutting chart indicate the size of the cut square (3" = 3" x 3").					
		4½"	**6"**	**7½"**	**9"**	**10½"**	**12"**
Light	A: 10 ◻→◪	1⅝"	1⅞"	2⅛"	2⅜"	2⅝"	2⅞"
	B: 8 ◻	1¼"	1½"	1¾"	2"	2¼"	2½"
Light 2	C: 4 ◻→◪	1⅝"	1⅞"	2⅛"	2⅜"	2⅝"	2⅞"
Dark	D: 14 ◻→◪	1⅝"	1⅞"	2⅛"	2⅜"	2⅝"	2⅞"

Try this: Use a medium instead of a light for B.

MAGIC CROSS

4-Unit Grid
Color Illustration: page 20

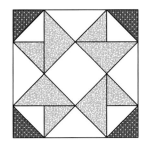
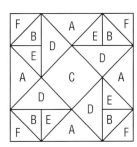

FOR 1 BLOCK:		FINISHED BLOCK SIZE Single dimensions in the cutting chart indicate the size of the cut square (3" = 3" x 3").					
		4"	**6"**	**8"**	**9"**	**10"**	**12"**
Light	A: 1 ⊠→⊠	3¼"	4¼"	5¼"	5¾"	6¼"	7¼"
	B: 2 ◻→◪	1⅞"	2⅜"	2⅞"	3⅛"	3⅜"	3⅞"
	C: 1 ◇	T7	T11	T14	T15	T16	T19
Medium	D: 1 ⊠→⊠	3¼"	4¼"	5¼"	5¾"	6¼"	7¼"
	E: 2 ◻→◪	1⅞"	2⅜"	2⅞"	3⅛"	3⅜"	3⅞"
Dark	F: 2 ◻→◪	1⅞"	2⅜"	2⅞"	3⅛"	3⅜"	3⅞"

Try this: Reverse the mediums and darks.

☐ *Light* ☐ *Light 2* ☐ *Medium* ☐ *Medium 2* ☐ *Dark*

MAGIC TRIANGLES

4-Unit Grid

Color Illustration: page 20

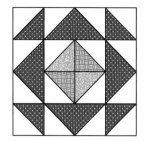 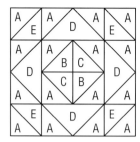 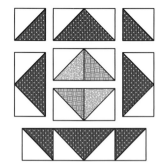

		FINISHED BLOCK SIZE *Single dimensions in the cutting chart indicate the size of the cut square (3" = 3" x 3").*					
FOR 1 BLOCK:		**4"**	**6"**	**8"**	**9"**	**10"**	**12"**
Light	A: 8 ◻→◺	1⅞"	2⅜"	2⅞"	3⅛"	3⅜"	3⅞"
Medium	B: 1 ◻→◺	1⅞"	2⅜"	2⅞"	3⅛"	3⅜"	3⅞"
Medium 2	C: 1 ◻→◺	1⅞"	2⅜"	2⅞"	3⅛"	3⅜"	3⅞"
Dark	D: 1 ⊠→⊠	3¼"	4¼"	5¼"	5¾"	6¼"	7¼"
	E: 2 ◻→◺	1⅞"	2⅜"	2⅞"	3⅛"	3⅜"	3⅞"
Try this:	Use one dark for D and a different dark for E.						

MALVINA'S CHAIN

3-Unit Grid

Color Illustration: page 20

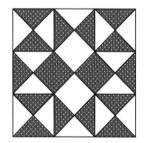 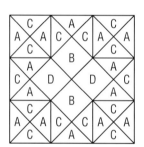 

		FINISHED BLOCK SIZE *Single dimensions in the cutting chart indicate the size of the cut square (3" = 3" x 3").*					
FOR 2 BLOCKS:		**4½"**	**6"**	**7½"**	**9"**	**10½"**	**12"**
Light	A: 7 ⊠→⊠	2¾"	3¼"	3¾"	4¼"	4¾"	5¼"
	B: 4 ◇	T5	T7	T9	T11	T12	T14
Dark	C: 7 ⊠→⊠	2¾"	3¼"	3¾"	4¼"	4¾"	5¼"
	D: 4 ◇	T5	T7	T9	T11	T12	T14
Try this:	Reverse the lights and darks in every other block.						

MAPLE STAR

6-Unit Grid
Color Illustration: page 20

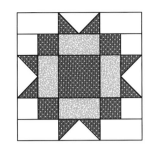
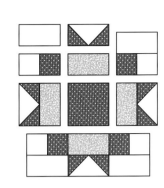

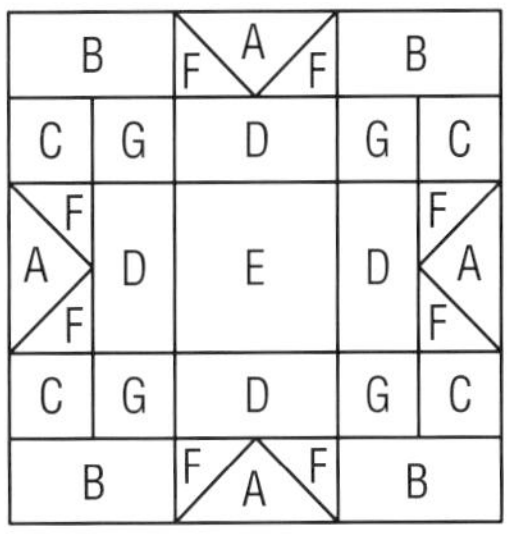

FINISHED BLOCK SIZE						
Single dimensions in the cutting chart indicate the size of the cut square (3" = 3" x 3").						
FOR 1 BLOCK:	**4½"**	**6"**	**7½"**	**9"**	**10½"**	**12"**
Light A: 1 ⊠→⊠	2¾"	3¼"	3¾"	4¼"	4¾"	5¼"
B: 4 ▭	1¼" x 2"	1½" x 2½"	1¾" x 3"	2" x 3½"	2¼" x 4"	2½" x 4½"
C: 4 □	1¼"	1½"	1¾"	2"	2¼"	2½"
Medium D: 4 ▭	1¼" x 2"	1½" x 2½"	1¾" x 3"	2" x 3½"	2¼" x 4"	2½" x 4½"
Dark E: 1 □	2"	2½"	3"	3½"	4"	4½"
F: 4 ◹→◺	1⅝"	1⅞"	2⅛"	2⅜"	2⅝"	2⅞"
G: 4 □	1¼"	1½"	1¾"	2"	2¼"	2½"

Try this: Reverse the lights and mediums in every other block.

MARGARET'S CHOICE

4-Unit Grid
Color Illustration: page 20

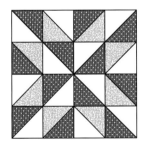
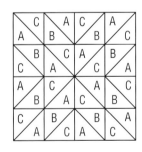
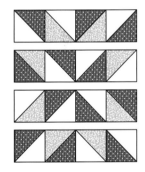

FINISHED BLOCK SIZE						
Single dimensions in the cutting chart indicate the size of the cut square (3" = 3" x 3").						
FOR 1 BLOCK:	**4"**	**6"**	**8"**	**9"**	**10"**	**12"**
Light A: 6 ◹→◺	1⅞"	2⅜"	2⅞"	3⅛"	3⅜"	3⅞"
Medium B: 4 ◹→◺	1⅞"	2⅜"	2⅞"	3⅛"	3⅜"	3⅞"
Dark C: 6 ◹→◺	1⅞"	2⅜"	2⅞"	3⅛"	3⅜"	3⅞"

Try this: Use several different darks for C.

MARTHA WASHINGTON STAR

4-Unit Grid

Color Illustration: page 20

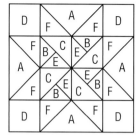
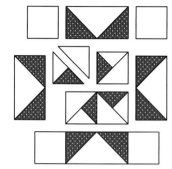

		FINISHED BLOCK SIZE *Single dimensions in the cutting chart indicate the size of the cut square (3" = 3" x 3").*					
FOR 1 BLOCK:		**4"**	**6"**	**8"**	**9"**	**10"**	**12"**
Light	A: 1 ⊠→⊠	3¼"	4¼"	5¼"	5¾"	6¼"	7¼"
	B: 1 ⊠→⊠	2¼"	2¾"	3¼"	3½"	3¾"	4¼"
	C: 2 ◻→◻	1⅞"	2⅜"	2⅞"	3⅛"	3⅜"	3⅞"
	D: 4 ◻	1½"	2"	2½"	2¾"	3"	3½"
Dark	E: 1 ⊠→⊠	2¼"	2¾"	3¼"	3½"	3¾"	4¼"
	F: 4 ◻→◻	1⅞"	2⅜"	2⅞"	3⅛"	3⅜"	3⅞"

Try this: Use a medium instead of a light for B and C.

MARYLAND BEAUTY

10-Unit Grid

Color Illustration: page 20

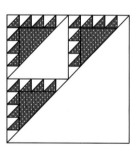
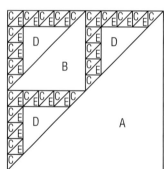
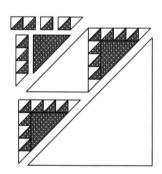

		FINISHED BLOCK SIZE *Single dimensions in the cutting chart indicate the size of the cut square (3" = 3" x 3").*					
FOR 2 BLOCKS:		**6¼"**	**7½"**	**8¾"**	**10"**	**12½"**	**13¾"**
Light	A: 1 ◻→◻	7⅛"	8⅜"	9⅝"	10⅞"	13⅜"	14⅝"
	B: 1 ◻→◻	4"	4⅝"	5¼"	5⅞"	7⅛"	7¾"
	C: 27 ◻→◻	1½"	1⅝"	1¾"	1⅞"	2⅛"	2¼"
Dark	D: 3 ◻→◻	2¾"	3⅛"	3½"	3⅞"	4⅝"	5"
	E: 21 ◻→◻	1½"	1⅝"	1¾"	1⅞"	2⅛"	2¼"

Try this: Use a large-scale medium print instead of a light for A.

MAY BASKET

5-Unit Grid

Color Illustration: page 20

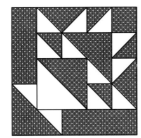
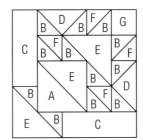
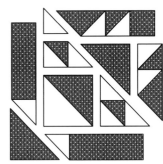

			FINISHED BLOCK SIZE *Single dimensions in the cutting chart indicate the size of the cut square (3" = 3" x 3").*					
FOR 2 BLOCKS:			**5"**	**6¼"**	**7½"**	**8¾"**	**10"**	**12½"**
Light	A: 1 ◻→◻		2⅞"	3⅜"	3⅞"	4⅜"	4⅞"	5⅞"
	B: 12 ◻→◻		1⅞"	2⅛"	2⅜"	2⅝"	2⅞"	3⅜"
Dark	C: 4 ▭		1½" x 3½"	1¾" x 4¼"	2" x 5"	2¼" x 5¾"	2½" x 6½"	3" x 8"
	D: 1 ⊠→⊠		3¼"	3¾"	4¼"	4¾"	5¼"	6¼"
	E: 3 ◻→◻		2⅞"	3⅜"	3⅞"	4⅜"	4⅞"	5⅞"
	F: 4 ◻→◻		1⅞"	2⅛"	2⅜"	2⅝"	2⅞"	3⅜"
	G: 2 ◻		1½"	1¾"	2"	2¼"	2½"	3"

Try this: Reverse the lights and darks.

MEMORY

6-Unit Grid

Color Illustration: page 20

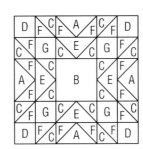

			FINISHED BLOCK SIZE *Single dimensions in the cutting chart indicate the size of the cut square (3" = 3" x 3").*					
FOR 1 BLOCK:			**4½"**	**6"**	**7½"**	**9"**	**10½"**	**12"**
Light	A: 1 ⊠→⊠		2¾"	3¼"	3¾"	4¼"	4¾"	5¼"
	B: 1 ◻		2"	2½"	3"	3½"	4"	4½"
	C: 8 ◻→◻		1⅝"	1⅞"	2⅛"	2⅜"	2⅝"	2⅞"
	D: 4 ◻		1¼"	1½"	1¾"	2"	2¼"	2½"
Dark	E: 1 ⊠→⊠		2¾"	3¼"	3¾"	4¼"	4¾"	5¼"
	F: 8 ◻→◻		1⅝"	1⅞"	2⅛"	2⅜"	2⅝"	2⅞"
	G: 4 ◻		1¼"	1½"	1¾"	2"	2¼"	2½"

Try this: Use a medium instead of a light for B.

MEMORY BLOCKS

10-Unit Grid
Color Illustration: page 20

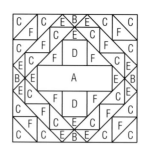

		FINISHED BLOCK SIZE *Single dimensions in the cutting chart indicate the size of the cut square (3" = 3" x 3").*					
FOR 1 BLOCK:		**5"**	**6¼"**	**7½"**	**8¾"**	**10"**	**12½"**
Light	A: 1 ▭	1½" x 3½"	1¾" x 4¼"	2" x 5"	2¼" x 5¾"	2½" x 6½"	3" x 8"
	B: 1 ⊠ → ⊠	2¼"	2½"	2¾"	3"	3¼"	3¾"
	C: 10 ◻ → ◹	1⅞"	2⅛"	2⅜"	2⅝"	2⅞"	3⅜"
	D: 2 ▢	1½"	1¾"	2"	2¼"	2½"	3"
Dark	E: 3 ⊠ → ⊠	2¼"	2½"	2¾"	3"	3¼"	3¾"
	F: 6 ◻ → ◹	1⅞"	2⅛"	2⅜"	2⅝"	2⅞"	3⅜"

Try this: Use an autographed rectangle for A.

MEMORY BLOCKS II

4-Unit Grid
Color Illustration: page 20

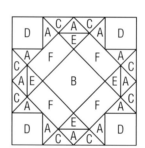

		FINISHED BLOCK SIZE *Single dimensions in the cutting chart indicate the size of the cut square (3" = 3" x 3").*					
FOR 1 BLOCK:		**4"**	**6"**	**8"**	**9"**	**10"**	**12"**
Light	A: 3 ⊠ → ⊠	2¼"	2¾"	3¼"	3½"	3¾"	4¼"
	B: 1 ◇	T7	T11	T14	T15	T16	T19
Medium	C: 2 ⊠ → ⊠	2¼"	2¾"	3¼"	3½"	3¾"	4¼"
	D: 4 ▢	1½"	2"	2½"	2¾"	3"	3½"
Dark	E: 1 ⊠ → ⊠	2¼"	2¾"	3¼"	3½"	3¾"	4¼"
	F: 4 ◇	T32	T41	T51	T56	T59	T67

Try this: Use a medium- or large-scale print for B.

MERRY GO ROUND

8-Unit Grid
Color Illustration: page 20

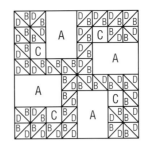
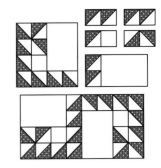

		FINISHED BLOCK SIZE *Single dimensions in the cutting chart indicate the size of the cut square (3" = 3" x 3").*					
FOR 1 BLOCK:		**6"**	**8"**	**9"**	**10"**	**12"**	**14"**
Light	A: 4 ▭	2" x 2¾"	2½" x 3½"	2¾" x 3⅞"	3" x 4¼"	3½" x 5"	4" x 5¾"
	B: 18 ◱→◩	1⅝"	1⅞"	2"	2⅛"	2⅜"	2⅝"
	C: 4 ▢	1¼"	1½"	1⅝"	1¾"	2"	2¼"
Dark	D: 18 ◱→◩	1⅝"	1⅞"	2"	2⅛"	2⅜"	2⅝"

Try this: Use many different darks for D.

MILKY WAY

8-Unit Grid
Color Illustration: page 20

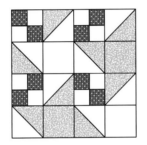
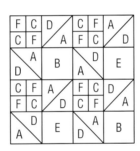
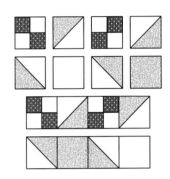

		FINISHED BLOCK SIZE *Single dimensions in the cutting chart indicate the size of the cut square (3" = 3" x 3").*					
FOR 1 BLOCK:		**6"**	**8"**	**9"**	**10"**	**12"**	**14"**
Light	A: 4 ◱→◩	2⅜"	2⅞"	3⅛"	3⅜"	3⅞"	4⅜"
	B: 2 ▢	2"	2½"	2¾"	3"	3½"	4"
	C: 8 ▢	1¼"	1½"	1⅝"	1¾"	2"	2¼"
Medium	D: 4 ◱→◩	2⅜"	2⅞"	3⅛"	3⅜"	3⅞"	4⅜"
	E: 2 ▢	2"	2½"	2¾"	3"	3½"	4"
Dark	F: 8 ▢	1¼"	1½"	1⅝"	1¾"	2"	2¼"

Try this: Use several different lights for A and several different mediums for D.

MILL WHEEL

4-Unit Grid

Color Illustration: page 20

 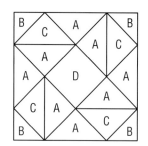 

FOR 1 BLOCK:		FINISHED BLOCK SIZE					
		Single dimensions in the cutting chart indicate the size of the cut square (3" = 3" x 3").					
		4"	6"	8"	9"	10"	12"
Light	A: 2 ⊠ → ⊠	3¼"	4¼"	5¼"	5¾"	6¼"	7¼"
	B: 2 ◺ → ◺	1⅞"	2⅜"	2⅞"	3⅛"	3⅜"	3⅞"
Dark	C: 1 ⊠ → ⊠	3¼"	4¼"	5¼"	5¾"	6¼"	7¼"
	D: 1 ◇	T7	T11	T14	T15	T16	T19

Try this: Use a medium instead of a light for the four A pieces that are part of the "wheel."

MILLENNIUM

12-Unit Grid

Color Illustration: page 20

 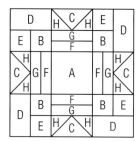 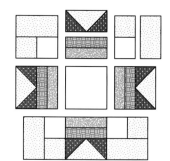

FOR 1 BLOCK:		FINISHED BLOCK SIZE					
		Single dimensions in the cutting chart indicate the size of the cut square (3" = 3" x 3").					
		6"	7½"	9"	12"	13½"	15"
Light	A: 1 ☐	2½"	3"	3½"	4½"	5"	5½"
	B: 4 ☐	1½"	1¾"	2"	2½"	2¾"	3"
Light 2	C: 1 ⊠ → ⊠	3¼"	3¾"	4¼"	5¼"	5¾"	6¼"
	D: 4 ▭	1½" x 2½"	1¾" x 3"	2" x 3½"	2½" x 4½"	2¾" x 5"	3" x 5½"
	E: 4 ☐	1½"	1¾"	2"	2½"	2¾"	3"
Medium	F: 4 ▭	1" x 2½"	1⅛" x 3"	1¼" x 3½"	1½" x 4½"	1⅝" x 5"	1¾" x 5½"
Medium 2	G: 4 ▭	1" x 2½"	1⅛" x 3"	1¼" x 3½"	1½" x 4½"	1⅝" x 5"	1¾" x 5½"
Dark	H: 4 ◺ → ◺	1⅞"	2⅛"	2⅜"	2⅞"	3⅛"	3⅜"

Try this: Reverse the light and light 2 in every other block.

MINERAL WELLS

8-Unit Grid

Color Illustration: page 20

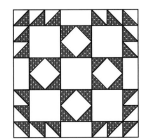 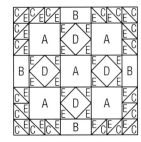 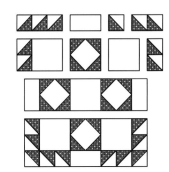

FOR 1 BLOCK:		**FINISHED BLOCK SIZE** *Single dimensions in the cutting chart indicate the size of the cut square (3" = 3" x 3").*					
		6"	**8"**	**9"**	**10"**	**12"**	**14"**
Light	A: 5 ▢	2"	2½"	2¾"	3"	3½"	4"
	B: 4 ▭	1¼" x 2"	1½" x 2½"	1⅝" x 2¾"	1¾" x 3"	2" x 3½"	2¼" x 4"
	C: 10 ◹ → ◺	1⅝"	1⅞"	2"	2⅛"	2⅜"	2⅝"
	D: 4 ◇	T5	T7	T8	T9	T11	T12
Dark	E: 18 ◹ → ◺	1⅝"	1⅞"	2"	2⅛"	2⅜"	2⅝"

Try this: Use one light for A and B and a different light for C and D.

MINNESOTA

5-Unit Grid

Color Illustration: page 20

 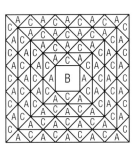 

FOR 1 BLOCK:		**FINISHED BLOCK SIZE** *Single dimensions in the cutting chart indicate the size of the cut square (3" = 3" x 3").*					
		5"	**6¼"**	**7½"**	**8¾"**	**10"**	**12½"**
Light	A: 12 ⊠ → ⧄	2¼"	2½"	2¾"	3"	3¼"	3¾"
	B: 1 ▢	1½"	1¾"	2"	2¼"	2½"	3"
Dark	C: 12 ⊠ → ⧄	2¼"	2½"	2¾"	3"	3¼"	3¾"

Try this: Use a medium instead of a light for B.

Light   Light 2   Medium   Medium 2   Dark

MISSOURI STAR

4-Unit Grid
Color Illustration: page 20

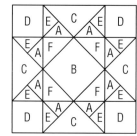

			FINISHED BLOCK SIZE				
		Single dimensions in the cutting chart indicate the size of the cut square (3" = 3" x 3").					
FOR 1 BLOCK:		**4"**	**6"**	**8"**	**9"**	**10"**	**12"**
Light	A: 2 ⊠ → ⊠	2¼"	2¾"	3¼"	3½"	3¾"	4¼"
	B: 1 ◇	T7	T11	T14	T15	T16	T19
Medium	C: 1 ⊠ → ⊠	3¼"	4¼"	5¼"	5¾"	6¼"	7¼"
	D: 4 ☐	1½"	2"	2½"	2¾"	3"	3½"
Dark	E: 2 ⊠ → ⊠	2¼"	2¾"	3¼"	3½"	3¾"	4¼"
	F: 2 ◻ → ◻	1⅞"	2⅜"	2⅞"	3⅛"	3⅜"	3⅞"

Try this: Reverse the mediums and darks in every other block.

MIXED T

6-Unit Grid
Color Illustration: page 20

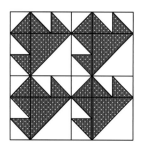
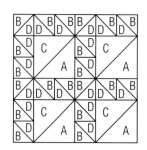
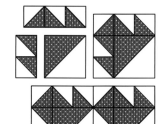

			FINISHED BLOCK SIZE				
		Single dimensions in the cutting chart indicate the size of the cut square (3" = 3" x 3").					
FOR 1 BLOCK:		**4½"**	**6"**	**7½"**	**9"**	**10½"**	**12"**
Light	A: 2 ◻ → ◻	2⅜"	2⅞"	3⅜"	3⅞"	4⅜"	4⅞"
	B: 10 ◻ → ◻	1⅝"	1⅞"	2⅛"	2⅜"	2⅝"	2⅞"
Dark	C: 2 ◻ → ◻	2⅜"	2⅞"	3⅜"	3⅞"	4⅜"	4⅞"
	D: 10 ◻ → ◻	1⅝"	1⅞"	2⅛"	2⅜"	2⅝"	2⅞"

Try this: Use a different fabric for each dark "T."

MOSAIC

6-Unit Grid

Color Illustration: page 20

 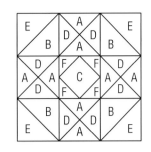 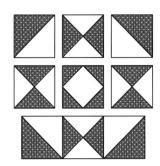

			FINISHED BLOCK SIZE Single dimensions in the cutting chart indicate the size of the cut square (3" = 3" x 3").					
FOR 1 BLOCK:			**4½"**	**6"**	**7½"**	**9"**	**10½"**	**12"**
Light	A: 2 ⊠→⊠		2¾"	3¼"	3¾"	4¼"	4¾"	5¼"
	B: 2 ◻→◻		2⅜"	2⅞"	3⅜"	3⅞"	4⅜"	4⅞"
	C: 1 ◇		T5	T7	T9	T11	T12	T14
Dark	D: 2 ⊠→⊠		2¾"	3¼"	3¾"	4¼"	4¾"	5¼"
	E: 2 ◻→◻		2⅜"	2⅞"	3⅜"	3⅞"	4⅜"	4⅞"
	F: 2 ◻→◻		1⅝"	1⅞"	2⅛"	2⅜"	2⅝"	2⅞"

Try this: Use a medium instead of a dark for E and F.

MOSAIC #3

4-Unit Grid

Color Illustration: page 20

 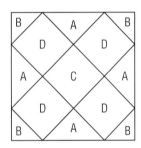 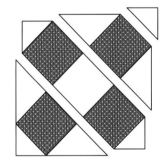

			FINISHED BLOCK SIZE Single dimensions in the cutting chart indicate the size of the cut square (3" = 3" x 3").					
FOR 1 BLOCK:			**4"**	**6"**	**8"**	**9"**	**10"**	**12"**
Light	A: 1 ⊠→⊠		3¼"	4¼"	5¼"	5¾"	6¼"	7¼"
	B: 2 ◻→◻		1⅞"	2⅜"	2⅞"	3⅛"	3⅜"	3⅞"
	C: 1 ◇		T7	T11	T14	T15	T16	T19
Dark	D: 4 ◇		T7	T11	T14	T15	T16	T19

Try this: Use several different darks for D.

MOSAIC #8

4-Unit Grid
Color Illustration: page 20

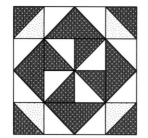
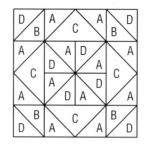
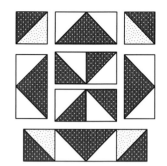

FOR 1 BLOCK:		**FINISHED BLOCK SIZE** *Single dimensions in the cutting chart indicate the size of the cut square (3" = 3" x 3").*					
		4"	**6"**	**8"**	**9"**	**10"**	**12"**
Light	A: 6 ☐ → ◩	1⅞"	2⅜"	2⅞"	3⅛"	3⅜"	3⅞"
Light 2	B: 2 ☐ → ◩	1⅞"	2⅜"	2⅞"	3⅛"	3⅜"	3⅞"
Dark	C: 1 ⊠ → ⊠	3¼"	4¼"	5¼"	5¾"	6¼"	7¼"
	D: 4 ☐ → ◩	1⅞"	2⅜"	2⅞"	3⅛"	3⅜"	3⅞"

Try this: Use a medium instead of a dark for C.

MOSAIC #10

4-Unit Grid
Color Illustration: page 21

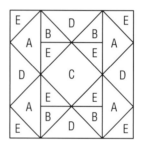

FOR 1 BLOCK:		**FINISHED BLOCK SIZE** *Single dimensions in the cutting chart indicate the size of the cut square (3" = 3" x 3").*					
		4"	**6"**	**8"**	**9"**	**10"**	**12"**
Light	A: 1 ⊠ → ⊠	3¼"	4¼"	5¼"	5¾"	6¼"	7¼"
	B: 2 ☐ → ◩	1⅞"	2⅜"	2⅞"	3⅛"	3⅜"	3⅞"
	C: 1 ◇	T7	T11	T14	T15	T16	T19
Dark	D: 1 ⊠ → ⊠	3¼"	4¼"	5¼"	5¾"	6¼"	7¼"
	E: 4 ☐ → ◩	1⅞"	2⅜"	2⅞"	3⅛"	3⅜"	3⅞"

Try this: Use a light and a medium instead of a light and a dark in every other block.

MOSAIC #11

4-Unit Grid

Color Illustration: page 21

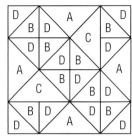

		FINISHED BLOCK SIZE *Single dimensions in the cutting chart indicate the size of the cut square (3" = 3" x 3").*					
FOR 2 BLOCKS:		**4"**	**6"**	**8"**	**9"**	**10"**	**12"**
Light	A: 2 ⊠ → ⊠	3¼"	4¼"	5¼"	5¾"	6¼"	7¼"
	B: 8 ◻ → ◺	1⅞"	2⅜"	2⅞"	3⅛"	3⅜"	3⅞"
Dark	C: 1 ⊠ → ⊠	3¼"	4¼"	5¼"	5¾"	6¼"	7¼"
	D: 12 ◻ → ◺	1⅞"	2⅜"	2⅞"	3⅛"	3⅜"	3⅞"

Try this: Use one light for A and a different light for B.

MOSAIC #12

4-Unit Grid

Color Illustration: page 21

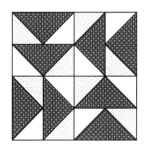
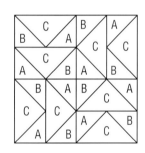

		FINISHED BLOCK SIZE *Single dimensions in the cutting chart indicate the size of the cut square (3" = 3" x 3").*					
FOR 1 BLOCK:		**4"**	**6"**	**8"**	**9"**	**10"**	**12"**
Light	A: 4 ◻ → ◺	1⅞"	2⅜"	2⅞"	3⅛"	3⅜"	3⅞"
Light 2	B: 4 ◻ → ◺	1⅞"	2⅜"	2⅞"	3⅛"	3⅜"	3⅞"
Dark	C: 2 ⊠ → ⊠	3¼"	4¼"	5¼"	5¾"	6¼"	7¼"

Try this: Use a medium instead of a dark for one of the C squares.

Light   Light 2   Medium   Medium 2   Dark

MOSAIC #19

4-Unit Grid

Color Illustration: page 21

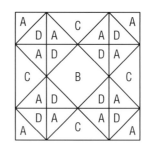

FOR 1 BLOCK:		FINISHED BLOCK SIZE *Single dimensions in the cutting chart indicate the size of the cut square (3" = 3" x 3").*					
		4"	6"	8"	9"	10"	12"
Light	A: 6 ◻ → ◺	1⅞"	2⅜"	2⅞"	3⅛"	3⅜"	3⅞"
	B: 1 ◇	T7	T11	T14	T15	T16	T19
Dark	C: 1 ⊠ → ⧅	3¼"	4¼"	5¼"	5¾"	6¼"	7¼"
	D: 4 ◻ → ◺	1⅞"	2⅜"	2⅞"	3⅛"	3⅜"	3⅞"

Try this: Reverse the lights and darks.

MOSAIC #21

4-Unit Grid

Color Illustration: page 21

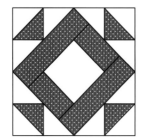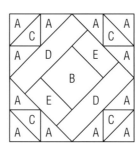

FOR 1 BLOCK:		FINISHED BLOCK SIZE *Single dimensions in the cutting chart indicate the size of the cut square (3" = 3" x 3").*					
		4"	6"	8"	9"	10"	12"
Light	A: 6 ◻ → ◺	1⅞"	2⅜"	2⅞"	3⅛"	3⅜"	3⅞"
	B: 1 ◇	T7	T11	T14	T15	T16	T19
Dark	C: 2 ◻ → ◺	1⅞"	2⅜"	2⅞"	3⅛"	3⅜"	3⅞"
	D: 2 ◇	T34	T43	T53	T58	T61	T69
	E: 2 ◇	T32	T41	T51	T56	T59	T67

Try this: Use one light for A and a different light or a medium for B.

MOSAIC ROSE

6-Unit Grid
Color Illustration: page 21

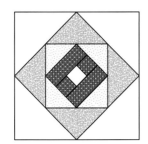
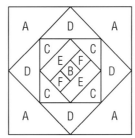

FOR 1 BLOCK:		FINISHED BLOCK SIZE *Single dimensions in the cutting chart indicate the size of the cut square (3" = 3" x 3").*					
		4½"	**6"**	**7½"**	**9"**	**10½"**	**12"**
Light	A: 2 ◻→◹	3⅛"	3⅞"	4⅝"	5⅜"	6⅛"	6⅞"
	B: 1 ◇	T1	T2	T4	T5	T6	T7
Light 2	C: 2 ◻→◹	2"	2⅜"	2¾"	3⅛"	3½"	3⅞"
Medium	D: 1 ⊠→⊠	3½"	4¼"	5"	5¾"	6½"	7¼"
Dark	E: 2 ◇	T29	T33	T37	T42	T47	T52
	F: 2 ◇	T1	T2	T4	T5	T6	T7

Try this: Reverse the medium and dark in every other block.

MRS. KELLER'S NINE PATCH

5-Unit Grid
Color Illustration: page 21

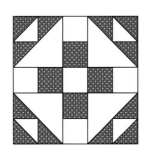

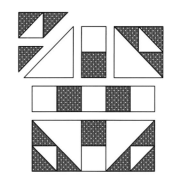

FOR 1 BLOCK:		FINISHED BLOCK SIZE *Single dimensions in the cutting chart indicate the size of the cut square (3" = 3" x 3").*					
		5"	**6¼"**	**7½"**	**8¾"**	**10"**	**12½"**
Light	A: 2 ◻→◹	2⅞"	3⅜"	3⅞"	4⅜"	4⅞"	5⅞"
	B: 2 ◻→◹	1⅞"	2⅛"	2⅜"	2⅝"	2⅞"	3⅜"
	C: 5 ◻	1½"	1¾"	2"	2¼"	2½"	3"
Dark	D: 6 ◻→◹	1⅞"	2⅛"	2⅜"	2⅝"	2⅞"	3⅜"
	E: 4 ◻	1½"	1¾"	2"	2¼"	2½"	3"

Try this: Use several mediums instead of a dark for D.

180

NAUTILUS

8-Unit Grid
Color Illustration: page 21

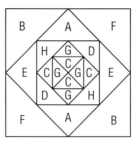

		FINISHED BLOCK SIZE *Single dimensions in the cutting chart indicate the size of the cut square (3" = 3" x 3").*					
FOR 2 BLOCKS:		**4"**	**6"**	**8"**	**9"**	**10"**	**12"**
Light	A: 1 ⊠→⊠	3¼"	4¼"	5¼"	5¾"	6¼"	7¼"
	B: 2 ◺→◺	2⅞"	3⅞"	4⅞"	5⅜"	5⅞"	6⅞"
	C: 2 ⊠→⊠	2¼"	2¾"	3¼"	3½"	3¾"	4¼"
	D: 2 ◺→◺	1⅞"	2⅜"	2⅞"	3⅛"	3⅜"	3⅞"
Dark	E: 1 ⊠→⊠	3¼"	4¼"	5¼"	5¾"	6¼"	7¼"
	F: 2 ◺→◺	2⅞"	3⅞"	4⅞"	5⅜"	5⅞"	6⅞"
	G: 2 ⊠→⊠	2¼"	2¾"	3¼"	3½"	3¾"	4¼"
	H: 2 ◺→◺	1⅞"	2⅜"	2⅞"	3⅛"	3⅜"	3⅞"

Try this: Use a medium instead of a light.

NEW ALBUM

4-Unit Grid
Color Illustration: page 21

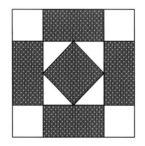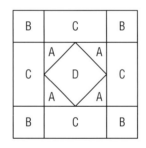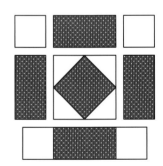

		FINISHED BLOCK SIZE *Single dimensions in the cutting chart indicate the size of the cut square (3" = 3" x 3").*					
FOR 1 BLOCK:		**4"**	**6"**	**8"**	**9"**	**10"**	**12"**
Light	A: 2 ◺→◺	1⅞"	2⅜"	2⅞"	3⅛"	3⅜"	3⅞"
	B: 4 ☐	1½"	2"	2½"	2¾"	3"	3½"
Dark	C: 4 ▭	1½" x 2½"	2" x 3½"	2½" x 4½"	2¾" x 5"	3" x 5½"	3½" x 6½"
	D: 1 ◇	T7	T11	T14	T15	T16	T19

Try this: Use a medium instead of a dark for D.

NEW ENGLAND BLOCK

5-Unit Grid

Color Illustration: page 21

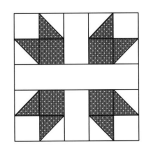 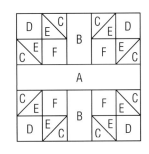 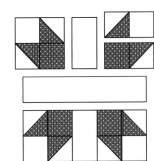

	FINISHED BLOCK SIZE					
	Single dimensions in the cutting chart indicate the size of the cut square (3" = 3" x 3").					
FOR 1 BLOCK:	**5"**	**6¼"**	**7½"**	**8¾"**	**10"**	**12½"**
Light A: 1 ▭	1½" x 5½"	1¾" x 6¾"	2" x 8"	2¼" x 9¼"	2½" x 10½"	3" x 13"
B: 2 ▭	1½" x 2½"	1¾" x 3"	2" x 3½"	2¼" x 4"	2½" x 4½"	3" x 5½"
C: 4 ◿ → ◹	1⅞"	2⅛"	2⅜"	2⅝"	2⅞"	3⅜"
D: 4 ☐	1½"	1¾"	2"	2¼"	2½"	3"
Dark E: 4 ◿ → ◹	1⅞"	2⅛"	2⅜"	2⅝"	2⅞"	3⅜"
F: 4 ☐	1½"	1¾"	2"	2¼"	2½"	3"

Try this: Use a different dark in every quadrant of the block.

NEW HOUR GLASS

6-Unit Grid

Color Illustration: page 21

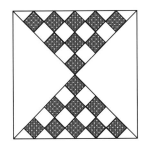 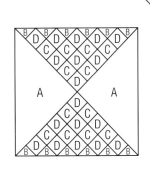 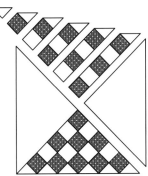

	FINISHED BLOCK SIZE					
	Single dimensions in the cutting chart indicate the size of the cut square (3" = 3" x 3").					
FOR 2 BLOCKS:	**4½"**	**6"**	**7½"**	**9"**	**10½"**	**12"**
Light A: 1 ⊠ → ⊠	5¾"	7¼"	8¾"	10¼"	11¾"	13¼"
B: 6 ⊠ → ⊠	2"	2¼"	2½"	2¾"	3"	3¼"
C: 24 ◇	T1	T2	T4	T5	T6	T7
Dark D: 36 ◇	T1	T2	T4	T5	T6	T7

Try this: Use many different darks for D.

NEW WATERWHEEL

9-Unit Grid
Color Illustration: page 21

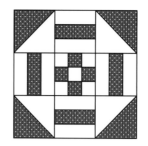
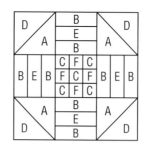
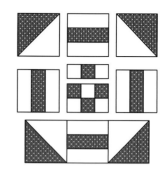

FOR 1 BLOCK:		**FINISHED BLOCK SIZE** Single dimensions in the cutting chart indicate the size of the cut square (3" = 3" x 3").					
		6¾"	**9"**	**10⅛"**	**11¼"**	**12⅜"**	**13½"**
Light	A: 2 ◻→◹	3⅛"	3⅞"	4¼"	4⅝"	5"	5⅜"
	B: 8 ▭	1¼" x 2¾"	1½" x 3½"	1⅝" x 3⅞"	1¾" x 4¼"	1⅞" x 4⅝"	2" x 5"
	C: 5 ◻	1¼"	1½"	1⅝"	1¾"	1⅞"	2"
Dark	D: 2 ◻→◹	3⅛"	3⅞"	4¼"	4⅝"	5"	5⅜"
	E: 4 ▭	1¼" x 2¾"	1½" x 3½"	1⅝" x 3⅞"	1¾" x 4¼"	1⅞" x 4⅝"	2" x 5"
	F: 4 ◻	1¼"	1½"	1⅝"	1¾"	1⅞"	2"

Try this: Reverse the lights and darks.

NEXT DOOR NEIGHBOR

4-Unit Grid
Color Illustration: page 21

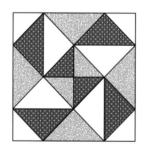
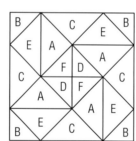

FOR 1 BLOCK:		**FINISHED BLOCK SIZE** Single dimensions in the cutting chart indicate the size of the cut square (3" = 3" x 3").					
		4"	**6"**	**8"**	**9"**	**10"**	**12"**
Light	A: 1 ⊠→⊠	3¼"	4¼"	5¼"	5¾"	6¼"	7¼"
	B: 2 ◻→◹	1⅞"	2⅜"	2⅞"	3⅛"	3⅜"	3⅞"
Medium	C: 1 ⊠→⊠	3¼"	4¼"	5¼"	5¾"	6¼"	7¼"
	D: 1 ◻→◹	1⅞"	2⅜"	2⅞"	3⅛"	3⅜"	3⅞"
Dark	E: 1 ⊠→⊠	3¼"	4¼"	5¼"	5¾"	6¼"	7¼"
	F: 1 ◻→◹	1⅞"	2⅜"	2⅞"	3⅛"	3⅜"	3⅞"

Try this: Reverse the mediums and the darks in every other block.

NINE PATCH STRAIGHT FURROW

3-Unit Grid
Color Illustration: page 21

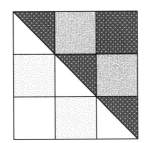
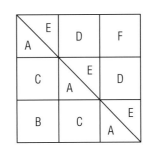
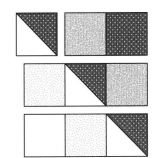

		FINISHED BLOCK SIZE *Single dimensions in the cutting chart indicate the size of the cut square (3" = 3" x 3").*					
FOR 2 BLOCKS:		**4½"**	**6"**	**7½"**	**9"**	**10½"**	**12"**
Light	A: 3 ▱→▱	2⅜"	2⅞"	3⅜"	3⅞"	4⅜"	4⅞"
	B: 2 □	2"	2½"	3"	3½"	4"	4½"
Light 2	C: 4 □	2"	2½"	3"	3½"	4"	4½"
Medium	D: 4 □	2"	2½"	3"	3½"	4"	4½"
Dark	E: 3 ▱→▱	2⅜"	2⅞"	3⅜"	3⅞"	4⅜"	4⅞"
	F: 2 □	2"	2½"	3"	3½"	4"	4½"

Try this: Use a different combination of fabrics for each block.

THE NORTH CAROLINA BEAUTY

5-Unit Grid
Color Illustration: page 21

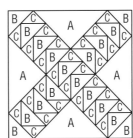

		FINISHED BLOCK SIZE *Single dimensions in the cutting chart indicate the size of the cut square (3" = 3" x 3").*					
FOR 1 BLOCK:		**5"**	**6¼"**	**7½"**	**8¾"**	**10"**	**12½"**
Light	A: 1 ⊠→⊠	4¼"	5"	5¾"	6½"	7¼"	8¾"
	B: 9 ▱→▱	1⅞"	2⅛"	2⅜"	2⅝"	2⅞"	3⅜"
Dark	C: 7 ⊠→⊠	2¼"	2½"	2¾"	3"	3¼"	3¾"

Try this: Use one light for A and a different light for B.

NORTHUMBERLAND STAR

4-Unit Grid
Color Illustration: page 21

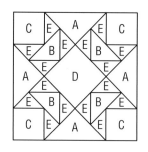

				FINISHED BLOCK SIZE					
				Single dimensions in the cutting chart indicate the size of the cut square (3" = 3" x 3").					
FOR 1 BLOCK:			**4"**	**6"**	**8"**	**9"**	**10"**	**12"**
Light	A: 1 ⊠→⊠		3¼"	4¼"	5¼"	5¾"	6¼"	7¼"
	B: 2 ◁→◁		1⅞"	2⅜"	2⅞"	3⅛"	3⅜"	3⅞"
	C: 4 ☐		1½"	2"	2½"	2¾"	3"	3½"
Medium	D: 1 ◇		T7	T11	T14	T15	T16	T19
Dark	E: 4 ⊠→⊠		2¼"	2¾"	3¼"	3½"	3¾"	4¼"

Try this: Use one light for A and C and a different light for B.

NORTHWIND

3-Unit Grid
Color Illustration: page 21

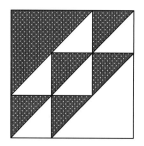
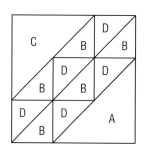
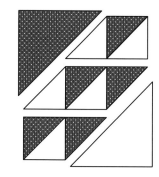

				FINISHED BLOCK SIZE					
				Single dimensions in the cutting chart indicate the size of the cut square (3" = 3" x 3").					
FOR 2 BLOCKS:			**4½"**	**6"**	**7½"**	**9"**	**10½"**	**12"**
Light	A: 1 ◁→◁		3⅞"	4⅞"	5⅞"	6⅞"	7⅞"	8⅞"
	B: 5 ◁→◁		2⅜"	2⅞"	3⅜"	3⅞"	4⅜"	4⅞"
Dark	C: 1 ◁→◁		3⅞"	4⅞"	5⅞"	6⅞"	7⅞"	8⅞"
	D: 5 ◁→◁		2⅜"	2⅞"	3⅜"	3⅞"	4⅜"	4⅞"

Try this: Use several different darks for D.

OCEAN WAVE

4-Unit Grid
Color Illustration: page 21

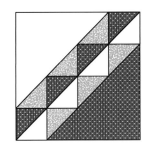
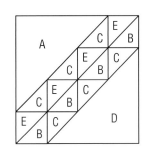
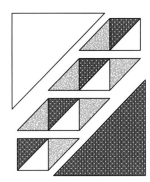

		FINISHED BLOCK SIZE _Single dimensions in the cutting chart indicate the size of the cut square (3" = 3" x 3")._					
FOR 2 BLOCKS:		**4"**	**6"**	**8"**	**9"**	**10"**	**12"**
Light	A: 1 ◻→◿	3⅞"	5⅜"	6⅞"	7⅝"	8⅜"	9⅞"
	B: 4 ◻→◿	1⅞"	2⅜"	2⅞"	3⅛"	3⅜"	3⅞"
Medium	C: 6 ◻→◿	1⅞"	2⅜"	2⅞"	3⅛"	3⅜"	3⅞"
Dark	D: 1 ◻→◿	3⅞"	5⅜"	6⅞"	7⅝"	8⅜"	9⅞"
	E: 4 ◻→◿	1⅞"	2⅜"	2⅞"	3⅛"	3⅜"	3⅞"

Try this: Use several different mediums for C.

ODD FELLOWS

5-Unit Grid
Color Illustration: page 21

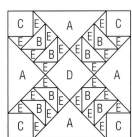

		FINISHED BLOCK SIZE _Single dimensions in the cutting chart indicate the size of the cut square (3" = 3" x 3")._					
FOR 1 BLOCK:		**5"**	**6¼"**	**7½"**	**8¾"**	**10"**	**12½"**
Light	A: 1 ⊠→⊠	4¼"	5"	5¾"	6½"	7¼"	8¾"
	B: 4 ◻→◿	1⅞"	2⅛"	2⅜"	2⅝"	2⅞"	3⅜"
	C: 4 ◻	1½"	1¾"	2"	2¼"	2½"	3"
	D: 1 ◇	T7	T9	T11	T12	T14	T16
Dark	E: 6 ⊠→⊠	2¼"	2½"	2¾"	3"	3¼"	3¾"

Try this: Use several different lights for B.

◻ Light	◻ Light 2	▦ Medium	▦ Medium 2	▦ Dark

ODD FELLOWS CHAIN

8-Unit Grid

Color Illustration: page 21

 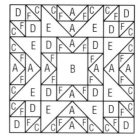 

	FINISHED BLOCK SIZE					
	Single dimensions in the cutting chart indicate the size of the cut square (3" = 3" x 3").					
FOR 1 BLOCK:	**6"**	**8"**	**9"**	**10"**	**12"**	**14"**
Light A: 3 ⊠ → ⊠	2¾"	3¼"	3½"	3¾"	4¼"	4¾"
B: 1 □	2"	2½"	2¾"	3"	3½"	4"
C: 8 ◻ → ◺	1⅝"	1⅞"	2"	2⅛"	2⅜"	2⅝"
D: 12 □	1¼"	1½"	1⅝"	1¾"	2"	2¼"
Dark E: 4 ◻ → ◺	2⅜"	2⅞"	3⅛"	3⅜"	3⅞"	4⅜"
F: 12 ◻ → ◺	1⅝"	1⅞"	2"	2⅛"	2⅜"	2⅝"

Try this: Use a medium instead of a dark for F.

ODD FELLOW'S CROSS

5-Unit Grid

Color Illustration: page 21

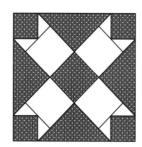 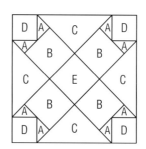 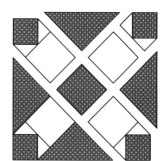

	FINISHED BLOCK SIZE					
	Single dimensions in the cutting chart indicate the size of the cut square (3" = 3" x 3").					
FOR 1 BLOCK:	**5"**	**6¼"**	**7½"**	**8¾"**	**10"**	**12½"**
Light A: 2 ⊠ → ⊠	2¼"	2½"	2¾"	3"	3¼"	3¾"
B: 4 ◇	T7	T9	T11	T12	T14	T16
Dark C: 1 ⊠ → ⊠	4¼"	5"	5¾"	6½"	7¼"	8¾"
D: 4 □	1½"	1¾"	2"	2¼"	2½"	3"
E: 1 ◇	T7	T9	T11	T12	T14	T16

Try this: Use a medium instead of a dark for C.

OHIO STAR

3-Unit Grid
Color Illustration: page 21

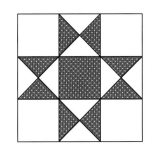
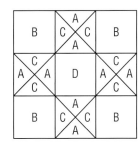
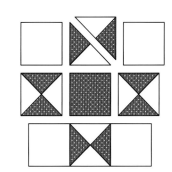

FOR 1 BLOCK:	FINISHED BLOCK SIZE *Single dimensions in the cutting chart indicate the size of the cut square (3" = 3" x 3").*					
	4½"	**6"**	**7½"**	**9"**	**10½"**	**12"**
Light A: 2 ⊠ → ⊠	2¾"	3¼"	3¾"	4¼"	4¾"	5¼"
B: 4 □	2"	2½"	3"	3½"	4"	4½"
Dark C: 2 ⊠ → ⊠	2¾"	3¼"	3¾"	4¼"	4¾"	5¼"
D: 1 □	2"	2½"	3"	3½"	4"	4½"

Try this: Use one dark for C and a medium or a different dark for D.

OLD FAVORITE

8-Unit Grid
Color Illustration: page 21

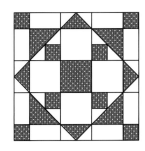

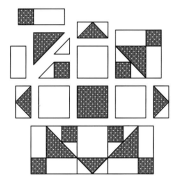

FOR 1 BLOCK:	FINISHED BLOCK SIZE *Single dimensions in the cutting chart indicate the size of the cut square (3" = 3" x 3").*					
	6"	**8"**	**9"**	**10"**	**12"**	**14"**
Light A: 4 □	2"	2½"	2¾"	3"	3½"	4"
B: 8 ▭	1¼" x 2"	1½" x 2½"	1⅝" x 2¾"	1¾" x 3"	2" x 3½"	2¼" x 4"
C: 8 ◻ → ◺	1⅝"	1⅞"	2"	2⅛"	2⅜"	2⅝"
Dark D: 1 ⊠ → ⊠	2¾"	3¼"	3½"	3¾"	4¼"	4¾"
E: 2 ◻ → ◺	2⅜"	2⅞"	3⅛"	3⅜"	3⅞"	4⅜"
F: 1 □	2"	2½"	2¾"	3"	3½"	4"
G: 8 □	1¼"	1½"	1⅝"	1¾"	2"	2¼"

Try this: Use a medium instead of a dark for G.

OLD GREY GOOSE

4-Unit Grid
Color Illustration: page 21

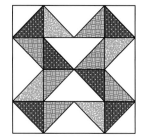 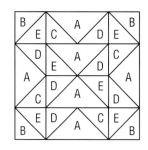 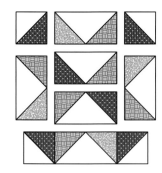

		FINISHED BLOCK SIZE *Single dimensions in the cutting chart indicate the size of the cut square (3" = 3" x 3").*					
FOR 2 BLOCKS:		**4"**	**6"**	**8"**	**9"**	**10"**	**12"**
Light	A: 3 ⊠ → ⊠	3¼"	4¼"	5¼"	5¾"	6¼"	7¼"
	B: 4 ◻ → ◻	1⅞"	2⅜"	2⅞"	3⅛"	3⅜"	3⅞"
Medium	C: 4 ◻ → ◻	1⅞"	2⅜"	2⅞"	3⅛"	3⅜"	3⅞"
Medium 2	D: 6 ◻ → ◻	1⅞"	2⅜"	2⅞"	3⅛"	3⅜"	3⅞"
Dark	E: 6 ◻ → ◻	1⅞"	2⅜"	2⅞"	3⅛"	3⅜"	3⅞"

Try this: Use a scrappy assortment of mediums and darks for C, D, and E.

OLD MAID'S PUZZLE

4-Unit Grid
Color Illustration: page 21

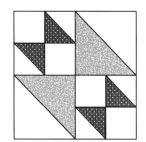 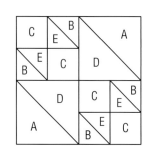 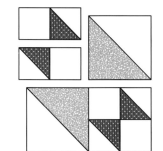

		FINISHED BLOCK SIZE *Single dimensions in the cutting chart indicate the size of the cut square (3" = 3" x 3").*					
FOR 1 BLOCK:		**4"**	**6"**	**8"**	**9"**	**10"**	**12"**
Light	A: 1 ◻ → ◻	2⅞"	3⅞"	4⅞"	5⅜"	5⅞"	6⅞"
	B: 2 ◻ → ◻	1⅞"	2⅜"	2⅞"	3⅛"	3⅜"	3⅞"
	C: 4 ◻	1½"	2"	2½"	2¾"	3"	3½"
Medium	D: 1 ◻ → ◻	2⅞"	3⅞"	4⅞"	5⅜"	5⅞"	6⅞"
Dark	E: 2 ◻ → ◻	1⅞"	2⅜"	2⅞"	3⅛"	3⅜"	3⅞"

Try this: Reverse the mediums and darks in every other block.

OLD MAID'S PUZZLE II

7-Unit Grid
Color Illustration: page 21

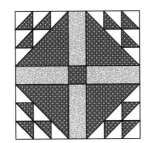 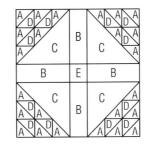 

		FINISHED BLOCK SIZE Single dimensions in the cutting chart indicate the size of the cut square (3" = 3" x 3").					
FOR 1 BLOCK:		**5¼"**	**7"**	**8¾"**	**10½"**	**12¼"**	**14"**
Light	A: 12 ◻→◹	1⅝"	1⅞"	2⅛"	2⅜"	2⅝"	2⅞"
Medium	B: 4 ▭	1¼" x 2¾"	1½" x 3½"	1¾" x 4¼"	2" x 5"	2¼" x 5¾"	2½" x 6½"
Dark	C: 2 ◻→◹	3⅛"	3⅞"	4⅝"	5⅜"	6⅛"	6⅞"
	D: 6 ◻→◹	1⅝"	1⅞"	2⅛"	2⅜"	2⅝"	2⅞"
	E: 1 ◻	1¼"	1½"	1¾"	2"	2¼"	2½"

Try this: Use a light instead of a medium for B.

OLD MAID'S RAMBLE

10-Unit Grid
Color Illustration: page 21

 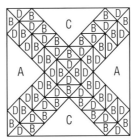 

		FINISHED BLOCK SIZE Single dimensions in the cutting chart indicate the size of the cut square (3" = 3" x 3").					
FOR 2 BLOCKS:		**5"**	**6¼"**	**7½"**	**8¾"**	**10"**	**12½"**
Light	A: 1 ⊠→⧖	4¼"	5"	5¾"	6½"	7¼"	8¾"
	B: 16 ⊠→⧖	2¼"	2½"	2¾"	3"	3¼"	3¾"
Dark	C: 1 ⊠→⧖	4¼"	5"	5¾"	6½"	7¼"	8¾"
	D: 16 ⊠→⧖	2¼"	2½"	2¾"	3"	3¼"	3¾"

Try this: Use several different darks for D.

THE OLD RUGGED CROSS

6-Unit Grid

Color Illustration: page 21

 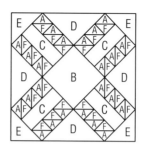 

FOR 1 BLOCK:		FINISHED BLOCK SIZE *Single dimensions in the cutting chart indicate the size of the cut square (3" = 3" x 3").*					
		4½"	6"	7½"	9"	10½"	12"
Light	A: 6 ⊠→⊠	2"	2¼"	2½"	2¾"	3"	3¼"
	B: 1 ◇	T8	T11	T13	T15	T17	T19
	C: 4 ◇	T29	T33	T37	T42	T47	T52
Medium	D: 1 ⊠→⊠	3½"	4¼"	5"	5¾"	6½"	7¼"
	E: 2 ◻→◻	2"	2⅜"	2¾"	3⅛"	3½"	3⅞"
Dark	F: 6 ⊠→⊠	2"	2¼"	2½"	2¾"	3"	3¼"
Try this: Reverse the mediums and darks in every other block.							

OLD TIME BLOCK

6-Unit Grid

Color Illustration: page 21

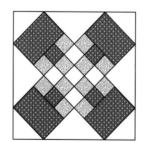 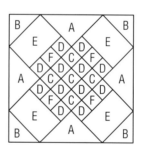 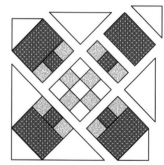

FOR 1 BLOCK:		FINISHED BLOCK SIZE *Single dimensions in the cutting chart indicate the size of the cut square (3" = 3" x 3").*					
		4½"	6"	7½"	9"	10½"	12"
Light	A: 1 ⊠→⊠	3½"	4¼"	5"	5¾"	6½"	7¼"
	B: 2 ◻→◻	2"	2⅜"	2¾"	3⅛"	3½"	3⅞"
	C: 5 ◇	T1	T2	T4	T5	T6	T7
Medium	D: 12 ◇	T1	T2	T4	T5	T6	T7
Dark	E: 4 ◇	T77	T78	T79	T80	T81	T82
	F: 4 ◇	T1	T2	T4	T5	T6	T7
Try this: Use several different mediums for D.							

ON THE SQUARE

9-Unit Grid
Color Illustration: page 21

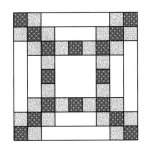
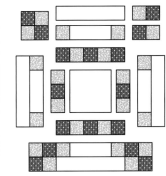

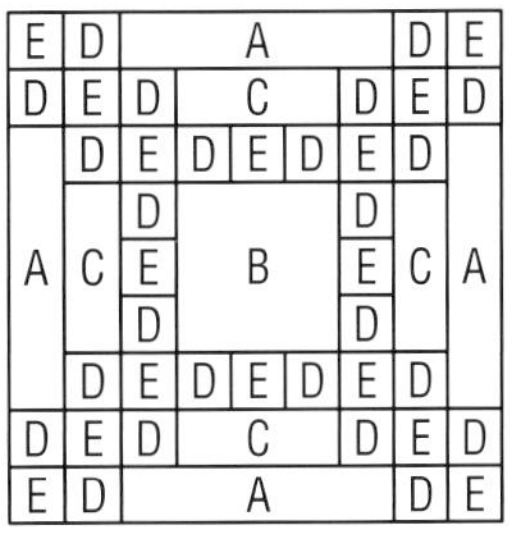

FOR 1 BLOCK:	FINISHED BLOCK SIZE *Single dimensions in the cutting chart indicate the size of the cut square (3" = 3" x 3").*					
	6¾"	**9"**	**10⅛"**	**11¼"**	**12⅜"**	**13½"**
Light A: 4 ▭	1¼" x 4¼"	1½" x 5½"	1⅝" x 6⅛"	1¾" x 6¾"	1⅞" x 7⅜"	2" x 8"
B: 1 ◻	2¾"	3½"	3⅞"	4¼"	4⅝"	5"
C: 4 ▭	1¼" x 2¾"	1½" x 3½"	1⅝" x 3⅞"	1¾" x 4¼"	1⅞" x 4⅝"	2" x 5"
Medium D: 24 ◻	1¼"	1½"	1⅝"	1¾"	1⅞"	2"
Dark E: 16 ◻	1¼"	1½"	1⅝"	1¾"	1⅞"	2"

Try this: Reverse the lights and darks.

ONE MORE BLOCK

6-Unit Grid
Color Illustration: page 22

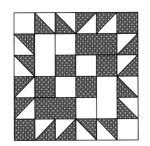
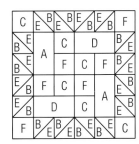
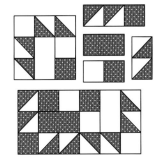

FOR 1 BLOCK:	FINISHED BLOCK SIZE *Single dimensions in the cutting chart indicate the size of the cut square (3" = 3" x 3").*					
	4½"	**6"**	**7½"**	**9"**	**10½"**	**12"**
Light A: 2 ▭	1¼" x 2"	1½" x 2½"	1¾" x 3"	2" x 3½"	2¼" x 4"	2½" x 4½"
B: 8 ◺→◳	1⅝"	1⅞"	2⅛"	2⅜"	2⅝"	2⅞"
C: 6 ◻	1¼"	1½"	1¾"	2"	2¼"	2½"
Dark D: 2 ▭	1¼" x 2"	1½" x 2½"	1¾" x 3"	2" x 3½"	2¼" x 4"	2½" x 4½"
E: 8 ◺→◳	1⅝"	1⅞"	2⅛"	2⅜"	2⅝"	2⅞"
F: 6 ◻	1¼"	1½"	1¾"	2"	2¼"	2½"

Try this: Use a different combination of lights and darks in each quadrant of the block.

AN ORIGINAL DESIGN

6-Unit Grid

Color Illustration: page 22

 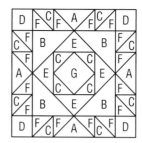 

FOR 1 BLOCK:		**FINISHED BLOCK SIZE** Single dimensions in the cutting chart indicate the size of the cut square (3" = 3" x 3").					
		4½"	**6"**	**7½"**	**9"**	**10½"**	**12"**
Light	A: 1 ⊠ → ⊠	2¾"	3¼"	3¾"	4¼"	4¾"	5¼"
	B: 2 ◲ → ◲	2⅜"	2⅞"	3⅜"	3⅞"	4⅜"	4⅞"
	C: 6 ◲ → ◲	1⅝"	1⅞"	2⅛"	2⅜"	2⅝"	2⅞"
	D: 4 ☐	1¼"	1½"	1¾"	2"	2¼"	2½"
Dark	E: 1 ⊠ → ⊠	2¾"	3¼"	3¾"	4¼"	4¾"	5¼"
	F: 8 ◲ → ◲	1⅝"	1⅞"	2⅛"	2⅜"	2⅝"	2⅞"
	G: 1 ◇	T5	T7	T9	T11	T12	T14

Try this: Use a medium instead of a dark for E.

OUR EDITOR

4-Unit Grid

Color Illustration: page 22

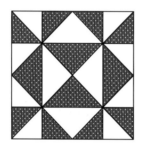 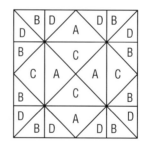 

FOR 1 BLOCK:		**FINISHED BLOCK SIZE** Single dimensions in the cutting chart indicate the size of the cut square (3" = 3" x 3").					
		4"	**6"**	**8"**	**9"**	**10"**	**12"**
Light	A: 1 ⊠ → ⊠	3¼"	4¼"	5¼"	5¾"	6¼"	7¼"
	B: 4 ◲ → ◲	1⅞"	2⅜"	2⅞"	3⅛"	3⅜"	3⅞"
Dark	C: 1 ⊠ → ⊠	3¼"	4¼"	5¼"	5¾"	6¼"	7¼"
	D: 4 ◲ → ◲	1⅞"	2⅜"	2⅞"	3⅛"	3⅜"	3⅞"

Try this: Use a medium instead of a light for A.

OUR VILLAGE GREEN

8-Unit Grid
Color Illustration: page 22

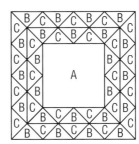

FOR 1 BLOCK:		FINISHED BLOCK SIZE *Single dimensions in the cutting chart indicate the size of the cut square (3" = 3" x 3").*					
		4"	**6"**	**8"**	**9"**	**10"**	**12"**
Light	A: 1 ☐	2½"	3½"	4½"	5"	5½"	6½"
	B: 6 ⊠ → ⊠	2¼"	2¾"	3¼"	3½"	3¾"	4¼"
Dark	C: 6 ⊠ → ⊠	2¼"	2¾"	3¼"	3½"	3¾"	4¼"

Try this: Use several different lights for B.

THE OZARK TRAIL

10-Unit Grid
Color Illustration: page 22

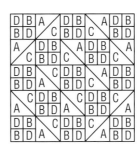
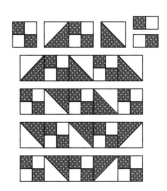

FOR 1 BLOCK:		FINISHED BLOCK SIZE *Single dimensions in the cutting chart indicate the size of the cut square (3" = 3" x 3").*					
		6¼"	**7½"**	**8¾"**	**10"**	**12½"**	**13¾"**
Light	A: 6 ◣ → ◣	2⅛"	2⅜"	2⅝"	2⅞"	3⅜"	3⅝"
	B: 26 ☐	1⅛"	1¼"	1⅜"	1½"	1¾"	1⅞"
Dark	C: 6 ◣ → ◣	2⅛"	2⅜"	2⅝"	2⅞"	3⅜"	3⅝"
	D: 26 ☐	1⅛"	1¼"	1⅜"	1½"	1¾"	1⅞"

Try this: Use one light for A and a different light or a medium for B.

PAPER PINWHEELS

4-Unit Grid

Color Illustration: page 22

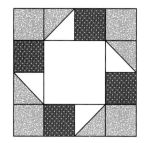

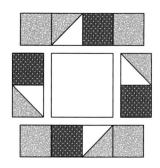

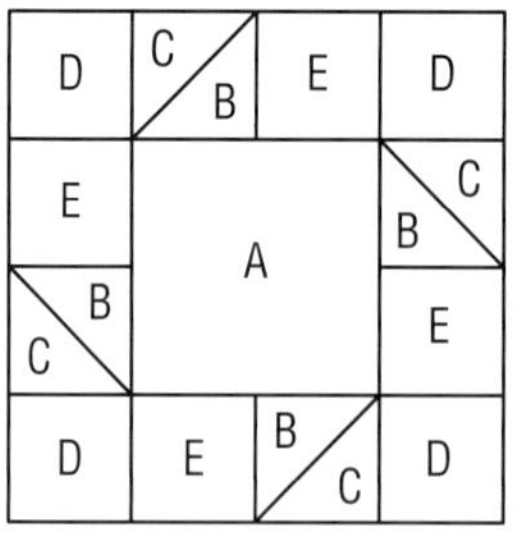

| FOR 1 BLOCK: | | FINISHED BLOCK SIZE | | | | | |
| | | Single dimensions in the cutting chart indicate the size of the cut square (3" = 3" x 3"). | | | | | |
		4"	6"	8"	9"	10"	12"
Light	A: 1 □	2½"	3½"	4½"	5"	5½"	6½"
	B: 2 ◪ → ◩	1⅞"	2⅜"	2⅞"	3⅛"	3⅜"	3⅞"
Medium	C: 2 ◪ → ◩	1⅞"	2⅜"	2⅞"	3⅛"	3⅜"	3⅞"
	D: 4 □	1½"	2"	2½"	2¾"	3"	3½"
Dark	E: 4 □	1½"	2"	2½"	2¾"	3"	3½"

Try this: Use one medium for C and a different medium for D.

PATH THRU THE WOODS

8-Unit Grid

Color Illustration: page 22

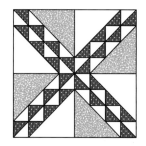

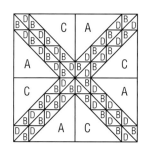

| FOR 1 BLOCK: | | FINISHED BLOCK SIZE | | | | | |
| | | Single dimensions in the cutting chart indicate the size of the cut square (3" = 3" x 3"). | | | | | |
		6"	8"	9"	10"	12"	14"
Light	A: 2 ◪ → ◩	3⅛"	3⅞"	4¼"	4⅝"	5⅜"	6⅛"
	B: 14 ◪ → ◩	1⅝"	1⅞"	2"	2⅛"	2⅜"	2⅝"
Medium	C: 2 ◪ → ◩	3⅛"	3⅞"	4¼"	4⅝"	5⅜"	6⅛"
Dark	D: 14 ◪ → ◩	1⅝"	1⅞"	2"	2⅛"	2⅜"	2⅝"

Try this: Use several different darks for D.

PAVEMENT PATTERN

4-Unit Grid
Color Illustration: page 22

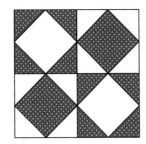 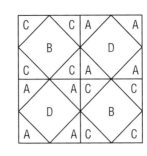 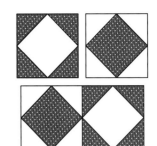

FOR 1 BLOCK:		FINISHED BLOCK SIZE *Single dimensions in the cutting chart indicate the size of the cut square (3" = 3" x 3").*					
		4"	6"	8"	9"	10"	12"
Light	A: 4 ☐→◺	1⅞"	2⅜"	2⅞"	3⅛"	3⅜"	3⅞"
	B: 2 ◇	T7	T11	T14	T15	T16	T19
Dark	C: 4 ☐→◺	1⅞"	2⅜"	2⅞"	3⅛"	3⅜"	3⅞"
	D: 2 ◇	T7	T11	T14	T15	T16	T19

Try this: Use a different combination of lights and darks in each quadrant of the block.

PEACE AND PLENTY

4-Unit Grid
Color Illustration: page 22

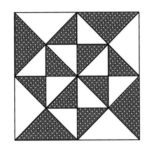 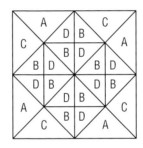 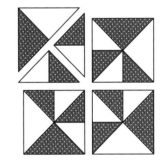

FOR 1 BLOCK:		FINISHED BLOCK SIZE *Single dimensions in the cutting chart indicate the size of the cut square (3" = 3" x 3").*					
		4"	6"	8"	9"	10"	12"
Light	A: 1 ☒→⊠	3¼"	4¼"	5¼"	5¾"	6¼"	7¼"
	B: 4 ☐→◺	1⅞"	2⅜"	2⅞"	3⅛"	3⅜"	3⅞"
Dark	C: 1 ☒→⊠	3¼"	4¼"	5¼"	5¾"	6¼"	7¼"
	D: 4 ☐→◺	1⅞"	2⅜"	2⅞"	3⅛"	3⅜"	3⅞"

Try this: Use a medium instead of a dark for D.

PENNSYLVANIA

6-Unit Grid

Color Illustration: page 22

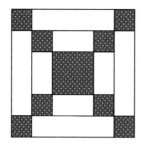

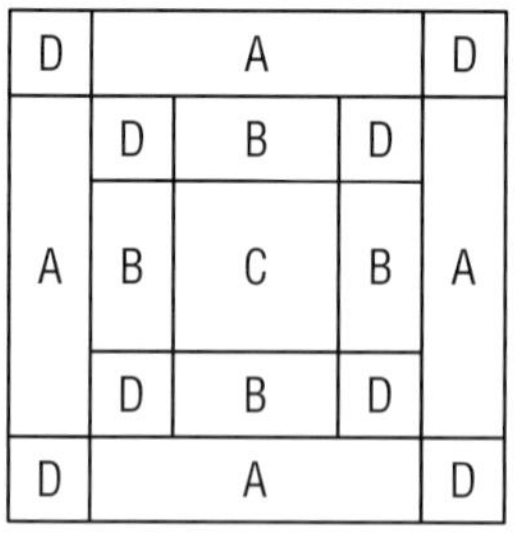

		FINISHED BLOCK SIZE *Single dimensions in the cutting chart indicate the size of the cut square (3" = 3" x 3").*					
FOR 1 BLOCK:		**4½"**	**6"**	**7½"**	**9"**	**10½"**	**12"**
Light	A: 4 ▭	1¼" x 3½"	1½" x 4½"	1¾" x 5½"	2" x 6½"	2¼" x 7½"	2½" x 8½"
	B: 4 ▭	1¼" x 2"	1½" x 2½"	1¾" x 3"	2" x 3½"	2¼" x 4"	2½" x 4½"
Dark	C: 1 ☐	2"	2½"	3"	3½"	4"	4½"
	D: 8 ☐	1¼"	1½"	1¾"	2"	2¼"	2½"
Try this:	Use a pictorial print for C.						

PERKIOMEN VALLEY

3-Unit Grid

Color Illustration: page 22

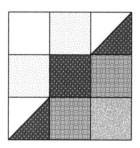

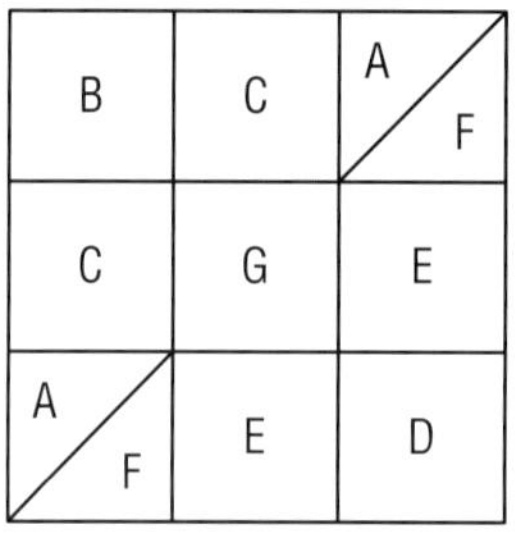

		FINISHED BLOCK SIZE *Single dimensions in the cutting chart indicate the size of the cut square (3" = 3" x 3").*					
FOR 1 BLOCK:		**4½"**	**6"**	**7½"**	**9"**	**10½"**	**12"**
Light	A: 1 ◻→◩	2⅜"	2⅞"	3⅜"	3⅞"	4⅜"	4⅞"
	B: 1 ☐	2"	2½"	3"	3½"	4"	4½"
Light 2	C: 2 ☐	2"	2½"	3"	3½"	4"	4½"
Medium	D: 1 ☐	2"	2½"	3"	3½"	4"	4½"
Medium 2	E: 2 ☐	2"	2½"	3"	3½"	4"	4½"
Dark	F: 1 ◻→◩	2⅜"	2⅞"	3⅜"	3⅞"	4⅜"	4⅞"
	G: 1 ☐	2"	2½"	3"	3½"	4"	4½"
Try this:	Use a scrappy assortment of lights and mediums for A–E.						

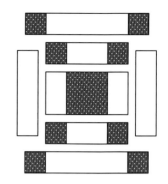

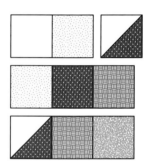

PHILADELPHIA PAVEMENT

5-Unit Grid
Color Illustration: page 22

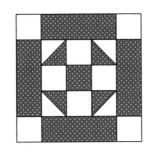 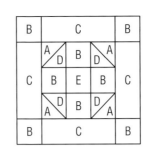 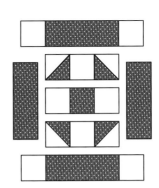

		FINISHED BLOCK SIZE					
		Single dimensions in the cutting chart indicate the size of the cut square (3" = 3" x 3").					
FOR 1 BLOCK:		**5"**	**6¼"**	**7½"**	**8¾"**	**10"**	**12½"**
Light	A: 2 ◻→◺	1⅞"	2⅛"	2⅜"	2⅝"	2⅞"	3⅜"
	B: 8 ◻	1½"	1¾"	2"	2¼"	2½"	3"
Dark	C: 4 ▭	1½" x 3½"	1¾" x 4¼"	2" x 5"	2¼" x 5¾"	2½" x 6½"	3" x 8"
	D: 2 ◻→◺	1⅞"	2⅛"	2⅜"	2⅝"	2⅞"	3⅜"
	E: 1 ◻	1½"	1¾"	2"	2¼"	2½"	3"

Try this: Reverse the lights and darks in every other block.

PICKET FENCE

6-Unit Grid
Color Illustration: page 22

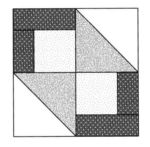 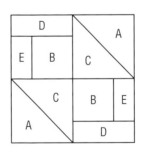 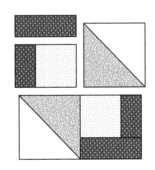

		FINISHED BLOCK SIZE					
		Single dimensions in the cutting chart indicate the size of the cut square (3" = 3" x 3").					
FOR 1 BLOCK:		**4½"**	**6"**	**7½"**	**9"**	**10½"**	**12"**
Light	A: 1 ◻→◺	3⅛"	3⅞"	4⅝"	5⅜"	6⅛"	6⅞"
Light 2	B: 2 ◻	2"	2½"	3"	3½"	4"	4½"
Medium	C: 1 ◻→◺	3⅛"	3⅞"	4⅝"	5⅜"	6⅛"	6⅞"
Dark	D: 2 ▭	1¼" x 2¾"	1½" x 3½"	1¾" x 4¼"	2" x 5"	2¼" x 5¾"	2½" x 6½"
	E: 2 ▭	1¼" x 2"	1½" x 2½"	1¾" x 3"	2" x 3½"	2¼" x 4"	2½" x 4½"

Try this: Use a different medium in every block.

PINE BURR

10-Unit Grid
Color Illustration: page 22

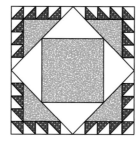
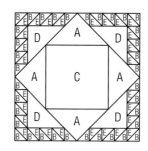
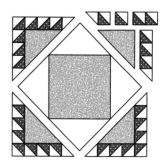

FOR 1 BLOCK:		**FINISHED BLOCK SIZE** *Single dimensions in the cutting chart indicate the size of the cut square (3" = 3" x 3").*					
		6¼"	**7½"**	**8¾"**	**10"**	**12½"**	**13¾"**
Light	A: 1 ⊠ → ⊠	4⅜"	5"	5⅝"	6¼"	7½"	8⅛"
	B: 18 ◺ → ◺	1½"	1⅝"	1¾"	1⅞"	2⅛"	2¼"
Medium	C: 1 ▢	3⅝"	4¼"	4⅞"	5½"	6¾"	7⅜"
	D: 2 ◺ → ◺	2¾"	3⅛"	3½"	3⅞"	4⅝"	5"
Dark	E: 14 ◺ → ◺	1½"	1⅝"	1¾"	1⅞"	2⅛"	2¼"

Try this: Use a large-scale print for C and D.

PINWHEEL

2-Unit Grid
Color Illustration: page 22

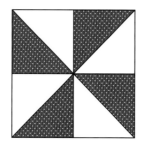
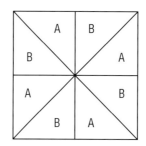
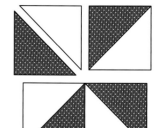

FOR 1 BLOCK:		**FINISHED BLOCK SIZE** *Single dimensions in the cutting chart indicate the size of the cut square (3" = 3" x 3").*					
		4"	**6"**	**8"**	**9"**	**10"**	**12"**
Light	A: 2 ◺ → ◺	2⅞"	3⅞"	4⅞"	5⅜"	5⅞"	6⅞"
Dark	B: 2 ◺ → ◺	2⅞"	3⅞"	4⅞"	5⅜"	5⅞"	6⅞"

Try this: Use a medium instead of a light for A in every other block.

PLAID

5-Unit Grid
Color Illustration: page 22

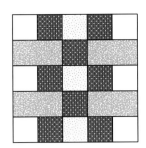

A	D	B	D	A
C		D		C
A	D	B	D	A
C		D		C
A	D	B	D	A

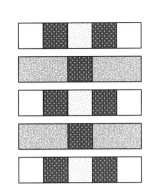

FOR 1 BLOCK:		FINISHED BLOCK SIZE					
		Single dimensions in the cutting chart indicate the size of the cut square (3" = 3" x 3").					
		5"	6¼"	7½"	8¾"	10"	12½"
Light	A: 6 ☐	1½"	1¾"	2"	2¼"	2½"	3"
Light 2	B: 3 ☐	1½"	1¾"	2"	2¼"	2½"	3"
Medium	C: 4 ▭	1½" x 2½"	1¾" x 3"	2" x 3½"	2¼" x 4"	2½" x 4½"	3" x 5½"
Dark	D: 8 ☐	1½"	1¾"	2"	2¼"	2½"	3"

Try this: Reverse the mediums and darks.

A PLAIN BLOCK

4-Unit Grid
Color Illustration: page 22

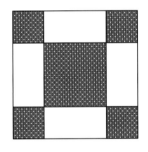

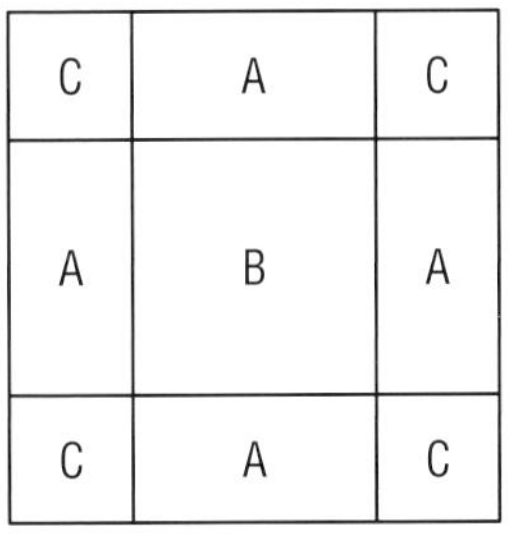 C	A	C
A	B	A
C	A	C

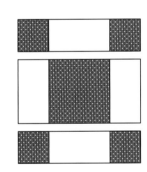

FOR 1 BLOCK:		FINISHED BLOCK SIZE					
		Single dimensions in the cutting chart indicate the size of the cut square (3" = 3" x 3").					
		4"	6"	8"	9"	10"	12"
Light	A: 4 ▭	1½" x 2½"	2" x 3½"	2½" x 4½"	2¾" x 5"	3" x 5½"	3½" x 6½"
Dark	B: 1 ☐	2½"	3½"	4½"	5"	5½"	6½"
	C: 4 ☐	1½"	2"	2½"	2¾"	3"	3½"

Try this: Reverse the lights and darks in every other block.

Light Light 2 Medium Medium 2 Dark

200

PORT AND STARBOARD

4-Unit Grid
Color Illustration: page 22

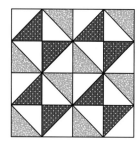 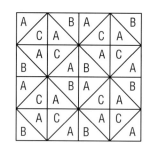 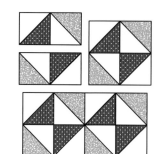

		FINISHED BLOCK SIZE					
		Single dimensions in the cutting chart indicate the size of the cut square (3" = 3" x 3").					
FOR 1 BLOCK:		**4"**	**6"**	**8"**	**9"**	**10"**	**12"**
Light	A: 8 ◻→◨	1⅞"	2⅜"	2⅞"	3⅛"	3⅜"	3⅞"
Medium	B: 4 ◻→◨	1⅞"	2⅜"	2⅞"	3⅛"	3⅜"	3⅞"
Dark	C: 4 ◻→◨	1⅞"	2⅜"	2⅞"	3⅛"	3⅜"	3⅞"
Try this:	Reverse the mediums and darks in every other block.						

PRACTICAL ORCHARD

3-Unit Grid
Color Illustration: page 22

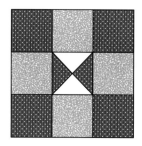 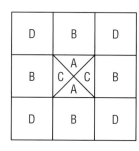 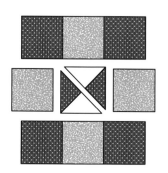

		FINISHED BLOCK SIZE					
		Single dimensions in the cutting chart indicate the size of the cut square (3" = 3" x 3").					
FOR 2 BLOCKS:		**4½"**	**6"**	**7½"**	**9"**	**10½"**	**12"**
Light	A: 1 ⊠→⊠	2¾"	3¼"	3¾"	4¼"	4¾"	5¼"
Medium	B: 8 ◻	2"	2½"	3"	3½"	4"	4½"
Dark	C: 1 ⊠→⊠	2¾"	3¼"	3¾"	4¼"	4¾"	5¼"
	D: 8 ◻	2"	2½"	3"	3½"	4"	4½"
Try this:	Reverse the darks and mediums in every other block.						

PREMIUM STAR

10-Unit Grid
Color Illustration: page 22

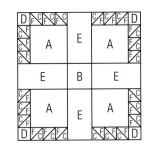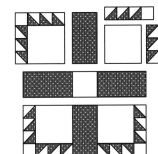

FOR 1 BLOCK:		**FINISHED BLOCK SIZE** *Single dimensions in the cutting chart indicate the size of the cut square (3" = 3" x 3").*					
		6¼"	**7½"**	**8¾"**	**10"**	**12½"**	**13¾"**
Light	A: 4 ☐	2⅜"	2¾"	3⅛"	3½"	4¼"	4⅝"
	B: 1 ☐	1¾"	2"	2¼"	2½"	3"	3¼"
	C: 12 ☐→◪	1½"	1⅝"	1¾"	1⅞"	2⅛"	2¼"
	D: 4 ☐	1⅛"	1¼"	1⅜"	1½"	1¾"	1⅞"
Dark	E: 4 ▭	1¾" x 3"	2" x 3½"	2¼" x 4"	2½" x 4½"	3" x 5½"	3¼" x 6"
	F: 12 ☐→◪	1½"	1⅝"	1¾"	1⅞"	2⅛"	2¼"

Try this: Reverse the lights and darks.

THE PRESIDENTIAL ARMCHAIR

9-Unit Grid
Color Illustration: page 22

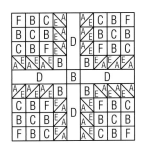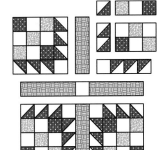

FOR 1 BLOCK:		**FINISHED BLOCK SIZE** *Single dimensions in the cutting chart indicate the size of the cut square (3" = 3" x 3").*					
		6¾"	**9"**	**10⅛"**	**11¼"**	**12⅜"**	**13½"**
Light	A: 12 ☐→◪	1⅝"	1⅞"	2"	2⅛"	2¼"	2⅜"
	B: 21 ☐	1¼"	1½"	1⅝"	1¾"	1⅞"	2"
Medium	C: 12 ☐	1¼"	1½"	1⅝"	1¾"	1⅞"	2"
Medium 2	D: 4 ▭	1¼" x 3½"	1½" x 4½"	1⅝" x 5"	1¾" x 5½"	1⅞" x 6"	2" x 6½"
Dark	E: 12 ☐→◪	1⅝"	1⅞"	2"	2⅛"	2¼"	2⅜"
	F: 8 ☐	1¼"	1½"	1⅝"	1¾"	1⅞"	2"

Try this: Use a different combination of darks and mediums in every quadrant of the block.

PRICKLY PEAR

7-Unit Grid
Color Illustration: page 22

 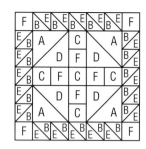 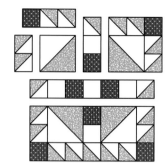

FOR 1 BLOCK:		FINISHED BLOCK SIZE *Single dimensions in the cutting chart indicate the size of the cut square (3" = 3" x 3").*					
		5¼"	7"	8¾"	10½"	12¼"	14"
Light	A: 2 ◻→◻	2⅜"	2⅞"	3⅜"	3⅞"	4⅜"	4⅞"
	B: 10 ◻→◻	1⅝"	1⅞"	2⅛"	2⅜"	2⅝"	2⅞"
	C: 5 ◻	1¼"	1½"	1¾"	2"	2¼"	2½"
Medium	D: 2 ◻→◻	2⅜"	2⅞"	3⅜"	3⅞"	4⅜"	4⅞"
	E: 10 ◻→◻	1⅝"	1⅞"	2⅛"	2⅜"	2⅝"	2⅞"
Dark	F: 8 ◻	1¼"	1½"	1¾"	2"	2¼"	2½"

Try this: Use several different mediums for E.

PROPELLER

5-Unit Grid
Color Illustration: page 22

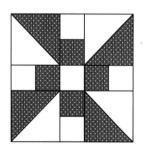 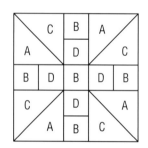 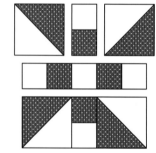

FOR 1 BLOCK:		FINISHED BLOCK SIZE *Single dimensions in the cutting chart indicate the size of the cut square (3" = 3" x 3").*					
		5"	6¼"	7½"	8¾"	10"	12½"
Light	A: 2 ◻→◻	2⅞"	3⅜"	3⅞"	4⅜"	4⅞"	5⅞"
	B: 5 ◻	1½"	1¾"	2"	2¼"	2½"	3"
Dark	C: 2 ◻→◻	2⅞"	3⅜"	3⅞"	4⅜"	4⅞"	5⅞"
	D: 4 ◻	1½"	1¾"	2"	2¼"	2½"	3"

Try this. Use a medium instead of a dark for C.

PROVIDENCE

5-Unit Grid
Color Illustration: page 22

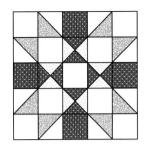
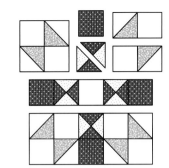

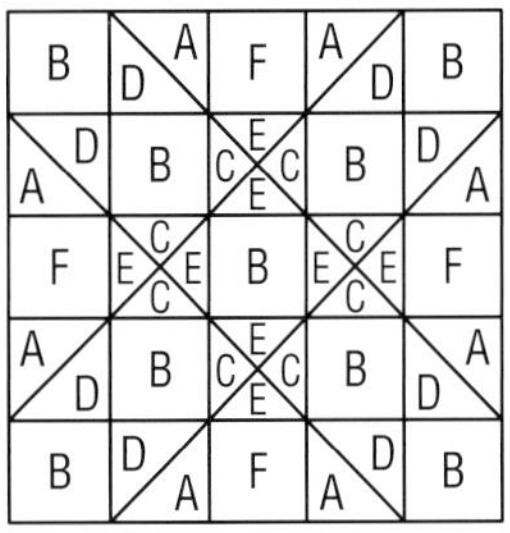

		FINISHED BLOCK SIZE *Single dimensions in the cutting chart indicate the size of the cut square (3" = 3" x 3").*					
FOR 1 BLOCK:		**5"**	**6¼"**	**7½"**	**8¾"**	**10"**	**12½"**
Light	A: 4 ◻→◩	1⅞"	2⅛"	2⅜"	2⅝"	2⅞"	3⅜"
	B: 9 ◻	1½"	1¾"	2"	2¼"	2½"	3"
Light 2	C: 2 ⊠→⊠	2¼"	2½"	2¾"	3"	3¼"	3¾"
Medium	D: 4 ◻→◩	1⅞"	2⅛"	2⅜"	2⅝"	2⅞"	3⅜"
Dark	E: 2 ⊠→⊠	2¼"	2½"	2¾"	3"	3¼"	3¾"
	F: 4 ◻	1½"	1¾"	2"	2¼"	2½"	3"

Try this: Reverse light 2 and the dark.

PUSS IN THE CORNER

6-Unit Grid
Color Illustration: page 22

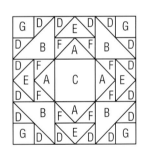

		FINISHED BLOCK SIZE *Single dimensions in the cutting chart indicate the size of the cut square (3" = 3" x 3").*					
FOR 1 BLOCK:		**4½"**	**6"**	**7½"**	**9"**	**10½"**	**12"**
Light	A: 1 ⊠→⊠	2¾"	3¼"	3¾"	4¼"	4¾"	5¼"
	B: 2 ◻→◩	2⅜"	2⅞"	3⅜"	3⅞"	4⅜"	4⅞"
	C: 1 ◻	2"	2½"	3"	3½"	4"	4½"
	D: 8 ◻→◩	1⅝"	1⅞"	2⅛"	2⅜"	2⅝"	2⅞"
Dark	E: 1 ⊠→⊠	2¾"	3¼"	3¾"	4¼"	4¾"	5¼"
	F: 4 ◻→◩	1⅝"	1⅞"	2⅛"	2⅜"	2⅝"	2⅞"
	G: 4 ◻	1¼"	1½"	1¾"	2"	2¼"	2½"

Try this: Use a medium instead of a light for B and C.

PUSS IN THE CORNER II

5-Unit Grid
Color Illustration: page 22

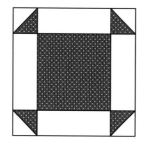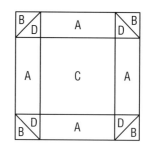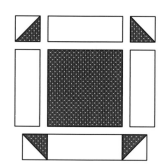

FOR 1 BLOCK:	FINISHED BLOCK SIZE *Single dimensions in the cutting chart indicate the size of the cut square (3" = 3" x 3").*					
	5"	**6¼"**	**7½"**	**8¾"**	**10"**	**12½"**
Light A: 4 ▭	1½" x 3½"	1¾" x 4¼"	2" x 5"	2¼" x 5¾"	2½" x 6½"	3" x 8"
B: 2 ◻→◹	1⅞"	2⅛"	2⅜"	2⅝"	2⅞"	3⅜"
Dark C: 1 ☐	3½"	4¼"	5"	5¾"	6½"	8"
D: 2 ◻→◹	1⅞"	2⅛"	2⅜"	2⅝"	2⅞"	3⅜"

Try this: Use a large-scale print for C.

PUSSY IN THE CORNER

6-Unit Grid
Color Illustration: page 22

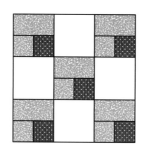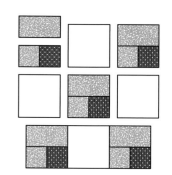

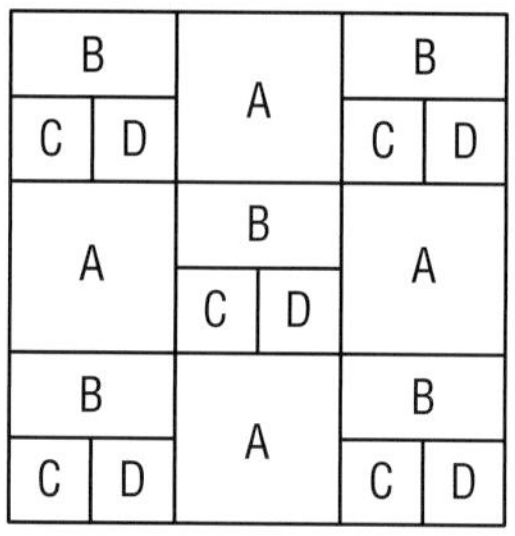

FOR 1 BLOCK:	FINISHED BLOCK SIZE *Single dimensions in the cutting chart indicate the size of the cut square (3" = 3" x 3").*					
	4½"	**6"**	**7½"**	**9"**	**10½"**	**12"**
Light A: 4 ☐	2"	2½"	3"	3½"	4"	4½"
Medium B: 5 ▭	1¼" x 2"	1½" x 2½"	1¾" x 3"	2" x 3½"	2¼" x 4"	2½" x 4½"
C: 5 ☐	1¼"	1½"	1¾"	2"	2¼"	2½"
Dark D: 5 ☐	1¼"	1½"	1¾"	2"	2¼"	2½"

Try this: Use several different lights for A.

PYRAMIDS

4-Unit Grid
Color Illustration: page 22

 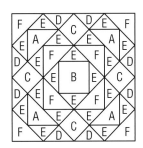 

FOR 1 BLOCK:		FINISHED BLOCK SIZE *Single dimensions in the cutting chart indicate the size of the cut square (3" = 3" x 3").*					
		4"	**6"**	**8"**	**9"**	**10"**	**12"**
Light	A: 2 ☐ → ◺	1⅞"	2⅜"	2⅞"	3⅛"	3⅜"	3⅞"
	B: 1 ☐	1½"	2"	2½"	2¾"	3"	3½"
	C: 4 ◇	T2	T5	T7	T8	T9	T11
Light 2	D: 2 ⊠ → ◪	2¼"	2¾"	3¼"	3½"	3¾"	4¼"
Medium	E: 5 ⊠ → ◪	2¼"	2¾"	3¼"	3½"	3¾"	4¼"
Dark	F: 4 ◻ → ◺	1⅞"	2⅜"	2⅞"	3⅛"	3⅜"	3⅞"

Try this: Reverse the mediums and darks.

QUILT IN LIGHT AND DARK

4-Unit Grid
Color Illustration: page 22

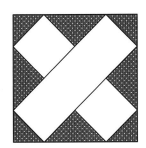 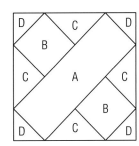 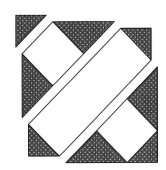

FOR 1 BLOCK:		FINISHED BLOCK SIZE *Single dimensions in the cutting chart indicate the size of the cut square (3" = 3" x 3").*					
		4"	**6"**	**8"**	**9"**	**10"**	**12"**
Light	A: 1 ▱	T52	T68	T73	T74	T75	T76
	B: 2 ◇	T7	T11	T14	T15	T16	T19
Dark	C: 1 ⊠ → ◪	3¼"	4¼"	5¼"	5¾"	6¼"	7¼"
	D: 2 ◻ → ◺	1⅞"	2⅜"	2⅞"	3⅛"	3⅜"	3⅞"

Try this: Reverse the lights and darks in every other block.

☐ *Light* ▧ *Light 2* ▨ *Medium* ▤ *Medium 2* ■ *Dark*

RAILROAD CROSSING

4-Unit Grid

Color Illustration: page 22

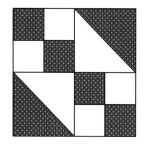
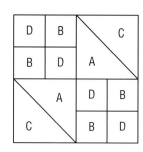
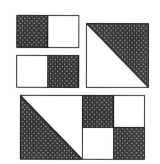

FOR 1 BLOCK:		FINISHED BLOCK SIZE					
		Single dimensions in the cutting chart indicate the size of the cut square (3" = 3" x 3").					
		4"	6"	8"	9"	10"	12"
Light	A: 1 ⬜→◪	2⅞"	3⅞"	4⅞"	5⅜"	5⅞"	6⅞"
	B: 4 ⬜	1½"	2"	2½"	2¾"	3"	3½"
Dark	C: 1 ⬜→◪	2⅞"	3⅞"	4⅞"	5⅜"	5⅞"	6⅞"
	D: 4 ⬜	1½"	2"	2½"	2¾"	3"	3½"

Try this: Use a medium instead of a dark for C.

RAMBLER

8-Unit Grid

Color Illustration: page 23

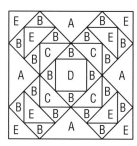

FOR 1 BLOCK:		FINISHED BLOCK SIZE					
		Single dimensions in the cutting chart indicate the size of the cut square (3" = 3" x 3").					
		4"	6"	8"	9"	10"	12"
Light	A: 1 ⬚→⊠	3¼"	4¼"	5¼"	5¾"	6¼"	7¼"
	B: 5 ⬚→⊠	2¼"	2¾"	3¼"	3½"	3¾"	4¼"
Medium	C: 2 ⬜→◪	1⅞"	2⅜"	2⅞"	3⅛"	3⅜"	3⅞"
	D: 1 ⬜	1½"	2"	2½"	2¾"	3"	3½"
Dark	E: 4 ⬜→◪	1⅞"	2⅜"	2⅞"	3⅛"	3⅜"	3⅞"

Try this: Use one light for A and a different light for B.

RED CROSS

8-Unit Grid
Color Illustration: page 23

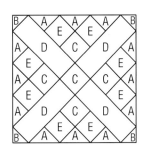

FOR 1 BLOCK:	FINISHED BLOCK SIZE *Single dimensions in the cutting chart indicate the size of the cut square (3" = 3" x 3").*					
	6"	**8"**	**9"**	**10"**	**12"**	**14"**
Light A: 3 ⊠ → ⊠	2¾"	3¼"	3½"	3¾"	4¼"	4¾"
B: 2 ◹ → ◺	1⅝"	1⅞"	2"	2⅛"	2⅜"	2⅝"
C: 5 ◇	T5	T7	T8	T9	T11	T12
Dark D: 4 ▱	T42	T52	T57	T60	T68	T71
E: 8 ◇	T5	T7	T8	T9	T11	T12

Try this: Use one light for A and B and a different light for C.

RED CROSS II

5-Unit Grid
Color Illustration: page 23

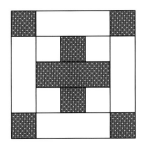
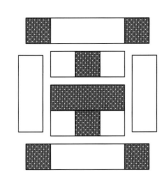

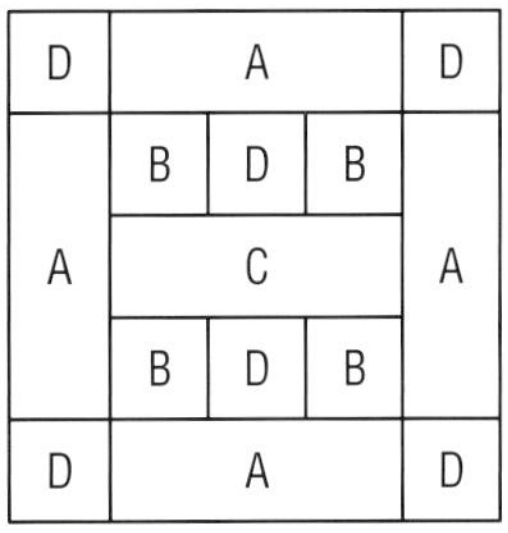

FOR 1 BLOCK:	FINISHED BLOCK SIZE *Single dimensions in the cutting chart indicate the size of the cut square (3" = 3" x 3").*					
	5"	**6¼"**	**7½"**	**8¾"**	**10"**	**12½"**
Light A: 4 ▭	1½" x 3½"	1¾" x 4¼"	2" x 5"	2¼" x 5¾"	2½" x 6½"	3" x 8"
B: 4 □	1½"	1¾"	2"	2¼"	2½"	3"
Dark C: 1 ▭	1½" x 3½"	1¾" x 4¼"	2" x 5"	2¼" x 5¾"	2½" x 6½"	3" x 8"
D: 6 □	1½"	1¾"	2"	2¼"	2½"	3"

Try this: Use a different light or a medium for B.

RED CROSS III

5-Unit Grid

Color Illustration: page 23

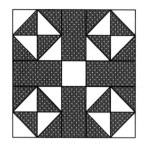 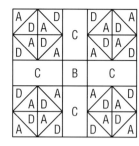 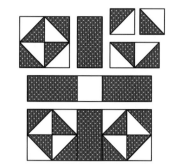

		FINISHED BLOCK SIZE *Single dimensions in the cutting chart indicate the size of the cut square (3" = 3" x 3").*					
FOR 1 BLOCK:		**5"**	**6¼"**	**7½"**	**8¾"**	**10"**	**12½"**
Light	A: 8 ◻→◁	1⅞"	2⅛"	2⅜"	2⅝"	2⅞"	3⅜"
	B: 1 ◻	1½"	1¾"	2"	2¼"	2½"	3"
Dark	C: 4 ▭	1½" x 2½"	1¾" x 3"	2" x 3½"	2¼" x 4"	2½" x 4½"	3" x 5½"
	D: 8 ◻→◁	1⅞"	2⅛"	2⅜"	2⅝"	2⅞"	3⅜"

Try this: Use a medium instead of a dark for C.

REMEMBER ME

2-Unit Grid

Color Illustration: page 23

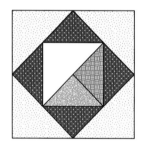 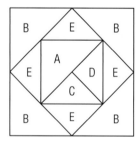 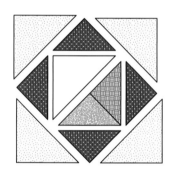

		FINISHED BLOCK SIZE *Single dimensions in the cutting chart indicate the size of the cut square (3" = 3" x 3").*					
FOR 4 BLOCKS:		**4"**	**6"**	**8"**	**9"**	**10"**	**12"**
Light	A: 2 ◻→◁	2⅞"	3⅞"	4⅞"	5⅜"	5⅞"	6⅞"
Light 2	B: 8 ◻→◁	2⅞"	3⅞"	4⅞"	5⅜"	5⅞"	6⅞"
Medium	C: 1 ⊠→⊠	3¼"	4¼"	5¼"	5¾"	6¼"	7¼"
Medium 2	D: 1 ⊠→⊠	3¼"	4¼"	5¼"	5¾"	6¼"	7¼"
Dark	E: 4 ⊠→⊠	3¼"	4¼"	5¼"	5¾"	6¼"	7¼"

Try this: Use a different combination of fabrics in every block.

RETURN OF THE SWALLOWS

4-Unit Grid

Color Illustration: page 23

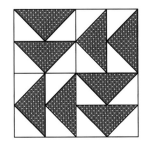
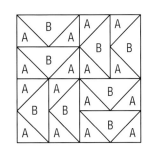
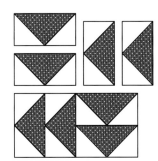

	FINISHED BLOCK SIZE *Single dimensions in the cutting chart indicate the size of the cut square (3" = 3" x 3").*					
FOR 1 BLOCK:	**4"**	**6"**	**8"**	**9"**	**10"**	**12"**
Light A: 8 ☐ → ◸	1⅞"	2⅜"	2⅞"	3⅛"	3⅜"	3⅞"
Dark B: 2 ⊠ → ⊠	3¼"	4¼"	5¼"	5¾"	6¼"	7¼"

Try this: Use several different lights for A.

REVERSE X

8-Unit Grid

Color Illustration: page 23

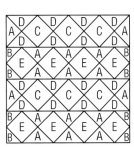

	FINISHED BLOCK SIZE *Single dimensions in the cutting chart indicate the size of the cut square (3" = 3" x 3").*					
FOR 1 BLOCK:	**6"**	**8"**	**9"**	**10"**	**12"**	**14"**
Light A: 4 ⊠ → ⊠	2¾"	3¼"	3½"	3¾"	4¼"	4¾"
B: 4 ☐ → ◸	1⅝"	1⅞"	2"	2⅛"	2⅜"	2⅝"
C: 6 ◇	T5	T7	T8	T9	T11	T12
Dark D: 4 ⊠ → ⊠	2¾"	3¼"	3½"	3¾"	4¼"	4¾"
E: 8 ◇	T5	T7	T8	T9	T11	T12

Try this: Use many different lights and darks.

RHODE ISLAND

6-Unit Grid

Color Illustration: page 23

 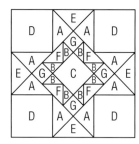 

		FINISHED BLOCK SIZE *Single dimensions in the cutting chart indicate the size of the cut square (3" = 3" x 3").*					
FOR 1 BLOCK:		**4½"**	**6"**	**7½"**	**9"**	**10½"**	**12"**
Light	A: 2 ⊠ → ⊠	2¾"	3¼"	3¾"	4¼"	4¾"	5¼"
	B: 2 ⊠ → ⊠	2"	2¼"	2½"	2¾"	3"	3¼"
	C: 1 ◇	T5	T7	T9	T11	T12	T14
Medium	D: 4 □	2"	2½"	3"	3½"	4"	4½"
Dark	E: 1 ⊠ → ⊠	2¾"	3¼"	3¾"	4¼"	4¾"	5¼"
	F: 2 ◻ → ◺	1⅝"	1⅞"	2⅛"	2⅜"	2⅝"	2⅞"
	G: 4 ◇	T1	T2	T4	T5	T6	T7

Try this: Use one light for A and a different light for B and C.

RIBBON QUILT

3-Unit Grid

Color Illustration: page 23

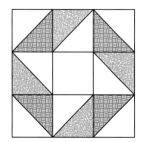 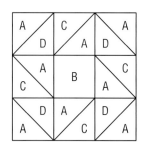 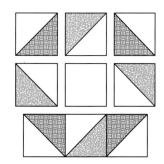

		FINISHED BLOCK SIZE *Single dimensions in the cutting chart indicate the size of the cut square (3" = 3" x 3").*					
FOR 1 BLOCK:		**4½"**	**6"**	**7½"**	**9"**	**10½"**	**12"**
Light	A: 4 ◻ → ◺	2⅜"	2⅞"	3⅜"	3⅞"	4⅜"	4⅞"
	B: 1 □	2"	2½"	3"	3½"	4"	4½"
Medium	C: 2 ◻ → ◺	2⅜"	2⅞"	3⅜"	3⅞"	4⅜"	4⅞"
Medium 2	D: 2 ◻ → ◺	2⅜"	2⅞"	3⅜"	3⅞"	4⅜"	4⅞"

Try this: Use one light for A and a different light for B.

RICHMOND

6-Unit Grid

Color Illustration: page 23

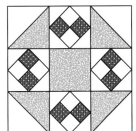
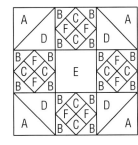

FOR 1 BLOCK:		FINISHED BLOCK SIZE Single dimensions in the cutting chart indicate the size of the cut square (3" = 3" x 3").					
		4½"	**6"**	**7½"**	**9"**	**10½"**	**12"**
Light	A: 2 ◻→◺	2⅜"	2⅞"	3⅜"	3⅞"	4⅜"	4⅞"
	B: 8 ◻→◺	1⅝"	1⅞"	2⅛"	2⅜"	2⅝"	2⅞"
	C: 8 ◇	T1	T2	T4	T5	T6	T7
Medium	D: 2 ◻→◺	2⅜"	2⅞"	3⅜"	3⅞"	4⅜"	4⅞"
	E: 1 ◻	2"	2½"	3"	3½"	4"	4½"
Dark	F: 8 ◇	T1	T2	T4	T5	T6	T7

Try this: Reverse the mediums and darks in every other block.

RIGHT AND LEFT

2-Unit Grid

Color Illustration: page 23

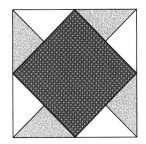
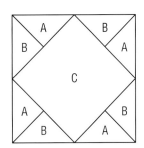
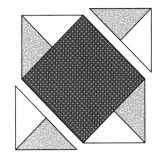

FOR 1 BLOCK:		FINISHED BLOCK SIZE Single dimensions in the cutting chart indicate the size of the cut square (3" = 3" x 3").					
		4"	**6"**	**8"**	**9"**	**10"**	**12"**
Light	A: 1 ⊠→⧖	3¼"	4¼"	5¼"	5¾"	6¼"	7¼"
Medium	B: 1 ⊠→⧖	3¼"	4¼"	5¼"	5¾"	6¼"	7¼"
Dark	C: 1 ◇	T14	T19	T23	T24	T25	T27

Try this: Use a large-scale print for C.

Light   Light 2   Medium   Medium 2   Dark

RIGHT HAND OF FRIENDSHIP

6-Unit Grid

Color Illustration: page 23

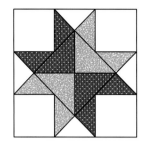
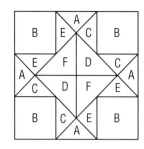

		FINISHED BLOCK SIZE Single dimensions in the cutting chart indicate the size of the cut square (3" = 3" x 3").					
FOR 1 BLOCK:		**4½"**	**6"**	**7½"**	**9"**	**10½"**	**12"**
Light	A: 1 ⊠ → ⊠	2¾"	3¼"	3¾"	4¼"	4¾"	5¼"
	B: 4 ☐	2"	2½"	3"	3½"	4"	4½"
Medium	C: 1 ⊠ → ⊠	2¾"	3¼"	3¾"	4¼"	4¾"	5¼"
	D: 1 ◻ → ◻	2⅜"	2⅞"	3⅜"	3⅞"	4⅜"	4⅞"
Dark	E: 1 ⊠ → ⊠	2¾"	3¼"	3¾"	4¼"	4¾"	5¼"
	F: 1 ◻ → ◻	2⅜"	2⅞"	3⅜"	3⅞"	4⅜"	4⅞"

Try this: Reverse the lights and darks in every other block.

RISING STAR

8-Unit Grid

Color Illustration: page 23

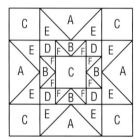
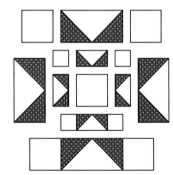

		FINISHED BLOCK SIZE Single dimensions in the cutting chart indicate the size of the cut square (3" = 3" x 3").					
FOR 1 BLOCK:		**6"**	**8"**	**9"**	**10"**	**12"**	**14"**
Light	A: 1 ⊠ → ⊠	4¼"	5¼"	5¾"	6¼"	7¼"	8¼"
	B: 1 ⊠ → ⊠	2¾"	3¼"	3½"	3¾"	4¼"	4¾"
	C: 5 ☐	2"	2½"	2¾"	3"	3½"	4"
	D: 4 ☐	1¼"	1½"	1⅝"	1¾"	2"	2¼"
Dark	E: 4 ◻ → ◻	2⅜"	2⅞"	3⅛"	3⅜"	3⅞"	4⅜"
	F: 4 ◻ → ◻	1⅝"	1⅞"	2"	2⅛"	2⅜"	2⅝"

Try this: Use one dark for E and a different dark for F.

RISING SUN

5-Unit Grid
Color Illustration: page 23

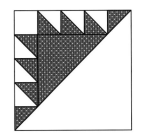
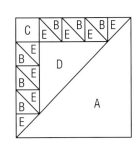
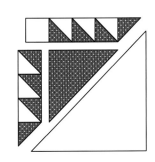

		FINISHED BLOCK SIZE *Single dimensions in the cutting chart indicate the size of the cut square (3" = 3" x 3").*					
FOR 2 BLOCKS:		**5"**	**6¼"**	**7½"**	**8¾"**	**10"**	**12½"**
Light	A: 1 ☐ → ◲	5⅞"	7⅛"	8⅜"	9⅝"	10⅞"	13⅜"
	B: 6 ☐ → ◲	1⅞"	2⅛"	2⅜"	2⅝"	2⅞"	3⅜"
	C: 2 ☐	1½"	1¾"	2"	2¼"	2½"	3"
Dark	D: 1 ☐ → ◲	3⅞"	4⅝"	5⅜"	6⅛"	6⅞"	8⅜"
	E: 8 ☐ → ◲	1⅞"	2⅛"	2⅜"	2⅝"	2⅞"	3⅜"

Try this: Use several different darks for E.

ROAD TO THE WHITE HOUSE

6-Unit Grid
Color Illustration: page 23

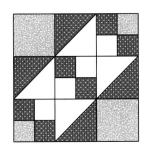
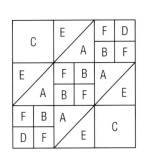

		FINISHED BLOCK SIZE *Single dimensions in the cutting chart indicate the size of the cut square (3" = 3" x 3").*					
FOR 1 BLOCK:		**4½"**	**6"**	**7½"**	**9"**	**10½"**	**12"**
Light	A: 2 ☐ → ◲	2⅜"	2⅞"	3⅜"	3⅞"	4⅜"	4⅞"
	B: 4 ☐	1¼"	1½"	1¾"	2"	2¼"	2½"
Medium	C: 2 ☐	2"	2½"	3"	3½"	4"	4½"
	D: 2 ☐	1¼"	1½"	1¾"	2"	2¼"	2½"
Dark	E: 2 ☐ → ◲	2⅜"	2⅞"	3⅜"	3⅞"	4⅜"	4⅞"
	F: 6 ☐	1¼"	1½"	1¾"	2"	2¼"	2½"

Try this: Use a different medium in every block.

☐ *Light*   ▦ *Light 2*   ▦ *Medium*   ▦ *Medium 2*   ▦ *Dark*

Robbing Peter to Pay Paul

6-Unit Grid
Color Illustration: page 23

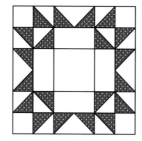
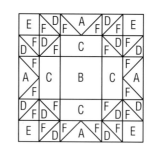
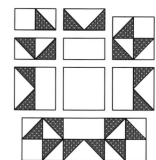

	FINISHED BLOCK SIZE					
	Single dimensions in the cutting chart indicate the size of the cut square (3" = 3" x 3").					
FOR 1 BLOCK:	**4½"**	**6"**	**7½"**	**9"**	**10½"**	**12"**
Light A: 1 ⊠ → ⊠	2¾"	3¼"	3¾"	4¼"	4¾"	5¼"
B: 1 ☐	2"	2½"	3"	3½"	4"	4½"
C: 4 ▭	1¼" x 2"	1½" x 2½"	1¾" x 3"	2" x 3½"	2¼" x 4"	2½" x 4½"
D: 6 ◻ → ◳	1⅝"	1⅞"	2⅛"	2⅜"	2⅝"	2⅞"
E: 4 ☐	1¼"	1½"	1¾"	2"	2¼"	2½"
Dark F: 10 ◻ → ◳	1⅝"	1⅞"	2⅛"	2⅜"	2⅝"	2⅞"

Try this: Use a medium instead of a light for B.

Rocky Glen

5-Unit Grid
Color Illustration: page 23

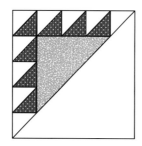
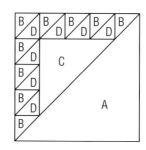
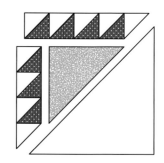

	FINISHED BLOCK SIZE					
	Single dimensions in the cutting chart indicate the size of the cut square (3" = 3" x 3").					
FOR 2 BLOCKS:	**5"**	**6¼"**	**7½"**	**8¾"**	**10"**	**12½"**
Light A: 1 ◻ → ◳	5⅞"	7⅛"	8⅜"	9⅝"	10⅞"	13⅜"
B: 9 ◻ → ◳	1⅞"	2⅛"	2⅜"	2⅝"	2⅞"	3⅜"
Medium C: 1 ◻ → ◳	3⅞"	4⅝"	5⅜"	6⅛"	6⅞"	8⅜"
Dark D: 7 ◻ → ◳	1⅞"	2⅛"	2⅜"	2⅝"	2⅞"	3⅜"

Try this: Use a large-scale print for C.

Rocky Glen II

10-Unit Grid

Color Illustration: page 23

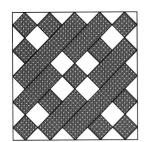

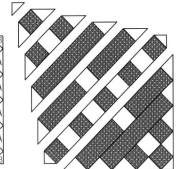

FOR 1 BLOCK:	FINISHED BLOCK SIZE Single dimensions in the cutting chart indicate the size of the cut square (3" = 3" x 3").					
	6¼"	7½"	8¾"	10"	12½"	13¾"
Light A: 4 ⊠ → ⊠	2½"	2¾"	3"	3¼"	3¾"	4"
B: 2 ◨ → ◪	1½"	1⅝"	1¾"	1⅞"	2⅛"	2¼"
C: 8 ◇	T4	T5	T6	T7	T9	T10
Dark D: 2 ▱	T39	T44	T49	T54	T62	T66
E: 4 ▱	T37	T42	T47	T52	T60	T64
F: 11 ◇	T4	T5	T6	T7	T9	T10

Try this: Use a different combination of lights and darks in every block.

Rocky Mountain Chain

10-Unit Grid

Color Illustration: page 23

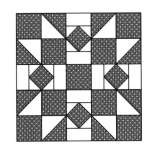
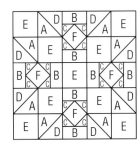
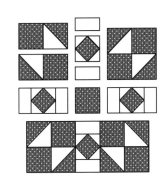

FOR 1 BLOCK:	FINISHED BLOCK SIZE Single dimensions in the cutting chart indicate the size of the cut square (3" = 3" x 3").					
	6¼"	7½"	8¾"	10"	12½"	13¾"
Light A: 4 ◨ → ◪	2⅛"	2⅜"	2⅝"	2⅞"	3⅜"	3⅝"
B: 8 ▭	1⅛" x 1¾"	1¼" x 2"	1⅜" x 2¼"	1½" x 2½"	1¾" x 3"	1⅞" x 3¼"
C: 8 ◨ → ◪	1½"	1⅝"	1¾"	1⅞"	2⅛"	2¼"
Dark D: 4 ◨ → ◪	2⅛"	2⅜"	2⅝"	2⅞"	3⅜"	3⅝"
E: 9 ▢	1¾"	2"	2¼"	2½"	3"	3¼"
F: 4 ◇	T4	T5	T6	T7	T9	T10

Try this: Use a medium instead of a light for C.

ROCKY ROAD

6-Unit Grid

Color Illustration: page 23

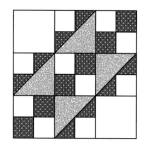
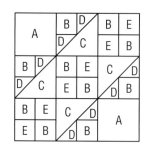
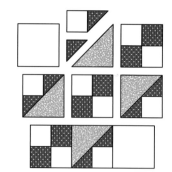

		FINISHED BLOCK SIZE					
		Single dimensions in the cutting chart indicate the size of the cut square (3" = 3" x 3").					
FOR 1 BLOCK:		**4½"**	**6"**	**7½"**	**9"**	**10½"**	**12"**
Light	A: 2 ☐	2"	2½"	3"	3½"	4"	4½"
	B: 10 ☐	1¼"	1½"	1¾"	2"	2¼"	2½"
Medium	C: 2 ◨ → ◪	2⅜"	2⅞"	3⅜"	3⅞"	4⅜"	4⅞"
Dark	D: 4 ◨ → ◪	1⅝"	1⅞"	2⅛"	2⅜"	2⅝"	2⅞"
	E: 6 ☐	1¼"	1½"	1¾"	2"	2¼"	2½"

Try this: Use one light for A and several different lights for B.

ROCKY ROAD TO CALIFORNIA

6-Unit Grid

Color Illustration: page 23

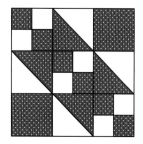
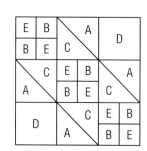

		FINISHED BLOCK SIZE					
		Single dimensions in the cutting chart indicate the size of the cut square (3" = 3" x 3").					
FOR 1 BLOCK:		**4½"**	**6"**	**7½"**	**9"**	**10½"**	**12"**
Light	A: 2 ◨ → ◪	2⅜"	2⅞"	3⅜"	3⅞"	4⅜"	4⅞"
	B: 6 ☐	1¼"	1½"	1¾"	2"	2¼"	2½"
Dark	C: 2 ◨ → ◪	2⅜"	2⅞"	3⅜"	3⅞"	4⅜"	4⅞"
	D: 2 ☐	2"	2½"	3"	3½"	4"	4½"
	E: 6 ☐	1¼"	1½"	1¾"	2"	2¼"	2½"

Try this: Use a medium instead of a dark for D and E.

ROCKY ROAD TO DUBLIN

6-Unit Grid
Color Illustration: page 23

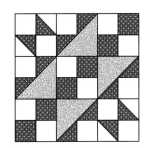 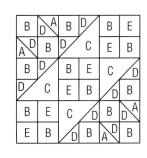 

FOR 1 BLOCK:		FINISHED BLOCK SIZE *Single dimensions in the cutting chart indicate the size of the cut square (3" = 3" x 3").*					
		4½"	6"	7½"	9"	10½"	12"
Light	A: 2 ◻→◹	1⅝"	1⅞"	2⅛"	2⅜"	2⅝"	2⅞"
	B: 14 ◻	1¼"	1½"	1¾"	2"	2¼"	2½"
Medium	C: 2 ◻→◹	2⅜"	2⅞"	3⅜"	3⅞"	4⅜"	4⅞"
Dark	D: 6 ◻→◹	1⅝"	1⅞"	2⅛"	2⅜"	2⅝"	2⅞"
	E: 6 ◻	1¼"	1½"	1¾"	2"	2¼"	2½"

Try this: Use one light for A and a different light for B.

ROLLING NINE PATCH

5-Unit Grid
Color Illustration: page 23

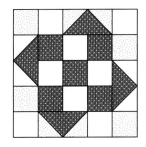 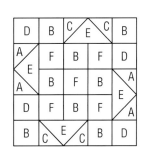 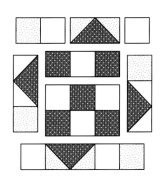

FOR 1 BLOCK:		FINISHED BLOCK SIZE *Single dimensions in the cutting chart indicate the size of the cut square (3" = 3" x 3").*					
		5"	6¼"	7½"	8¾"	10"	12½"
Light	A: 2 ◻→◹	1⅞"	2⅛"	2⅜"	2⅝"	2⅞"	3⅜"
	B: 8 ◻	1½"	1¾"	2"	2¼"	2½"	3"
Light 2	C: 2 ◻→◹	1⅞"	2⅛"	2⅜"	2⅝"	2⅞"	3⅜"
	D: 4 ◻	1½"	1¾"	2"	2¼"	2½"	3"
Dark	E: 1 ⊠→⊠	3¼"	3¾"	4¼"	4¾"	5¼"	6¼"
	F: 5 ◻	1½"	1¾"	2"	2¼"	2½"	3"

Try this: Use a different combination of fabrics in every block.

ROLLING PINWHEEL

6-Unit Grid
Color Illustration: page 23

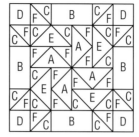

		FINISHED BLOCK SIZE					
		Single dimensions in the cutting chart indicate the size of the cut square (3" = 3" x 3").					
FOR 1 BLOCK:		**4½"**	**6"**	**7½"**	**9"**	**10½"**	**12"**
Light	A: 1 ⊠ → ⊠	2¾"	3¼"	3¾"	4¼"	4¾"	5¼"
	B: 4 ▭	1¼" x 2"	1½" x 2½"	1¾" x 3"	2" x 3½"	2¼" x 4"	2½" x 4½"
	C: 8 ◻ → ◪	1⅝"	1⅞"	2⅛"	2⅜"	2⅝"	2⅞"
	D: 4 ▢	1¼"	1½"	1¾"	2"	2¼"	2½"
Dark	E: 1 ⊠ → ⊠	2¾"	3¼"	3¾"	4¼"	4¾"	5¼"
	F: 8 ◻ → ◪	1⅝"	1⅞"	2⅛"	2⅜"	2⅝"	2⅞"

Try this: Reverse the lights and darks.

ROLLING SQUARES

6-Unit Grid
Color Illustration: page 23

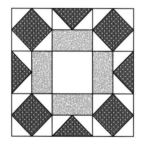
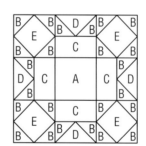
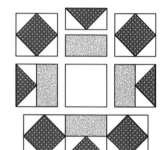

		FINISHED BLOCK SIZE					
		Single dimensions in the cutting chart indicate the size of the cut square (3" = 3" x 3").					
FOR 1 BLOCK:		**4½"**	**6"**	**7½"**	**9"**	**10½"**	**12"**
Light	A: 1 ▢	2"	2½"	3"	3½"	4"	4½"
	B: 12 ◻ → ◪	1⅝"	1⅞"	2⅛"	2⅜"	2⅝"	2⅞"
Medium	C: 4 ▭	1¼" x 2"	1½" x 2½"	1¾" x 3"	2" x 3½"	2¼" x 4"	2½" x 4½"
Dark	D: 1 ⊠ → ⊠	2¾"	3¼"	3¾"	4¼"	4¾"	5¼"
	E: 4 ◇	T5	T7	T9	T11	T12	T14

Try this: Reverse the mediums and darks.

ROLLING STONE

6-Unit Grid
Color Illustration: page 23

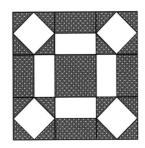
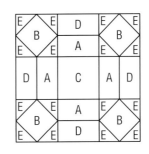
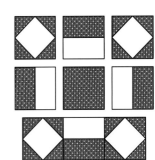

		FINISHED BLOCK SIZE *Single dimensions in the cutting chart indicate the size of the cut square (3" = 3" x 3").*					
FOR 1 BLOCK:		**4½"**	**6"**	**7½"**	**9"**	**10½"**	**12"**
Light	A: 4 ▭	1¼" x 2"	1½" x 2½"	1¾" x 3"	2" x 3½"	2¼" x 4"	2½" x 4½"
	B: 4 ◇	T5	T7	T9	T11	T12	T14
Dark	C: 1 ▢	2"	2½"	3"	3½"	4"	4½"
	D: 4 ▭	1¼" x 2"	1½" x 2½"	1¾" x 3"	2" x 3½"	2¼" x 4"	2½" x 4½"
	E: 8 ◺→◳	1⅝"	1⅞"	2⅛"	2⅜"	2⅝"	2⅞"

Try this: Reverse the lights and darks in every other block.

THE ROSEBUD

8-Unit Grid
Color Illustration: page 23

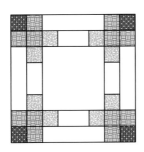
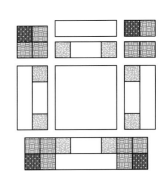

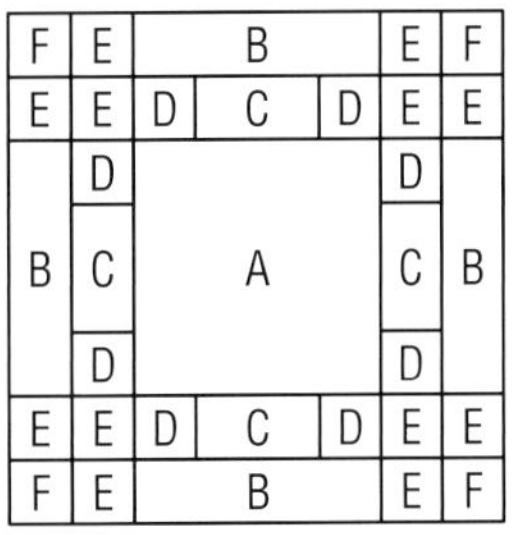

		FINISHED BLOCK SIZE *Single dimensions in the cutting chart indicate the size of the cut square (3" = 3" x 3").*					
FOR 1 BLOCK:		**6"**	**8"**	**9"**	**10"**	**12"**	**14"**
Light	A: 1 ▢	3½"	4½"	5"	5½"	6½"	7½"
	B: 4 ▭	1¼" x 3½"	1½" x 4½"	1⅝" x 5"	1¾" x 5½"	2" x 6½"	2¼" x 7½"
	C: 4 ▭	1¼" x 2"	1½" x 2½"	1⅝" x 2¾"	1¾" x 3"	2" x 3½"	2¼" x 4"
Medium	D: 8 ▢	1¼"	1½"	1⅝"	1¾"	2"	2¼"
Medium 2	E: 12 ▢	1¼"	1½"	1⅝"	1¾"	2"	2¼"
Dark	F: 4 ▢	1¼"	1½"	1⅝"	1¾"	2"	2¼"

Try this: Use a different combination of mediums and darks in every block.

ROUND THE CORNER

5-Unit Grid

Color Illustration: page 23

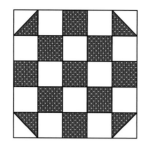

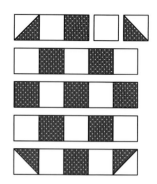

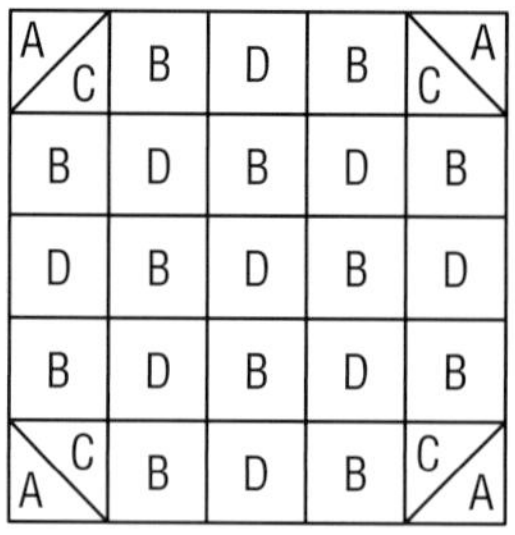

FOR 1 BLOCK:		**FINISHED BLOCK SIZE** *Single dimensions in the cutting chart indicate the size of the cut square (3" = 3" x 3").*					
		5"	**6¼"**	**7½"**	**8¾"**	**10"**	**12½"**
Light	A: 2 ◻→◹	1⅞"	2⅛"	2⅜"	2⅝"	2⅞"	3⅜"
	B: 12 ◻	1½"	1¾"	2"	2¼"	2½"	3"
Dark	C: 2 ◻→◹	1⅞"	2⅛"	2⅜"	2⅝"	2⅞"	3⅜"
	D: 9 ◻	1½"	1¾"	2"	2¼"	2½"	3"

Try this: Use a medium instead of a dark for C.

RUINS OF JERICHO

8-Unit Grid

Color Illustration: page 23

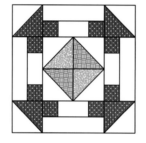

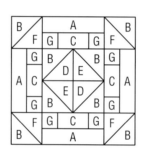

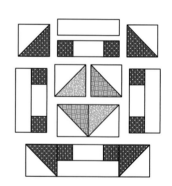

FOR 1 BLOCK:		**FINISHED BLOCK SIZE** *Single dimensions in the cutting chart indicate the size of the cut square (3" = 3" x 3").*					
		6"	**8"**	**9"**	**10"**	**12"**	**14"**
Light	A: 4 ▭	1¼" x 3½"	1½" x 4½"	1⅝" x 5"	1¾" x 5½"	2" x 6½"	2¼" x 7½"
	B: 4 ◻→◹	2⅜"	2⅞"	3⅛"	3⅜"	3⅞"	4⅜"
	C: 4 ▭	1¼" x 2"	1½" x 2½"	1⅝" x 2¾"	1¾" x 3"	2" x 3½"	2¼" x 4"
Medium	D: 1 ◻→◹	2⅜"	2⅞"	3⅛"	3⅜"	3⅞"	4⅜"
Medium 2	E: 1 ◻→◹	2⅜"	2⅞"	3⅛"	3⅜"	3⅞"	4⅜"
Dark	F: 2 ◻→◹	2⅜"	2⅞"	3⅛"	3⅜"	3⅞"	4⅜"
	G: 8 ◻	1¼"	1½"	1⅝"	1¾"	2"	2¼"

Try this: Use one light for A and C and a different light for B.

SAIL BOATS

6-Unit Grid

Color Illustration: page 23

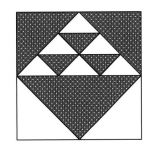
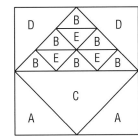

			FINISHED BLOCK SIZE *Single dimensions in the cutting chart indicate the size of the cut square (3" = 3" x 3").*					
FOR 4 BLOCKS:			**4½"**	**6"**	**7½"**	**9"**	**10½"**	**12"**
Light	A: 4 ◻→◻		3⅛"	3⅞"	4⅝"	5⅜"	6⅛"	6⅞"
	B: 6 ⊠→⊠		2¾"	3¼"	3¾"	4¼"	4¾"	5¼"
Dark	C: 1 ⊠→⊠		5¾"	7¼"	8¾"	10¼"	11¾"	13¼"
	D: 4 ◻→◻		3⅛"	3⅞"	4⅝"	5⅜"	6⅛"	6⅞"
	E: 3 ⊠→⊠		2¾"	3¼"	3¾"	4¼"	4¾"	5¼"

Try this: Use several different mediums or darks for E.

SALLY'S FAVORITE

4-Unit Grid

Color Illustration: page 24

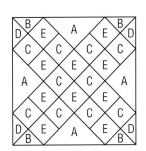

			FINISHED BLOCK SIZE *Single dimensions in the cutting chart indicate the size of the cut square (3" = 3" x 3").*					
FOR 1 BLOCK:			**4"**	**6"**	**8"**	**9"**	**10"**	**12"**
Light	A: 1 ⊠→⊠		3¼"	4¼"	5¼"	5¾"	6¼"	7¼"
	B: 1 ⊠→⊠		2¼"	2¾"	3¼"	3½"	3¾"	4¼"
	C: 10 ◇		T2	T5	T7	T8	T9	T11
Dark	D: 1 ⊠→⊠		2¼"	2¾"	3¼"	3½"	3¾"	4¼"
	E: 10 ◇		T2	T5	T7	T8	T9	T11

Try this: Use a medium instead of a light for A.

Light   Light 2   Medium   Medium 2   Dark

SALT LAKE CITY

4-Unit Grid

Color Illustration: page 24

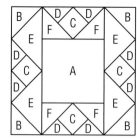

		FINISHED BLOCK SIZE					
		Single dimensions in the cutting chart indicate the size of the cut square (3" = 3" x 3").					
FOR 1 BLOCK:		**4"**	**6"**	**8"**	**9"**	**10"**	**12"**
Light	A: 1 □	2½"	3½"	4½"	5"	5½"	6½"
	B: 2 □ → ◩	1⅞"	2⅜"	2⅞"	3⅛"	3⅜"	3⅞"
	C: 4 ◇	T2	T5	T7	T8	T9	T11
Medium	D: 2 ⊠ → ◪	2¼"	2¾"	3¼"	3½"	3¾"	4¼"
Dark	E: 1 ⊠ → ◪	3¼"	4¼"	5¼"	5¾"	6¼"	7¼"
	F: 2 □ → ◩	1⅞"	2⅜"	2⅞"	3⅛"	3⅜"	3⅞"

Try this: Use one light for A and C and a different light for B.

A SALUTE TO THE COLORS

4-Unit Grid

Color Illustration: page 24

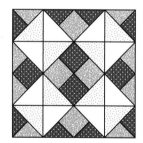
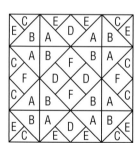

		FINISHED BLOCK SIZE					
		Single dimensions in the cutting chart indicate the size of the cut square (3" = 3" x 3").					
FOR 1 BLOCK:		**4"**	**6"**	**8"**	**9"**	**10"**	**12"**
Light	A: 4 □ → ◩	1⅞"	2⅜"	2⅞"	3⅛"	3⅜"	3⅞"
Light 2	B: 4 □ → ◩	1⅞"	2⅜"	2⅞"	3⅛"	3⅜"	3⅞"
Medium	C: 2 ⊠ → ◪	2¼"	2¾"	3¼"	3½"	3¾"	4¼"
	D: 4 ◇	T2	T5	T7	T8	T9	T11
Dark	E: 2 ⊠ → ◪	2¼"	2¾"	3¼"	3½"	3¾"	4¼"
	F: 4 ◇	T2	T5	T7	T8	T9	T11

Try this: Use a different combination of fabrics in every block.

SARAH'S CHOICE

4-Unit Grid
Color Illustration: page 24

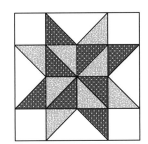
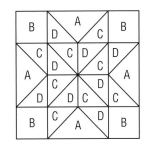
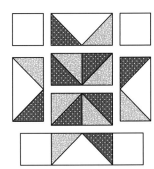

FOR 1 BLOCK:			FINISHED BLOCK SIZE *Single dimensions in the cutting chart indicate the size of the cut square (3" = 3" x 3").*					
			4"	**6"**	**8"**	**9"**	**10"**	**12"**
Light	A: 1 ⊠ → ⊠		3¼"	4¼"	5¼"	5¾"	6¼"	7¼"
	B: 4 ☐		1½"	2"	2½"	2¾"	3"	3½"
Medium	C: 4 ◺ → ◿		1⅞"	2⅜"	2⅞"	3⅛"	3⅜"	3⅞"
Dark	D: 4 ◺ → ◿		1⅞"	2⅜"	2⅞"	3⅛"	3⅜"	3⅞"

Try this: Use one light for A and a different light for B.

SAWTOOTH

6-Unit Grid
Color Illustration: page 24

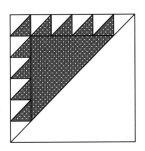
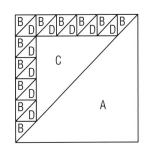
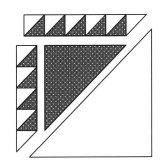

FOR 2 BLOCKS:			FINISHED BLOCK SIZE *Single dimensions in the cutting chart indicate the size of the cut square (3" = 3" x 3").*					
			4½"	**6"**	**7½"**	**9"**	**10½"**	**12"**
Light	A: 1 ◺ → ◿		5⅜"	6⅞"	8⅜"	9⅞"	11⅜"	12⅞"
	B: 11 ◺ → ◿		1⅝"	1⅞"	2⅛"	2⅜"	2⅝"	2⅞"
Dark	C: 1 ◺ → ◿		3⅞"	4⅞"	5⅞"	6⅞"	7⅞"	8⅞"
	D: 9 ◺ → ◿		1⅝"	1⅞"	2⅛"	2⅜"	2⅝"	2⅞"

Try this: Use a large-scale print for A.

Light | Light 2 | Medium | Medium 2 | Dark

Sawtooth II

5-Unit Grid
Color Illustration: page 24

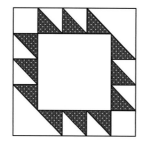
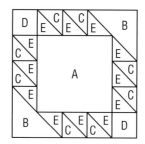
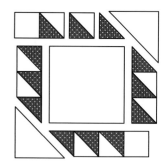

		FINISHED BLOCK SIZE *Single dimensions in the cutting chart indicate the size of the cut square (3" = 3" x 3").*					
FOR 1 BLOCK:		**5"**	**6¼"**	**7½"**	**8¾"**	**10"**	**12½"**
Light	A: 1 □	3½"	4¼"	5"	5¾"	6½"	8"
	B: 1 ◻ → ◪	2⅞"	3⅜"	3⅞"	4⅜"	4⅞"	5⅞"
	C: 4 ◻ → ◪	1⅞"	2⅛"	2⅜"	2⅝"	2⅞"	3⅜"
	D: 2 □	1½"	1¾"	2"	2¼"	2½"	3"
Dark	E: 6 ◻ → ◪	1⅞"	2⅛"	2⅜"	2⅝"	2⅞"	3⅜"

Try this: Use a large-scale print for A.

Sawtooth Star

4-Unit Grid
Color Illustration: page 24

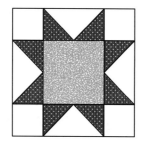
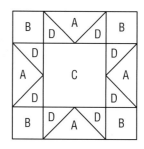
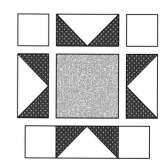

		FINISHED BLOCK SIZE *Single dimensions in the cutting chart indicate the size of the cut square (3" = 3" x 3").*					
FOR 1 BLOCK:		**4"**	**6"**	**8"**	**9"**	**10"**	**12"**
Light	A: 1 ⊠ → ⊠	3¼"	4¼"	5¼"	5¾"	6¼"	7¼"
	B: 4 □	1½"	2"	2½"	2¾"	3"	3½"
Medium	C: 1 □	2½"	3½"	4½"	5"	5½"	6½"
Dark	D: 4 ◻ → ◪	1⅞"	2⅜"	2⅞"	3⅛"	3⅜"	3⅞"

Try this: Use a large-scale print for C.

SCHOOL GIRL'S PUZZLE

4-Unit Grid
Color Illustration: page 24

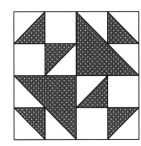
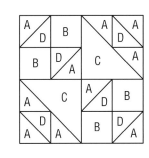
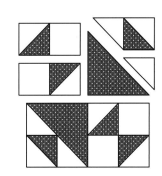

FOR 1 BLOCK:			**FINISHED BLOCK SIZE** Single dimensions in the cutting chart indicate the size of the cut square (3" = 3" x 3").					
			4"	**6"**	**8"**	**9"**	**10"**	**12"**
Light	A: 5 ◻→◺		1⅞"	2⅜"	2⅞"	3⅛"	3⅜"	3⅞"
	B: 4 ◻		1½"	2"	2½"	2¾"	3"	3½"
Dark	C: 1 ◻→◺		2⅞"	3⅞"	4⅞"	5⅜"	5⅞"	6⅞"
	D: 3 ◻→◺		1⅞"	2⅜"	2⅞"	3⅛"	3⅜"	3⅞"

Try this: Use a medium instead of a dark for D.

SCOTCH SQUARES

4-Unit Grid
Color Illustration: page 24

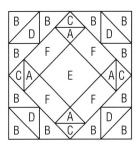
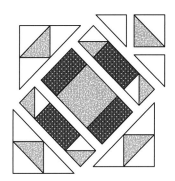

FOR 1 BLOCK:			**FINISHED BLOCK SIZE** Single dimensions in the cutting chart indicate the size of the cut square (3" = 3" x 3").					
			4"	**6"**	**8"**	**9"**	**10"**	**12"**
Light	A: 1 ⊠→⧆		2¼"	2¾"	3¼"	3½"	3¾"	4¼"
	B: 6 ◻→◺		1⅞"	2⅜"	2⅞"	3⅛"	3⅜"	3⅞"
Medium	C: 1 ⊠→⧆		2¼"	2¾"	3¼"	3½"	3¾"	4¼"
	D: 2 ◻→◺		1⅞"	2⅜"	2⅞"	3⅛"	3⅜"	3⅞"
	E: 1 ◇		T7	T11	T14	T15	T16	T19
Dark	F: 4 ▱		T32	T41	T51	T56	T59	T67

Try this: Reverse the lights and mediums in every other block.

☐ *Light* ▥ *Light 2* ▦ *Medium* ▤ *Medium 2* ▨ *Dark*

Scot's Plaid

4-Unit Grid
Color Illustration: page 24

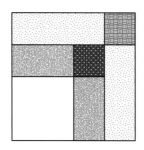 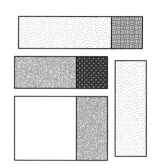

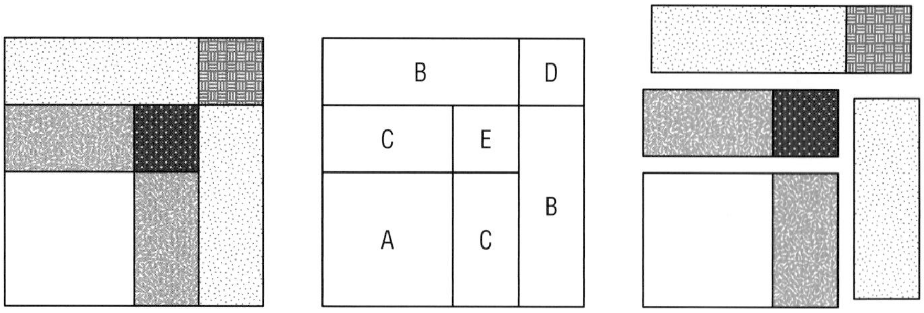

		FINISHED BLOCK SIZE					
		Single dimensions in the cutting chart indicate the size of the cut square (3" = 3" x 3").					
FOR 1 BLOCK:		**4"**	**6"**	**8"**	**9"**	**10"**	**12"**
Light	A: 1 ☐	2½"	3½"	4½"	5"	5½"	6½"
Light 2	B: 2 ▭	1½" x 3½"	2" x 5"	2½" x 6½"	2¾" x 7¼"	3" x 8"	3½" x 9½"
Medium	C: 2 ▭	1½" x 2½"	2" x 3½"	2½" x 4½"	2¾" x 5"	3" x 5½"	3½" x 6½"
Medium 2	D: 1 ☐	1½"	2"	2½"	2¾"	3"	3½"
Dark	E: 1 ☐	1½"	2"	2½"	2¾"	3"	3½"

Try this: Use a dark instead of medium 2 for D.

Shoo Fly

3-Unit Grid
Color Illustration: page 24

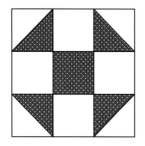 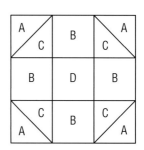 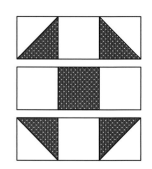

		FINISHED BLOCK SIZE					
		Single dimensions in the cutting chart indicate the size of the cut square (3" = 3" x 3").					
FOR 1 BLOCK:		**4½"**	**6"**	**7½"**	**9"**	**10½"**	**12"**
Light	A: 2 ◻→◹	2⅜"	2⅞"	3⅜"	3⅞"	4⅜"	4⅞"
	B: 4 ☐	2"	2½"	3"	3½"	4"	4½"
Dark	C: 2 ◻→◹	2⅜"	2⅞"	3⅜"	3⅞"	4⅜"	4⅞"
	D: 1 ☐	2"	2½"	3"	3½"	4"	4½"

Try this: Reverse the lights and darks.

THE SICKLE

4-Unit Grid
Color Illustration: page 24

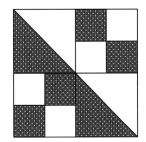

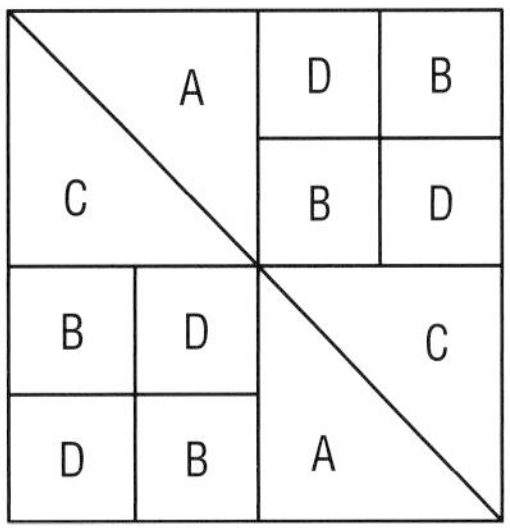

		FINISHED BLOCK SIZE *Single dimensions in the cutting chart indicate the size of the cut square (3" = 3" x 3").*					
FOR 1 BLOCK:		**4"**	**6"**	**8"**	**9"**	**10"**	**12"**
Light	A: 1 ☐→◨	2⅞"	3⅞"	4⅞"	5⅜"	5⅞"	6⅞"
	B: 4 ☐	1½"	2"	2½"	2¾"	3"	3½"
Dark	C: 1 ☐→◨	2⅞"	3⅞"	4⅞"	5⅜"	5⅞"	6⅞"
	D: 4 ☐	1½"	2"	2½"	2¾"	3"	3½"

Try this: Use a medium instead of a light for A.

THE SILENT STAR

3-Unit Grid
Color Illustration: page 24

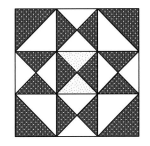
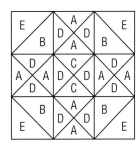

		FINISHED BLOCK SIZE *Single dimensions in the cutting chart indicate the size of the cut square (3" = 3" x 3").*					
FOR 2 BLOCKS:		**4½"**	**6"**	**7½"**	**9"**	**10½"**	**12"**
Light	A: 4 ☒→⊠	2¾"	3¼"	3¾"	4¼"	4¾"	5¼"
	B: 4 ☐→◨	2⅜"	2⅞"	3⅜"	3⅞"	4⅜"	4⅞"
Light 2	C: 1 ☒→⊠	2¾"	3¼"	3¾"	4¼"	4¾"	5¼"
Dark	D: 5 ☒→⊠	2¾"	3¼"	3¾"	4¼"	4¾"	5¼"
	E: 4 ☐→◨	2⅜"	2⅞"	3⅜"	3⅞"	4⅜"	4⅞"

Try this: Use a medium instead of a dark for E.

SIMPLE FLOWER BASKET

4-Unit Grid
Color Illustration: page 24

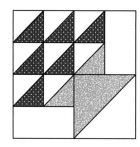
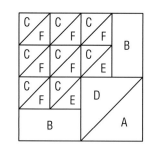
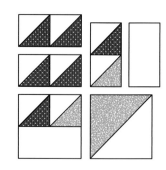

		FINISHED BLOCK SIZE					
		Single dimensions in the cutting chart indicate the size of the cut square (3" = 3" x 3").					
FOR 2 BLOCKS:			**4"**	**6"**	**8"**	**9"**	**10"**	**12"**
Light	A: 1 ⬜→◩		2⅞"	3⅞"	4⅞"	5⅜"	5⅞"	6⅞"
	B: 4 ▭		1½" x 2½"	2" x 3½"	2½" x 4½"	2¾" x 5"	3" x 5½"	3½" x 6½"
	C: 8 ⬜→◩		1⅞"	2⅜"	2⅞"	3⅛"	3⅜"	3⅞"
Medium	D: 1 ⬜→◩		2⅞"	3⅞"	4⅞"	5⅜"	5⅞"	6⅞"
	E: 2 ⬜→◩		1⅞"	2⅜"	2⅞"	3⅛"	3⅜"	3⅞"
Dark	F: 6 ⬜→◩		1⅞"	2⅜"	2⅞"	3⅛"	3⅜"	3⅞"

Try this: Use several different darks for F.

SIMPLEX STAR

3-Unit Grid
Color Illustration: page 24

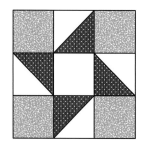
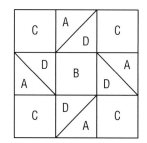
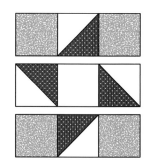

			FINISHED BLOCK SIZE					
			Single dimensions in the cutting chart indicate the size of the cut square (3" = 3" x 3").					
FOR 1 BLOCK:			**4½"**	**6"**	**7½"**	**9"**	**10½"**	**12"**
Light	A: 2 ⬜→◩		2⅜"	2⅞"	3⅜"	3⅞"	4⅜"	4⅞"
	B: 1 ⬜		2"	2½"	3"	3½"	4"	4½"
Medium	C: 4 ⬜		2"	2½"	3"	3½"	4"	4½"
Dark	D: 2 ⬜→◩		2⅜"	2⅞"	3⅜"	3⅞"	4⅜"	4⅞"

Try this: Reverse the mediums and darks in every other block.

SINGLE CHAIN AND KNOT

10-Unit Grid

Color Illustration: page 24

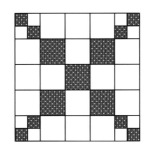

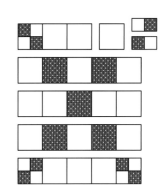

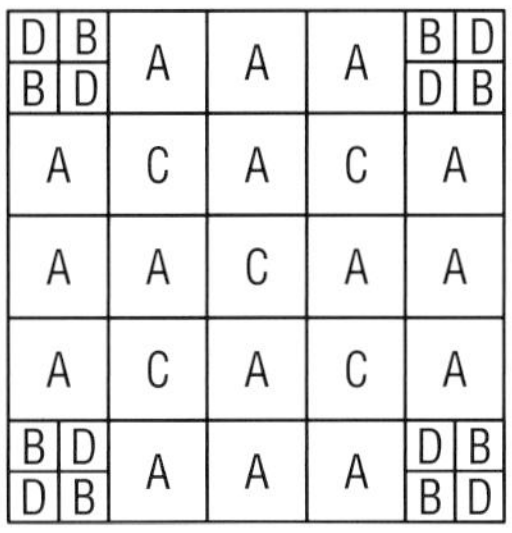

		FINISHED BLOCK SIZE					
		Single dimensions in the cutting chart indicate the size of the cut square (3" = 3" x 3").					
FOR 1 BLOCK:		**6¼"**	**7½"**	**8¾"**	**10"**	**12½"**	**13¾"**
Light	A: 16 □	1¾"	2"	2¼"	2½"	3"	3¼"
	B: 8 □	1⅛"	1¼"	1⅜"	1½"	1¾"	1⅞"
Dark	C: 5 □	1¾"	2"	2¼"	2½"	3"	3¼"
	D: 8 □	1⅛"	1¼"	1⅜"	1½"	1¾"	1⅞"

Try this: Use a scrappy assortment of lights for A.

SMOKEHOUSE

6-Unit Grid

Color Illustration: page 24

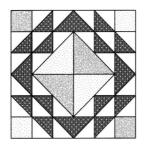

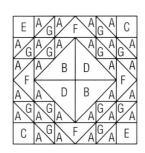

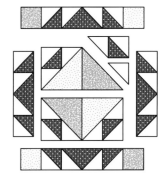

		FINISHED BLOCK SIZE					
		Single dimensions in the cutting chart indicate the size of the cut square (3" = 3" x 3").					
FOR 1 BLOCK:		**4½"**	**6"**	**7½"**	**9"**	**10½"**	**12"**
Light	A: 14 □ → ◹	1⅝"	1⅞"	2⅛"	2⅜"	2⅝"	2⅞"
Light 2	B: 1 □ → ◹	2⅜"	2⅞"	3⅜"	3⅞"	4⅜"	4⅞"
	C: 2 □	1¼"	1½"	1¾"	2"	2¼"	2½"
Medium	D: 1 □ → ◹	2⅜"	2⅞"	3⅜"	3⅞"	4⅜"	4⅞"
	E: 2 □	1¼"	1½"	1¾"	2"	2¼"	2½"
Dark	F: 1 ⊠ → ◱	2¾"	3¼"	3¾"	4¼"	4¾"	5¼"
	G: 6 □ → ◹	1⅝"	1⅞"	2⅛"	2⅜"	2⅝"	2⅞"

Try this: Use a different light 2 and medium in every block.

SNAIL'S TRAIL

8-Unit Grid

Color Illustration: page 24

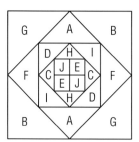

FOR 2 BLOCKS:		FINISHED BLOCK SIZE *Single dimensions in the cutting chart indicate the size of the cut square (3" = 3" x 3").*					
		6"	**8"**	**9"**	**10"**	**12"**	**14"**
Light	A: 1 ⊠ → ⊠	4¼"	5¼"	5¾"	6¼"	7¼"	8¼"
	B: 2 ◻ → ◺	3⅞"	4⅞"	5⅜"	5⅞"	6⅞"	7⅞"
	C: 1 ⊠ → ⊠	2¾"	3¼"	3½"	3¾"	4¼"	4¾"
	D: 2 ◻ → ◺	2⅜"	2⅞"	3⅛"	3⅜"	3⅞"	4⅜"
	E: 4 ◻	1¼"	1½"	1⅝"	1¾"	2"	2¼"
Dark	F: 1 ⊠ → ⊠	4¼"	5¼"	5¾"	6¼"	7¼"	8¼"
	G: 2 ◻ → ◺	3⅞"	4⅞"	5⅜"	5⅞"	6⅞"	7⅞"
	H: 1 ⊠ → ⊠	2¾"	3¼"	3½"	3¾"	4¼"	4¾"
	I: 2 ◻ → ◺	2⅜"	2⅞"	3⅛"	3⅜"	3⅞"	4⅜"
	J: 4 ◻	1¼"	1½"	1⅝"	1¾"	2"	2¼"

Try this: Use a different fabric for each "trail."

SNOWY OWL

6-Unit Grid
Color Illustration: page 24

 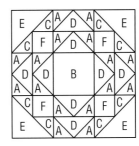 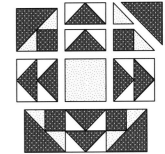

FOR 1 BLOCK:		FINISHED BLOCK SIZE *Single dimensions in the cutting chart indicate the size of the cut square (3" = 3" x 3").*					
		4½"	6"	7½"	9"	10½"	12"
Light	A: 8 ▢→◩	1⅝"	1⅞"	2⅛"	2⅜"	2⅝"	2⅞"
Light 2	B: 1 ▢	2"	2½"	3"	3½"	4"	4½"
	C: 4 ▢→◩	1⅝"	1⅞"	2⅛"	2⅜"	2⅝"	2⅞"
Dark	D: 2 ⊠→⊠	2¾"	3¼"	3¾"	4¼"	4¾"	5¼"
	E: 2 ▢→◩	2⅜"	2⅞"	3⅜"	3⅞"	4⅜"	4⅞"
	F: 4 ▢	1¼"	1½"	1¾"	2"	2¼"	2½"

Try this: Use a medium instead of a dark for E.

SOUTHERN BELLE

2-Unit Grid
Color Illustration: page 24

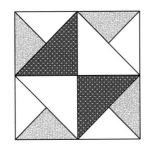 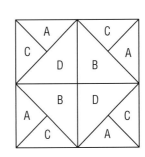 

FOR 1 BLOCK:		FINISHED BLOCK SIZE *Single dimensions in the cutting chart indicate the size of the cut square (3" = 3" x 3").*					
		4"	6"	8"	9"	10"	12"
Light	A: 1 ⊠→⊠	3¼"	4¼"	5¼"	5¾"	6¼"	7¼"
	B: 1 ▢→◩	2⅞"	3⅞"	4⅞"	5⅜"	5⅞"	6⅞"
Medium	C: 1 ⊠→⊠	3¼"	4¼"	5¼"	5¾"	6¼"	7¼"
Dark	D: 1 ▢→◩	2⅞"	3⅞"	4⅞"	5⅜"	5⅞"	6⅞"

Try this: Use one light for A and a different light for B.

SPINNER

4-Unit Grid

Color Illustration: page 24

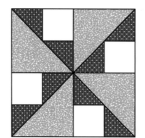 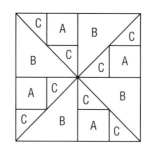 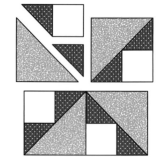

FOR 1 BLOCK:	FINISHED BLOCK SIZE Single dimensions in the cutting chart indicate the size of the cut square (3" = 3" x 3").					
	4"	**6"**	**8"**	**9"**	**10"**	**12"**
Light A: 4 ☐	1½"	2"	2½"	2¾"	3"	3½"
Medium B: 2 ◻→◹	2⅞"	3⅞"	4⅞"	5⅜"	5⅞"	6⅞"
Dark C: 4 ◻→◹	1⅞"	2⅜"	2⅞"	3⅛"	3⅜"	3⅞"

Try this: Reverse the mediums and lights.

SPINNING TOPS

5-Unit Grid

Color Illustration: page 24

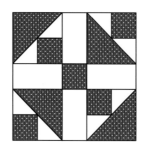 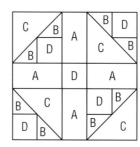 

FOR 1 BLOCK:	FINISHED BLOCK SIZE Single dimensions in the cutting chart indicate the size of the cut square (3" = 3" x 3").					
	5"	**6¼"**	**7½"**	**8¾"**	**10"**	**12½"**
Light A: 4 ▭	1½" x 2½"	1¾" x 3"	2" x 3½"	2¼" x 4"	2½" x 4½"	3" x 5½"
B: 4 ◻→◹	1⅞"	2⅛"	2⅜"	2⅝"	2⅞"	3⅜"
Dark C: 2 ◻→◹	2⅞"	3⅜"	3⅞"	4⅜"	4⅞"	5⅞"
D: 5 ☐	1½"	1¾"	2"	2¼"	2½"	3"

Try this: Use one dark for C and a medium or a different dark for D.

SPLIT NINE PATCH

3-Unit Grid
Color Illustration: page 24

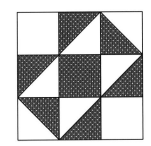 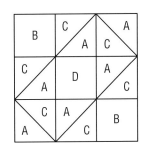 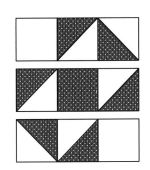

| | | FINISHED BLOCK SIZE *Single dimensions in the cutting chart indicate the size of the cut square (3" = 3" x 3").* | | | | | |
		4½"	6"	7½"	9"	10½"	12"
Light	A: 3 ◻→◪	2⅜"	2⅞"	3⅜"	3⅞"	4⅜"	4⅞"
	B: 2 ◻	2"	2½"	3"	3½"	4"	4½"
Dark	C: 3 ◻→◪	2⅜"	2⅞"	3⅜"	3⅞"	4⅜"	4⅞"
	D: 1 ◻	2"	2½"	3"	3½"	4"	4½"

FOR 1 BLOCK:

Try this: Use one light for A and a different light for B.

SPOOL AND BOBBIN

4-Unit Grid
Color Illustration: page 24

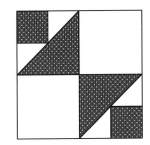 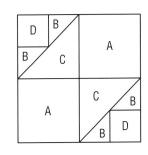 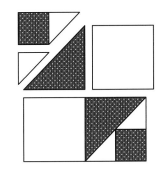

| | | FINISHED BLOCK SIZE *Single dimensions in the cutting chart indicate the size of the cut square (3" = 3" x 3").* | | | | | |
		4"	6"	8"	9"	10"	12"
Light	A: 2 ◻	2½"	3½"	4½"	5"	5½"	6½"
	B: 2 ◻→◪	1⅞"	2⅜"	2⅞"	3⅛"	3⅜"	3⅞"
Dark	C: 1 ◻→◪	2⅞"	3⅞"	4⅞"	5⅜"	5⅞"	6⅞"
	D: 2 ◻	1½"	2"	2½"	2¾"	3"	3½"

FOR 1 BLOCK:

Try this: Use a medium instead of a dark for D.

Spring and Fall

10-Unit Grid

Color Illustration: page 24

 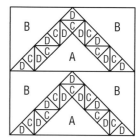 

	FINISHED BLOCK SIZE					
	Single dimensions in the cutting chart indicate the size of the cut square (3" = 3" x 3").					
FOR 2 BLOCKS:	**6¼"**	**7½"**	**8¾"**	**10"**	**12½"**	**13¾"**
Light A: 1 ⊠→⊠	5"	5¾"	6½"	7¼"	8¾"	9½"
B: 4 ◻→◻	4"	4⅝"	5¼"	5⅞"	7⅛"	7¾"
C: 7 ⊠→⊠	2½"	2¾"	3"	3¼"	3¾"	4"
Dark D: 9 ⊠→⊠	2½"	2¾"	3"	3¼"	3¾"	4"

Try this: Use many different darks for D.

Spring Has Come

8-Unit Grid

Color Illustration: page 24

 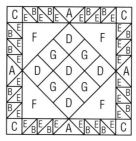 

	FINISHED BLOCK SIZE					
	Single dimensions in the cutting chart indicate the size of the cut square (3" = 3" x 3").					
FOR 1 BLOCK:	**6"**	**8"**	**9"**	**10"**	**12"**	**14"**
Light A: 1 ⊠→⊠	2¾"	3¼"	3½"	3¾"	4¼"	4¾"
B: 8 ◻→◻	1⅝"	1⅞"	2"	2⅛"	2⅜"	2⅝"
C: 4 ◻	1¼"	1½"	1⅝"	1¾"	2"	2¼"
D: 5 ◇	T5	T7	T8	T9	T11	T12
Medium E: 12 ◻→◻	1⅝"	1⅞"	2"	2⅛"	2⅜"	2⅝"
Dark F: 2 ◻→◻	3⅛"	3⅞"	4¼"	4⅝"	5⅜"	6⅛"
G: 4 ◇	T5	T7	T8	T9	T11	T12

Try this: Use a medium instead of a dark for F.

SQUARE AND STAR

4-Unit Grid
Color Illustration: page 24

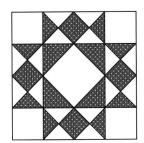 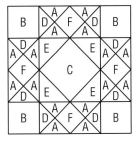 

		FINISHED BLOCK SIZE					
		Single dimensions in the cutting chart indicate the size of the cut square (3" = 3" x 3").					
FOR 1 BLOCK:			**4"**	**6"**	**8"**	**9"**	**10"**	**12"**
Light	A: 4 ⊠ → ⊠		2¼"	2¾"	3¼"	3½"	3¾"	4¼"
	B: 4 □		1½"	2"	2½"	2¾"	3"	3½"
	C: 1 ◇		T7	T11	T14	T15	T16	T19
Dark	D: 2 ⊠ → ⊠		2¼"	2¾"	3¼"	3½"	3¾"	4¼"
	E: 2 ◻ → ◻		1⅞"	2⅜"	2⅞"	3⅛"	3⅜"	3⅞"
	F: 4 ◇		T2	T5	T7	T8	T9	T11

Try this: Use a medium instead of a dark for F.

THE SQUARE DEAL

8-Unit Grid
Color Illustration: page 24

 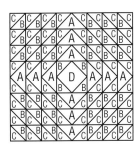 

		FINISHED BLOCK SIZE					
		Single dimensions in the cutting chart indicate the size of the cut square (3" = 3" x 3").					
FOR 1 BLOCK:			**6"**	**8"**	**9"**	**10"**	**12"**	**14"**
Light	A: 3 ⊠ → ⊠		2¾"	3¼"	3½"	3¾"	4¼"	4¾"
	B: 20 ◻ → ◻		1⅝"	1⅞"	2"	2⅛"	2⅜"	2⅝"
Dark	C: 30 ◻ → ◻		1⅝"	1⅞"	2"	2⅛"	2⅜"	2⅝"
	D: 1 ◇		T5	T7	T8	T9	T11	T12

Try this: Use many different darks for C.

SQUARE ON SQUARE

8-Unit Grid
Color Illustration: page 24

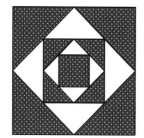 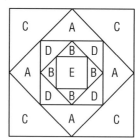 

FOR 1 BLOCK:		FINISHED BLOCK SIZE					
		Single dimensions in the cutting chart indicate the size of the cut square (3" = 3" x 3").					
		4"	6"	8"	9"	10"	12"
Light	A: 1 ⊠ → ⊠	3¼"	4¼"	5¼"	5¾"	6¼"	7¼"
	B: 1 ⊠ → ⊠	2¼"	2¾"	3¼"	3½"	3¾"	4¼"
Dark	C: 2 ◩ → ◩	2⅞"	3⅞"	4⅞"	5⅜"	5⅞"	6⅞"
	D: 2 ◩ → ◩	1⅞"	2⅜"	2⅞"	3⅛"	3⅜"	3⅞"
	E: 1 ☐	1½"	2"	2½"	2¾"	3"	3½"

Try this: Reverse the lights and darks in every other block.

SQUARE SURROUNDED

8-Unit Grid
Color Illustration: page 24

 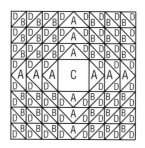 

FOR 1 BLOCK:		FINISHED BLOCK SIZE					
		Single dimensions in the cutting chart indicate the size of the cut square (3" = 3" x 3").					
		6"	8"	9"	10"	12"	14"
Light	A: 3 ⊠ → ⊠	2¾"	3¼"	3½"	3¾"	4¼"	4¾"
	B: 18 ◩ → ◩	1⅝"	1⅞"	2"	2⅛"	2⅜"	2⅝"
Dark	C: 1 ☐	2"	2½"	2¾"	3"	3½"	4"
	D: 30 ◩ → ◩	1⅝"	1⅞"	2"	2⅛"	2⅜"	2⅝"

Try this: Reverse the lights and darks.

SQUARES AND STRIPS

11-Unit Grid

Color Illustration: page 25

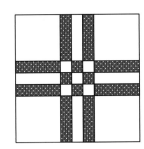
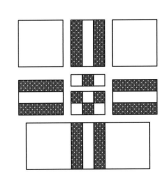

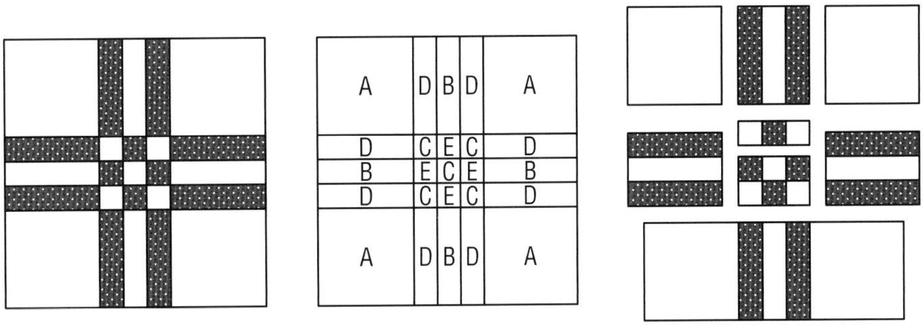

| FOR 1 BLOCK: | FINISHED BLOCK SIZE | | | | | |
| | Single dimensions in the cutting chart indicate the size of the cut square (3" = 3" x 3"). | | | | | |
	6⅞"	**8¼"**	**9⅝"**	**11"**	**12⅜"**	**15⅛"**
Light A: 4 □	3"	3½"	4"	4½"	5"	6"
B: 4 ▭	1⅛" x 3"	1¼" x 3½"	1⅜" x 4"	1½" x 4½"	1⅝" x 5"	1⅞" x 6"
C: 5 □	1⅛"	1¼"	1⅜"	1½"	1⅝"	1⅞"
Dark D: 8 ▭	1⅛" x 3"	1¼" x 3½"	1⅜" x 4"	1½" x 4½"	1⅝" x 5"	1⅞" x 6"
E: 4 □	1⅛"	1¼"	1⅜"	1½"	1⅝"	1⅞"

Try this: Reverse the lights and darks in every other block.

ST. JOHN PAVEMENT

5-Unit Grid

Color Illustration: page 25

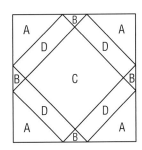
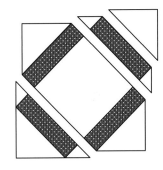

| FOR 1 BLOCK: | FINISHED BLOCK SIZE | | | | | |
| | Single dimensions in the cutting chart indicate the size of the cut square (3" = 3" x 3"). | | | | | |
	5"	**6¼"**	**7½"**	**8¾"**	**10"**	**12½"**
Light A: 2 ◨→◩	2⅞"	3⅜"	3⅞"	4⅜"	4⅞"	5⅞"
B: 1 ⊠→⧅	2¼"	2½"	2¾"	3"	3¼"	3¾"
C: 1 ◇	T14	T16	T19	T21	T23	T25
Dark D: 4 ▱	T34	T38	T43	T48	T53	T61

Try this: Use a medium- or large-scale print for C.

□ Light ▦ Light 2 ▨ Medium ▥ Medium 2 ▩ Dark

THE STAR AND BLOCK

4-Unit Grid

Color Illustration: page 25

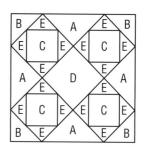

FOR 1 BLOCK:		**FINISHED BLOCK SIZE** Single dimensions in the cutting chart indicate the size of the cut square (3" = 3" x 3").					
		4"	**6"**	**8"**	**9"**	**10"**	**12"**
Light	A: 1 ⊠ → ⊠	3¼"	4¼"	5¼"	5¾"	6¼"	7¼"
	B: 2 ◹ → ◺	1⅞"	2⅜"	2⅞"	3⅛"	3⅜"	3⅞"
	C: 4 ▢	1½"	2"	2½"	2¾"	3"	3½"
	D: 1 ◇	T7	T11	T14	T15	T16	T19
Dark	E: 4 ⊠ → ⊠	2¼"	2¾"	3¼"	3½"	3¾"	4¼"

Try this: Use a different dark fabric in each corner of the block.

STAR AND PINWHEELS

4-Unit Grid

Color Illustration: page 25

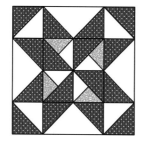
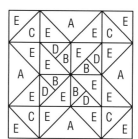
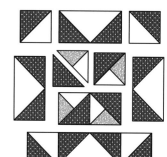

FOR 1 BLOCK:		**FINISHED BLOCK SIZE** Single dimensions in the cutting chart indicate the size of the cut square (3" = 3" x 3").					
		4"	**6"**	**8"**	**9"**	**10"**	**12"**
Light	A: 1 ⊠ → ⊠	3¼"	4¼"	5¼"	5¾"	6¼"	7¼"
	B: 1 ⊠ → ⊠	2¼"	2¾"	3¼"	3½"	3¾"	4¼"
	C: 2 ◹ → ◺	1⅞"	2⅜"	2⅞"	3⅛"	3⅜"	3⅞"
Medium	D: 1 ⊠ → ⊠	2¼"	2¾"	3¼"	3½"	3¾"	4¼"
Dark	E: 8 ◹ → ◺	1⅞"	2⅜"	2⅞"	3⅛"	3⅜"	3⅞"

Try this: Reverse the lights and mediums in every other block.

STAR OF VIRGINIA

6-Unit Grid
Color Illustration: page 25

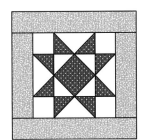 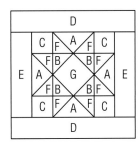 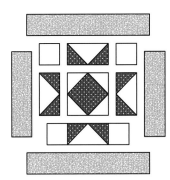

		FINISHED BLOCK SIZE *Single dimensions in the cutting chart indicate the size of the cut square (3" = 3" x 3").*					
FOR 1 BLOCK:		**4½"**	**6"**	**7½"**	**9"**	**10½"**	**12"**
Light	A: 1 ⊠ → ⊠	2¾"	3¼"	3¾"	4¼"	4¾"	5¼"
	B: 2 ◲ → ◳	1⅝"	1⅞"	2⅛"	2⅜"	2⅝"	2⅞"
	C: 4 □	1¼"	1½"	1¾"	2"	2¼"	2½"
Medium	D: 2 ▭	1¼" x 5"	1½" x 6½"	1¾" x 8"	2" x 9½"	2¼" x 11"	2½" x 12½"
	E: 2 ▭	1¼" x 3½"	1½" x 4½"	1¾" x 5½"	2" x 6½"	2¼" x 7½"	2½" x 8½"
Dark	F: 4 ◲ → ◳	1⅝"	1⅞"	2⅛"	2⅜"	2⅝"	2⅞"
	G: 1 ◇	T5	T7	T9	T11	T12	T14

Try this: Reverse the mediums and darks in every other block.

STAR PUZZLE

4-Unit Grid
Color Illustration: page 25

 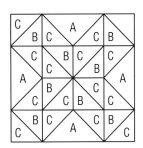 

		FINISHED BLOCK SIZE *Single dimensions in the cutting chart indicate the size of the cut square (3" = 3" x 3").*					
FOR 1 BLOCK:		**4"**	**6"**	**8"**	**9"**	**10"**	**12"**
Light	A: 1 ⊠ → ⊠	3¼"	4¼"	5¼"	5¾"	6¼"	7¼"
	B: 4 ◲ → ◳	1⅞"	2⅜"	2⅞"	3⅛"	3⅜"	3⅞"
Dark	C: 8 ◲ → ◳	1⅞"	2⅜"	2⅞"	3⅛"	3⅜"	3⅞"

Try this: Use a medium instead of a light for A and B.

Light · Light 2 · Medium · Medium 2 · Dark

STAR X

3-Unit Grid
Color Illustration: page 25

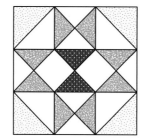 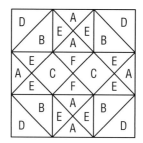 

		FINISHED BLOCK SIZE Single dimensions in the cutting chart indicate the size of the cut square (3" = 3" x 3").					
FOR 2 BLOCKS:		**4½"**	**6"**	**7½"**	**9"**	**10½"**	**12"**
Light	A: 3 ⊠ → ⊠	2¾"	3¼"	3¾"	4¼"	4¾"	5¼"
	B: 4 ◺ → ◺	2⅜"	2⅞"	3⅜"	3⅞"	4⅜"	4⅞"
	C: 4 ◇	T5	T7	T9	T11	T12	T14
Light 2	D: 4 ◺ → ◺	2⅜"	2⅞"	3⅜"	3⅞"	4⅜"	4⅞"
Medium	E: 4 ⊠ → ⊠	2¾"	3¼"	3¾"	4¼"	4¾"	5¼"
Dark	F: 1 ⊠ → ⊠	2¾"	3¼"	3¾"	4¼"	4¾"	5¼"

Try this: Use a dark instead of light 2 for D.

STARRY PATH

4-Unit Grid
Color Illustration: page 25

 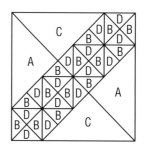 

		FINISHED BLOCK SIZE Single dimensions in the cutting chart indicate the size of the cut square (3" = 3" x 3").					
FOR 2 BLOCKS:		**4"**	**6"**	**8"**	**9"**	**10"**	**12"**
Light	A: 1 ⊠ → ⊠	4¼"	5¾"	7¼"	8"	8¾"	10¼"
	B: 7 ⊠ → ⊠	2¼"	2¾"	3¼"	3½"	3¾"	4¼"
Medium	C: 1 ⊠ → ⊠	4¼"	5¾"	7¼"	8"	8¾"	10¼"
Dark	D: 7 ⊠ → ⊠	2¼"	2¾"	3¼"	3½"	3¾"	4¼"

Try this: Use several different darks for D.

Stepping Stones

6-Unit Grid

Color Illustration: page 25

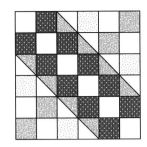
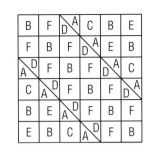
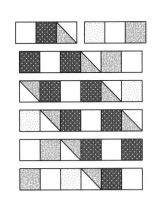

		FINISHED BLOCK SIZE					
		Single dimensions in the cutting chart indicate the size of the cut square (3" = 3" x 3").					
FOR 1 BLOCK:		**4½"**	**6"**	**7½"**	**9"**	**10½"**	**12"**
Light	A: 4 ◻ → ◻	1⅝"	1⅞"	2⅛"	2⅜"	2⅝"	2⅞"
	B: 10 ◻	1¼"	1½"	1¾"	2"	2¼"	2½"
Light 2	C: 4 ◻	1¼"	1½"	1¾"	2"	2¼"	2½"
Medium	D: 4 ◻ → ◻	1⅝"	1⅞"	2⅛"	2⅜"	2⅝"	2⅞"
	E: 4 ◻	1¼"	1½"	1¾"	2"	2¼"	2½"
Dark	F: 10 ◻	1¼"	1½"	1¾"	2"	2¼"	2½"

Try this: Use a scrappy assortment of light fabrics for C and a scrappy assortment of medium fabrics for E.

Steps to the Altar

6-Unit Grid

Color Illustration: page 25

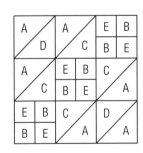
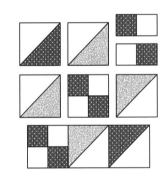

		FINISHED BLOCK SIZE					
		Single dimensions in the cutting chart indicate the size of the cut square (3" = 3" x 3").					
FOR 1 BLOCK:		**4½"**	**6"**	**7½"**	**9"**	**10½"**	**12"**
Light	A: 3 ◻ → ◻	2⅜"	2⅞"	3⅜"	3⅞"	4⅜"	4⅞"
	B: 6 ◻	1¼"	1½"	1¾"	2"	2¼"	2½"
Medium	C: 2 ◻ → ◻	2⅜"	2⅞"	3⅜"	3⅞"	4⅜"	4⅞"
Dark	D: 1 ◻ → ◻	2⅜"	2⅞"	3⅜"	3⅞"	4⅜"	4⅞"
	E: 6 ◻	1¼"	1½"	1¾"	2"	2¼"	2½"

Try this: Use one light for A and a different light for B.

| | Light | | Light 2 | | Medium | | Medium 2 | | Dark |

STILES AND PATHS

9-Unit Grid
Color Illustration: page 25

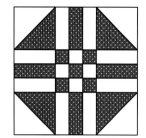
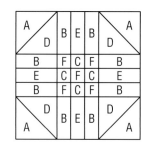

FOR 1 BLOCK:		FINISHED BLOCK SIZE *Single dimensions in the cutting chart indicate the size of the cut square (3" = 3" x 3").*					
		6¾"	9"	10⅛"	11¼"	12⅜"	13½"
Light	A: 2 ◻→◨	3⅛"	3⅞"	4¼"	4⅝"	5"	5⅜"
	B: 8 ▭	1¼" x 2¾"	1½" x 3½"	1⅝" x 3⅞"	1¾" x 4¼"	1⅞" x 4⅝"	2" x 5"
	C: 4 ◻	1¼"	1½"	1⅝"	1¾"	1⅞"	2"
Dark	D: 2 ◻→◨	3⅛"	3⅞"	4¼"	4⅝"	5"	5⅜"
	E: 4 ▭	1¼" x 2¾"	1½" x 3½"	1⅝" x 3⅞"	1¾" x 4¼"	1⅞" x 4⅝"	2" x 5"
	F: 5 ◻	1¼"	1½"	1⅝"	1¾"	1⅞"	2"

Try this: Use a medium instead of a dark in every other block.

STORM SIGNAL

6-Unit Grid
Color Illustration: page 25

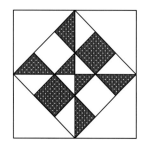
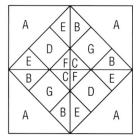

FOR 1 BLOCK:		FINISHED BLOCK SIZE *Single dimensions in the cutting chart indicate the size of the cut square (3" = 3" x 3").*					
		4½"	6"	7½"	9"	10½"	12"
Light	A: 2 ◻→◨	3⅛"	3⅞"	4⅝"	5⅜"	6⅛"	6⅞"
	B: 1 ⊠→⊠	2¾"	3¼"	3¾"	4¼"	4¾"	5¼"
	C: 1 ◻→◨	1⅝"	1⅞"	2⅛"	2⅜"	2⅝"	2⅞"
	D: 2 ◇	T5	T7	T9	T11	T12	T14
Dark	E: 1 ⊠→⊠	2¾"	3¼"	3¾"	4¼"	4¾"	5¼"
	F: 1 ◻→◨	1⅝"	1⅞"	2⅛"	2⅜"	2⅝"	2⅞"
	G: 2 ◇	T5	T7	T9	T11	T12	T14

Try this: Use a medium instead of a light for A.

STRENGTH IN UNION

5-Unit Grid
Color Illustration: page 25

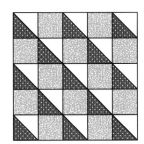 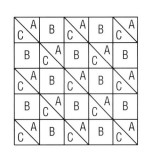 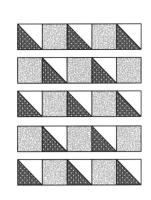

FOR 2 BLOCKS:	FINISHED BLOCK SIZE Single dimensions in the cutting chart indicate the size of the cut square (3" = 3" x 3").					
	5"	6¼"	7½"	8¾"	10"	12½"
Light A: 13 ◸→◺	1⅞"	2⅛"	2⅜"	2⅝"	2⅞"	3⅜"
Medium B: 24 □	1½"	1¾"	2"	2¼"	2½"	3"
Dark C: 13 ◸→◺	1⅞"	2⅛"	2⅜"	2⅝"	2⅞"	3⅜"

Try this: Use several different mediums for B and several different darks for C.

STRIP HEART

8-Unit Grid
Color Illustration: page 25

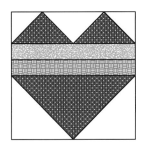 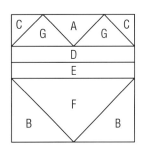 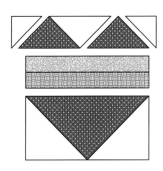

FOR 4 BLOCKS:	FINISHED BLOCK SIZE Single dimensions in the cutting chart indicate the size of the cut square (3" = 3" x 3").					
	6"	8"	9"	10"	12"	14"
Light A: 1 ⊠→⊠	4¼"	5¼"	5¾"	6¼"	7¼"	8¼"
B: 4 ◸→◺	3⅞"	4⅞"	5⅜"	5⅞"	6⅞"	7⅞"
C: 4 ◸→◺	2⅜"	2⅞"	3⅛"	3⅜"	3⅞"	4⅜"
Medium D: 4 ▭	1¼" x 6½"	1½" x 8½"	1⅝" x 9½"	1¾" x 10½"	2" x 12½"	2¼" x 14½"
Medium 2 E: 4 ▭	1¼" x 6½"	1½" x 8½"	1⅝" x 9½"	1¾" x 10½"	2" x 12½"	2¼" x 14½"
Dark F: 1 ⊠→⊠	7¼"	9¼"	10¼"	11¼"	13¼"	15¼"
G: 2 ⊠→⊠	4¼"	5¼"	5¾"	6¼"	7¼"	8¼"

Try this: Use a different combination of mediums in every block.

SUGAR BOWL

4-Unit Grid

Color Illustration: page 25

 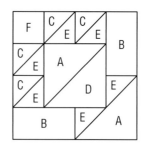 

FOR 2 BLOCKS:		FINISHED BLOCK SIZE *Single dimensions in the cutting chart indicate the size of the cut square (3" = 3" x 3").*					
		4"	6"	8"	9"	10"	12"
Light	A: 2 ◻→◻	2⅞"	3⅞"	4⅞"	5⅜"	5⅞"	6⅞"
	B: 4 ▭	1½" x 2½"	2" x 3½"	2½" x 4½"	2¾" x 5"	3" x 5½"	3½" x 6½"
	C: 4 ◻→◻	1⅞"	2⅜"	2⅞"	3⅛"	3⅜"	3⅞"
Dark	D: 1 ◻→◻	2⅞"	3⅞"	4⅞"	5⅜"	5⅞"	6⅞"
	E: 6 ◻→◻	1⅞"	2⅜"	2⅞"	3⅛"	3⅜"	3⅞"
	F: 2 ◻	1½"	2"	2½"	2¾"	3"	3½"

Try this: Use several different darks for E.

SUMMER SOLSTICE

4-Unit Grid

Color Illustration: page 25

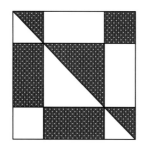 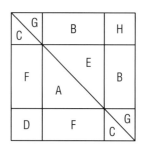 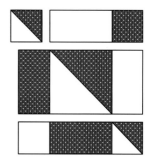

FOR 2 BLOCKS:		FINISHED BLOCK SIZE *Single dimensions in the cutting chart indicate the size of the cut square (3" = 3" x 3").*					
		4"	6"	8"	9"	10"	12"
Light	A: 1 ◻→◻	2⅞"	3⅞"	4⅞"	5⅜"	5⅞"	6⅞"
	B: 4 ▭	1½" x 2½"	2" x 3½"	2½" x 4½"	2¾" x 5"	3" x 5½"	3½" x 6½"
	C: 2 ◻→◻	1⅞"	2⅜"	2⅞"	3⅛"	3⅜"	3⅞"
	D: 2 ◻	1½"	2"	2½"	2¾"	3"	3½"
Dark	E: 1 ◻→◻	2⅞"	3⅞"	4⅞"	5⅜"	5⅞"	6⅞"
	F: 4 ▭	1½" x 2½"	2" x 3½"	2½" x 4½"	2¾" x 5"	3" x 5½"	3½" x 6½"
	G: 2 ◻→◻	1⅞"	2⅜"	2⅞"	3⅛"	3⅜"	3⅞"
	H: 2 ◻	1½"	2"	2½"	2¾"	3"	3½"

Try this: Use a medium instead of a light in every other block.

SUMMER WINDS

6-Unit Grid

Color Illustration: page 25

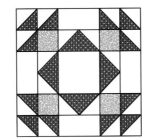
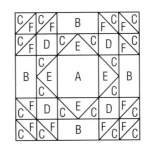
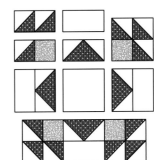

	FINISHED BLOCK SIZE *Single dimensions in the cutting chart indicate the size of the cut square (3" = 3" x 3").*					
FOR 1 BLOCK:	**4½"**	**6"**	**7½"**	**9"**	**10½"**	**12"**
Light A: 1 □	2"	2½"	3"	3½"	4"	4½"
B: 4 ▭	1¼" x 2"	1½" x 2½"	1¾" x 3"	2" x 3½"	2¼" x 4"	2½" x 4½"
C: 10 ◩→◪	1⅝"	1⅞"	2⅛"	2⅜"	2⅝"	2⅞"
Medium D: 4 □	1¼"	1½"	1¾"	2"	2¼"	2½"
Dark E: 1 ⊠→⊠	2¾"	3¼"	3¾"	4¼"	4¾"	5¼"
F: 6 ◩→◪	1⅝"	1⅞"	2⅛"	2⅜"	2⅝"	2⅞"

Try this: Use one light for A and B and a different light for C.

SUNNY LANES

8-Unit Grid

Color Illustration: page 25

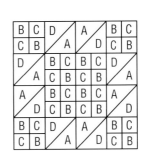
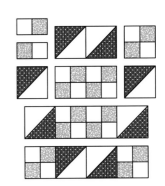

	FINISHED BLOCK SIZE *Single dimensions in the cutting chart indicate the size of the cut square (3" = 3" x 3").*					
FOR 1 BLOCK:	**6"**	**8"**	**9"**	**10"**	**12"**	**14"**
Light A: 4 ◩→◪	2⅜"	2⅞"	3⅛"	3⅜"	3⅞"	4⅜"
B: 16 □	1¼"	1½"	1⅝"	1¾"	2"	2¼"
Medium C: 16 □	1¼"	1½"	1⅝"	1¾"	2"	2¼"
Dark D: 4 ◩→◪	2⅜"	2⅞"	3⅛"	3⅜"	3⅞"	4⅜"

Try this: Use several different mediums for C.

Sunshine

8-Unit Grid

Color Illustration: page 25

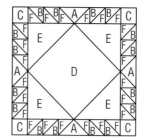

		FINISHED BLOCK SIZE					
		Single dimensions in the cutting chart indicate the size of the cut square (3" = 3" x 3").					
FOR 1 BLOCK:		**6"**	**8"**	**9"**	**10"**	**12"**	**14"**
Light	A: 1 ⊠ → ⊠	2¾"	3¼"	3½"	3¾"	4¼"	4¾"
	B: 8 ◨ → ◨	1⅝"	1⅞"	2"	2⅛"	2⅜"	2⅝"
	C: 4 □	1¼"	1½"	1⅝"	1¾"	2"	2¼"
	D: 1 ◇	T15	T19	T20	T22	T24	T26
Dark	E: 2 ◨ → ◨	3⅛"	3⅞"	4¼"	4⅝"	5⅜"	6⅛"
	F: 12 ◨ → ◨	1⅝"	1⅞"	2"	2⅛"	2⅜"	2⅝"

Try this: Use a medium- or large-scale print for D.

Surprise Package

7-Unit Grid

Color Illustration: page 25

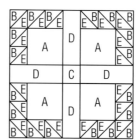
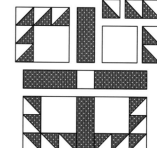

		FINISHED BLOCK SIZE					
		Single dimensions in the cutting chart indicate the size of the cut square (3" = 3" x 3").					
FOR 1 BLOCK:		**5¼"**	**7"**	**8¾"**	**10½"**	**12¼"**	**14"**
Light	A: 4 □	2"	2½"	3"	3½"	4"	4½"
	B: 10 ◨ → ◨	1⅝"	1⅞"	2⅛"	2⅜"	2⅝"	2⅞"
	C: 1 □	1¼"	1½"	1¾"	2"	2¼"	2½"
Dark	D: 4 ▭	1¼" x 2¾"	1½" x 3½"	1¾" x 4¼"	2" x 5"	2¼" x 5¾"	2½" x 6½"
	E: 10 ◨ → ◨	1⅝"	1⅞"	2⅛"	2⅜"	2⅝"	2⅞"

Try this: Use a medium instead of a dark for D.

SWAMP ANGEL

3-Unit Grid
Color Illustration: page 25

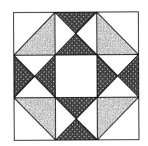
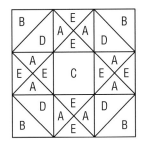
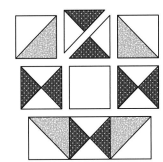

			FINISHED BLOCK SIZE				
			Single dimensions in the cutting chart indicate the size of the cut square (3" = 3" x 3").				
FOR 1 BLOCK:			**4½"**	**6"**	**7½"**	**9"**	**10½"**	**12"**
Light	A: 2 ⊠ → ⊠		2¾"	3¼"	3¾"	4¼"	4¾"	5¼"
	B: 2 ◻ → ◺		2⅜"	2⅞"	3⅜"	3⅞"	4⅜"	4⅞"
	C: 1 ◻		2"	2½"	3"	3½"	4"	4½"
Medium	D: 2 ◻ → ◺		2⅜"	2⅞"	3⅜"	3⅞"	4⅜"	4⅞"
Dark	E: 2 ⊠ → ⊠		2¾"	3¼"	3¾"	4¼"	4¾"	5¼"

Try this: Reverse the mediums and darks in every other block.

T SQUARE

8-Unit Grid
Color Illustration: page 25

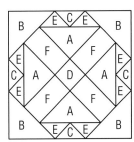

			FINISHED BLOCK SIZE				
			Single dimensions in the cutting chart indicate the size of the cut square (3" = 3" x 3").				
FOR 1 BLOCK:			**6"**	**8"**	**9"**	**10"**	**12"**	**14"**
Light	A: 1 ⊠ → ⊠		4¼"	5¼"	5¾"	6¼"	7¼"	8¼"
	B: 2 ◻ → ◺		3⅛"	3⅞"	4¼"	4⅝"	5⅜"	6⅛"
	C: 1 ⊠ → ⊠		2¾"	3¼"	3½"	3¾"	4¼"	4¾"
	D: 1 ◇		T5	T7	T8	T9	T11	T12
Dark	E: 2 ⊠ → ⊠		2¾"	3¼"	3½"	3¾"	4¼"	4¾"
	F: 4 ◇		T41	T51	T56	T59	T67	T70

Try this: Use one light for A and D and a different light for B and C.

☐ *Light*   ▦ *Light 2*   ▦ *Medium*   ▦ *Medium 2*   ■ *Dark*

TEMPLE COURT

8-Unit Grid

Color Illustration: page 25

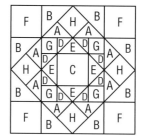

FOR 1 BLOCK:		**FINISHED BLOCK SIZE** Single dimensions in the cutting chart indicate the size of the cut square (3" = 3" x 3").					
		6"	**8"**	**9"**	**10"**	**12"**	**14"**
Light	A: 2 ⊠→⊠	2¾"	3¼"	3½"	3¾"	4¼"	4¾"
	B: 4 ◺→◺	2⅜"	2⅞"	3⅛"	3⅜"	3⅞"	4⅜"
	C: 1 ◻	2"	2½"	2¾"	3"	3½"	4"
	D: 4 ◺→◺	1⅝"	1⅞"	2"	2⅛"	2⅜"	2⅝"
Dark	E: 1 ⊠→⊠	2¾"	3¼"	3½"	3¾"	4¼"	4¾"
	F: 4 ◻	2"	2½"	2¾"	3"	3½"	4"
	G: 4 ◻	1¼"	1½"	1⅝"	1¾"	2"	2¼"
	H: 4 ◇	T5	T7	T8	T9	T11	T12

Try this: Use a medium instead of a light for A.

TEXAS PUZZLE

9-Unit Grid

Color Illustration: page 25

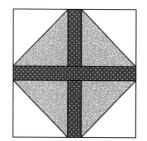
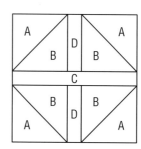
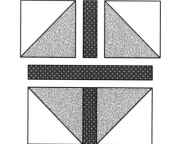

FOR 1 BLOCK:		**FINISHED BLOCK SIZE** Single dimensions in the cutting chart indicate the size of the cut square (3" = 3" x 3").					
		6¾"	**9"**	**10⅛"**	**11¼"**	**12⅜"**	**13½"**
Light	A: 2 ◺→◺	3⅞"	4⅞"	5⅜"	5⅞"	6⅜"	6⅞"
Medium	B: 2 ◺→◺	3⅞"	4⅞"	5⅜"	5⅞"	6⅜"	6⅞"
Dark	C: 1 ▭	1¼" x 7¼"	1½" x 9½"	1⅝" x 10⅝"	1¾" x 11¾"	1⅞" x 12⅞"	2" x 14"
	D: 2 ▭	1¼" x 3½"	1½" x 4½"	1⅝" x 5"	1¾" x 5½"	1⅞" x 6"	2" x 6½"

Try this: Use a different combination of mediums and lights in every block.

THREE AND SIX

3-Unit Grid
Color Illustration: page 25

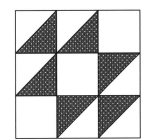 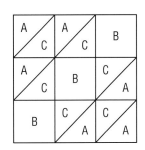 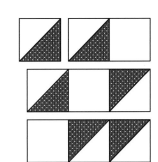

FOR 1 BLOCK:		FINISHED BLOCK SIZE *Single dimensions in the cutting chart indicate the size of the cut square (3" = 3" x 3").*					
		4½"	6"	7½"	9"	10½"	12"
Light	A: 3 ◻ → ◻	2⅜"	2⅞"	3⅜"	3⅞"	4⅜"	4⅞"
	B: 3 ◻	2"	2½"	3"	3½"	4"	4½"
Dark	C: 3 ◻ → ◻	2⅜"	2⅞"	3⅜"	3⅞"	4⅜"	4⅞"

Try this: Use a different dark in every block.

THRIFTY

6-Unit Grid
Color Illustration: page 25

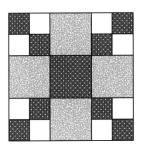 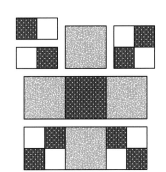

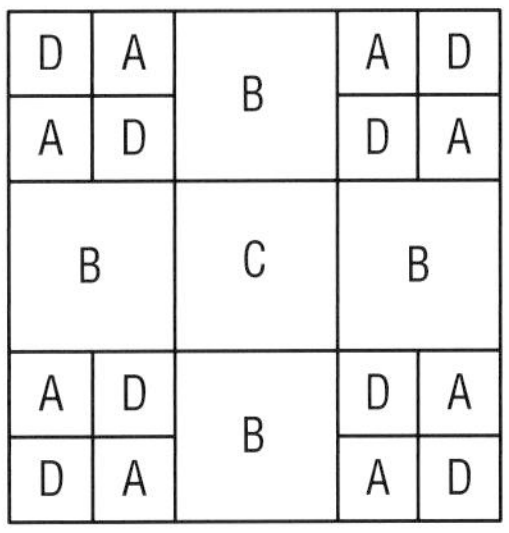

FOR 1 BLOCK:		FINISHED BLOCK SIZE *Single dimensions in the cutting chart indicate the size of the cut square (3" = 3" x 3").*					
		4½"	6"	7½"	9"	10½"	12"
Light	A: 8 ◻	1¼"	1½"	1¾"	2"	2¼"	2½"
Medium	B: 4 ◻	2"	2½"	3"	3½"	4"	4½"
Dark	C: 1 ◻	2"	2½"	3"	3½"	4"	4½"
	D: 8 ◻	1¼"	1½"	1¾"	2"	2¼"	2½"

Try this: Reverse the lights and mediums.

THUNDER AND LIGHTNING

6-Unit Grid

Color Illustration: page 25

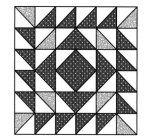
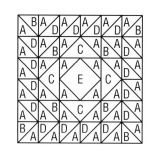
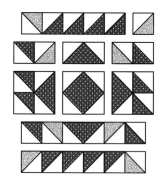

			FINISHED BLOCK SIZE Single dimensions in the cutting chart indicate the size of the cut square (3" = 3" x 3").					
FOR 1 BLOCK:			**4½"**	**6"**	**7½"**	**9"**	**10½"**	**12"**
Light	A: 18 ◻→◹		1⅝"	1⅞"	2⅛"	2⅜"	2⅝"	2⅞"
Medium	B: 4 ◻→◹		1⅝"	1⅞"	2⅛"	2⅜"	2⅝"	2⅞"
Dark	C: 1 ⊠→⊠		2¾"	3¼"	3¾"	4¼"	4¾"	5¼"
	D: 8 ◻→◹		1⅝"	1⅞"	2⅛"	2⅜"	2⅝"	2⅞"
	E: 1 ◇		T5	T7	T9	T11	T12	T14

Try this: Use one dark for C and E and a different dark for D.

TINTED CHAINS

8-Unit Grid

Color Illustration: page 25

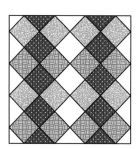
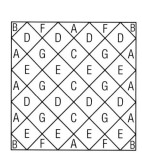
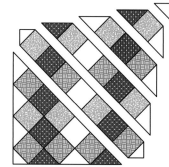

			FINISHED BLOCK SIZE Single dimensions in the cutting chart indicate the size of the cut square (3" = 3" x 3").					
FOR 1 BLOCK:			**6"**	**8"**	**9"**	**10"**	**12"**	**14"**
Light	A: 2 ⊠→⊠		2¾"	3¼"	3½"	3¾"	4¼"	4¾"
	B: 2 ◻→◹		1⅝"	1⅞"	2"	2⅛"	2⅜"	2⅝"
	C: 3 ◇		T5	T7	T8	T9	T11	T12
Medium	D: 8 ◇		T5	T7	T8	T9	T11	T12
Medium 2	E: 8 ◇		T5	T7	T8	T9	T11	T12
Dark	F: 1 ⊠→⊠		2¾"	3¼"	3½"	3¾"	4¼"	4¾"
	G: 6 ◇		T5	T7	T8	T9	T11	T12

Try this: Use many different fabrics for D and E.

TOAD IN A PUDDLE

4-Unit Grid

Color Illustration: page 25

 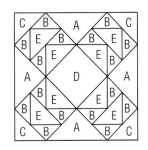 

FOR 1 BLOCK:		**FINISHED BLOCK SIZE** Single dimensions in the cutting chart indicate the size of the cut square (3" = 3" x 3").					
		4"	**6"**	**8"**	**9"**	**10"**	**12"**
Light	A: 1 ⊠ → ⊠	3¼"	4¼"	5¼"	5¾"	6¼"	7¼"
	B: 4 ⊠ → ⊠	2¼"	2¾"	3¼"	3½"	3¾"	4¼"
	C: 2 ◻ → ◹	1⅞"	2⅜"	2⅞"	3⅛"	3⅜"	3⅞"
	D: 1 ◇	T7	T11	T14	T15	T16	T19
Dark	E: 4 ◻ → ◹	1⅞"	2⅜"	2⅞"	3⅛"	3⅜"	3⅞"

Try this: Use a medium instead of a light for A and C.

TOMBSTONE QUILT

4-Unit Grid

Color Illustration: page 25

 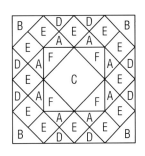 

FOR 1 BLOCK:		**FINISHED BLOCK SIZE** Single dimensions in the cutting chart indicate the size of the cut square (3" = 3" x 3").					
		4"	**6"**	**8"**	**9"**	**10"**	**12"**
Light	A: 2 ⊠ → ⊠	2¼"	2¾"	3¼"	3½"	3¾"	4¼"
	B: 2 ◻ → ◹	1⅞"	2⅜"	2⅞"	3⅛"	3⅜"	3⅞"
	C: 1 ◇	T7	T11	T14	T15	T16	T19
Medium	D: 2 ⊠ → ⊠	2¼"	2¾"	3¼"	3½"	3¾"	4¼"
	E: 12 ◇	T2	T5	T7	T8	T9	T11
Dark	F: 2 ◻ → ◹	1⅞"	2⅜"	2⅞"	3⅛"	3⅜"	3⅞"

Try this: Use several different mediums for E.

TONGANOXIE NINE PATCH

7-Unit Grid
Color Illustration: page 26

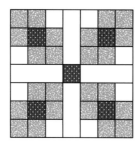
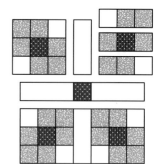

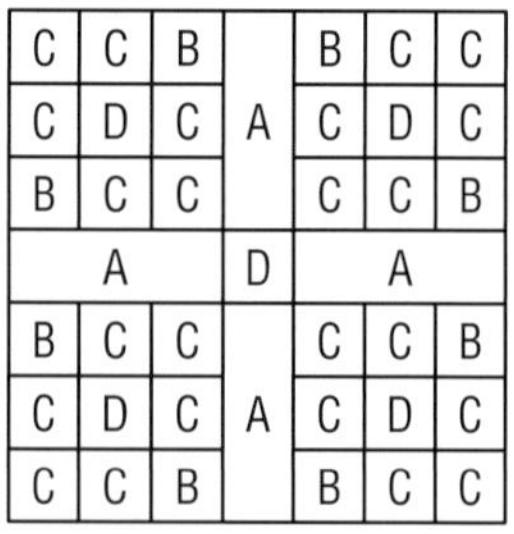

C	C	B		B	C	C
C	D	C	A	C	D	C
B	C	C		C	C	B
		A		D		A
B	C	C		C	C	B
C	D	C	A	C	D	C
C	C	B		B	C	C

	FINISHED BLOCK SIZE					
	Single dimensions in the cutting chart indicate the size of the cut square (3" = 3" x 3").					
FOR 1 BLOCK:	**5¼"**	**7"**	**8¾"**	**10½"**	**12¼"**	**14"**
Light A: 4 ▭	1¼" x 2¾"	1½" x 3½"	1¾" x 4¼"	2" x 5"	2¼" x 5¾"	2½" x 6½"
B: 8 ☐	1¼"	1½"	1¾"	2"	2¼"	2½"
Medium C: 24 ☐	1¼"	1½"	1¾"	2"	2¼"	2½"
Dark D: 5 ☐	1¼"	1½"	1¾"	2"	2¼"	2½"

Try this: Use several different mediums for C.

TRAIL OF TEARS

4-Unit Grid
Color Illustration: page 26

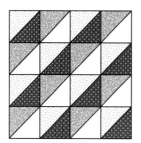
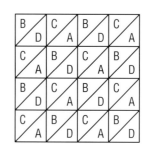
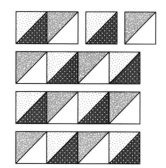

B / D	C / A	B / D	C / A
C / A	B / D	C / A	B / D
B / D	C / A	B / D	C / A
C / A	B / D	C / A	B / D

	FINISHED BLOCK SIZE					
	Single dimensions in the cutting chart indicate the size of the cut square (3" = 3" x 3").					
FOR 1 BLOCK:	**4"**	**6"**	**8"**	**9"**	**10"**	**12"**
Light A: 4 ◻→◪	1⅞"	2⅜"	2⅞"	3⅛"	3⅜"	3⅞"
Light 2 B: 4 ◻→◪	1⅞"	2⅜"	2⅞"	3⅛"	3⅜"	3⅞"
Medium C: 4 ◻→◪	1⅞"	2⅜"	2⅞"	3⅛"	3⅜"	3⅞"
Dark D: 4 ◻→◪	1⅞"	2⅜"	2⅞"	3⅛"	3⅜"	3⅞"

Try this: Use a scrappy assortment of fabrics for B, C, and D.

TRIANGLE

6-Unit Grid
Color Illustration: page 26

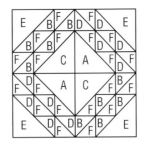

		FINISHED BLOCK SIZE					
		Single dimensions in the cutting chart indicate the size of the cut square (3" = 3" x 3").					
FOR 1 BLOCK:		**4½"**	**6"**	**7½"**	**9"**	**10½"**	**12"**
Light	A: 1 ◻→◸	2⅜"	2⅞"	3⅜"	3⅞"	4⅜"	4⅞"
	B: 5 ◻→◸	1⅝"	1⅞"	2⅛"	2⅜"	2⅝"	2⅞"
Light 2	C: 1 ◻→◸	2⅜"	2⅞"	3⅜"	3⅞"	4⅜"	4⅞"
	D: 5 ◻→◸	1⅝"	1⅞"	2⅛"	2⅜"	2⅝"	2⅞"
Dark	E: 2 ◻→◸	2⅜"	2⅞"	3⅜"	3⅞"	4⅜"	4⅞"
	F: 10 ◻→◸	1⅝"	1⅞"	2⅛"	2⅜"	2⅝"	2⅞"

Try this: Use a different combination of fabrics in each quadrant of the block.

TRIANGLE SQUARES

4-Unit Grid
Color Illustration: page 26

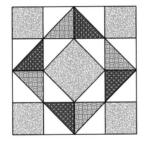
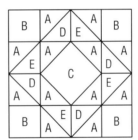
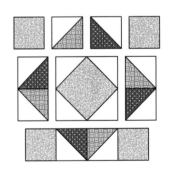

		FINISHED BLOCK SIZE					
		Single dimensions in the cutting chart indicate the size of the cut square (3" = 3" x 3").					
FOR 1 BLOCK:		**4"**	**6"**	**8"**	**9"**	**10"**	**12"**
Light	A: 6 ◻→◸	1⅞"	2⅜"	2⅞"	3⅛"	3⅜"	3⅞"
Medium	B: 4 ◻	1½"	2"	2½"	2¾"	3"	3½"
	C: 1 ◇	T7	T11	T14	T15	T16	T19
Medium 2	D: 2 ◻→◸	1⅞"	2⅜"	2⅞"	3⅛"	3⅜"	3⅞"
Dark	E: 2 ◻→◸	1⅞"	2⅜"	2⅞"	3⅛"	3⅜"	3⅞"

Try this: Use a different combination of fabrics in every block.

TRIANGLES

6-Unit Grid

Color Illustration: page 26

 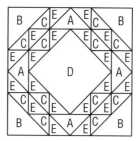 

		FINISHED BLOCK SIZE					
		Single dimensions in the cutting chart indicate the size of the cut square (3" = 3" x 3").					
FOR 1 BLOCK:		4½"	6"	7½"	9"	10½"	12"
Light	A: 1 ⊠ → ⊠	2¾"	3¼"	3¾"	4¼"	4¾"	5¼"
	B: 2 ◹ → ◺	2⅜"	2⅞"	3⅜"	3⅞"	4⅜"	4⅞"
	C: 6 ◹ → ◺	1⅝"	1⅞"	2⅛"	2⅜"	2⅝"	2⅞"
	D: 1 ◇	T11	T14	T16	T19	T21	T23
Dark	E: 10 ◹ → ◺	1⅝"	1⅞"	2⅛"	2⅜"	2⅝"	2⅞"

Try this: Use one light for A and C and a different light or a medium for B and D.

TRIPLET

3-Unit Grid

Color Illustration: page 26

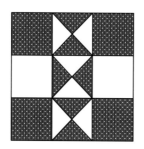 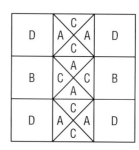 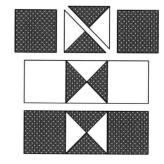

		FINISHED BLOCK SIZE					
		Single dimensions in the cutting chart indicate the size of the cut square (3" = 3" x 3").					
FOR 2 BLOCKS:		4½"	6"	7½"	9"	10½"	12"
Light	A: 3 ⊠ → ⊠	2¾"	3¼"	3¾"	4¼"	4¾"	5¼"
	B: 4 ☐	2"	2½"	3"	3½"	4"	4½"
Dark	C: 3 ⊠ → ⊠	2¾"	3¼"	3¾"	4¼"	4¾"	5¼"
	D: 8 ☐	2"	2½"	3"	3½"	4"	4½"

Try this: Reverse the lights and darks in every other block.

TRUE BLUE

6-Unit Grid

Color Illustration: page 26

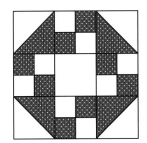
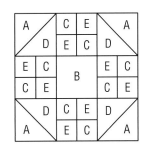
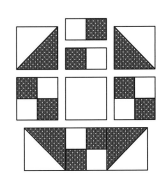

FOR 1 BLOCK:		FINISHED BLOCK SIZE *Single dimensions in the cutting chart indicate the size of the cut square (3" = 3" x 3").*					
		4½"	**6"**	**7½"**	**9"**	**10½"**	**12"**
Light	A: 2 ☐→☑	2⅜"	2⅞"	3⅜"	3⅞"	4⅜"	4⅞"
	B: 1 ☐	2"	2½"	3"	3½"	4"	4½"
	C: 8 ☐	1¼"	1½"	1¾"	2"	2¼"	2½"
Dark	D: 2 ☐→☑	2⅜"	2⅞"	3⅜"	3⅞"	4⅜"	4⅞"
	E: 8 ☐	1¼"	1½"	1¾"	2"	2¼"	2½"

Try this: Use one dark for D and a medium or a different dark for E.

TURKEY IN THE STRAW

8-Unit Grid

Color Illustration: page 26

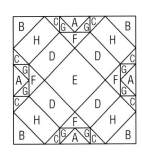

FOR 1 BLOCK:		FINISHED BLOCK SIZE *Single dimensions in the cutting chart indicate the size of the cut square (3" = 3" x 3").*					
		6"	**8"**	**9"**	**10"**	**12"**	**14"**
Light	A: 1 ☒→☒	2¾"	3¼"	3½"	3¾"	4¼"	4¾"
	B: 2 ☐→☑	2⅜"	2⅞"	3⅛"	3⅜"	3⅞"	4⅜"
	C: 4 ☐→☑	1⅝"	1⅞"	2"	2⅛"	2⅜"	2⅝"
	D: 4 ◇	T41	T51	T56	T59	T67	T70
Medium	E: 1 ◇	T11	T14	T15	T16	T19	T21
Dark	F: 1 ☒→☒	2¾"	3¼"	3½"	3¾"	4¼"	4¾"
	G: 4 ☐→☑	1⅝"	1⅞"	2"	2⅛"	2⅜"	2⅝"
	H: 4 ◇	T41	T51	T56	T59	T67	T70

Try this: Use a medium instead of a dark for F and G.

TURNSTILE

2-Unit Grid
Color Illustration: page 26

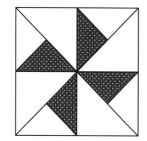
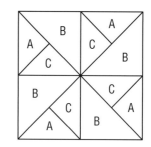
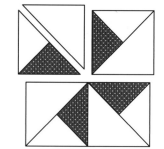

FOR 1 BLOCK:		FINISHED BLOCK SIZE Single dimensions in the cutting chart indicate the size of the cut square (3" = 3" x 3").					
		4"	6"	8"	9"	10"	12"
Light	A: 1 ⊠ → ⊠	3¼"	4¼"	5¼"	5¾"	6¼"	7¼"
	B: 2 ◻ → ◹	2⅞"	3⅞"	4⅞"	5⅜"	5⅞"	6⅞"
Dark	C: 1 ⊠ → ⊠	3¼"	4¼"	5¼"	5¾"	6¼"	7¼"

Try this: Use a medium instead of a light for A.

TWELVE CROWNS

12-Unit Grid
Color Illustration: page 26

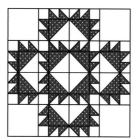
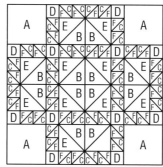
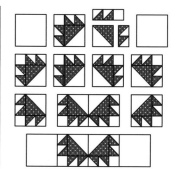

FOR 1 BLOCK:		FINISHED BLOCK SIZE Single dimensions in the cutting chart indicate the size of the cut square (3" = 3" x 3").					
		6"	7½"	9"	12"	13½"	15"
Light	A: 4 ◻	2"	2⅜"	2¾"	3½"	3⅞"	4¼"
	B: 6 ◻ → ◹	1⅞"	2⅛"	2⅜"	2⅞"	3⅛"	3⅜"
	C: 24 ◻ → ◹	1⅜"	1½"	1⅝"	1⅞"	2"	2⅛"
	D: 12 ◻	1"	1⅛"	1¼"	1½"	1⅝"	1¾"
Dark	E: 6 ◻ → ◹	1⅞"	2⅛"	2⅜"	2⅞"	3⅛"	3⅜"
	F: 24 ◻ → ◹	1⅜"	1½"	1⅝"	1⅞"	2"	2⅛"

Try this: Use a different fabric combination for each "crown."

TWELVE TRIANGLES

4-Unit Grid
Color Illustration: page 26

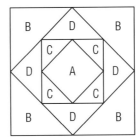

FOR 1 BLOCK:		FINISHED BLOCK SIZE *Single dimensions in the cutting chart indicate the size of the cut square (3" = 3" x 3").*					
		4"	**6"**	**8"**	**9"**	**10"**	**12"**
Light	A: 1 ◇	T7	T11	T14	T15	T16	T19
Light 2	B: 2 ▢→◲	2⅞"	3⅞"	4⅞"	5⅜"	5⅞"	6⅞"
Medium	C: 2 ▢→◲	1⅞"	2⅜"	2⅞"	3⅛"	3⅜"	3⅞"
Dark	D: 1 ⊠→⧈	3¼"	4¼"	5¼"	5¾"	6¼"	7¼"

Try this: Use a different combination of fabrics in every block.

TWINKLING STAR

12-Unit Grid
Color Illustration: page 26

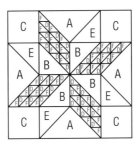

FOR 1 BLOCK:		FINISHED BLOCK SIZE *Single dimensions in the cutting chart indicate the size of the cut square (3" = 3" x 3").*					
		6"	**7½"**	**9"**	**10½"**	**12"**	**15"**
Light	A: 1 ⊠→⧈	4¼"	5"	5¾"	6½"	7¼"	8¾"
	B: 2 ▢→◲	2⅜"	2¾"	3⅛"	3½"	3⅞"	4⅝"
	C: 4 ▢	2"	2⅜"	2¾"	3⅛"	3½	4¼"
	D: 18 ▢→◲	1⅜"	1½"	1⅝"	1¾"	1⅞"	2⅛"
Dark	E: 2 ▢→◲	2⅜"	2¾"	3⅛"	3½"	3⅞"	4⅝"
	F: 18 ▢→◲	1⅜"	1½"	1⅝"	1¾"	1⅞"	2⅛"

Try this: Use several different darks for F.

UNDERGROUND RAILROAD

6-Unit Grid

Color Illustration: page 26

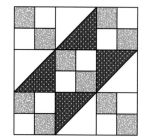
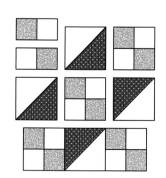

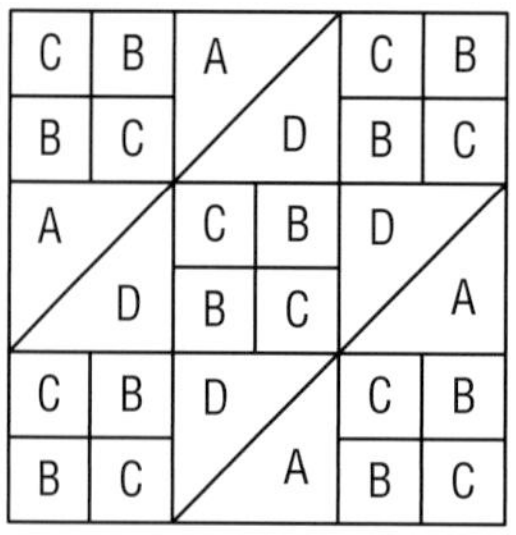

	FINISHED BLOCK SIZE					
	Single dimensions in the cutting chart indicate the size of the cut square (3" = 3" x 3").					
FOR 1 BLOCK:	**4½"**	**6"**	**7½"**	**9"**	**10½"**	**12"**
Light A: 2 ◻→◨	2⅜"	2⅞"	3⅜"	3⅞"	4⅜"	4⅞"
B: 10 ◻	1¼"	1½"	1¾"	2"	2¼"	2½"
Medium C: 10 ◻	1¼"	1½"	1¾"	2"	2¼"	2½"
Dark D: 2 ◻→◨	2⅜"	2⅞"	3⅜"	3⅞"	4⅜"	4⅞"

Try this: Use several different mediums for C.

UNION

6-Unit Grid

Color Illustration: page 26

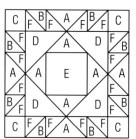

	FINISHED BLOCK SIZE					
	Single dimensions in the cutting chart indicate the size of the cut square (3" = 3" x 3").					
FOR 1 BLOCK:	**4½"**	**6"**	**7½"**	**9"**	**10½"**	**12"**
Light A: 2 ⊠→⊠	2¾"	3¼"	3¾"	4¼"	4¾"	5¼"
B: 4 ◻→◨	1⅝"	1⅞"	2⅛"	2⅜"	2⅝"	2⅞"
C: 4 ◻	1¼"	1½"	1¾"	2"	2¼"	2½"
Dark D: 2 ◻→◨	2⅜"	2⅞"	3⅜"	3⅞"	4⅜"	4⅞"
E: 1 ◻	2"	2½"	3"	3½"	4"	4½"
F: 8 ◻→◨	1⅝"	1⅞"	2⅛"	2⅜"	2⅝"	2⅞"

Try this: Use a medium instead of a dark for D.

UNION SQUARE

3-Unit Grid
Color Illustration: page 26

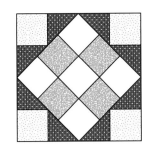
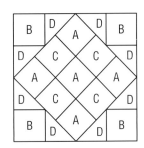
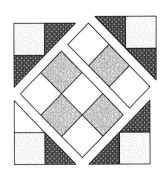

FOR 1 BLOCK:		**FINISHED BLOCK SIZE** Single dimensions in the cutting chart indicate the size of the cut square (3" = 3" x 3").					
		4½"	**6"**	**7½"**	**9"**	**10½"**	**12"**
Light	A: 5 ◇	T5	T7	T9	T11	T12	T14
Light 2	B: 4 □	1⅝"	2"	2⅜"	2¾"	3⅛"	3½"
Medium	C: 4 ◇	T5	T7	T9	T11	T12	T14
Dark	D: 4 ◻→◺	2"	2⅜"	2¾"	3⅛"	3½"	3⅞"

Try this: Reverse the mediums and darks in every other block.

UNNAMED STAR

8-Unit Grid
Color Illustration: page 26

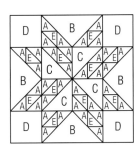

FOR 1 BLOCK:		**FINISHED BLOCK SIZE** Single dimensions in the cutting chart indicate the size of the cut square (3" = 3" x 3").					
		6"	**8"**	**9"**	**10"**	**12"**	**14"**
Light	A: 18 ◻→◺	1⅝"	1⅞"	2"	2⅛"	2⅜"	2⅝"
Dark	B: 1 ⊠→⧖	4¼"	5¼"	5¾"	6¼"	7¼"	8¼"
	C: 2 ◻→◺	2⅜"	2⅞"	3⅛"	3⅜"	3⅞"	4⅜"
	D: 4 □	2"	2½"	2¾"	3"	3½"	4"
	E: 6 ◻→◺	1⅝"	1⅞"	2"	2⅛"	2⅜"	2⅝"

Try this: Reverse the lights and darks.

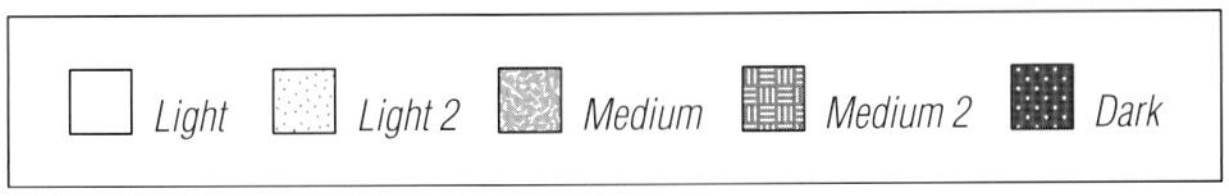

□ Light   ▨ Light 2   ▦ Medium   ▦ Medium 2   ▨ Dark

VERMONT

4-Unit Grid

Color Illustration: page 26

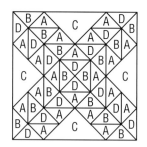

			FINISHED BLOCK SIZE				
			Single dimensions in the cutting chart indicate the size of the cut square (3" = 3" x 3").				
FOR 2 BLOCKS:		**4"**	**6"**	**8"**	**9"**	**10"**	**12"**
Light	A: 10 ⊠ → ⊠	2¼"	2¾"	3¼"	3½"	3¾"	4¼"
Medium	B: 7 ⊠ → ⊠	2¼"	2¾"	3¼"	3½"	3¾"	4¼"
Dark	C: 2 ⊠ → ⊠	3¼"	4¼"	5¼"	5¾"	6¼"	7¼"
	D: 7 ⊠ → ⊠	2¼"	2¾"	3¼"	3½"	3¾"	4¼"
Try this:	Use one dark for C and a different dark for D.						

VINES AT THE WINDOW

8-Unit Grid

Color Illustration: page 26

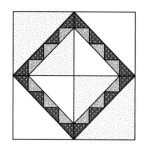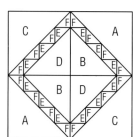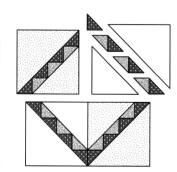

			FINISHED BLOCK SIZE				
			Single dimensions in the cutting chart indicate the size of the cut square (3" = 3" x 3").				
FOR 1 BLOCK:		**6"**	**8"**	**9"**	**10"**	**12"**	**14"**
Light	A: 1 ◻ → ◻	3⅞"	4⅞"	5⅜"	5⅞"	6⅞"	7⅞"
	B: 1 ◻ → ◻	3⅛"	3⅞"	4¼"	4⅝"	5⅜"	6⅛"
Light 2	C: 1 ◻ → ◻	3⅞"	4⅞"	5⅜"	5⅞"	6⅞"	7⅞"
	D: 1 ◻ → ◻	3⅛"	3⅞"	4¼"	4⅝"	5⅜"	6⅛"
Medium	E: 6 ◻ → ◻	1⅝"	1⅞"	2"	2⅛"	2⅜"	2⅝"
Dark	F: 8 ◻ → ◻	1⅝"	1⅞"	2"	2⅛"	2⅜"	2⅝"
Try this:	Use several different mediums for E.						

WAGON TRACKS

6-Unit Grid
Color Illustration: page 26

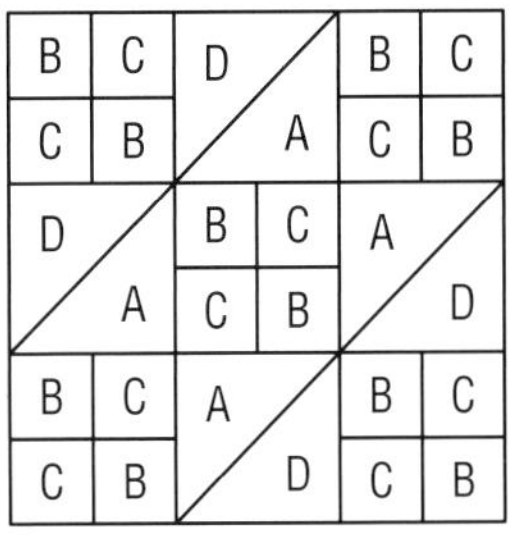

FOR 1 BLOCK:		**FINISHED BLOCK SIZE** Single dimensions in the cutting chart indicate the size of the cut square (3" = 3" x 3").					
		4½"	**6"**	**7½"**	**9"**	**10½"**	**12"**
Light	A: 2 ◻→◪	2⅜"	2⅞"	3⅜"	3⅞"	4⅜"	4⅞"
	B: 10 ◻	1¼"	1½"	1¾"	2"	2¼"	2½"
Medium	C: 10 ◻	1¼"	1½"	1¾"	2"	2¼"	2½"
Dark	D: 2 ◻→◪	2⅜"	2⅞"	3⅜"	3⅞"	4⅜"	4⅞"

Try this: Use one light for A and a different light for B.

WAMPUM BLOCK

6-Unit Grid
Color Illustration: page 26

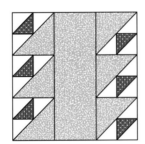

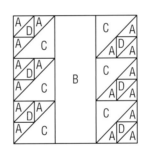

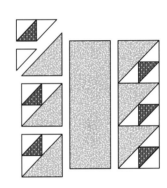

FOR 1 BLOCK:		**FINISHED BLOCK SIZE** Single dimensions in the cutting chart indicate the size of the cut square (3" = 3" x 3").					
		4½"	**6"**	**7½"**	**9"**	**10½"**	**12"**
Light	A: 9 ◻→◪	1⅝"	1⅞"	2⅛"	2⅜"	2⅝"	2⅞"
Medium	B: 1 ▭	2" x 5"	2½" x 6½"	3" x 8"	3½" x 9½"	4" x 11"	4½" x 12½"
	C: 3 ◻→◪	2⅜"	2⅞"	3⅜"	3⅞"	4⅜"	4⅞"
Dark	D: 3 ◻→◪	1⅝"	1⅞"	2⅛"	2⅜"	2⅝"	2⅞"

Try this: Use a dark instead of a medium for B.

WANDERING LOVER

9-Unit Grid
Color Illustration: page 26

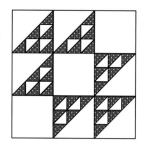 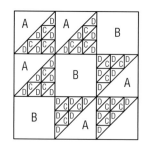 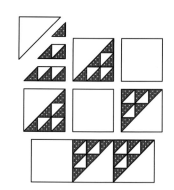

FOR 1 BLOCK:		FINISHED BLOCK SIZE *Single dimensions in the cutting chart indicate the size of the cut square (3" = 3" x 3").*					
		6¾"	**9"**	**10⅛"**	**11¼"**	**12⅜"**	**13½"**
Light	A: 3 ◻ → ◺	3⅛"	3⅞"	4¼"	4⅝"	5"	5⅜"
	B: 3 ◻	2¾"	3½"	3⅞"	4¼"	4⅝"	5"
	C: 9 ◻ → ◺	1⅝"	1⅞"	2"	2⅛"	2¼"	2⅜"
Dark	D: 18 ◻ → ◺	1⅝"	1⅞"	2"	2⅛"	2¼"	2⅜"

Try this: Use several different darks for D.

WASHINGTON PAVEMENT

8-Unit Grid
Color Illustration: page 26

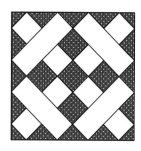 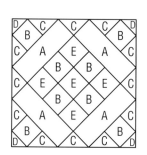 

FOR 1 BLOCK:		FINISHED BLOCK SIZE *Single dimensions in the cutting chart indicate the size of the cut square (3" = 3" x 3").*					
		6"	**8"**	**9"**	**10"**	**12"**	**14"**
Light	A: 4 ◇	T42	T52	T57	T60	T68	T71
	B: 8 ◇	T5	T7	T8	T9	T11	T12
Dark	C: 3 ⊠ → ⧖	2¾"	3¼"	3½"	3¾"	4¼"	4¾"
	D: 2 ◻ → ◺	1⅝"	1⅞"	2"	2⅛"	2⅜"	2⅝"
	E: 5 ◇	T5	T7	T8	T9	T11	T12

Try this: Use a different combination of lights and darks in every block.

WATER WHEEL

6-Unit Grid
Color Illustration: page 26

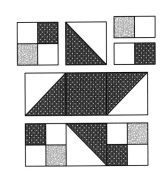

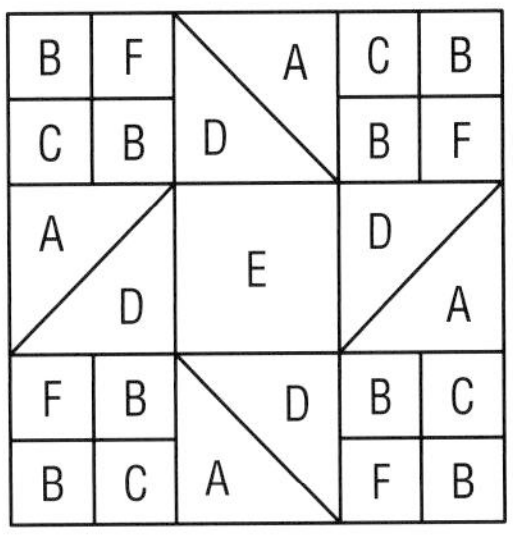

FOR 1 BLOCK:			FINISHED BLOCK SIZE *Single dimensions in the cutting chart indicate the size of the cut square (3" = 3" x 3").*					
			4½"	**6"**	**7½"**	**9"**	**10½"**	**12"**
Light	A: 2 ☐→◩		2⅜"	2⅞"	3⅜"	3⅞"	4⅜"	4⅞"
	B: 8 ☐		1¼"	1½"	1¾"	2"	2¼"	2½"
Medium	C: 4 ☐		1¼"	1½"	1¾"	2"	2¼"	2½"
Dark	D: 2 ☐→◩		2⅜"	2⅞"	3⅜"	3⅞"	4⅜"	4⅞"
	E: 1 ☐		2"	2½"	3"	3½"	4"	4½"
	F: 4 ☐		1¼"	1½"	1¾"	2"	2¼"	2½"

Try this: Use a different medium in each block.

WAVES OF THE SEA

8-Unit Grid
Color Illustration: page 26

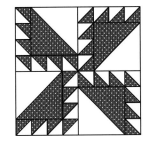
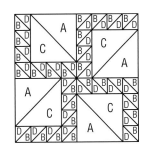

FOR 1 BLOCK:			FINISHED BLOCK SIZE *Single dimensions in the cutting chart indicate the size of the cut square (3" = 3" x 3").*					
			6"	**8"**	**9"**	**10"**	**12"**	**14"**
Light	A: 2 ☐→◩		3⅛"	3⅞"	4¼"	4⅝"	5⅜"	6⅛"
	B: 14 ☐→◩		1⅝"	1⅞"	2"	2⅛"	2⅜"	2⅝"
Dark	C: 2 ☐→◩		3⅛"	3⅞"	4¼"	4⅝"	5⅜"	6⅛"
	D: 14 ☐→◩		1⅝"	1⅞"	2"	2⅛"	2⅜"	2⅝"

Try this: Use a large-scale print for C.

THE WEDDING RING

4-Unit Grid
Color Illustration: page 26

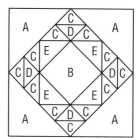

		FINISHED BLOCK SIZE *Single dimensions in the cutting chart indicate the size of the cut square (3" = 3" x 3").*					
FOR 1 BLOCK:		**4"**	**6"**	**8"**	**9"**	**10"**	**12"**
Light	A: 2 ◻→◹	2⅞"	3⅞"	4⅞"	5⅜"	5⅞"	6⅞"
	B: 1 ◇	T7	T11	T14	T15	T16	T19
Medium	C: 3 ⊠→⧅	2¼"	2¾"	3¼"	3½"	3¾"	4¼"
Dark	D: 1 ⊠→⧅	2¼"	2¾"	3¼"	3½"	3¾"	4¼"
	E: 2 ◻→◹	1⅞"	2⅜"	2⅞"	3⅛"	3⅜"	3⅞"

Try this: Use one light for A and a different light for B.

WEST WIND

3-Unit Grid
Color Illustration: page 26

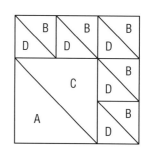

		FINISHED BLOCK SIZE *Single dimensions in the cutting chart indicate the size of the cut square (3" = 3" x 3").*					
FOR 2 BLOCKS:		**4½"**	**6"**	**7½"**	**9"**	**10½"**	**12"**
Light	A: 1 ◻→◹	3⅞"	4⅞"	5⅞"	6⅞"	7⅞"	8⅞"
	B: 5 ◻→◹	2⅜"	2⅞"	3⅜"	3⅞"	4⅜"	4⅞"
Dark	C: 1 ◻→◹	3⅞"	4⅞"	5⅞"	6⅞"	7⅞"	8⅞"
	D: 5 ◻→◹	2⅜"	2⅞"	3⅜"	3⅞"	4⅜"	4⅞"

Try this: Use a medium instead of a dark for C.

WHEEL OF CHANCE

5-Unit Grid
Color Illustration: page 26

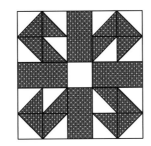
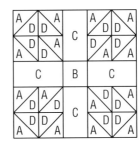
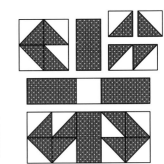

FOR 1 BLOCK:		**FINISHED BLOCK SIZE** Single dimensions in the cutting chart indicate the size of the cut square (3" = 3" x 3").					
		5"	**6¼"**	**7½"**	**8¾"**	**10"**	**12½"**
Light	A: 8 ◻→◺	1⅞"	2⅛"	2⅜"	2⅝"	2⅞"	3⅜"
	B: 1 ◻	1½"	1¾"	2"	2¼"	2½"	3"
Dark	C: 4 ▭	1½" x 2½"	1¾" x 3"	2" x 3½"	2¼" x 4"	2½" x 4½"	3" x 5½"
	D: 8 ◻→◺	1⅞"	2⅛"	2⅜"	2⅝"	2⅞"	3⅜"

Try this: Use one medium for C and several different darks for D.

WHEEL OF TIME

4-Unit Grid
Color Illustration: page 26

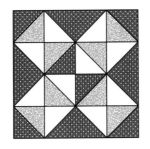
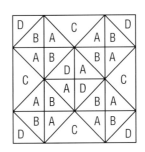
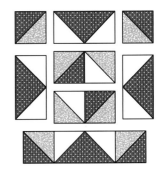

FOR 1 BLOCK:		**FINISHED BLOCK SIZE** Single dimensions in the cutting chart indicate the size of the cut square (3" = 3" x 3").					
		4"	**6"**	**8"**	**9"**	**10"**	**12"**
Light	A: 5 ◻→◺	1⅞"	2⅜"	2⅞"	3⅛"	3⅜"	3⅞"
Medium	B: 4 ◻→◺	1⅞"	2⅜"	2⅞"	3⅛"	3⅜"	3⅞"
Dark	C: 1 ⊠→⧅	3¼"	4¼"	5¼"	5¾"	6¼"	7¼"
	D: 3 ◻→◺	1⅞"	2⅜"	2⅞"	3⅛"	3⅜"	3⅞"

Try this: Reverse the mediums and darks in every other block.

◻ Light   ▦ Light 2   ▩ Medium   ▦ Medium 2   ■ Dark

WHIRLING FIVE PATCH

5-Unit Grid
Color Illustration: page 26

 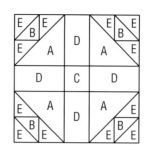 

FOR 1 BLOCK:	FINISHED BLOCK SIZE — *Single dimensions in the cutting chart indicate the size of the cut square (3" = 3" x 3").*					
	5"	6¼"	7½"	8¾"	10"	12½"
Light A: 2 ▢→◨	2⅞"	3⅜"	3⅞"	4⅜"	4⅞"	5⅞"
B: 2 ▢→◨	1⅞"	2⅛"	2⅜"	2⅝"	2⅞"	3⅜"
C: 1 ▢	1½"	1¾"	2"	2¼"	2½"	3"
Dark D: 4 ▭	1½" x 2½"	1¾" x 3"	2" x 3½"	2¼" x 4"	2½" x 4½"	3" x 5½"
E: 6 ▢→◨	1⅞"	2⅛"	2⅜"	2⅝"	2⅞"	3⅜"

Try this: Use several different darks for E.

WHIRLING SQUARE

9-Unit Grid
Color Illustration: page 26

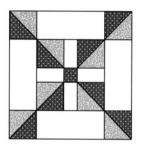 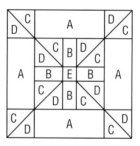 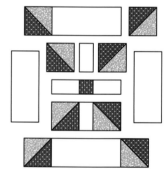

FOR 1 BLOCK:	FINISHED BLOCK SIZE — *Single dimensions in the cutting chart indicate the size of the cut square (3" = 3" x 3").*					
	6¾"	9"	10⅛"	11¼"	12⅜"	13½"
Light A: 4 ▭	2" x 4¼"	2½" x 5½"	2¾" x 6⅛"	3" x 6¾"	3¼" x 7⅜"	3½" x 8"
B: 4 ▭	1¼" x 2"	1½" x 2½"	1⅝" x 2¾"	1¾" x 3"	1⅞" x 3¼"	2" x 3½"
Medium C: 4 ▢→◨	2⅜"	2⅞"	3⅛"	3⅜"	3⅝"	3⅞"
Dark D: 4 ▢→◨	2⅜"	2⅞"	3⅛"	3⅜"	3⅝"	3⅞"
E: 1 ▢	1¼"	1½"	1⅝"	1¾"	1⅞"	2"

Try this: Use a scrappy assortment of mediums and darks for C and D.

WHIRLWIND

10-Unit Grid

Color Illustration: page 27

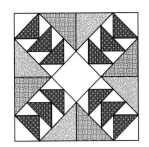 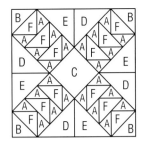 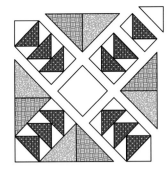

FOR 1 BLOCK:		FINISHED BLOCK SIZE *Single dimensions in the cutting chart indicate the size of the cut square (3" = 3" x 3").*					
		6¼"	7½"	8¾"	10"	12½"	13¾"
Light	A: 6 ⊠ → ⊠	2½"	2¾"	3"	3¼"	3¾"	4"
	B: 2 ◻ → ◸	2⅛"	2⅜"	2⅝"	2⅞"	3⅜"	3⅝"
	C: 1 ◇	T9	T11	T12	T14	T16	T18
Medium	D: 2 ◻ → ◸	2¾"	3⅛"	3½"	3⅞"	4⅝"	5"
Medium 2	E: 2 ◻ → ◸	2¾"	3⅛"	3½"	3⅞"	4⅝"	5"
Dark	F: 6 ◻ → ◸	2⅛"	2⅜"	2⅝"	2⅞"	3⅜"	3⅝"

Try this: Use several different lights for A.

WHITE HEMSTITCH

8-Unit Grid

Color Illustration: page 27

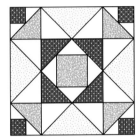 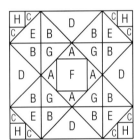 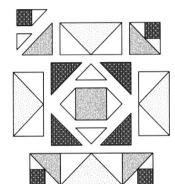

FOR 1 BLOCK:		FINISHED BLOCK SIZE *Single dimensions in the cutting chart indicate the size of the cut square (3" = 3" x 3").*					
		6"	8"	9"	10"	12"	14"
Light	A: 1 ⊠ → ⊠	2¾"	3¼"	3½"	3¾"	4¼"	4¾"
	B: 4 ◻ → ◸	2⅜"	2⅞"	3⅛"	3⅜"	3⅞"	4⅜"
	C: 4 ◻ → ◸	1⅝"	1⅞"	2"	2⅛"	2⅜"	2⅝"
Light 2	D: 1 ⊠ → ⊠	4¼"	5¼"	5¾"	6¼"	7¼"	8¼"
Medium	E: 2 ◻ → ◸	2⅜"	2⅞"	3⅛"	3⅜"	3⅞"	4⅜"
	F: 1 ◻	2"	2½"	2¾"	3"	3½"	4"
Dark	G: 2 ◻ → ◸	2⅜"	2⅞"	3⅛"	3⅜"	3⅞"	4⅜"
	H: 4 ◻	1¼"	1½"	1⅝"	1¾"	2"	2¼"

Try this: Reverse the mediums and darks in every other block.

WILD DUCK

4-Unit Grid

Color Illustration: page 27

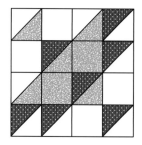
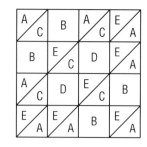
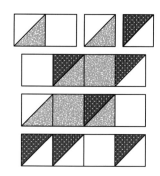

			FINISHED BLOCK SIZE Single dimensions in the cutting chart indicate the size of the cut square (3" = 3" x 3").				
FOR 2 BLOCKS:			**4"**	**6"**	**8"**	**9"**	**10"**	**12"**
Light	A: 8 ⬜➔◪	1⅞"	2⅜"	2⅞"	3⅛"	3⅜"	3⅞"
	B: 8 ⬜	1½"	2"	2½"	2¾"	3"	3½"
Medium	C: 5 ⬜➔◪	1⅞"	2⅜"	2⅞"	3⅛"	3⅜"	3⅞"
	D: 4 ⬜	1½"	2"	2½"	2¾"	3"	3½"
Dark	E: 7 ⬜➔◪	1⅞"	2⅜"	2⅞"	3⅛"	3⅜"	3⅞"

Try this: Use a different combination of mediums and darks in every block.

WILD GOOSE

4-Unit Grid

Color Illustration: page 27

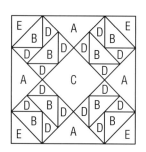

			FINISHED BLOCK SIZE Single dimensions in the cutting chart indicate the size of the cut square (3" = 3" x 3").				
FOR 1 BLOCK:			**4"**	**6"**	**8"**	**9"**	**10"**	**12"**
Light	A: 1 ⊠➔⊠	3¼"	4¼"	5¼"	5¾"	6¼"	7¼"
	B: 4 ⬜➔◪	1⅞"	2⅜"	2⅞"	3⅛"	3⅜"	3⅞"
	C: 1 ◇	T7	T11	T14	T15	T16	T19
Dark	D: 4 ⊠➔⊠	2¼"	2¾"	3¼"	3½"	3¾"	4¼"
	E: 2 ⬜➔◪	1⅞"	2⅜"	2⅞"	3⅛"	3⅜"	3⅞"

Try this: Reverse the lights and darks.

WILD GOOSE CHASE

8-Unit Grid

Color Illustration: page 27

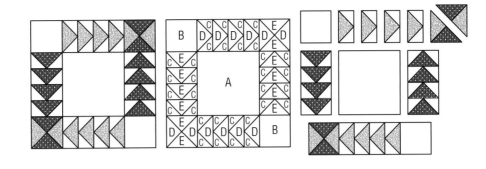

		FINISHED BLOCK SIZE					
		Single dimensions in the cutting chart indicate the size of the cut square (3" = 3" x 3").					
FOR 1 BLOCK:		**6"**	**8"**	**9"**	**10"**	**12"**	**14"**
Light	A: 1 ☐	3½"	4½"	5"	5½"	6½"	7½"
	B: 2 ☐	2"	2½"	2¾"	3"	3½"	4"
	C: 16 ◺→◹	1⅝"	1⅞"	2"	2⅛"	2⅜"	2⅝"
Medium	D: 3 ⊠→⧆	2¾"	3¼"	3½"	3¾"	4¼"	4¾"
Dark	E: 3 ⊠→⧆	2¾"	3¼"	3½"	3¾"	4¼"	4¾"
Try this:	Use several different mediums and darks.						

WILD GOOSE CHASE II

6-Unit Grid

Color Illustration: page 27

 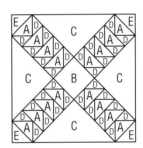 

		FINISHED BLOCK SIZE					
		Single dimensions in the cutting chart indicate the size of the cut square (3" = 3" x 3").					
FOR 1 BLOCK:		**4½"**	**6"**	**7½"**	**9"**	**10½"**	**12"**
Light	A: 8 ◺→◹	1⅝"	1⅞"	2⅛"	2⅜"	2⅝"	2⅞"
	B: 1 ◇	T5	T7	T9	T11	T12	T14
Medium	C: 1 ⊠→⧆	4¼"	5¼"	6¼"	7¼"	8¼"	9¼"
Dark	D: 8 ⊠→⧆	2"	2¼"	2½"	2¾"	3"	3¼"
	E: 2 ◺→◹	1⅝"	1⅞"	2⅛"	2⅜"	2⅝"	2⅞"
Try this:	Reverse the lights and the medium.						

WILD GOOSE CHASE III

6-Unit Grid
Color Illustration: page 27

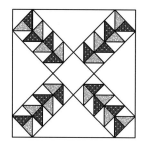 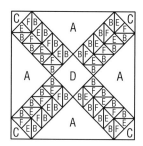 

		FINISHED BLOCK SIZE					
		Single dimensions in the cutting chart indicate the size of the cut square (3" = 3" x 3").					
FOR 1 BLOCK:		**4½"**	**6"**	**7½"**	**9"**	**10½"**	**12"**
Light	A: 1 ⊠→⊠	4¼"	5¼"	6¼"	7¼"	8¼"	9¼"
	B: 8 ⊠→⊠	2"	2¼"	2½"	2¾"	3"	3¼"
	C: 2 ◻→◻	1⅝"	1⅞"	2⅛"	2⅜"	2⅝"	2⅞"
	D: 1 ◇	T5	T7	T9	T11	T12	T14
Medium	E: 4 ⊠→⊠	2"	2¼"	2½"	2¾"	3"	3¼"
Dark	F: 4 ⊠→⊠	2"	2¼"	2½"	2¾"	3"	3¼"
Try this:	Use many different fabrics for E and F.						

WILLOW HAVEN

4-Unit Grid
Color Illustration: page 27

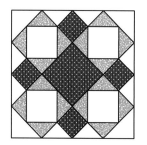 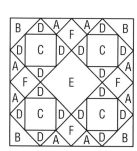 

		FINISHED BLOCK SIZE					
		Single dimensions in the cutting chart indicate the size of the cut square (3" = 3" x 3").					
FOR 1 BLOCK:		**4"**	**6"**	**8"**	**9"**	**10"**	**12"**
Light	A: 2 ⊠→⊠	2¼"	2¾"	3¼"	3½"	3¾"	4¼"
	B: 2 ◻→◻	1⅞"	2⅜"	2⅞"	3⅛"	3⅜"	3⅞"
	C: 4 ◻	1½"	2"	2½"	2¾"	3"	3½"
Medium	D: 4 ⊠→⊠	2¼"	2¾"	3¼"	3½"	3¾"	4¼"
Dark	E: 1 ◇	T7	T11	T14	T15	T16	T19
	F: 4 ◇	T2	T5	T7	T8	T9	T11
Try this:	Use one dark for E and a different dark for F.						

WINDBLOWN SQUARE

4-Unit Grid
Color Illustration: page 27

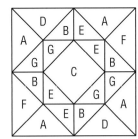

	FINISHED BLOCK SIZE					
	Single dimensions in the cutting chart indicate the size of the cut square (3" = 3" x 3").					
FOR 2 BLOCKS:	**4"**	**6"**	**8"**	**9"**	**10"**	**12"**
Light A: 2 ⊠ → ⊠	3¼"	4¼"	5¼"	5¾"	6¼"	7¼"
B: 4 ◺ → ◸	1⅞"	2⅜"	2⅞"	3⅛"	3⅜"	3⅞"
C: 2 ◇	T7	T11	T14	T15	T16	T19
Medium D: 1 ⊠ → ⊠	3¼"	4¼"	5¼"	5¾"	6¼"	7¼"
E: 4 ◺ → ◸	1⅞"	2⅜"	2⅞"	3⅛"	3⅜"	3⅞"
Dark F: 1 ⊠ → ⊠	3¼"	4¼"	5¼"	5¾"	6¼"	7¼"
G: 4 ◺ → ◸	1⅞"	2⅜"	2⅞"	3⅛"	3⅜"	3⅞"

Try this: Use one light for A and C and a different light for B.

WINDMILL

10-Unit Grid
Color Illustration: page 27

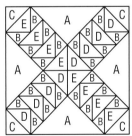

	FINISHED BLOCK SIZE					
	Single dimensions in the cutting chart indicate the size of the cut square (3" = 3" x 3").					
FOR 1 BLOCK:	**5"**	**6¼"**	**7½"**	**8¾"**	**10"**	**12½"**
Light A: 1 ⊠ → ⊠	4¼"	5"	5¾"	6½"	7¼"	8¾"
B: 6 ⊠ → ⊠	2¼"	2½"	2¾"	3"	3¼"	3¾"
C: 2 ◺ → ◸	1⅞"	2⅛"	2⅜"	2⅝"	2⅞"	3⅜"
Medium D: 4 ◺ → ◸	1⅞"	2⅛"	2⅜"	2⅝"	2⅞"	3⅜"
Dark E: 4 ◺ → ◸	1⅞"	2⅛"	2⅜"	2⅝"	2⅞"	3⅜"

Try this: Use several different mediums and darks for D and E.

WINDMILL II

4-Unit Grid
Color Illustration: page 27

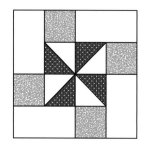 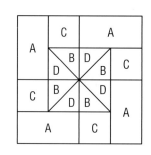 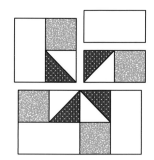

		FINISHED BLOCK SIZE Single dimensions in the cutting chart indicate the size of the cut square (3" = 3" x 3").					
FOR 1 BLOCK:		**4"**	**6"**	**8"**	**9"**	**10"**	**12"**
Light	A: 4 ▭	1½" x 2½"	2" x 3½"	2½" x 4½"	2¾" x 5"	3" x 5½"	3½" x 6½"
	B: 2 ◹→◺	1⅞"	2⅜"	2⅞"	3⅛"	3⅜"	3⅞"
Medium	C: 4 ▢	1½"	2"	2½"	2¾"	3"	3½"
Dark	D: 2 ◹→◺	1⅞"	2⅜"	2⅞"	3⅛"	3⅜"	3⅞"

Try this: Use several different mediums for C.

WINDMILL III

8-Unit Grid
Color Illustration: page 27

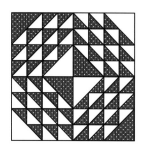 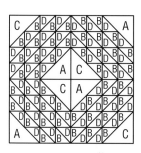 

		FINISHED BLOCK SIZE Single dimensions in the cutting chart indicate the size of the cut square (3" = 3" x 3").					
FOR 1 BLOCK:		**6"**	**8"**	**9"**	**10"**	**12"**	**14"**
Light	A: 2 ◹→◺	2⅜"	2⅞"	3⅛"	3⅜"	3⅞"	4⅜"
	B: 24 ◹→◺	1⅝"	1⅞"	2"	2⅛"	2⅜"	2⅝"
Dark	C: 2 ◹→◺	2⅜"	2⅞"	3⅛"	3⅜"	3⅞"	4⅜"
	D: 24 ◹→◺	1⅝"	1⅞"	2"	2⅛"	2⅜"	2⅝"

Try this: Use many different darks for D.

WINDMILL SQUARE

4-Unit Grid

Color Illustration: page 27

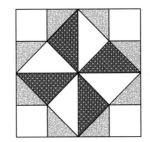
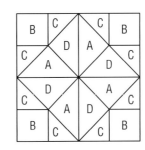
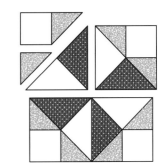

FOR 1 BLOCK:		FINISHED BLOCK SIZE *Single dimensions in the cutting chart indicate the size of the cut square (3" = 3" x 3").*					
		4"	**6"**	**8"**	**9"**	**10"**	**12"**
Light	A: 1 ⊠→⊠	$3\frac{1}{4}$"	$4\frac{1}{4}$"	$5\frac{1}{4}$"	$5\frac{3}{4}$"	$6\frac{1}{4}$"	$7\frac{1}{4}$"
	B: 4 ▢	$1\frac{1}{2}$"	2"	$2\frac{1}{2}$"	$2\frac{3}{4}$"	3"	$3\frac{1}{2}$"
Medium	C: 4 ◩→◪	$1\frac{7}{8}$"	$2\frac{3}{8}$"	$2\frac{7}{8}$"	$3\frac{1}{8}$"	$3\frac{3}{8}$"	$3\frac{7}{8}$"
Dark	D: 1 ⊠→⊠	$3\frac{1}{4}$"	$4\frac{1}{4}$"	$5\frac{1}{4}$"	$5\frac{3}{4}$"	$6\frac{1}{4}$"	$7\frac{1}{4}$"

Try this: Use one light for A and a different light for B.

WINDOWS AND DOORS

10-Unit Grid

Color Illustration: page 27

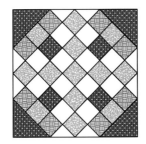
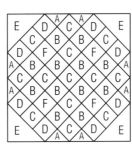
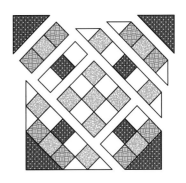

FOR 1 BLOCK:		FINISHED BLOCK SIZE *Single dimensions in the cutting chart indicate the size of the cut square (3" = 3" x 3").*					
		$6\frac{1}{4}$"	**$7\frac{1}{2}$"**	**$8\frac{3}{4}$"**	**10"**	**$12\frac{1}{2}$"**	**$13\frac{3}{4}$"**
Light	A: 2 ⊠→⊠	$2\frac{1}{2}$"	$2\frac{3}{4}$"	3"	$3\frac{1}{4}$"	$3\frac{3}{4}$"	4"
	B: 12 ◇	T4	T5	T6	T7	T9	T10
Medium	C: 13 ◇	T4	T5	T6	T7	T9	T10
Medium 2	D: 8 ◇	T4	T5	T6	T7	T9	T10
Dark	E: 2 ◩→◪	$2\frac{3}{4}$"	$3\frac{1}{8}$"	$3\frac{1}{2}$"	$3\frac{7}{8}$"	$4\frac{5}{8}$"	5"
	F: 4 ◇	T4	T5	T6	T7	T9	T10

Try this: Use many different mediums for C and D.

▢ Light ▨ Light 2 ▨ Medium ▨ Medium 2 ■ Dark

THE WINGED 9 PATCH

8-Unit Grid
Color Illustration: page 27

 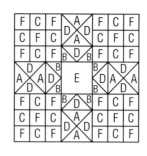 

FOR 1 BLOCK:			FINISHED BLOCK SIZE					
			Single dimensions in the cutting chart indicate the size of the cut square (3" = 3" x 3").					
			6"	**8"**	**9"**	**10"**	**12"**	**14"**
Light	A: 2 ⊠ → ⊠		2¾"	3¼"	3½"	3¾"	4¼"	4¾"
	B: 4 ◻ → ◻		1⅝"	1⅞"	2"	2⅛"	2⅜"	2⅝"
	C: 16 ◻		1¼"	1½"	1⅝"	1¾"	2"	2¼"
Dark	D: 3 ⊠ → ⊠		2¾"	3¼"	3½"	3¾"	4¼"	4¾"
	E: 1 ◻		2"	2½"	2¾"	3"	3½"	4"
	F: 20 ◻		1¼"	1½"	1⅝"	1¾"	2"	2¼"

Try this: Use a medium instead of a dark for F.

WINGED SQUARE

6-Unit Grid
Color Illustration: page 27

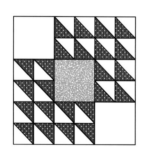 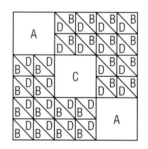 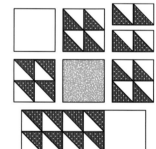

FOR 1 BLOCK:			FINISHED BLOCK SIZE					
			Single dimensions in the cutting chart indicate the size of the cut square (3" = 3" x 3").					
			4½"	**6"**	**7½"**	**9"**	**10½"**	**12"**
Light	A: 2 ◻		2"	2½"	3"	3½"	4"	4½"
	B: 12 ◻ → ◻		1⅝"	1⅞"	2⅛"	2⅜"	2⅝"	2⅞"
Medium	C: 1 ◻		2"	2½"	3"	3½"	4"	4½"
Dark	D: 12 ◻ → ◻		1⅝"	1⅞"	2⅛"	2⅜"	2⅝"	2⅞"

Try this: Use a different combination of mediums and darks in every block.

WISHING RING

5-Unit Grid
Color Illustration: page 27

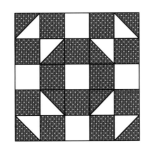
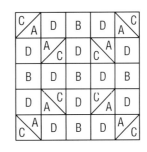
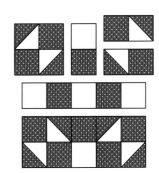

FOR 1 BLOCK:		**FINISHED BLOCK SIZE** Single dimensions in the cutting chart indicate the size of the cut square (3" = 3" x 3").					
		5"	**6¼"**	**7½"**	**8¾"**	**10"**	**12½"**
Light	A: 4 ◻→◻	1⅞"	2⅛"	2⅜"	2⅝"	2⅞"	3⅜"
	B: 5 ◻	1½"	1¾"	2"	2¼"	2½"	3"
Dark	C: 4 ◻→◻	1⅞"	2⅛"	2⅜"	2⅝"	2⅞"	3⅜"
	D: 12 ◻	1½"	1¾"	2"	2¼"	2½"	3"

Try this: Reverse the lights and darks.

WOODLAND PATH

10-Unit Grid
Color Illustration: page 27

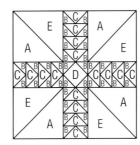
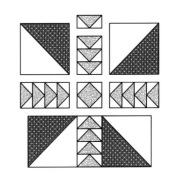

FOR 1 BLOCK:		**FINISHED BLOCK SIZE** Single dimensions in the cutting chart indicate the size of the cut square (3" = 3" x 3").					
		6¼"	**7½"**	**8¾"**	**10"**	**12½"**	**13¾"**
Light	A: 2 ◻→◻	3⅜"	3⅞"	4⅜"	4⅞"	5⅞"	6⅜"
	B: 18 ◻→◻	1½"	1⅝"	1¾"	1⅞"	2⅛"	2¼"
Medium	C: 4 ⊠→⊠	2½"	2¾"	3"	3¼"	3¾"	4"
	D: 1 ◇	T4	T5	T6	T7	T9	T10
Dark	E: 2 ◻→◻	3⅜"	3⅞"	4⅜"	4⅞"	5⅞"	6⅜"

Try this: Use one light for A and a different light for B.

WORLD'S FAIR PUZZLE

8-Unit Grid

Color Illustration: page 27

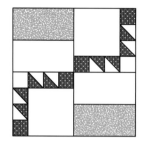 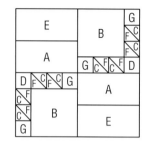 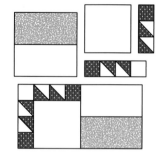

		FINISHED BLOCK SIZE Single dimensions in the cutting chart indicate the size of the cut square (3" = 3" x 3").					
FOR 1 BLOCK:		**6"**	**8"**	**9"**	**10"**	**12"**	**14"**
Light	A: 2 ▭	2" x 3½"	2½" x 4½"	2¾" x 5"	3" x 5½"	3½" x 6½"	4" x 7½"
	B: 2 □	2¾"	3½"	3⅞"	4¼"	5"	5¾"
	C: 4 ◨→◩	1⅝"	1⅞"	2"	2⅛"	2⅜"	2⅝"
	D: 2 □	1¼"	1½"	1⅝"	1¾"	2"	2¼"
Medium	E: 2 ▭	2" x 3½"	2½" x 4½"	2¾" x 5"	3" x 5½"	3½" x 6½"	4" x 7½"
Dark	F: 4 ◨→◩	1⅝"	1⅞"	2"	2⅛"	2⅜"	2⅝"
	G: 4 □	1¼"	1½"	1⅝"	1¾"	2"	2¼"

Try this: Use a different medium in every block.

WRENCH

5-Unit Grid

Color Illustration: page 27

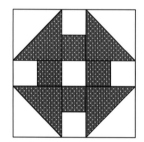 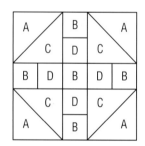 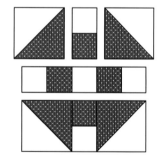

		FINISHED BLOCK SIZE Single dimensions in the cutting chart indicate the size of the cut square (3" = 3" x 3").					
FOR 1 BLOCK:		**5"**	**6¼"**	**7½"**	**8¾"**	**10"**	**12½"**
Light	A: 2 ◨→◩	2⅞"	3⅜"	3⅞"	4⅜"	4⅞"	5⅞"
	B: 5 □	1½"	1¾"	2"	2¼"	2½"	3"
Dark	C: 2 ◨→◩	2⅞"	3⅜"	3⅞"	4⅜"	4⅞"	5⅞"
	D: 4 □	1½"	1¾"	2"	2¼"	2½"	3"

Try this: Reverse the lights and darks in every other block.

THE X

10-Unit Grid
Color Illustration: page 27

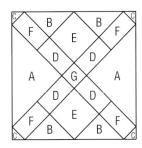

		FINISHED BLOCK SIZE *Single dimensions in the cutting chart indicate the size of the cut square (3" = 3" x 3").*					
FOR 2 BLOCKS:		**6¼"**	**7½"**	**8¾"**	**10"**	**12½"**	**13¾"**
Light	A: 1 ▨ → ▨	6¼"	7¼"	8¼"	9¼"	11¼"	12¼"
	B: 2 ▨ → ▨	3¾"	4¼"	4¾"	5¼"	6¼"	6¾"
	C: 4 ◺ → ◹	1½"	1⅝"	1¾"	1⅞"	2⅛"	2¼"
	D: 8 ◇	T36	T41	T46	T51	T59	T63
Dark	E: 4 ◇	T9	T11	T12	T14	T16	T18
	F: 8 ◇	T36	T41	T46	T51	T59	T63
	G: 2 ◇	T4	T5	T6	T7	T9	T10

Try this: Use a medium instead of a light for D.

X QUARTET

4-Unit Grid
Color Illustration: page 27

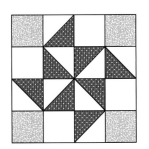
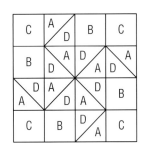
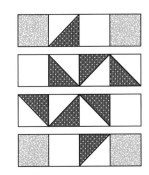

		FINISHED BLOCK SIZE *Single dimensions in the cutting chart indicate the size of the cut square (3" = 3" x 3").*					
FOR 1 BLOCK:		**4"**	**6"**	**8"**	**9"**	**10"**	**12"**
Light	A: 4 ◺ → ◹	1⅞"	2⅜"	2⅞"	3⅛"	3⅜"	3⅞"
	B: 4 ▢	1½"	2"	2½"	2¾"	3"	3½"
Medium	C: 4 ▢	1½"	2"	2½"	2¾"	3"	3½"
Dark	D: 4 ◺ → ◹	1⅞"	2⅜"	2⅞"	3⅛"	3⅜"	3⅞"

Try this: Reverse the mediums and darks in every other block.

☐ *Light*　▦ *Light 2*　▦ *Medium*　▦ *Medium 2*　■ *Dark*

YANKEE PUZZLE

4-Unit Grid
Color Illustration: page 27

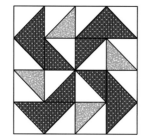
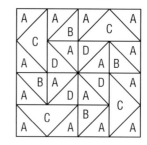
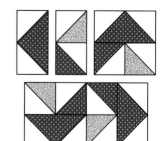

FOR 1 BLOCK:		**FINISHED BLOCK SIZE** Single dimensions in the cutting chart indicate the size of the cut square (3" = 3" x 3").					
		4"	**6"**	**8"**	**9"**	**10"**	**12"**
Light	A: 8 ◱ → ◺	1⅞"	2⅜"	2⅞"	3⅛"	3⅜"	3⅞"
Medium	B: 2 ◱ → ◺	1⅞"	2⅜"	2⅞"	3⅛"	3⅜"	3⅞"
Dark	C: 1 ⊠ → ⊠	3¼"	4¼"	5¼"	5¾"	6¼"	7¼"
	D: 2 ◱ → ◺	1⅞"	2⅜"	2⅞"	3⅛"	3⅜"	3⅞"

Try this: Use several different lights for A

YEAR'S FAVORITE

4-Unit Grid
Color Illustration: page 27

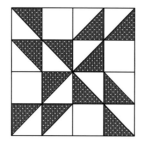
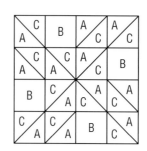
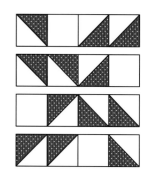

FOR 1 BLOCK:		**FINISHED BLOCK SIZE** Single dimensions in the cutting chart indicate the size of the cut square (3" = 3" x 3").					
		4"	**6"**	**8"**	**9"**	**10"**	**12"**
Light	A: 6 ◱ → ◺	1⅞"	2⅜"	2⅞"	3⅛"	3⅜"	3⅞"
	B: 4 ▢	1½"	2"	2½"	2¾"	3"	3½"
Dark	C: 6 ◱ → ◺	1⅞"	2⅜"	2⅞"	3⅛"	3⅜"	3⅞"

Try this: Use several different darks for C.

ZENOBIA'S PUZZLE

8-Unit Grid

Color Illustration: page 27

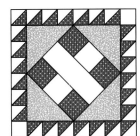
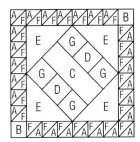

FOR 1 BLOCK:			FINISHED BLOCK SIZE Single dimensions in the cutting chart indicate the size of the cut square (3" = 3" x 3").					
			6"	**8"**	**9"**	**10"**	**12"**	**14"**
Light	A: 13 ▱ → ▱		1⅝"	1⅞"	2"	2⅛"	2⅜"	2⅝"
	B: 2 ☐		1¼"	1½"	1⅝"	1¾"	2"	2¼"
	C: 1 ◇		T42	T52	T57	T60	T68	T71
	D: 2 ◇		T5	T7	T8	T9	T11	T12
Medium	E: 2 ▱ → ▱		3⅛"	3⅞"	4¼"	4⅝"	5⅜"	6⅛"
Dark	F: 13 ▱ → ▱		1⅝"	1⅞"	2"	2⅛"	2⅜"	2⅝"
	G: 4 ◇		T5	T7	T8	T9	T11	T12

Try this: Reverse the lights and darks in every other block.

ZIGZAG

5-Unit Grid

Color Illustration: page 27

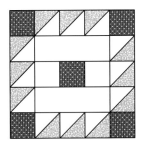
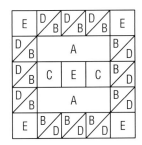
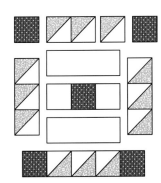

FOR 1 BLOCK:			FINISHED BLOCK SIZE Single dimensions in the cutting chart indicate the size of the cut square (3" = 3" x 3").					
			5"	**6¼"**	**7½"**	**8¾"**	**10"**	**12½"**
Light	A: 2 ▭		1½" x 3½"	1¾" x 4¼"	2" x 5"	2¼" x 5¾"	2½" x 6½"	3" x 8"
	B: 6 ▱ → ▱		1⅞"	2⅛"	2⅜"	2⅝"	2⅞"	3⅜"
	C: 2 ☐		1½"	1¾"	2"	2¼"	2½"	3"
Medium	D: 6 ▱ → ▱		1⅞"	2⅛"	2⅜"	2⅝"	2⅞"	3⅜"
Dark	E: 5 ☐		1½"	1¾"	2"	2¼"	2½"	3"

Try this: Reverse the mediums and darks in every other block.

TEMPLATES

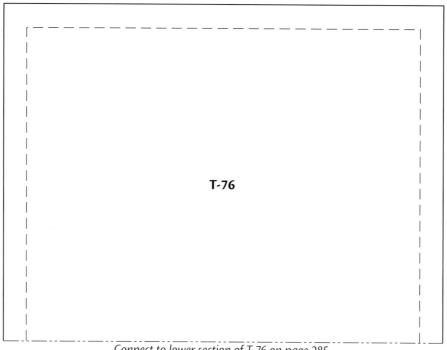

T-76

Connect to lower section of T-76 on page 285.

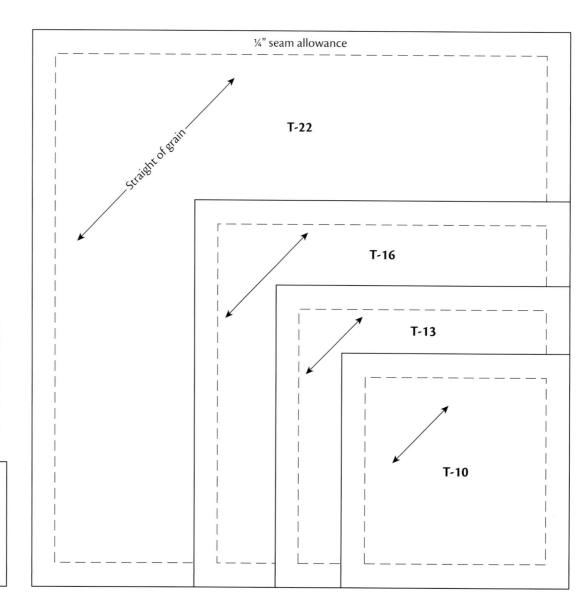

¼" seam allowance

T-22

Straight of grain

T-16

T-13

T-10

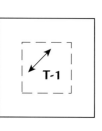

T-1

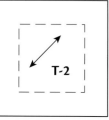

T-2

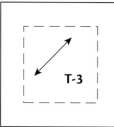

T-3

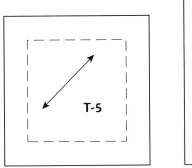

T-5

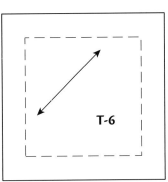

T-6

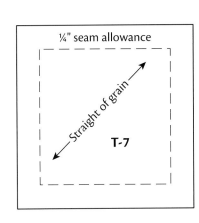

¼" seam allowance

Straight of grain

T-7

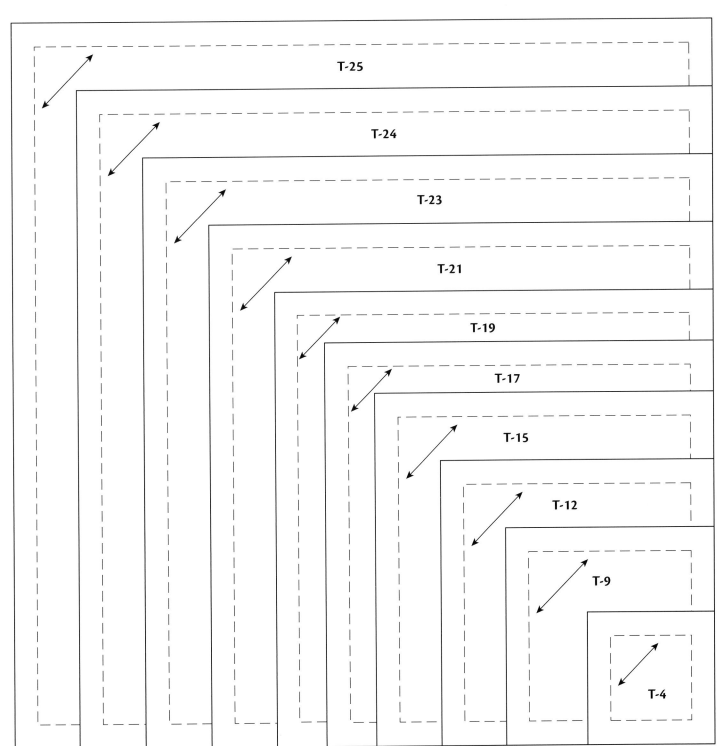

T-25

T-24

T-23

T-21

T-19

T-17

T-15

T-12

T-9

T-4

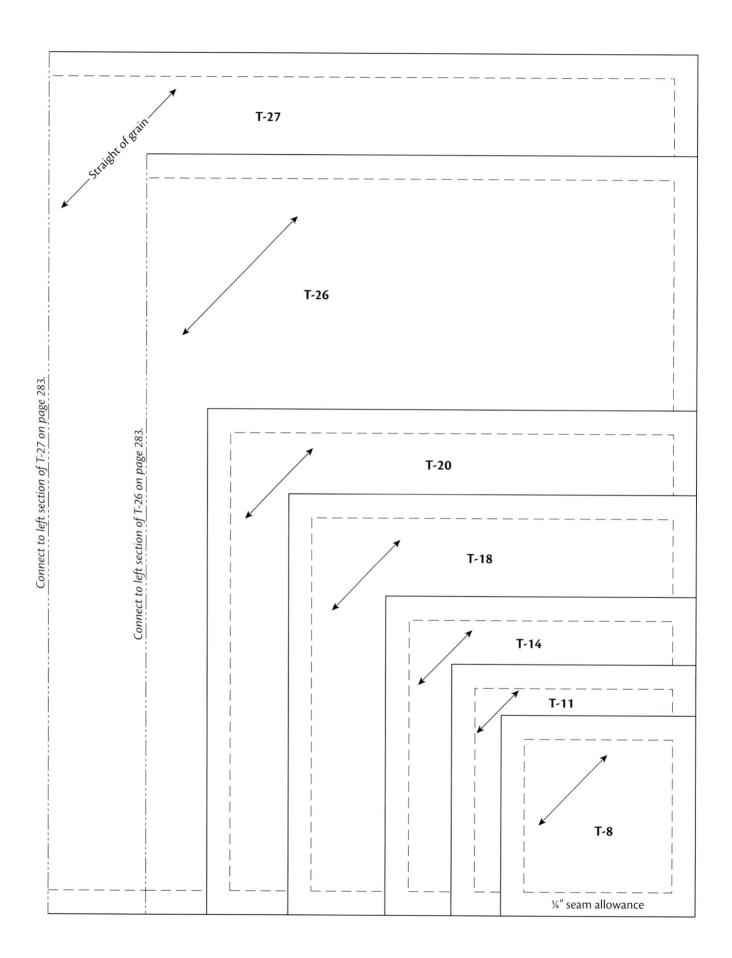

T-27

T-26

T-20

T-18

T-14

T-11

T-8

Straight of grain

Connect to left section of T-27 on page 283.

Connect to left section of T-26 on page 283.

¼" seam allowance

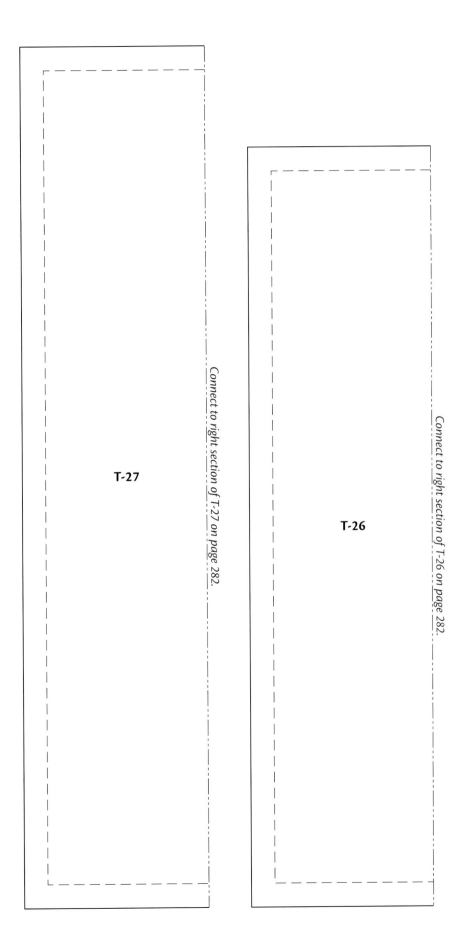

T-27

T-26

Connect to right section of T-27 on page 282.

Connect to right section of T-26 on page 282.

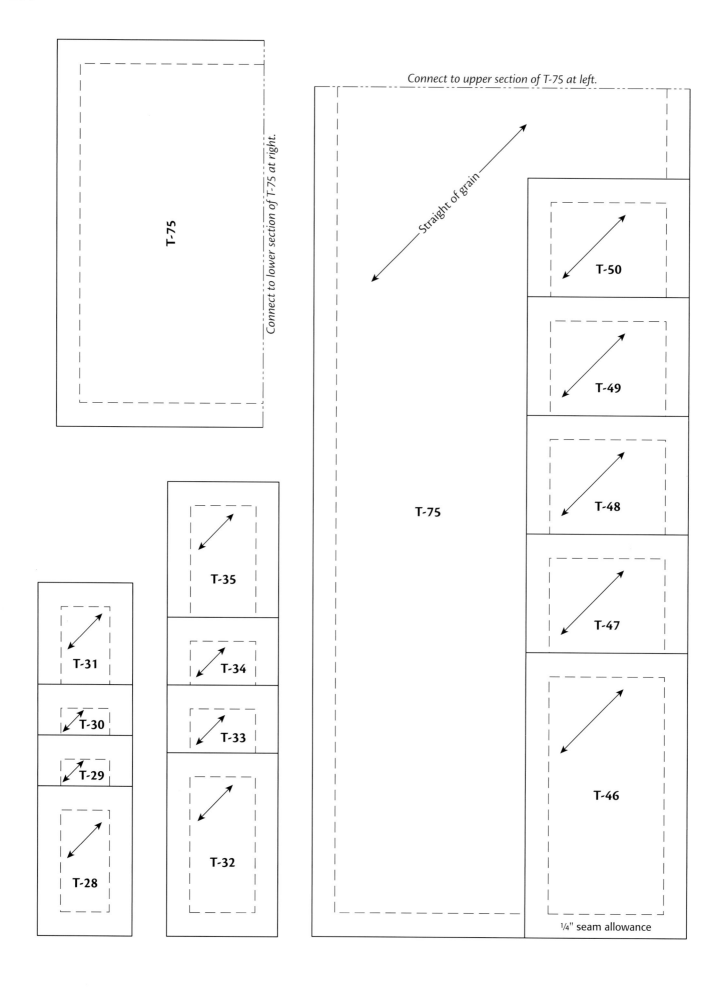

T-75

Connect to lower section of T-75 at right.

Connect to upper section of T-75 at left.

Straight of grain

T-75

T-50

T-49

T-48

T-47

T-46

¼" seam allowance

T-35

T-34

T-33

T-32

T-31

T-30

T-29

T-28

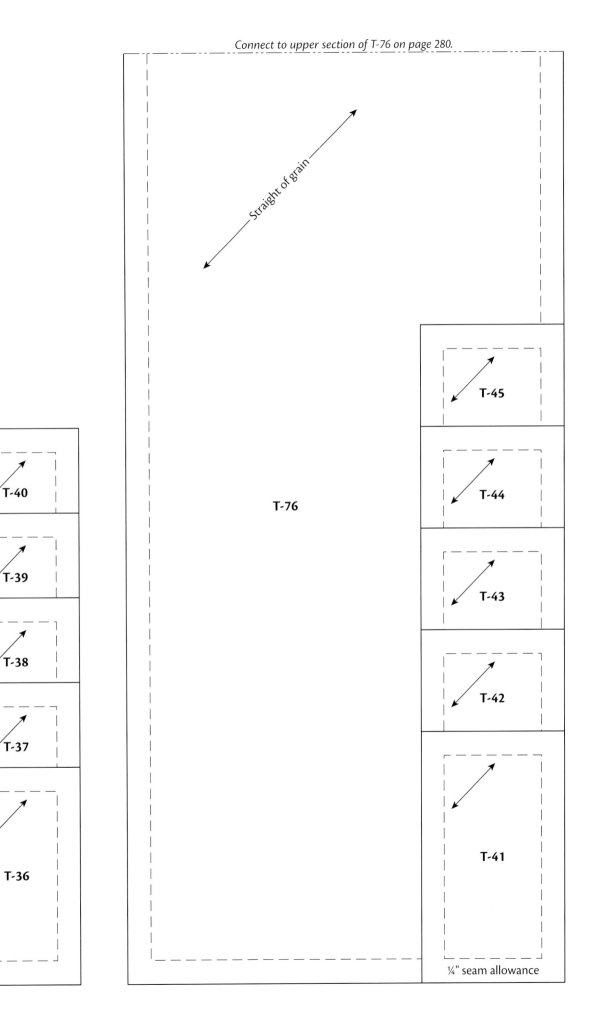

Connect to upper section of T-76 on page 280.

Straight of grain

T-76

T-45

T-44

T-43

T-42

T-41

¼" seam allowance

T-40

T-39

T-38

T-37

T-36

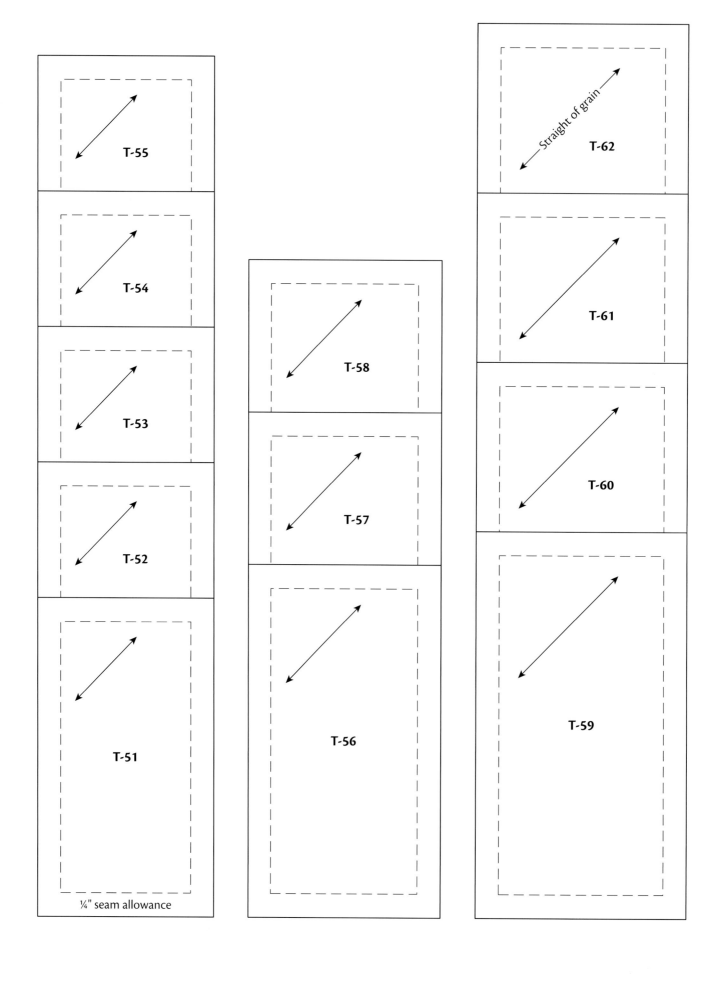

T-55

T-54

T-53

T-52

T-51

¼" seam allowance

T-58

T-57

T-56

Straight of grain   T-62

T-61

T-60

T-59

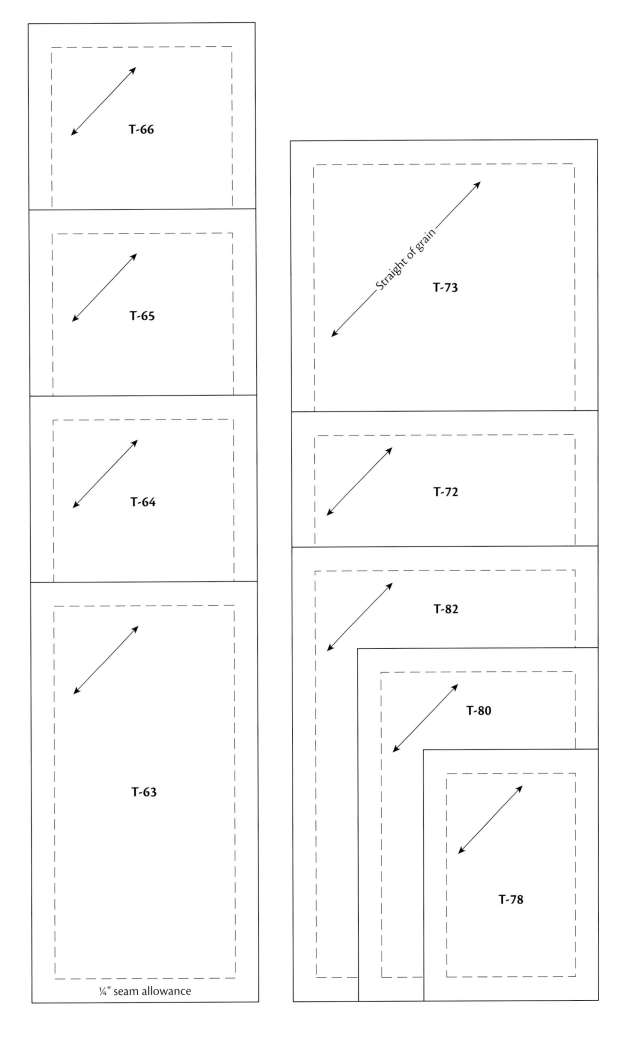

T-66

T-65

T-64

T-63

¼" seam allowance

Straight of grain

T-73

T-72

T-82

T-80

T-78

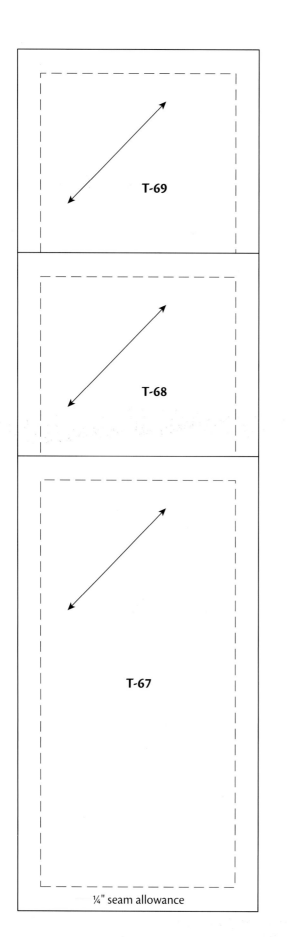

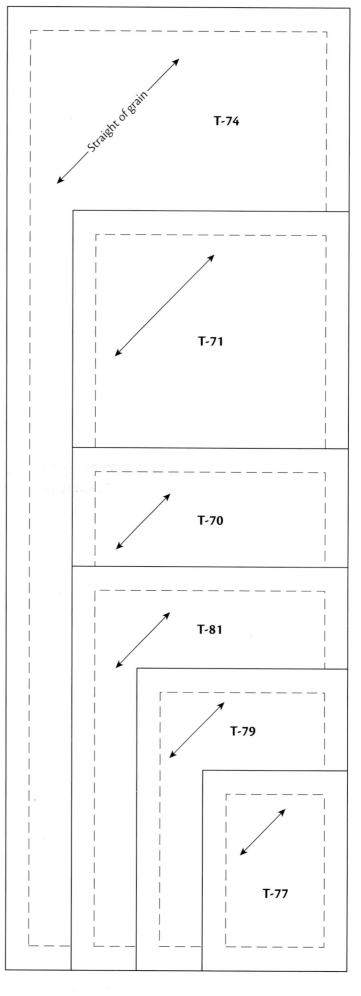